Bernard Taylor was bor
Swindon, London and
teacher, painter (with se
credit) and actor, as well
produced on the stage
published seven novels.

By the same author

Novels

The Godsend
Sweetheart, Sweetheart
The Reaping
The Moorstone Sickness
The Kindness of Strangers
Madeleine
Mother's Boys

Non-fiction

Perfect Murder (with Stephen Knight)
Murder at the Priory (with Kate Clarke)

BERNARD TAYLOR

Cruelly Murdered

Constance Kent and the killing at Road Hill House

GRAFTON BOOKS

A Division of the Collins Publishing Group

LONDON GLASGOW
TORONTO SYDNEY AUCKLAND

Grafton Books
A Division of the Collins Publishing Group
8 Grafton Street, London W1X 3LA

Published by Grafton Books 1989

First published in Great Britain by
Souvenir Press Ltd 1979

ISBN 0-586-20286-2

Printed and bound in Great Britain by
Collins, Glasgow

Set in Times

This is for Kate (my Kit) and Roy

CONTENTS

PART THREE

THE ANSWERS

PART FOUR

THE AFTER-YEARS

ACKNOWLEDGEMENTS

In researching this book I have been greatly aided by a number of persons; their help I would like to acknowledge here.

To Mr. and Mrs. J. G. Yates of Langham House, Rode; Mr. and Mrs. A. Macdonald-Buchanan of Baynton House, Coulston, and Mr. and Mrs. S. M. Wills of the Manor House, Walton-in-Gordano, my thanks for their kind hospitality.

I am grateful for the help of the late Professor Keith Simpson; and to the Home Office for granting me access to their file on the case, a file not previously seen by any member of the public. In having these papers made available for my study I was given every possible assistance by Mr. H. G. Pearson, Mr. Peter Bradshaw and Miss. Mary White.

I would also like to thank Mr. G. Davison and Mr. E. C. Harris of the Lord Chancellor's Office, Detective Chief Inspector Douglas Campbell, the late Mr. Ivor Cantle, Roy Purkess and the late Stephen Knight. My thanks also to Michael Lane who so kindly lent me papers from the estate of the late John Rhode.

My gratitude is due also to Mrs. Laurene Brittan of the Australian High Commission, Prof. Maurice G. Rathbone of the Wiltshire County Archives, Canon Ralph E. Dudley, Sir John Eardley-Wilmot, Mrs. Jacqueline Taylor, Mr. and Mrs. Samuel Colbourne, Mr. and Mrs. Tom Barnes, Rev. John Milburn, Mr. Telford Stone, Mrs. S. M. J. Middleton, Mrs. M. M. Rowe, Mr. A. M. Carr of the Shropshire County Library, Canon H. G. Bear, Rev. Clifford Hayward, Rev. T. C. Secombe, Miss. Hilda M. Woolley, Mr. Michael Lansdown of *The Wiltshire Times*, Mrs. Katherine Ridley of Madame Tussaud's, Joseph Gaute, J. C. G. Hammond, Basil Donne-Smith, Glyn Hardwicke, the late John Hill, and the staff of the Hammersmith Public Libraries.

There are those further afield, in Australia, whom I must thank. They are: Miss. Catherine Hurst of the Maitland City Library, Mrs. J. Youldon of the Maitland Historical Society, Miss. Patricia

Reynolds of the State Library of Victoria, Miss. Suzanne Mourot of the Mitchell Library, NSW; Mrs. Cecily Ellis, Mrs. Jean Uhl, Miss. N. Sewell of the Alfred Hospital, Melbourne, Mr. William Mantle of Parramatta, NSW; and Dr. Anne M. Mitchell of Melbourne.

I would also like to thank the descendants of Samuel Savill Kent.

For kind permission to quote from the works of other writers I would like to thank the following publishing houses, agents or trustees with regard to the works given against their names:

Geoffrey Bles: *The Case of Constance Kent* (John Rhode)

John Farquharson, Ltd: *Saint—With Red Hands?* (Yseult Bridges)

George Harrap & Co. Ltd: *Murder and its Motives* (F. Tennyson Jesse)

The Public Trustee, Harwood Will Trust: *Comments on Cain* (F. Tennyson Jesse)

To those who helped me but whose names have not been included above I apologize and offer my thanks now.

BERNARD TAYLOR

AUTHOR'S NOTE

This new edition of my book gives me the opportunity not only to correct a few minor errors that crept into the original edition but also to make a valuable addition in the form of an extra appendix. As is stated in the text, in 1929 Geoffrey Bles, the publisher of John Rhode's *The Case of Constance Kent*, received a lengthy anonymous letter from Australia giving a great deal of fascinating information on Constance. Parts of this letter—which became known as the *Sydney Document*—were later published in an essay by John Rhode in *The Anatomy of Murder* (see Bibliography), following which the original letter was destroyed by enemy action. Fortunately, however, a typewritten copy had been made (though quite forgotten), and this came to me along with other papers during the last stages of my writing on the case.

As the reader will see, I have quoted frequently from the letter—with a little necessary editing here and there—throughout the text. Needless to say, I regard the document as a most valuable item and in view of this feel that it should be included, in total, in this new edition of the book. In this way the letter may be preserved. So, its text (with its odd punctuation) copied faithfully from the original typescript, the unedited letter (the *Sydney Document*) can be found as *Appendix II*.

On another matter: it will be noted that the second name of Francis Savill Kent varies in certain instances in the literature of the crime. In most newspapers of the time the spelling appears as *Savile*, as indeed Constance herself spelled it on occasion. There is nothing remarkable in this. William Savill Kent later adopted the spelling of his own second name as *Saville*, while Constance herself was also to vary the spelling of her second name, changing the *Emily* to *Emilie*. In this book, however, I have used the spelling of the victim's name as it appears on his death certificate and gravestone, i. e. *Savill*.

The two surgeons who figure in the case, Stapleton and Parsons, should of course be correctly addressed as *Mister*; however, to more clearly define them in their roles as medical men I have referred to them throughout the text as *Doctor*.

For the sake of brevity *The Somerset and Wilts Journal* is referred to in the text as *The Journal*; and *The Trowbridge and North Wilts Advertiser* as *The Advertiser*.

Unless otherwise acknowledged, the photographs are my copyright.

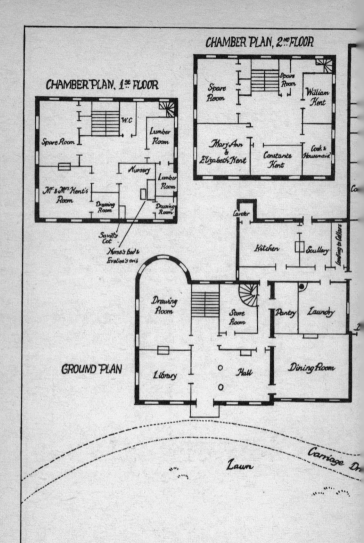

CHAMBER PLAN, 2.ᴺᴰ FLOOR

Spare
Room

Spare
Room

William
Kent

Mary Ann
&
Elizabeth Kent

Constance
Kent

Cook &
Housemaid

CHAMBER PLAN, 1ˢᵀ FLOOR

W.C

Spare Room

Lumber
Room

Nursery

Lumber
Room

Mr & Mrs Kent's
Room

Drawing
Room

Drawing
Room

Savill's
Cot.

Nurse's bed &
Evelina's on's

Carter

Kitchen

Scullery

Landing to Cellars

Co

Drawing
Room

Store
Room

Pantry

Laundry

GROUND PLAN

Library

Hall

Dining Room

2

Lawn

Carriage Dr

Plan of *ROAD HILL HOUSE* at the time of the

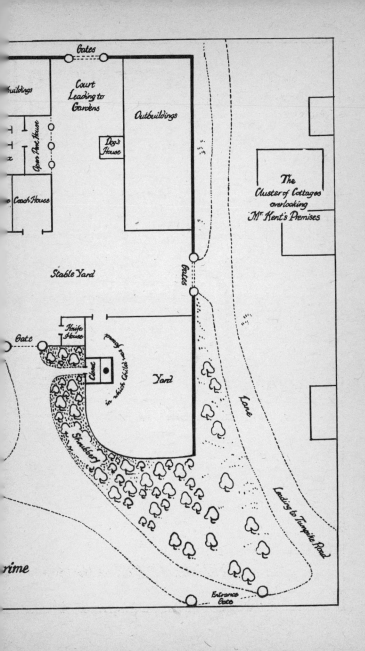

Gates

Court Leading to Gardens

Outbuildings

Buildings

Dogs House

Open Part House

Coach House

The Cluster of Cottages overlooking Mr Kent's Premises

Stable Yard

Gates

Gate

Knife House

Passage in which Child was found

Closet

Yard

Shrubbery

Lane

Leading to Turnpike Road

rime

Entrance Gate

INTRODUCTION

It is difficult to conceive of a more grotesque happening than that which occurred one midsummer night in Road (now Rode), a tiny village on the borders of Wiltshire and Somerset.

The crime, apart from its horrific nature, was also singular in that the details, as they became known, only served to enclose the truth more deeply in a shroud of mystery. As more evidence was revealed so, it seemed, the mystery deepened; that which should have illumined only cast the truth further into shadow, and even when, years later, it appeared that the truth was at last to be known, no one was at all sure that they did, indeed, have the truth.

The mystery began when the mutilated corpse of a child was discovered, his almost-decapitated body hidden in the privy in the grounds of an imposing house occupied by a respected civil-servant and his large family. The shocking news of the murder stunned the neighbourhood and, subsequently, the entire nation, and although various efforts were made to bring the culprit or culprits to justice they were to no avail. If justice was not being deliberately thwarted it was certainly not being helped either; the story of the investigations presents pictures of blunder after blunder, of inaction and precipitate action, of missed opportunities and official ineptitude and stupidity.

Three persons were suspected, two of whom were charged with the crime and then released again, and as time passed it was feared that the mystery would never be solved. And then, suddenly, five years later, there burst like a thunderclap upon the lulled population an answer. The police and the public alike breathed a sigh of relief; at last, they believed, the mystery was at an end.

Not so; the very nature of that "answer" and the events surrounding it gave rise to a furthur mystery. If that one who had confessed to the crime was truly guilty then how could so many vital questions remain unanswered? But perhaps that confession was a lie—but if so, why should it be?

These and other questions have haunted people every since the murder: Who in the dead of that summer night crept through those carpeted hallways? Who lifted the victim from his warm cot and wielded the blade?

The murder has given rise to several books. The first, *The Great Crime of 1860*, was published in 1861 and written by Joseph Stapleton, one of the participants in the drama. Since then there have been two others, *The Case of Constance Kent* (1928) by John Rhode, and *Saint—With Red Hands?* (1954) by Yseult Bridges.*

The three books are very different. Joseph Stapleton, writing years before the trial and constrained by fears of libel, could only hint at what he believed to be the truth of the matter. His book is a laborious work, full of philosophical meanderings, though it contains a great deal of very vital information for anyone who is prepared to persevere. That by John Rhodes is a more straightforward piece, being little more than an honest account drawn from newspaper reports, but offering no solutions or conclusions beyond those officially given.

The third book, that by the late Yseult Bridges, I found of particular interest. Presenting a story very different from that generally accepted, her widely read book had come to be seen in some quarters as almost the last word on the subject. And I was no less impressed with it than were her other readers; indeed, I was quite sure that she had the answer. So impressed was I with her theory that I considered adapting her book as a drama for television. Before I could begin such a task, however, I felt that there were several items in her account which needed clarification. With this in mind I set out to do a certain amount of basic research.

Very soon afterwards, in the course of those early researches, I was astonished, and not a little disappointed, to find that Yseult Bridges' account was, as a piece of factual writing, completely unreliable.

The first causes for doubting its veracity came when looking up

---

* Yseult Bridges's book was published in the USA by Rinehart, 1955, under the title *The Tragedy of Road Hill House*.

such fundamental information as the ages and birthdates of the principle characters. To my surprise I found that the *true* ages and dates were often at great variance with those quoted in Mrs. Bridges' book.

These inventions, however, were relatively trivial. It was when her 'creativeness' got in the way of important facts that it became truly disconcerting. Following on from those first inventions of dates and ages further inventions came thick and fast. Obviously anxious to prove her theory, she appears to have manipulated the facts to suit her case. In two particular instances involving testimonies given by two of the witnesses she manipulated vital evidence—rewriting the testimony given by one, Sergeant Watts, and ignoring the testimony given by the other, Sarah Kerslake. These, however, are mere examples. In short it is enough to say that her account of a young, saintly girl sacrificing herself for another person has about as much relation to fact as does *Little Red Riding Hood*.

However, when all is said, perhaps I should be grateful, for those researches of mine quickly led me to the realization that the *true* story of Constance Kent and the mystery behind the Road murder had never been told; as a result, abandoning all thought of adapting Mrs. Bridges' book, I decided to write my own.

In my subsequent researches I made a careful study of all the published accounts of the case, including contemporary newspaper reports. I examined the records of New Scotland Yard, those held by the Lord Chancellor and also, with special and most kind permission, that file held by the Home Office, a file which is officially closed until the year 2002. I also met and consulted the descendants of Samuel Savill Kent.

One thing I became very much aware of during my researches was the great and enduring fascination held by the Road murder. And it is hardly surprising; the story is surely unique, and that particular fascination it owns is rarely found in murder cases. For one thing all the ingredients for classic mystery and intrigue are there; the setting alone—a large house standing on the edge of a small country village—might be taken from the pages of some detective whodunnit, while the time—the Victorian era—is perfect again: a time of gas—and oil-lamps, before the telephone and the motor-car, and before the advent of more sophisticated means of criminal detection. Add, too, the fact that in that Gothic atmosphere of hidden passions and brooding resentment there slept, on the night of the killing, twelve persons—nine adults and three small children; twelve persons, one of whom, before the day broke, was to be cruelly put to death.

In the following pages I present my solution to the mystery that surrounds the killing at Road Hill House, and in advancing my theory I quote the relevant testimonies *verbatim*, and use *all* the evidence available—for surely any theory that relies on a careful *selection* of facts must be worse than useless. The answer I give, the particular theory presented as a result of my investigations, has never been exposed before, but to my mind it is the only one that fits all the facts.

This book, then, must tell of those inhabitants of Road Hill House. But in particular it must tell the story of one individual member of the Kent household, Constance.

Constance Kent.

She is given no name in the birth register at the General Register Office, London. Beneath the records of those other babies born with the surname Kent—the Emmas, the Georges, the Sarahs—there is one entry where, in the column for *Christian Name*, is simply written the word *Female*, with the added information that her birth was registered in Honiton, Devonshire. The words are inscribed on yellowing, dog-eared parchment, in black ink, in a tall, angular, sloping hand, long gone from fashion. The entry, in its anonymity, almost fades into the page. It is perhaps ironic, therefore, that the name of that then-unnamed female child was destined to become, for a short while, one of the best-known names in England.

Constance Kent . . . Her name, like the comet that shone on the night of the killing, came out of obscurity, brilliantly blazed for a brief span and then faded, leaving behind it only the shadow, the mystery.

The Road murder . . . one of the strangest among the romances of crime. It might figure a hundred years hence as a story unequalled for ghastly attractiveness, and exercise the ingenuity of our great-grandchildren, as it did our own.

The Times, 26th April, 1865.

Cruelly Murdered

Part One

PRELUDE TO A CRIME

As to the family, we do know that it has been a very unhappy one.

W. N. Mallam, physician to the Kent family.

Chapter 1

MR. AND MRS. SAMUEL KENT

When talk of the brutal crime was on everyone's lips and the gossip-mongers were impatient for further revelations, rumour was spread about that Samuel Kent was of royal blood. He was, said the whisperers, the illegitimate son of Queen Victoria's father, the Duke of Kent.

The murder and its astonishing sequel was so shocking and so incredible that it seems strange that anyone should ever feel the need to dress it up. But there, scandal breeds more scandal, and such was the case with the crime at Road.

However, to begin at the beginning. The events leading up to the killing start with Samuel Kent himself and, since there is no evidence to support the idea of his royal parentage one must begin the story with what is acknowledged to be fact.

He was born in 1801, the son of a prosperous carpet-manufacturer, Samuel Luck Kent, who pursued his business at London Wall. His mother, from whom he took his second name, Savill (a name he was so proudly to pass on to several of his own children), was the daughter of property owners in Colchester.

Young Samuel Savill Kent received a good education and at the age of twenty-five, after acquiring valuable experience in his father's carpet-making business, left it to take up a partnership in a firm of dry-salters, North and Company, of Aldermanbury, a nearby street in the City of London.

It was about this time that he met the young woman who was to become his first wife. She was Mary Ann Windus, eldest daughter of Thomas Windus, a wealthy coach-builder of Bishopsgate Street, an educated, cultured man who, in 1845, was to become a Fellow of the Royal Society of Antiquaries.

On the 8th of January, 1829, at St. John's church, Hackney, Samuel Kent and Mary Ann Windus were married. He was twenty-eight; she twenty-one. Afterwards they set up house in Artillery

Place, Finsbury Square, then a select residential area in the City. Their first child, Thomas Savill, was born the following December, only to die from convulsions a year later. The two daughters who were born after him, however—Mary Ann Alice in October, 1831, and Elizabeth in December, 1832—were strong and both thrived.

It was not long after the birth of Elizabeth that Mr. Kent's own health declined and he was forced to give up his business partnership. The house in Artillery Place was likewise disposed of and he and his wife and two daughters moved to Sidmouth on the Devon coast. There in the clean air of the English Channel, and far from the fog- and smoke-filled city he subsequently recovered and turned his mind to procuring a new means of livelihood. Seeking some post that would suit his abilities and his ambition (the latter, it appears, was the greater), he was fortunate enough to be offered a highly-paid governmental post of Sub-Inspector of Factories.

Wool was once the very foundation of England's wealth and strength and the South-West was good sheep-farming country; consequently many wool factories had sprung up in the area, and this was where the efforts of Samuel Kent were to be concentrated. His job, as an inspector—a post not long created—was to implement the Factory Act of 1833 which, apart from being new and revolutionary was also extremely unpopular. Part of the purpose of the Act was the protection of young children who, hitherto, had been employed in the factories at a very tender age. These children had been exploited by their parents and their employers alike; if a child was old enough to repeatedly tug on a string and so operate a flap for the circulation of air then that child was employable and a valuable commodity. The new Factory Act, forbidding employment of any child under the age of nine, was hated by the exploiters of those children: the employers were deprived of their cheap labour, and the parents of the pittances their children earned.

Due to the very strong feelings against the Act the enforcement of the new, highly unpopular laws was not an easy task. Therefore it was necessary to grant the inspectors certain powers; they could administer oaths and, acting in a judicial capacity, hear complaints and impose penalties provided under the Act. The men selected for such sought-after positions were therefore chosen carefully, the government seeking those of a certain class and education who could be assumed to be above the temptations of bribery and corruption, and to operate with pragmatism, fairness and tact. Samuel Kent was considered to be of this stamp.

He pursued his new responsibilities with zeal. From Cliff Cottage, his house in Sidmouth, his work took him by train and by horse-drawn carriage on a ceaseless round of journeys over parts of Devon, Somerset, Wiltshire and Dorset. And the work suited him. Apart from being lucrative it went well with his ambitious nature; he was only thirty-three and in the years to come he could hope to gain promotion—specifically to a much-desired seat on the Board of Factory Inspectors. Also, young as he was, he was regarded as being on a par with the local magistrates, and this suited his self-esteem.

J. W. Stapleton, writing years later in *The Great Crime of 1860*, would have his readers believe that there was no one better at his job than was his friend Mr. Kent, but this doesn't appear to have been the general view. John Rhode writes of him as "a not over-intelligent person with an overbearing manner, derived in all probability from an inflated idea of his own importance". He says that Kent "was never distinguished; he blundered with strange persistence when faced with emergency; yet somehow he managed to maintain a certain dignity. . . ."[1]

The description rings true. Certainly that inflated idea of his own importance is illustrated by his choice of living-accommodation. After Cliff Cottage, and up to the time of the crime, he invariably chose houses that were far too big and above his means. These gave to the outside world a picture of prosperity and grandeur which his bank account found it increasingly difficult to keep up with. He managed by stringently economizing *within* the home, on the household budget and his children's educational expenses; while at the same time he was accused—and not without foundation—of being financially unreliable.

While he was still based in Sidmouth, though, his expenses would still have been within his means; he would have been a respected man, and relatively happy; those accusations that would later be levelled against him, of gross immorality, every shade of cruelty—and *murder*, were not yet to be even dreamed of.

Although Mr. Kent and his wife are said to have been happy

[1] *The Case of Constance Kent.*

together in the early years of their marriage it becomes apparent that as time went by he showed less and less interest in her.

The move to the coast had dramatically changed for both of them their respective lifestyles, and it was Mrs. Kent who came off the loser. While her husband moved about in the course of his work, entertaining and cultivating new friends, she stayed at home with her two small daughters. Had she been in London she could have turned for company to her family or friends but, being newly arrived in Sidmouth, pregnant again and knowing no one, she was driven more and more on to her own resources.

Except for the gratification of his sexual needs, it seems that Kent gradually ceased to regard her as any positive part of his life; and where his sexual gratification was concerned it is doubtful that she was ever consulted on the matter. In those times it amounted to an acknowledged case of a husband's rights and a wife's duty, and it is clear that Kent, in claiming his rights, showed little or no thought for his wife's feelings, either mental or physical—and her constitution was by no means robust. She was more than once threatened with pulmonary consumption, it is said, and in 1835, whilst pregnant with her fourth child, she was so ill that it was feared she would die. She survived, though, as did her child, Edward Windus, born in the April of that year.

Although Mrs. Kent recovered her physical health to some degree she was, if we are to believe her husband, left with some mental illness. At the time of the crime, years later, he was to broadcast information to this effect, saying that following Edward's birth he had had his wife examined by a certain Dr. Blackall, physician to St. Thomas's Lunatic Asylum, Exeter, who gave it as his opinion that Mrs. Kent showed a weakness of intellect and was suffering from "various though harmless delusions". According to Mr. Kent his wife's condition had continued to deteriorate to the point where she had become totally incapable of running the household, was seen to be incurably insane and, in the end, had to be kept in confinement.

It must be borne in mind, though, that Mr. Kent did not make known this "situation" until 1860—a time when it well suited his predicament. Also, as Dr. Blackall was by that time dead there was no one to contradict Mr. Kent's assertions.

Even so, it must be acknowledged that Mrs. Kent may well have suffered from some mental incapacity, though to what degree, and whether it was caused by inherent mental weakness or to the strain of her physical and emotional suffering cannot be known. There was mental illness on her mother's side, it is true, but it is also true that during her married life Mrs. Kent was assaulted variously by physical illness, endless pregnancies and acute—and continuing—emotional stress. Regarding this latter: to face disdain and total rejection every day of one's life cannot be easy, and this she certainly had to do. In fact, the picture of her existence after arriving in Sidmouth seems to be that of a woman submerged almost to the point of extinction by circumstances beyond her control.

Mr. Kent's pronouncements on his wife's "imbecility" are negated to an extent by his own admission that for many years she correctly fulfilled her household duties and took her place in society, which certainly indicates that her condition—at least during the earlier years—was not as alarming as he would have one believe. Add to this the fact that right up until 1845 he slept with her and gave her children in monotonous and uncomfortable succession. (Also, this latter, when taken into account with his averments of her insanity, does not say much for *his* rational thought—or his self-control.)

Post-natal depression is a common enough ailment, and that more serious malady that can follow a birth, puerperal insanity, is by no means that rare. Although such illnesses do not generally last for more than a few weeks it is known that some cases can go on for months.

What is reported of Mrs. Kent's "odd" behaviour following Edward's birth is almost classically symptomatic of puerperal insanity, among the symptoms of which are exhausted bodily condition, weak pulse, delusions and, sometimes, suicidal tendencies.

Now, consider the following:

Over a period of approximately fifteen years Mrs. Kent, apart from suffering several miscarriages, gave birth to ten children. They were:

Thomas Savill, born December, 1829; died January, 1831.
Mary Ann Alice, born October, 1831.
Elizabeth, born December, 1832.
Edward Windus, born April, 1835.
Henry Savill, born February, 1837; died May, 1838.

Ellen, born September, 1839; died December, 1839.
John Savill, born March, 1841; died July, 1841.
Julia, born April, 1842; died September, 1842.
Constance Emily, born February, 1844.
William Savill, born July, 1845.

Ten children, five of whom died within fifteen months of birth. Such a list makes for sad reading. Those were the days, though, before antibiotics and other sophisticated medicine, and besides that there were no maternity hospitals, so mothers and their babies usually had to place themselves solely in the hands of local midwives and casual nurses, very often women whose ineptitude was only matched by their ignorance.

But bearing in mind that succession of pregnancies and miscarriages, Mrs. Kent's sorrow at seeing four of her children buried in almost as many years, her poor health and the increasing neglect by an uncaring husband, and it is not surprising to be told that in the end she was totally unable to cope, either mentally or physically and, being unable to cope, completely gave up.

For the last eight or nine years of her life Mrs. Kent became more and more reclusive until at last she rarely ventured out, keeping instead to her own room and relying for her only happiness upon the visits of her children.

Mary Ann and Elizabeth, it might be mentioned here, always insisted that their mother was *not* insane, while a less subjective opinion—and probably therefore more valid—is that given by a certain woman bearing the strangely Dickensian name of Harriet Gollop, who was parlour-maid to the Kents as late as 1850. She believed, she was to state, that Mrs. Kent was indeed a very unhappy woman, but nevertheless she "considered her perfectly sane".

By that year, 1850, Mrs. Kent had long since ceased taking any part in the running of the household. But by then Mary Pratt the governess was immovably ensconced there, and she had taken to her mistress's former task with eagerness.

With Mary Pratt's entry into the household there had come on the scene another protagonist in the drama that was later to unfold; a drama unparalleled in the chronicles of crime.

Chapter 2

THE GOVERNESS

Mary Drewe Pratt was born in Tiverton, Devon, in the summer of 1820, the third of four children born to Francis Pratt, a grocer, and his wife Mary. It is reported that she received a good education and that previous to her employment by Mr. Kent had been governess—on a daily, visiting basis—in the families of a local clergyman and a solicitor.

The precise date of her entry into the Kent household is not known, though it was almost certainly in 1840, and before her twentieth birthday. She was hired ostensibly as governess to Mary Ann and Elizabeth, their previous governess having recently left the household. It is said that she was recommended to Mr. Kent by a Sidmouth surgeon, a Mr. Walker, and that Mr. Kent subsequently hired her as "domestic governess" after going to Tiverton and interviewing the girl and her parents. She had been living at home up until this time and, if *The Journal* was right, she was probably glad of the chance to get away. That newspaper reported that her father, Francis Pratt, had given up his successful grocery business for farming only to find that his new occupation "was not successful in a pecuniary view". This, apparently, "led him to indulge in habits of intemperance, and he became reduced in circumstances. . . ." Later, when he died, it was said, his "wife and family were unprovided for".

That the nineteen-year-old Mary Pratt's arrival at Cliff Cottage brought pleasure and satisfaction to Mr. Kent cannot be doubted. She was extremely capable, clever and pretty, and she also possessed youth and vitality, qualities which the unhappy Mrs. Kent no longer owned. She seems to have been blessed with little sensitivity, but she had an abundance of ambition, and with her efficiency and her charm she was very soon to become, in Mr. Kent's eyes, indispensable. In no time at all he had become completely infatuated.

Although he was so head-over-heels in love with the young

CERTIFIED COPY OF AN ENTRY OF BIRTH

		REGISTRATION DISTRICT			Honit

__1844.__ BIRTH in the Sub-district of _Ottery St Mar_

Columns:—	1	2	3	4	5
No.	When and where born	Name, if any	Sex	Name, and surname of father	Name, surna maiden su of mot
136	Sixth of February 1844 Cliff Cottage Sidmouth	—	Girl	Samuel Savill Kent	Mary k forme wind

CERTIFIED to be a true copy of an entry in the certified copy of a Register of E

Given at the GENERAL REGISTER OFFICE, LONDON, under the Seal of the said Office,

BC 952381

This certificate is issued in pursuance of the Births and Deaths Registration Act Section 34 provides that any certified copy of an entry purporting to be sealed c or death to which it relates without any further or other proof of the entry, and unless it is sealed or stamped as aforesaid.
CAUTION:—Any person who (1) falsifies any of the particulars on this certificate,

Constance's birth certificate.

governess, Kent nevertheless continued to share his wife's bed, nightly leaving the arms of his mistress for the resigned, dutiful acceptance of his unhappy wife, who still continued to bear his children—children born of his sexual frustration and her meek obedience.

Her ninth child, a daughter, was born on the 6th of February, 1844, and on the 5th of June that year was baptized Constance Emily.

Like so many of her unfortunate antecedent siblings, Constance is said to have begun life as a weak, sickly infant, though later she developed into a strong, healthy child; which change in her physical state Dr. Stapleton attributes to Mary Pratt. It is possible. Mary Pratt was to be responsible for *many* changes in the Kent house-

Given at the GENERAL REGISTER OFFICE, LONDON.

Application Number....... 3̶4̶9̶.̶2̶...H ....

	in the *County of Devon*			
	7	8	9	10*
~~ion~~ ~~er~~	Signature, description and residence of informant	When registered	Signature of registrar	Name entered after registration
~~int-~~ ~~ent~~ ~~tones~~	*Mary ann Kent* *Mother* *Sidmouth*	*Twentieth* *of* *February* *1844*	*Edwd* *Carter* *Registrar*	—

trict above mentioned.

~~d~~ day of *August* 19̶7̶7̶.

*See note overleaf.

hold, changes more far-reaching than anyone at the time could ever have imagined.

During the period of his wife's child-bearing years Kent had vacated himself from their bedroom only at those times of her many confinements. However, after the birth of her last child, William, born in July, 1845, Mrs. Kent had her bed to herself (mercifully, one might say), while her husband took permanently a room in another part of the house. There is no reason to believe, though, that his move was prompted by consideration for his wife's feelings and her ill-health—mental and physical. No, the room he adopted was close to the one occupied by Mary Pratt. Mrs. Kent was not consciously being given the rest she had long desperately needed, she was being discarded, even as an outlet for her husband's sexual needs. And while she was increasingly ignored, and so encouraged to become even more reclusive, so the governess continued to take over the position of mistress of the house, growing in favour and influence, until she filled that role completely.

It was not very long before there was much gossip concerning Kent and Mary Pratt—and that gossip grew rife. Not surprisingly—the servants were well aware of the situation as, surely, Mrs. Kent was also. That Edward was aware of it at a fairly early stage is certain. The Sydney Document[1] reports:

> The eldest son, who was training at a naval school, came home for his holidays about a year before Sidmouth was left. Rising early one morning he met his father coming out of the governess's room which was next to his. Highly indignant, he did not mince his words to his father, who promptly sent him back to school. Soon after the two elder girls were sent to two different boarding schools. The governess's position was much canvassed in the town.

Edward and the governess, it seems, had never liked each other, and it is reasonable to assume that the boy's feelings of antipathy sprang from resentment on his mother's behalf. However, while Edward could be dealt with, obviously the local population could not, and as the gossip spread so Kent was increasingly threatened by it. His jealously guarded governmental position demanded that he be above reproach—or at least be regarded as such—and this was no longer the case. Subsequently, in 1848, a meeting took place between himself and a certain Mr. Howell, a friend who was also his official superior and one of the members of the illustrious Factory Commission. Following this meeting Mr. Kent took his wife, his children and the governess and moved to Somerset where he had taken the lease of Walton Manor, a gracious, secluded mansion in the tiny village of Walton-in-Gordano, not far from Clevedon and some seventy-odd miles from Sidmouth, the scene of the gossip.

J. W. Stapleton says that the choice of this secluded Somerset residence was determined "by the consideration of Mrs. Kent's state of mind", though the move can have made little difference to

[1] An anonymous document written in February, 1929, and sent from Sydney, Australia, to Geoffrey Bles, publisher of John Rhode's book, *The Case of Constance Kent*. It is discussed in the final chapter of this book.

her, except to give her a change of view from her windows. In truth
the only ones to derive benefit from the upheaval were Kent and
Mary Pratt—around Walton Manor they were not known, the nature
of the *ménage* was not known and, in a strange place, more shielded
from prying eyes and wagging tongues, Kent, in his position of
responsibility, would feel more secure.

Any sense of new found security, however, did not last. Even in
Walton-in-Gordano the new arrivals were not safe from gossip.
Whispers of scandal followed them from Sidmouth in time and
these, allied to the knowledge owned by the new servants in the
house, did not for long keep the situation a secret.

One of those servants was the parlour-maid Harriet Gollop who,
ten years later when the crime was being investigated, gave information to Sergeant Tanner of the Metropolitan Police. She told him
that Mary Pratt's room had been close to Mr. Kent's room and
that all the servants were aware of the nature of the relationship
between them. She went on to say that "Mrs. Kent knew of the
relationship between her husband and Mary Pratt, and was very
unhappy and miserable". In addition to saying that Mrs. Kent was
"a very ladylike person", and that she considered her "perfectly
sane", the former parlour-maid went on to state: "Miss Pratt had
the entire control of the children, and Mr. Kent gave directions to
all the servants to consider *Miss Pratt* as their mistress."

It is certain that Mary Ann and Elizabeth were also cognizant of
the situation. They were not long at boarding school and living
within the family circle again would have been faced with countless
indications of what was happening. They must have questioned,
albeit silently, a state of affairs in which their mother was wholeheartedly encouraged to be a recluse while the governess ran the
house and replaced Mrs. Kent as the object of Mr. Kent's affections.
Says the Sydney Document:

> Mrs. Kent had a bed, bathroom and sitting-room to herself at
> the other end of the house, but when in winter a fire was for-
> bidden in her sitting-room she sat in the dining-room with her
> two eldest daughters and the eldest boy, when home, and her
> youngest son to whom she was devotedly attached. Mr. Kent and
> the governess occupied the library where Constance had her
> lessons, but all generally met at meals.

Today we may ask why Mrs. Kent did not assert herself, for clearly she was most unhappy at being placed in the background. But times have changed, and at that time where would such an assertion get her? It was quite clear to her that she was unloved by her husband; more than that, was a burden on him. She could do little but meekly suffer her lot. At that time husbands and wives tended to put up with their miseries and stay together. Separation was not a move considered lightly, while the difficulties involved in obtaining a divorce made such a monumental step almost out of the question. No, Mrs. Kent had to be resigned to her situation; whatever happiness she desired she must seek through her children.

And nor were those children, it must be noted, unaffected by the relationship between their father and the governess. They were, and not least in the way in which they came to be denied companionship from outside. The Sydney Document tells us that whereas "a good deal of company was kept at Sidmouth, there was none afterwards; only the gentlemen who came down for the shooting", and that "the few relatives who visited got into disgrace over the governess and their stay was brief". We learn too that the development of any more personal relationships was also sometimes thwarted. For instance, Mary Ann and Elizabeth had made friends with some young people from two neighbouring families, but as these families would not call at the house orders were issued to the Kent girls that the meetings must cease. The document also tells us:

> The same ban was placed on the younger children. One day when Constance and her brother were supposed to be attending to their little gardens behind some shrubbery they heard some merry laughter from a neighbouring garden. They went to the hedge and looked over longingly at the children playing with some visitors. They were invited to join but were afraid. They were seen and their disobedience punished; the little gardens were uprooted and trampled down. Constance made some futile efforts to revive hers.

In 1851 William, whose health was somewhat delicate, was sent away to a school run by relatives of the governess. Mrs. Kent was never to see her youngest son again. However, she still had Mary Ann and Elizabeth, and occasionally Edward, and in the company of her elder children she found great comfort.

Constance, of course, was also in the house, but *her* presence there only brought to her mother added sorrow.

It must be remembered that the governess had tended and cared for Constance from the moment of her birth and notwithstanding her strict treatment of the child she was closer to her than was the child's own mother. It was the governess to whom Constance ran when she was unhappy and it was the governess who had by far the greater influence over her.

So firmly ensconced was Mary Pratt in the household, so sure was she of her power in her situation that she did not hesitate to make clear her own feelings regarding the unhappy Mrs. Kent. She despised her, totally, and treated her with ridicule and contempt. Her feelings were probably born of envy and jealousy, but whatever their source she gave vent to them.

She was not, however, content with expressing her own feelings of scorn. She began, from the earliest time, to indoctrinate the small child Constance with the same feelings towards the unfortunate woman. Constance, very young and impressionable, naturally allied herself with that person closest to her—the mother-figure, Mary Pratt—and very soon had learned to despise and dislike her own mother. Says the Sydney Document:

> The governess always spoke of Mrs. Kent with a sneer, calling her a Certain Person, ridiculing her. Constance was sometimes rude to her mother and would tell the governess what she had said. The governess would make no comment other than a Mona Lisa smile.

Mrs. Kent and her youngest daughter were daily growing further and further apart.

That was Constance's first tragedy.

When sowing the seeds of it Mary Pratt could never have dreamed that one day it would bear a second, and much more bitter, fruit.

Chapter 3

A FINE AND PRIVATE PLACE

Constance, at such a young age, could not have been aware of the nature of the relationship between her father and the governess. The closeness of those two adults and the reclusiveness of her mother was a situation that was, for her, the norm; it was a situation she had known all her life. She was very fond of Mary Pratt and the governess's presence in the house was not a factor she would question—*then*. Any untoward incidents that she observed—and there must have been many—would not have struck her as significant; it would only be later on that those incidents, lingering in the memory, would be examined and seen more clearly for what they meant. The Sydney Document speaks of Constance later recalling certain happenings that, as she became more sexually aware, took on a new significance:

She slept in a room inside that of the governess, who always locked the door between when she came to bed. Mr. Kent's bed- and dressing-room were on the other side and when he was away the governess said she was frightened to be alone and Constance had to sleep with her. Also, why did her mother, when speaking to her, often call herself, "your poor mamma", which the govern- ess said was silly? Why was the governess taken out for drives and her mother never? Why was her father in the library with the governess while the rest of the family was with her mother? She remembered many little incidents which seemed strange. One was during a thunderstorm when the governess acted as though she were frightened and rushed over to the father who drew her down on his knee and kissed her. The governess exclaimed: "Oh, not before the child!"

For the time being, though, life continued on a fairly even course, the relative calm only slightly ruffled by Constance's outbursts as she showed her growing resentment of authority. In this case that authority came with her schoolwork under the tuition of the governess. From the Sydney Document we learn:

> The governess had a theory that once a child said a letter or spelt a word right it could not forget it, and she conscientiously believed it was her duty to treat any lapse as obstinacy. The letter H gave Constance many hours of confinement in a room while she listened longingly to the music of the scythe on the lawn outside. When words were to be mastered punishments became more severe. Two days were spent shut up in a room with dry bread and milk and water for tea. At other times she would be stood up in a corner in the hall, sobbing, "I want to be good. I do, I do," till she came to the conclusion that goodness was impossible for a child and she could only hope to grow up quickly as grown-ups were never naughty. At times she gave way to furious fits of temper and was locked away in a distant room and sometimes in a cellar, that her noise might not annoy people.

There were two strong personalities here, that of the woman and the child, and their clashes did not augur well for the future. At the moment, though, in spite of the tantrums and the punishments, the affection between them remained.

In 1851 the sum of £1,000 was settled (through Mrs. Kent) on Constance, the money to be held in trust for her until she should come of age at twenty-one. The endowment came from Mrs. Kent's family, the Winduses, similar amounts having earlier been settled on Mary Ann and Elizabeth.

That same year Edward, now sixteen, left the naval school at Gosport and went to Bristol where he was placed under the care and guidance of a private naval tutor, "from whose establishment it was now designed that he should enter the merchant service".[1] Edward was apparently most unhappy at this change but nevertheless had no choice but to submit to his father's decision—a decision brought about by the need to conserve finances. There cannot be any doubt that Mr. Kent would not have taken such a step had not his situation demanded such measures, but at the same time it must

[1] J. W. Stapleton.

be correct to say that he gave little or no thought to the personal desires of his children—while yet demanding from them the strictest obedience.

This same attitude seems to have prevailed wherever he was held as a superior. In his work, where tact was a necessity of the first order, he appears to have been singularly lacking in that quality and frequently found himself violently at odds with the employers at the local cloth factories.

Still, while his children, his servants and his professional subordinates found him a difficult man to deal with, the fact is equally clear that Mary Pratt did not. She continued to hold him in total thrall, and rather than let her go he was prepared to risk the opprobrium of his superiors, the respect inherent in his position, and the contentment of his children. Even so, however, he had to make concessions.

Early in 1852 he decided that another change of scene was essential. The gossip surrounding the nature of the Walton-in-Gordano *ménage* was making life intolerable, and not only as regards his professional interests but also in respect of his social pursuits.

By far the greatest consideration, however, had to be given to the security of his professional position and, being approached once more by his superior, Mr. Howell, and unable to find any other way out of his dilemma, Mr. Kent found no alternative but to once again run from the scene of the calumny. According to Dr. Stapleton it was openly stated that the departure was made "to screen him from public censure as regard to his cruel indifference to her" (his wife) "and his misconduct in regard to the governess".

They went this time to Wiltshire, moving a distance—as the crow flies—of some thirty-six miles, to East Coulston, a tiny village nestling in the hills on the northern edge of Salisbury Plain.

The narrow road that approaches the village from Westbury, the nearest town, winds through leafy avenues where trees crowd the high banks. From the road the carriage drive sweeps between the pillars of the lodge gates, through meadows and into the grounds of Baynton House, moving up to its wide front door in a snaking curve beside green lawns and a wide ornamental lake where rushes fringe the banks.

The spacious, well-kept grounds of the beautiful twenty-room mansion are secluded by screens of yew hedges, birches and elms.

The setting is tranquil; one can walk the length of the carriage drive and hear only the cawing of rooks.

And that new seclusion was what Samuel Kent needed. Although Baynton House was situated much too far from Westbury Station for convenience; although the house itself was larger than he needed and too expensive for his means, it nevertheless provided that desperately needed respite from the gossip and the watchful eyes; it was another retreat where he would, hopefully, at last, be free from criticism.

The move was made at the end of March.

Mrs. Kent, driving up to the house to take up another period of melancholy loneliness, could look over her shoulder and see, beyond the lawns and the water, the walls of the tiny grey-stone church of St. Thomas à Becket, the grounds of which abutted the grounds of her new home. Her rooms in the house would be the last she would occupy. Perhaps from their windows she could gaze out and see the little church's cemetery, and there, on its north side, her final resting place.

It must have been around the time of the move to Baynton House that Constance began to realize how wrongly she had felt and behaved towards her mother. It was not a sudden realization but a gradual dawning of awareness. Often she had heard conversations between her sisters and elder brother on the subject of their mother's unhappiness and whereas once she had remained unaffected by them in time they had made their mark upon her. She became aware at last that her father treated her mother with complete indifference, while at the same time he gave all his affection to the governess. She became aware that her mother had suffered, was suffering still, and that she, Constance, through her thoughtless, callous behaviour, had added to that suffering. Now, watching her mother, witnessing her resignation and total rejection, and seeing still how the governess disparaged and despised her, she became swamped by contrition and guilt. She was filled with love for her mother and with dislike for the governess, for she it was who surely was the cause of all the unhappiness and mental and emotional anguish her mother had endured. The governess it was who, in the child's eyes, had "robbed that mother of the affection both of a husband and a daughter". The child would never feel love for the governess again.

Constance was then eight years old. Being yet so young she could still, perhaps, make up to her mother for the wrong that had been done to her.

But time was not on her side.

Only weeks after the arrival at Baynton House Mary Pratt left on the 1st of May to visit her father who was ill in Devonshire. On the following day Mrs Kent became desperately sick with excruciating pains in the stomach. A local doctor who was called in was unable to save her and three days later, in great agony, she died.

Immediately on hearing the news, Mary Pratt left her father's sick bed and returned to East Coulston where, on the 11th, along with other members of the Kent family, she attended Mrs. Kent's burial next to the tiny church.

The governess's own father died just four days later on the 15th.

Having paid so little attention to his wife during her lifetime Kent, now, with her death, paid lip-service to her remembrance. The stone that was laid over her grave bears the inscription:

SACRED TO THE MEMORY OF MARY ANN,
THE WIFE OF S. SAVILL KENT, ESQUIRE OF BAYNTON HOUSE,
WHO DIED MAY 5TH 1852 AGED 44 YEARS

The unhappy life of Mary Ann Kent had, no doubt, been a great burden on her husband. Perhaps, though, as he stood above her grave while the Reverend John Clapp intoned a prayer he imagined that his troubles were at last over.

His troubles had hardly begun.

In eight years he would be standing once more in that same spot, watching as another coffin was lowered into the earth. Another name would be cut into that same stone, while on the head of Samuel Kent would rest the weight of a secret he dare not divulge.

Chapter 4

THE FAMILY

I n no time at all word of Mrs. Kent's death reached those areas where the family had previously lived, and some recipients of the news were not slow to spread the rumour that Mr. Kent and the governess had been responsible for Mrs. Kent's end—that the pair had actually engineered it. Some years later these whispered hints would be heard again, but for now Mr. Kent, if he heard the whispers, could rise above them.

Edward was at sea for most of the period of mourning following his mother's death. He had entered the service of the West India Royal Mail Steam Packet Company, preparing to serve a year under sail as fifth officer, a humble rank, and the lowest, but the necessary first step in his career. While he was away the rest of the family remained in the seclusion of Baynton House, as also did Mary Pratt who, "in the delicate and unusual position in which she consented to remain in Mr. Kent's family",[1] continued to run the house and give lessons to Constance and William—the latter back amongst his kin once more.

Although William, it appears, gave the governess no trouble, Constance on the other hand did, and her increasingly bad behaviour saw her undergoing frequent punishments. On this subject the Sydney Document says:

> Constance did not take her punishments very seriously; she generally managed to get some amusement out of them. Once after being particularly provocative and passionate, the governess put her down in a dark wine cellar. She fell on a heap of straw and fancied herself in the dungeon of a great castle, a prisoner taken in battle fighting for Bonnie Prince Charlie and to be taken to the block next morning. When the governess unlocked the door and told her to come up she was looking rather pleased over her fancies. The governess asked what she was smiling about. "Oh," she said, "only the funny rats."

[1] J. W. Stapleton.

"What rats?" said the governess. She did not know there were any there.

"They do not hurt," said Constance, "only dance and play about."

After that to her disappointment she was shut in the beer cellar, a light room but with a window too high to look out of. She managed to pull the spigot out of a cask of beer. After that she was locked up in one of two spare rooms at the end of a vestibule and shut off by double doors. She liked the big room for it had a large four-poster bed she could climb about, but the little room was dreary. The rooms had a legend attached to them and were said to be haunted, and on a certain date a blue fire burned in the fireplace.

At one time at Baynton House Constance's place of punishment was in one of the empty garrets. The house was built in the shape of an E, and there was a parapet round the best part of the house. She used to climb out of the window and up the bend to the top of the roof and slide down the other side. She tied an old fur across her chest to act the monkey and called it playing Cromwell. To return she got through the window of another garret. The governess was puzzled at always finding the door unlocked with the key left in. The servants were questioned but of course knew nothing. One day she found Constance and her brother out on the leads and told them not to do it as it was dangerous. Next time when Constance did her climb she found the window fastened. She could not climb back the way she came, but just where the parapet ended was the window of a room where the groom slept. She leaned across and climbed through, and though she upset and broke a jug on the washstand, the cat got the credit. Afterwards she heard that her father did not approve of the window being fastened to trap her and said that when unruly she could be shut in the study, a room where her father wrote and kept his papers. Being on the ground floor she easily got out of the window and passed her time climbing trees in the shrubbery.

There was now no sign at all of that closeness that had once existed between Constance and Mary Pratt. With the death of Mrs. Kent any vestige of the affection the child had felt for the governess had vanished, its place being taken by a bitterly growing hatred. The widening rift that henceforth grew between the two might at later times have been patched up to some degree, but it was never to be healed.

Where the Kent children had found only grief in their mother's passing, that same event can have brought to Mary Pratt only happiness and relief. It is understandable; the woman who had previously stood in the way of that happiness was no longer an obstacle.

Mary Pratt was thirty-two years old, and the last twelve years of her life had been spent in the Kent household. What, during those twelve years had she seen as her future? What promises and blandishments had Mr. Kent pressed upon her as she had seen the years going by with no prospect of any change for the better? What, she must have asked herself and her lover, was to become of her? Supposing Mrs. Kent should live on into old age—then where would that leave Mary Pratt who was but twelve years her junior? Already the governess was well over the first flush of youth—and her youth and vitality had been among her main attractions. With dread she must have seen the very strong possibility that, with no legal claim on Mr. Kent's affections, some other woman would in time appear, some servant perhaps—as she officially was still—but a younger, prettier woman, and that she herself would be replaced, discarded, just as Mrs. Kent had been. And if that should happen she would be left with less than she had begun.

Yes, it was a good thing for Mary Pratt that Mrs. Kent died when she did, for the subsequent deaths, very soon afterwards, of both the governess's parents left her with no home to return to should she even desire it. With Mrs. Kent's demise, though, Mary Pratt's immediate worries came to an end.

Fifteen months later—as soon as the period of mourning was over, and as early as Victorian decency allowed—the family travelled to Lewisham where, at St. Mary's church on the 11th of August (1853), the governess and Mr. Kent were made husband and wife. The bride was married from her uncle's house nearby, such a venue having been chosen, probably, with a view to avoiding unwelcome publicity; that the couple felt a conscious need to avoid gossip is indicated by the fact that for the purpose of the register the bride gave her residence as Lewisham.

Constance and her two sisters were bridesmaids, following the governess up the aisle and returning down it in the wake of their stepmother.

Edward was away at sea at the time of the marriage and was kept in complete ignorance of it until he returned to Baynton House some weeks afterwards. He was shocked, angry and hurt at the news that greeted him and after a very unpleasant scene in which he strongly expressed himself towards his stepmother "in terms of dislike and resentment", he left the house and returned at once to Bristol. There he rejoined his ship, the *Kenilworth*, which, having been hired by the government as a transport in the Crimean War, set sail for Balaclava. His dramatic and abrupt departure could not have endeared to Constance and her siblings that one whom they saw as being responsible for it—their stepmother—and the resulting prevailing ambience did not portend well for the future.

The second Mrs. Kent, though, soon had more personal and pressing matters to concern her: she had found that she was pregnant. In June of the following year, 1854, she gave birth to her first child. It was stillborn. However, though her hopes for motherhood had been temporarily dashed they were soon to be raised again for very soon after her confinement was over she found that she was pregnant once more.

If the birth of a dead child had caused Mr. Kent any sorrow it was nothing to that which he experienced in November of that same year when he received the dread news that Edward, along with all hands of the *Kenilworth*, had drowned off the coast of Balaclava. Samuel Kent was truly heartbroken and made frequent inquiries of the ship-owners and of Lloyd's in the hope that the news might be contradicted. But it was not, and after a month had passed he was forced to accept as fact the loss of his most loved son.

What made acceptance even more bitter was the fact that he and Edward had parted in great anger and that since their parting they had not communicated with one another by so much as a single written word.

It was at the point of Mr. Kent's acceptance of his son's death, though, that there occurred one of those strange twists of fate which would be scorned by any writer of fiction. Mr. Kent was preparing, with his wife, to drive to Bath to buy mourning—he was actually just stepping into the carriage—when the village postman came towards him and put into his hand a letter. It was from Edward. He had, after all, survived.

His account of his escape is best told in his own words:

R.M.S. *Trent*, at Balaclava.
Nov. 17th, 1854.

My dear Papa,—I know that you will be very glad to hear of my providential escape from shipwreck on the 14th of November. The *Kenilworth* was lying at anchor off Balaclava when a most fearful gale sprang up about seven o'clock, and in an hour's time increased to a terrible hurricane. About 9.45 the *Kenilworth* parted from her anchors, and was dashed to pieces on the rocks in the course of a very few minutes. Only myself and six of the crew were saved, and twenty-three lost. I am the only officer that is saved.

Captain Ponsonby, of the royal mail steamer *Trent*, when he heard that I was saved, sent for me, and, as there was an officer wanting on board the *Trent*, he has made me acting fifth officer. I should think that the best thing that could be done now would be to write to the directors and try and get the appointment confirmed; as I suppose all further hopes of going in another sailing-ship must be given up. I have lost everything but a shirt and trousers, and my watch, which I had on me when cast ashore. Very fortunately for me the R.M.S. *Avon* was lying in Balaclava; and Mr. Langdon, the officer who was so kind to me when I was on board the *Magdalena*, is on board her, and he has given me some shirts and a suit of clothes, and lent me £4 to get what I wanted. Several other ships have met with the same fate as ours, and the loss of life has been most considerable. Captain Ponsonby is very kind to me. I knew him when he was chief officer in the Company. He is also very intimate with Mr. Arthur Windus, who always asks after me when he sees Captain Ponsonby; so the Captain seems interested in my behalf. I must now conclude with love to all.

I remain your affectionate son,
Edward Kent.

When Edward returned to England the quarrel with his father and stepmother was patched up and the period of his leave was

pleasant and harmonious. Later, his appointment on the flagship
Trent being confirmed, he joined her on her voyages to the West
Indies, frequently coming home on leave.

There can be little doubt that the birth of Mary Amelia in the
summer of 1855 changed even further the relationship that existed
between the second Mrs. Kent and her stepchildren. John Rhode
writes of Mrs. Kent: "she appears to have been a rather selfish
woman, the scope of whose affections was strictly limited. While
she may, as governess, have genuinely lavished these affections upon
Mr. Kent's children, no sooner had she become a mother herself
than her attention was wholly centred upon her own children."
Well, not an uncommon situation, but nonetheless difficult for those
children who find themselves suddenly pushed into the background.
Certainly for the younger Kent children the early years with their
stepmother must have been especially difficult; for Constance in
particular; it can only have caused her growing hatred to become
even more bitter.

Mary Ann and Elizabeth, it should be noted, would have been
less affected by the change in Mary Pratt's status, though even so
they still had their problems. These were inherent in the domestic
situation, a situation that had long before sprung from their father's
wish to escape censure and which had resulted in their being denied
any kind of social life. Neither girl was ever to marry—a fact which
is hardly surprising when one considers that they were deprived of
practically any opportunity. During their most eligible years they
were living in near-isolation and forced to shun society. By the time
they were able to do as they wished it was too late; both were well
past marriageable age and even should an opportunity have arisen
it is doubtful that they would have been equipped to deal with it.

It was not any long time after her marriage that the second Mrs.
Kent took up once more her old attitude of scorn with regard to her
predecessor.

It did not matter that Mary Drewe Kent was now the legal wife
of Mr. Kent and the legal mistress of the beautiful Baynton House;
in the eyes of so many—at a time when class distinctions were far
more rigidly defined than they are now—she was still little more
than a fortunate, ambitious upstart. And of her own lowly origins

she must have been acutely aware. The first Mrs. Kent was acknowledged to have been a gentle, gracious woman, from a wealthy, much-respected family, and the one-time governess must have been faced, time and again, with reminders of her predecessor's origins. The only way that she—the grocer's daughter—could elevate herself was to denigrate her husband's late wife, and this she continued to do. Her own lingering sense of guilt—supposing that she possessed it—might also have played a part in her hostile attitude; there is much truth in the saying, "Guilt turns to hostility", and where Mary Drewe Kent was concerned she had much to feel guilty about.

And there was, of course, only one sure way in which the character of the dead Mrs. Kent *could* be criticized—and this was through her somewhat questionable mental state; it was a mental state that Mary Drewe Kent had doubtless contributed to, yet nevertheless she did not hesitate to use it as a weapon against the dead woman's memory—and, obliquely, against the children that the woman had borne.

If Mary Drewe Kent had been guided more by sense than by sensibility the hurt she had caused in the past might have been mended, and she might well have averted the tragedy that was to come. But no, she went ahead, continuing in her scornful way, not caring or not seeing that her malicious attitude only aggravated the old wounds, making them more painful.

It cannot be mere coincidence that Constance's father and stepmother were finding the child increasingly difficult to handle. Says J. W. Stapleton:

> The conduct and behaviour of the child is complained of as having been at this period occasionally very troublesome and bad, sometimes even insolent. Her ears are said to have been boxed; but her general punishment was simply banishment from the parlour to the hall.

Constance was giving clear indication of the hurt and anger she felt, and still Mrs. Kent went on with her provocations.

There was to be a reckoning, and the cost would be dear.

Chapter 5

THE FUGITIVES

Later in 1855 Mr. Kent decided that he had had enough of Baynton House and began to look for other accommodation. According to Dr. Stapleton one of the main reasons for the desired change of scene was the inconvenient situation of Baynton House—it lying at too great a distance from the nearest railway station at Westbury and also from the various bases of manufacture over which Mr. Kent exercised his particular control. This, it was said, caused unnecessary expense to the department in which he was employed. Stapleton also says that Mr. Howell, Kent's friend and official superior, reminded Kent that it was time that Mary Ann and Elizabeth were "introduced into society of their own rank" and that Mr. Kent himself should take his own rightful place in that society once more.

It is in the latter that part of the *true* reason for the move can be found. In East Coulston Mr. Kent was not accorded any of that respect which he believed to be his due—a situation brought about by his late domestic affairs which had been the talk of the locality. And the same, of course, went for Mrs. Kent. She was seen as a woman who had been elevated from servant of the house to mistress of the house—not by any laudable means, either—and as such would probably never be socially accepted. Residence in a different area could change all that; she would enter her next home as the rightful, and accepted, wife of Mr. Kent and should, therefore, receive the respect she desired; they both would.

Another reason understood to be behind the planned move was that Baynton House was on too grand a scale for Mr. Kent's pocket; a less financially-draining residence was a total necessity. Mr. Kent had a yearly salary of £800, supplemented by a smaller private income, and this was insufficient for his lifestyle in a great house "adequate to the wants and pretensions of a country gentleman of considerable and independent fortune". These words, from Dr.

Stapleton, show that even *that* gentleman was critical of his friend's affectations.

So it was, then, that in the autumn of 1855, having disposed of the lease of Baynton House, Mr. Kent and his family moved some ten miles distant to Road, a tiny village straddling the Wiltshire/ Somerset border. There they took up the occupancy of Road Hill House which, although having about the same number of rooms as Baynton House, was built on a slightly smaller scale. Nevertheless, it was still beyond his means. Still, perhaps his finances were a lesser consideration when compared with his and his wife's need to be socially accepted.

Mr. Kent had given out that one of his reasons for leaving the near-isolation of Baynton House was consideration for his elder daughters' want of social intercourse, but for this the new venue would have been but little improvement on the old. Road is a small village now and it was even smaller then when its population was fewer than seven hundred. The nearest towns of any size are Trow-bridge and Frome, each about five miles away in opposite directions, while the city of Bath lies about ten miles to the north-west. Such distances are minor by today's reckonings, but in those days, before the bus and the motor-car, the only means of local travel was by horse or one's own two feet. Consequently, when Mary Ann and Elizabeth took up residence at Road Hill House they cannot have looked forward to much social diversion.

As Samuel Kent must be held partly responsible for that situation so, to a great extent, he was to blame for the lack of accept-ance suffered by Constance and William on their arrival in the village. He had made a bad start at the time of taking the lease on the house, and the unpleasant impression he created did not bode well for his future dealings with his neighbours.

The first incident to count against him took place before the family had even moved in. While Mr. Kent was visiting his newly-leased property he discovered in the grounds one Abraham Nutt, a neighbour, stealing apples. As the property had been empty for some time it appears that many of the nearby inhabitants, adults and children, had regarded such behaviour as quite acceptable, not seeing it as a criminal offence. Mr. Kent did, however, and he at once instigated legal proceedings which resulted in a successful prosecution of the culprit.

Next, having moved into the house he made an attempt to "secure his own privacy and that of his servants"[1] by erecting a substantial fence along one side of his property which was bordered by a narrow lane. On the other side of this lane stood several cottages, and his erection of the fence was a "protection against the oversight and intrusion of the inmates of those cottages".[2] The cottagers, though, it is said, took umbrage at the act, and before their feelings had had a chance to cool Mr. Kent managed to antagonize them still further. As Dr. Stapleton says:

> Beyond the enclosed grounds of Road Hill House the land slopes on one side gradually down into a beautiful and watered valley. In the river which intersects this valley Mr. Kent secured that right of fishing over a certain extent of its course. He cultivated and protected the fish, put up warnings against trespassers and reserved the right of fishing exclusively to himself and his friends. In this same river the inmates of the cottages also had been accustomed to find their amusement; and they at once resented a monopoly which deprived them of their dish of trout. Poaching commenced, and, on the other side, watching and threats of punishment.

Dr. Stapleton then goes on to say that Constance and William "were called after in their walks and on their way to church, by the cottagers' children; [and were] frequently molested by them". This being the case then the move from Baynton House cannot have promised much pleasure to the younger children either.

These two, Constance and William, were sent to boarding-schools in Bath early in 1856. Their stepmother, having started her own family, now cared even less for, and felt less inclined to instruct, her stepchildren. Not only did she have the baby Mary Amelia, but she had found herself pregnant once more. This situation would not make her eager to continue to suffer Constance's troublesome behaviour, and was probably partly responsible for the decision to send the children away.

---

[1] J. W. Stapleton.
[2] *Ibid.*

On the subject of Constance's life at school the Sydney Document reports:

At school she was happier with companions, but as she was always resentful of authority she was still ever in trouble and looked on as a black sheep. She gave nicknames to her teachers and made rhymes on them which were not complimentary, increasing her unpopularity with them, though there were exceptions. Of these was one of the masters who attended the school. He had a great quantity of black hair and a rugged countenance; she named him "Bear in a Bush", and when taken to a fashionable chapel for Bible class she called the minister "The Octagon Magpie"—from the shape of the building. When the men were told of their nicknames, though, they only laughed, and the minister, thinking he might bring some good out of her, took some extra pains with her. However, seeing that the other girls were jealous she gave stupid replies on purpose, and so fell from grace. Then she thought to turn religious and got two of her companions to join her in learning chapters of the Bible, but it did not act to make her good as she had hoped. She was given to read a book by Baxter which convinced her that she had committed the unforgivable sin, so it was useless to try any more. Also about this time she read a book on evolution by Darwin and much scandalized her family by expressing her belief in his theory of creation.

From the same source we learn that Constance did not always go home for her holidays, and that

on one occasion when she did so no one took any notice; she might have just come in from a walk. She was sitting at a window, rather disconsolate, when her stepmother wanted her to do some mending. She refused, and her stepmother said, "Do you know, but only for me you would have remained at school. When I said you were coming one of your sisters exclaimed, 'What, that tiresome girl!' So you see, *they* do not want you."

The above incident shows that Mrs. Kent was very capable of making a conscious effort to encourage some positive communication with Constance. Being rather blinkered to anything outside her own special situation it is more than likely that she simply did not, could not, understand her youngest step-daughter's impossible behaviour.

But apart from the interesting insight it gives into the more human
and sympathetic side of Mrs. Kent's character, the episode clearly
indicates that Mary Ann and Elizabeth—perhaps understandably
in the circumstances—also found Constance's presence often very
trying and disruptive.

For some time following her return from Miss Duckworth's school,
Manor House, in that summer of 1856, Constance complained of
weak ankles and pain in her legs. She was duly examined by Dr.
Parsons, the family's physician, in the belief that her legs might be
injured or diseased, and following his directions put on lace stockings to combat the lameness she complained of. Apparently she was
excused all exercise, particularly "much walking", and when an
excursion was made to the Bath flower-show she was taken around
it in a wheel-chair.

There is, however, a question as to whether Constance was indeed
suffering from some unspecified but painful malady of the legs or
whether the whole thing was an act from start to finish.

If it was an act then it could have been motivated by a desire
for attention, to evince sympathy, caring and love from her father
—of his lack of affection for her she must have been very much
aware; on the other hand it could well be that her act (if it was
such) was simply to *divert* attention from a certain scheme she had
in mind. All that is certain is that, when the time came, her "weak
ankles" had gained enough strength to carry her for a distance of
many miles.

Constance's plan came into operation one afternoon that summer.
It is reported that the term of her and William's holidays was
actually over and that the two children had been kept at home
pending their father's return from a business trip to Devonshire.
The reason *behind* their being kept at home, however—which is not
generally known—is that Mr. Kent, finding it increasingly difficult
to keep up with boarding-school expenses, had reluctantly decided
that the children must once again be taught at home by their stepmother.

Constance, though, had other ideas. The prospect of once again
having to stay at home with her stepmother was not to be borne,
and with matters coming to a head with some punishment received

for misbehaviour, she decided to make her escape. We are told that she was also motivated by the fact that

> she longed for a more active life than the one she led, which was so dull and monotonous. She was not wanted; everyone was against her. She had read of women disguised as men earning their living and never being found out till they were dead. She felt fit and strong and made up her mind to dress as a boy and get a billet as cabin boy on the first ship that would take her. She thought there would not be much fuss if she disappeared . . . so she persuaded her young brother to join her in her wild enterprise.[3]

Some hours after lunch it was suddenly discovered that she and William had not been seen about the house or grounds for a considerable time. At once an alarm was raised and a search made for them; to no avail; the children had gone.

Earlier, so it transpired, Constance had mended some of William's old clothes, added to them with items of her own making, and hidden the whole lot in a hedge. Then, on the afternoon in question, after retrieving the bundle, she took it to a rarely-used privy that stood in thick yew shrubbery near the house, took off her own clothes and changed into the boy's. To complete her disguise she then—with William's help—cut off her long tawny hair and thrust it, along with her own discarded clothing, down into the privy's vault.[4] This done, the boy and the girl made their furtive escape from the grounds and, looking to all outward appearances like two brothers, set off on the road to the north-west.

At the time of their flight Constance was twelve-and-a-half years old and William just eleven. Many children at some time in their young lives conceive the romantic notion of running away from home but rarely does their distress or resolve carry them much

---

[3] The Sydney Document.

[4] Whilst in Road I was told by one of its residents that following the Kents' departure from Road a metal box containing Constance's hair was dug up from what had been her garden. There is no evidence to show that it had ever belonged to Constance, however; on the contrary it is disproved by the fact that in September, 1860, every inch of her garden was dug up with nothing being revealed (see p. 205), and also by Constance's own words, to the effect that she herself cast her shorn hair into the privy's vault (see p. 162).

beyond the front gate. With Constance, however—with William in tow—the flight from home was no mere passing whim of the moment brought about merely by some trivial or imaginary injustice. It is clear that she must have been desperate to escape, and if nothing else were ever known about her this episode alone would speak volumes for her single-mindedness and strength of will. It also shows that she was well capable of devising a plan and, if unhampered by circumstances beyond her control, of seeing that plan through. She was to demonstrate this strength of purpose many times in the years to come.

Her plan in this instance was to get to Bristol where she and William might find a ship that would take them from England. Their brother Edward, having gained promotion to fourth officer, had been transferred to the intercolonial steamer, the *Clyde*, on a route connecting the smaller West Indian islands with Barbados (an appointment which promised to keep him away from home for at least another two years), and thoughts of his career abroad probably contributed to Constance's aims so that she imagined they could somehow find him and join him in his freedom.

By late evening the pair had reached Bath, about ten miles from home and somewhat less than half-way to Bristol. There at the Greyhound Hotel Constance asked for food and a room for the night. She, being shorter than William, was taken to be the younger of the two and, whilst William stood silently by it was the "younger boy" who did all the talking. The landlord, suspicious, suspected that the two children were runaways and began to question them, but Constance refused to give her name and even denied knowing her companion, saying they had only recently met, by chance, on the road. J. W. Stapleton says that "Constance was very self-possessed, and even insolent, in her manner and language", but that William "soon broke down and burst into tears".

The landlord, leaving Constance in the care of another adult, took William to the local police station where the boy was questioned by the inspector there. It wasn't long before the true story came out. His companion, William said, was actually his sister who had dressed herself in his clothes and cut short her hair. Their aim was to go to sea. All the cash they had between them was eighteen-pence. . . .

Contrite and tearful, William was taken back to the hotel where it was arranged that he should have a bed for the night while Constance—clearly determined and unrepentant—was given a bed in the station's detention room. As she was taken away, it is said, William wept bitterly at being parted from her.

The following week *The Devizes Advertiser* wrote an account of the children's adventure. It was headed *A Little Romance*, and concluded:

> . . . The next morning their story was confirmed by the arrival of a servant in livery in search of them, and he was heartily glad to find them, having, he said, broken down three horses in pursuing them in other directions. . . . The little girl, we are told, behaved like a little hero, acting the part of a boy to the admiration of all who saw her. We learn from Mr. Inspector Norris, who was on duty at the time, that Miss Kent manifested great shrewdness and resolution. The boy's clothes she wore were too small for her, and she carried a small stick, which she used as if she had been accustomed to it. . . .

The officers at the station might have been filled with admiration for Constance, but her parents were to be less favourably impressed. Back at home the two children awaited the return of their father from Devonshire, and when he appeared later in the day they were duly confronted with his wrath. William, says Dr. Stapleton, "at once expressed the greatest sorrow and contrition, and sobbed bitterly", while Constance, quite intractable, was kept in solitary confinement for many days, giving "no evidence of regret or shame at her conduct". At last, though, she told her father what had been her aim in running away—that she had wanted, with William, to leave England. "I wished," she said, "to be independent."

It is hardly surprising that Mr. Kent should have been so angry. In the past he had gone to great lengths to escape censure and it was at Road that—apart from those minor squabbles with the neighbours—for the first time in years he had been free of it. Now, within months of his arrival there he had become, through the truancy of his children, the scandal of the neighbourhood.

The news of the escapade—through local gossip and the newspapers—spread rapidly over a wide area and the public waited expectantly for some statement from Mr. Kent which would satisfactorily explain his children's clearly indicated desire to get away from home. Not only the public, either; after all, Mr. Kent gained his livelihood partly through the care and protection of children and suddenly a doubt had been raised as to whether he was up to the task even within his own domestic circle. Where the example he set should have been of the very highest, that example was found to be questionable, and unless he could give some reasonable explanation to account for the episode the questions would remain.

He never did give any acceptable explanation and four years later when Dr. Stapleton was writing his book those questions were still unanswered. He wrote:

> It ought not to be difficult to account for such an extraordinary proceeding on the part of two young and tender children. It was to be expected certainly the parents . . . would have been found as able, as they should have been desirous, to furnish some explanation more probable, more sufficient, more satisfactory, than simple love of adventure on the part of those children. . . . Nor, while it remains unexplained, can any fair or reasonable comment be made of that criticism which, on the part of the public and the authorities, has supposed some defect in their education, and moral discipline, and domestic treatment. . . . A painful doubt rests upon the public mind in reference to all.

When one remembers that Dr. Stapleton wrote his book in order to mend the damaged reputation of his friend Mr. Kent, then any *criticism* he makes of Mr. Kent should be taken very seriously indeed. Children do not try to escape from an environment in which they are happy and loved, and it was clear to everyone that Constance and William did not feel they were.[5]

One outcome of the children's truancy was that they were both sent away to boarding-schools once more, William to one in Worcester and Constance to that distant school run by relatives of her stepmother. This latter move, however, did not prove a success and in a short time the girl had managed to antagonize her new teachers. According to the Sydney Document:

---

[5] It is believed that Constance and William's flight from home inspired Charles Dickens. In his book *Edwin Drood* (1870) Helena Landless and her brother Neville run away from their stepfather—Helena having first cut off her hair and disguised herself as a boy.

They were extremely proper and she delighted in shocking them; it was only too easy. She was considered blasphemous because she would always speak of Sara Bernhardt as La Divine Sara. She was not with them long as they considered her incorrigible.

From there Constance was sent to school in Hertfordshire, from where she was rarely allowed home for her holidays.

About the end of August, just a few weeks after Constance and William's escape-attempt, Mrs. Kent gave birth to a son. He was baptized Francis Savill, his first name after Mrs. Kent's father. Due, however, to Mr. Kent's inordinate pride in his own second name, the baby was known as Savill from the time of his birth.

With this new addition to the family, by all accounts a handsome, healthy baby, the needs of the members of the first family were thrust even more into the background. William in particular suffered, for not only was he further deprived of affection but he had also to bear the humiliation of having his own qualities unfavourably compared with those of his baby half-brother.

This was about the time also when Constance, now in her early teens, began to brood much upon the memories of her late mother, and with the startling awareness brought on by the onset of puberty saw the reality of the father-mother-governess triangle for what it had been. The result of that awareness was that her hatred for her stepmother was given new life and grew deeper still.

In other respects also she was very far from happy. Although she had gained some advantage in being at boarding-school she well knew that such a move had not been planned for *her* benefit; she was, she believed, being kept away from home; she and William, she was sure, were discriminated against—and only because they were members of the first family.

William, it seems, was the only one with whom Constance felt any real kinship. They were close in age—only fifteen months apart—and were probably drawn still closer together by their mutual feeling that from the second family they had been set apart.

Constance loved her brother dearly and later in her life she was to demonstrate, with incredible courage, just how true and deep this affection was.

William apart, though, her youthful relationships were not very positive, and from all we know of the young Constance Kent a picture emerges of a basically unhappy, often sullen girl; a girl thwarted in her need to receive affection and equally in her need to give it.

Notwithstanding Constance's continually troublesome behaviour, however, the four years following her attempt at escape were, for the Kent family, on the surface, relatively without incident. But for one tragic exception.

At the beginning of July, 1858, Edward, on board his ship the *Clyde*, fell ill with a fever. After a few days he rallied—his temperature falling closer to normal and the aches in his legs decreasing; it was hoped that he might recover. But then his pulse slowed again and he took on that sickly hue that pointed to yellow fever—for such his sickness was. When he began to vomit blood and to bleed freely from his nose he knew he had but little time to live, and on the 10th, in the presence of his friend Robert Parr of the sister ship *Atrato*, and the ship's surgeon, Elijah Pring, he made his will.[6]

Edward Windus Kent directed that his estate—which realized almost £300—should be shared by his siblings. His much loved Mary Ann and Elizabeth each inherited a third of the sum total while the remaining third was divided equally between William and Constance.

Soon after signing his name to the document he went into a coma. The following day, there at Havana, he died. He was just twenty-three.

[6] Yseult Bridges states that Edward left the sum of £150 to be divided equally among his three sisters. This is not so. Mrs. Bridges further states – trying to promote the belief that Constance was his favourite sister – that Edward also bequeathed her their mother's Bible. This is another invention, as the briefest examination of Edward's will clearly shows; it is available at Somerset House for anyone to see. Incidentally, his will was undated, and was the subject of probate later in the year.

Chapter 6

ROAD HILL HOUSE

The village of Road (or Rode as its name is now spelt) is noted on the map for having a bird sanctuary. At the beginning of 1860, though, it had no such claim to fame, being just another sleepy little English village with little to distinguish it from so many others. That fame in which it was so soon to be steeped could not, at the start of that fateful year, even have been dreamed of. Not that murder had not touched the inhabitants of that place and the villages surrounding it; it *had*—over a period of twenty years there had occurred five cut-throat murders in the vicinity—and the perpetrator or perpetrators had never been caught. Even so, all those five killings together could not cause a stir like that brought about by the killing at Road Hill House.

Although the main part of the village was in Somerset, Road Hill House, at that time, stood just over the border in the county of Wiltshire[1]—a situation which, when panic was running high, was to create its own special problems. An imposing, gracious residence, built in 1790, it stands looking out over the village from its hillside vantage point. Today the house is secluded by walls and tall trees but in those earlier times it could be gazed upon by any passer-by, while at the same time entrance to its immediate grounds was easily accessible to anyone. After the seclusion of Baynton House Mr. Kent must have felt very much exposed in his home at Road; it is hardly surprising, therefore, so jealously guarding his privacy as he did, that he should have erected that fence that was the cause of so much bad feeling between himself and his close neighbours.

Then, as now, the front aspect of the house faced a large, well-kept lawn, close to one corner of which, in 1860, grew a yew shrubbery. It was in this shrubbery where stood the privy from which point Constance and William had made their attempt at escape some four years earlier.

[1] The county boundary has been altered in the intervening years and the house now stands enclosed by the Somerset border.

Although the gardens have undergone considerable changes over the years the house itself has altered little and the accompanying plan gives an accurate picture of it as it was at the time of the crime. Ironically, at that time—when it mattered most—no similar accurate plan was available—for the simple reason that Mr. Kent refused to allow one to be taken.

As can be seen, the ground floor of the house is much larger than the two upper floors, the dining-room and the servants' working areas spreading beyond the main body of the building. The ground floor consisted of, on the left of the wide hall, the library and, beyond that, the drawing-room. The rest of that floor was comprised of the dining-room, the kitchen, the scullery, the pantry and a laundry room.

The first and second floors held the bedrooms of the household. The members of the second family and the children's nursemaid occupied the first floor, while the servants and the first family were housed on the second. All three floors were connected by two staircases: the main one reaching up from the hall, and the back stairs—the foot of which was close to the kitchen quarters.

Outside at the rear of the house the back door opened onto a stable yard where the coach-houses, stables and outbuildings were situated, this whole area being enclosed by a wall and further secured by gates that were locked at night. For added protection a large Newfoundland dog was kennelled towards the rear of the yard.

Road Hill House with its nineteen rooms and various outbuildings is a most imposing residence by today's standards, and in 1860 when the gulf that separated the classes was so much wider its effect on the relatively poor villagers was probably quite awe-inspiring.

And Mr. Kent lived well in that house. The seclusion of his first wife while at the same time he had conducted a scandalous affair with the children's governess had forced upon him an unwelcome retirement from the good life for too many years. So now, with Baynton House and his marital problems hopefully behind him he could, at Road, once again take up the threads of that more convivial existence he had so much missed. He could begin to entertain his colleagues once more, and also seek the company of those prominent local men whose friendship might previously have been denied him. And apparently his hopes for acceptance were meeting with some success. Dr. Stapleton, writing of those first four years at Road, says that over "this period Mr. and Mrs. Kent and their family had accorded to them that place and welcome in the society of their own rank to which the station of Mr. Kent so unquestionably entitled them".

Even so, although Mr. Kent's present "respectable state of marriage" might have released him from one particular theme of gossip, he was by no means free of it on other counts. The common opinion that he had lived beyond his means at Baynton House touched him yet again at Road Hill House. John Rhode says:

> The fact that Mr. Kent took so large a house, although he had apparently very little means beyond the salary attached to his office, occasioned a certain amount of remark. Local gossip insisted that he was living beyond his means, and asserted that his position afforded him opportunities for receiving bribes which helped to fill the gulf between his expenditure and his income.

Also, and somewhat strangely, Dr. Stapleton, though seemingly pleased that his friend had been accorded his "rightful place in society", still felt compelled to make the comment: "Whether at this time Mr. Kent was living at Road Hill House in a style and at an expense unwarranted by his income, is a matter which it is quite irrelevant and impertinent to discuss."

Well, Mr. Kent *was* still living well beyond his means. A certain Mr. William Gee, writing from Freshford, near Bath, endorsed the popular opinion in a letter he wrote to Sir Richard Mayne of the Metropolitan Police just two months after the crime. I quote from his eloquent letter:

> . . . As to Mr. Kent himself, I learn from the widow of a schoolmaster, a friend of mine, that four years ago he was so straitened as not to be able to pay the bills of the son, £15 or £20 halfyearly, and I cannot reconcile his occupying so handsome a mansion, second to few in the neighbourhood, with the way he behaved to a poor teacher.

The time that Mr. Gee refers to was the summer of 1856, that summer when Constance and William, sick at the prospect of long confinement with their stepmother, set off on the road towards Bristol.

Incidentally, it appears that William's late mentor, that "poor teacher", never did get his money.

Mr. Kent's financial circumstances were not the only cause of gossip, though. He had servant problems, too, and these were also the source of much comment. Wrote Dr. Stapleton: "It was known from some cause or other, whether from their own misconduct or from domestic mismanagement, a constant succession of female servants prevailed at Road Hill House." True. A contemporary estimate has it that in the first four years of the Kents' occupancy of Road Hill House almost *two hundred female servants came and went!* The kernel of the gossip surrounding this parade of ever-changing faces was, according to Dr. Stapleton, that Mr. Kent's female servants "were the constant objects and victims of his pursuit", and although Stapleton tries to scotch the notion with his overkill, clearly there were many who believed there was solid foundation for the rumour—that Mr. Kent, while perhaps not behaving in quite so outrageous a manner had, nevertheless, been guilty of certain indiscretions. Mr. Hughes, Bath's Chief Constable, later made inquiries into the matter, after which saying that he had "examined upwards of twenty witnesses", all of whom had denied that there was any truth in the rumour.

And who knows now what the truth was? Mr. Hughes's inquiries were carried out many months after the crime and when the great furore was at last dying down. Also, although the women he questioned refuted the allegations it could well be argued that twenty-odd out of nearly two hundred is hardly a significant number. Besides that, no girl in her right mind would, in those Victorian days, risk her future happiness and present livelihood by admitting that her past employer had taken, or tried to take, sexual liberties with her! The stigma resulting from such an admission could well prove disastrous.

It is clear, therefore, with one thing and another, that Mr. Kent was not without his problems. However, where his financial difficulties were concerned it appeared that the year 1860 might see an end to them.

In that year he would be fifty-nine years of age, and he had held the post of Sub-Inspector for twenty-five of those years. Now, at long last, there was a vacant post of *full* Inspector on the Board of

Factory Commissioners, and Mr. Kent's age and long years of service would make him an eligible candidate.

He could take no chances. Apart from the high cost of running Road Hill House he had an increasingly large family to support. Not only did the care and education of Constance and William have to be seen to, but there were now three young children by his second marriage to tend (the youngest, Eveline, had been born in October, 1858), while his wife was pregnant yet again. Samuel Kent was desperate for that promotion, and the measures he took to gain it are indicative of his desperation.

To support his application for the vacant post he drew up a paper of recommendation and spent several months getting "some two hundred magistrates, chiefly resident in Wilts, Somerset, Dorset and Devon",[2] to put their signatures to it.

He was still awaiting the outcome of his application when the tragedy struck.

[2] J. W. Stapleton.

Chapter 7

THE EVE OF THE CRIME

Following the summer term of 1859 Constance was removed from her boarding-school near London and enrolled, for the remainder of that year, as a day pupil at a school in Beckington which was run by a Miss Scott and her assistant Miss Williamson. That this arrangement was prompted by consideration for Constance's well-being is doubtful—it was in all probability dictated by the state of Mr. Kent's finances; but anyway, for the first time in four years Constance was once again resident at home.

Not for long, though. It would appear that this situation—having her close to her family again—was not in any way a success, for when she returned to school after the Christmas holidays it was as a boarder. Now Beckington is only about two miles from Road, and the fact that the girl was boarded out practically on her own doorstep was the cause of some local gossip, apart from which the rather odd situation must have given rise to comment among her schoolfellows. Whatever, Constance was resentful of the arrangement— and what it implied—and she was not soon to forget it. Still, in spite of her feelings she did well at the Beckington school and when she returned home on the 17th of June for the start of her summer holidays she carried with her the second prize for good conduct.

She was sixteen years old now. A physically healthy, strong girl of just less than average height. She had a broad face, deep-set eyes and, while by no means pretty, had her attractions in a fresh complexion and a quantity of rich, golden brown hair.

William, during these latter years, had also had a change of school, being now a boarder in Gloucestershire. On his holidays at Road he was often seen by the villagers as he walked about wheeling the baby Eveline in her pram—a chore which he loathed and which, to a boy almost fifteen years of age, must have been the cause of much self-consciousness. Further to this he was now no longer allowed to use the main stairs in the house. His boots made too much mess said his stepmother, so, like the servants, he must use the back staircase.

This new arrangement could only add to the general opinion that great partiality was shown to the members of the second family. And it was no mere empty gossip; it *was so*. Dr. W. Mallam, Savill's godfather and one-time medical attendant to the Kent family, knew well the situation at Road Hill House; years later he was to tell Inspector Williamson of Scotland Yard that

> the children of the first Mrs. Kent were slighted by Mr. and Mrs. Kent . . . and if it is necessary that this should be proved, Miss Mary Ann will be the best person to do it.[1]

It would appear, therefore, that Mary Ann also knew and felt a good deal more than she openly expressed.

On Friday, the 29th of June, the three servants resident at Road Hill House were the cook-general, Sarah Kerslake; the young housemaid, Sarah Cox, and the children's nurse, Elizabeth Gough.

The latter had joined Mr. Kent's household some eight months before, following the first two positions she had held in domestic service—initially as a nursemaid and secondly in the more elevated capacity of lady's maid. This third post, at Road, seeing her as a nursemaid again, marked something in the way of a retrogressive step on the ladder of success. By all accounts she was an attractive, well-dressed, well-spoken girl with dark eyes and a fair complexion, her looks only marred by the fact that she had lost one of her front teeth. Almost twenty-three years old, she was the eldest daughter of William Gough, a respected Isleworth baker.

She was responsible for looking after the three youngest Kent children, Mary Amelia, aged five, Savill, not yet four, and Eveline, not quite two, the two latter children sleeping with the nurse in the nursery and Mary Amelia in a cot in her parents' room.

Elizabeth Gough also had other, minor tasks to perform that called upon her experience as lady's maid, regularly helping Mrs. Kent to dress and do her hair, while for her work in the nursery she had the assistance of fourteen-year-old Emily Doel, a local girl who came in daily from seven in the morning till seven in the evening; she it was who was called upon to do the heavier work in the

[1] Quoted in Inspector Williamson's report of the 8th of June, 1865.

nursery, the fetching-and-carrying of the water and the scrubbing
of the floors.

The other members of the Road Hill House staff were Mrs. Mary
Holcomb, who came in on Saturdays and Mondays to do the scrubbing in the kitchen area, and the three daily outdoor men. These
were Mrs. Holcomb's son James the groom-gardener (he "worked
when required"—his hours often running from five in the morning
till seven in the evening!); his elderly casual helper Daniel Oliver
from nearby Beckington, and, also from Beckington, the odd-job
boy, John Alloway. For Alloway, Friday would see his penultimate
day's work at Road Hill House. The week previously he had asked
Mr. Kent for a rise in wages, and on his request being refused had
given a week's notice.

Elizabeth Gough had an early start to her day that Friday as Henry
Noler, a sweep, was coming from Trowbridge at six to sweep the
hotplate flue in the scullery and then the kitchen and nursery chim-
neys. She paid him his 4s. 6d. when he had finished and then, along
with Emily Doel, set about clearing out the nursery and giving it a
thorough cleaning. Young Savill, though, whose routine had also
been disrupted by the sweep's visit, proved increasingly fretful and
difficult to cope with and as time went on he became more and
more demanding, hampering the two girls in their task so that in
the end, having had more than enough, Elizabeth Gough picked him
up and carried him downstairs to his mother. There she asked Mrs.
Kent to take charge of him till the work in the nursery was done,
which Mrs. Kent agreed to do, though telling the nurse:

"But you must put him down; you know he is too heavy for me
to carry."

Mrs. Kent was eight months pregnant, and Savill was a very well
developed child for his age. Spoiled by his indulgent parents and
the favourite of both of them, his well-being was most jealously
guarded so that any slight negative variation from his usual robust
state of health was viewed with concern. And this occasion was no
exception. Mrs. Kent, thinking his peevishness might be due to some
minor physical disorder, at once despatched a message to Dr.
Parsons, the family's medical attendant, asking him to prescribe a
mild purge for her son.

Although Savill was her favourite, Mrs. Kent was fiercely protective of all her three young children and she had frequently instructed all the nurses who had been in her employ that if any child was ill or anything occurred to cause the slightest concern, she, Mrs. Kent, was to be informed immediately. Said Mrs. Kent, on numerous occasions: "I would rather be called for a trivial cause than not be called when I was wanted."

When the odd-job boy returned from seeing Dr. Parsons he brought with him a calomel pill with the instructions that it should be administered to Master Savill when he went to bed.

Alloway had other errands to run that day; one of which was to run to the house of the elderly Tom Fricker—general labourer and jack-of-all-trades—and inquire after Mr. Kent's dark-lantern which had been taken there on Wednesday for the fitting of a new pane of glass. Mr. Kent had left Road on Tuesday for a business trip and before leaving had given instructions to Sarah Kerslake that his lantern must be mended and ready for his return on Friday. Now Alloway collected it and brought it back with him to Road Hill House.

William, following his own pursuits, left the house after lunch that Friday and Constance, sent on an errand to Beckington, followed him soon afterwards. They met and walked back together from Beckington later that afternoon and, at the house once more, Constance took Savill out into the grounds to play. The two could be seen "romping" together on the grass. Savill was fond of his stepsister and she appeared to be fond of him. On her return from school she had brought home for him a coloured picture she had purchased while he, more recently, had been making bead rings as a present for her.

It was to a scene of some domestic harmony, therefore, that Mr. Kent returned later that afternoon, and that same pleasant atmosphere was still in evidence when the nurse went in search of Savill to put him to bed. She found him in the library, sitting on the knee of his father who, at his desk, was drafting a report on the findings of his recently completed factory inspection.

The outdoor servants had all left at seven o'clock—Holcomb securely locking the garden door behind them—so when the nurse took the child up to the nursery not long before eight only the three resident servants and the nine family members were still on the premises.

Mrs. Kent had instructed that Savill should be given the aperient pill some little while before and now she looked in on him as he lay quietly in his cot in one corner of the room. Eveline, the youngest, was in her own crib alongside the nurse's bed. Satisfied, Mrs. Kent left the nursery and went to her own room where she saw Mary Amelia settled for the night. After that she went back downstairs.

Later, as was her custom while the nurse was having her supper, Mrs. Kent went again to look in on her children. All were sleeping soundly.

The drawing-room, whose carpet was covered with white drugget, was rarely used, and just after nine o'clock Cox entered the room and fastened the hooks and iron bars that secured the shutters over the three sash windows. When that was done she left, closing the door behind her.

The family at this time were in the dining-room drinking tea and it was there at 9.45 that Cox, Kerslake and Gough went to join them for evening prayers. Afterwards the nurse followed the other two servants to the kitchen where the teapot was refilled, the cook and the housemaid sitting to drink their tea while Elizabeth Gough remained standing. When she had finished she put down her cup and went upstairs to the nursery.

Mr. Kent, soon afterwards, appeared in the kitchen to get the dog's food which he carried out into the back yard. There, aided by the light of the newly repaired lantern, he undid the chain that secured the dog, allowing the animal his freedom to wander at will within the precincts of the walls. When this was done Mr. Kent returned to the house where, in the dining-room, Constance and William were on the point of leaving for their beds.

Very soon after their departure Mrs. Kent once more went upstairs. A comet had recently made its appearance and now at the nursery door Mrs. Kent called softly to the nurse to come and look at it. Together the two women climbed the few steps to an upper landing where, side by side, at the rear window, they stood gazing out at the night sky. They remained there only a few moments though, and after Elizabeth Gough had remarked how sweetly Savill was sleeping she and her mistress bade each other goodnight and went their separate ways, Elizabeth Gough returning to the nursery and Mrs. Kent to the dining-room.

At about 10.45 Elizabeth said her goodnights to her father and stepmother and went up to her bedroom on the top floor. Mary Ann joined her there just a few minutes later. Leaving her elder sister preparing for bed Elizabeth slipped out of the room and, quietly opening Constance's door—which was next to her own—checked that the girl's candle was out. Satisfied that all was well she then turned, walked around the landing to the other side and listened for a moment outside William's room. There, too, all seemed peaceful; there was no sound, and no thread of light was visible beneath his closed door. Elizabeth then descended the few stairs to the window on the lower landing where she stood gazing out at the summer night. For a minute or two she stayed looking at the comet then, turning, went back up to her room where Mary Ann secured the lock on the door. Mary Ann was the first in bed, and she was soon asleep. When Elizabeth blew out the candle and lay down beside her sleeping sister it was almost midnight.

Earlier, at 10.30, the two Sarahs, Cox and Kerslake, had begun their final tasks of the day. Cox had already secured the drawing-room window and shutters and now she locked and bolted its door. This done, she continued on her usual nightly tour, methodically locking the rest of the doors and windows at the front of the house. As Cox was busy with her chores Kerslake, having left the knife-box outside the back door ready for Alloway first thing in the morning, locked up the kitchen and the back part of the house.

By 10.45 they had finished and were moving towards the back stairs. There at its foot Kerslake turned to lock the door behind her and then together the two women, very tired after their arduous day's work, climbed up to the room they shared next to Constance's. Their long day was at last over. Once in bed they were soon asleep.

On the floor below the nursery door stood ajar. This was in case Mary Amelia, sleeping in her parents' room just across the landing, might awaken and cry out; should this happen then Elizabeth Gough, in the nursery, would hear her.

Mrs. Kent had not remained long in the dining-room and at about eleven o'clock, leaving her husband there alone, she too was on her way to bed. Outside the nursery door she paused, listened for a moment and then very softly pulled the door shut. Turning, she crossed the landing and entered her own room.

Elizabeth Gough, emerging from her dressing-room, was aware

of the soft closing of the nursery door. In the warm glow of the
nightlight she looked down at the sleeping children. Eveline was
quite peaceful. And Savill too; he lay with his face turned towards
the wall, his head resting on his arm. The time was five-past-eleven.

Now only Mr. Kent was still downstairs and it only remained for
him to carry out his customary task of checking on the security of
the house. This he would do as usual with the aid of his dark-
lantern, going round the darkened rooms and seeing that the locks
and bolts were fastened.

Up to that time, within variations of a few minutes either way,
the movements of the members of Road Hill House are quite well
accounted for. But at what time Mr. Kent joined his wife in their
room can only be surmised. Nor can it ever be known at what time
he at last went to sleep that night. If indeed he did.

Although within Road Hill House work had finished for the day, for
some others, outside, work was by no means over. P.C. Urch was
one of them, and he, a member of the Somerset Constabulary
stationed at Road, was on duty until ten minutes before one o'clock.
He was later to state in evidence that, passing by Road Hill House
shortly before that time, he had seen the usual "light in the hall
and nursery" (other police testimony substantiated that the gas-light
in the hall *always* burned throughout the night) and that he had
also "heard Mr. Kent's dog bark furiously".

That brief spasm of barking reached, too, ears within the grounds
of Road Hill House, while, further away in the nearby meadows
one Joe Moon and his companion also heard it. These two men,
workers at a local limekiln, were then on the banks of the river
Frome, Moon taking up his net in preparation to poaching one of
Mr. Kent's trout. As the dog's noise shattered the stillness the men
paused in their work, Moon remarking to his friend: "There must
be something wrong at Mr. Kent's—the dog is barking so."

For Moon and his companion it was a fine night to be out, and
that year had seen less than its usual share of fine nights. January
had come in with heavy rain, gales and high winds, and nor had
the weather much improved as the months went by into the gloom
and discomfort of the *soidisant* summer; the rainfall had been
twenty-five per cent higher than the average while the temperature
had remained discouragingly well below. Nearing the end of June,

however, there had been several fine days which, it was hoped, might be a sign that there was to be a change for the better. But not so. Never since registers had been instituted were there four such summer months as that June, July, August and September of 1860.

For the Kent family their lives were to follow a similar pattern. And a darker one.

Could it be that there was truth in the ancient belief that the appearance of a comet heralded catastrophe?—since earliest times the sight of such an apparition in the heavens had created the greatest dread. But no; surely that was merely an outworn superstition; certainly members of the Road Hill House *ménage* had not been disturbed by the sight; on the contrary it had fascinated and gladdened them.

And yet while that comet had been making its way across the sky, and while P.C. Urch was making his way homeward, catastrophe had struck. One member of the Kent household had been laid at the very point of death. Only minutes later, by the hour of one, he would be far beyond any aid.

For several of those other eleven inmates of Road Hill House the comet signalled the passing of their peace of mind for months and years to come – for some of them for the rest of their lives.

Part Two

THE CRIME

What a night's work was that 29th of June, 1860!

The Trowbridge and North Wilts Advertiser;
29th April, 1865.

Chapter 8

THE DISCOVERY: SATURDAY, 30th of JUNE

A bright morning. At five o'clock young James Holcomb left the cottage where he lived with his mother, crossed the narrow lane and unlocked the garden door of Road Hill House. It was to him a morning like most other mornings, and after tethering the dog he set about his day's work; there were the horse and cows to be tended, also some mowing to be done.

Inside the house Sarah Kerslake, who had briefly awakened at five o'clock and gone back to sleep again, now awoke once more and saw that it was a quarter-to-six. She aroused Sarah Cox who was still sleeping at her side and the two women got up, dressed, and prepared to start another day. When they were ready they set off downstairs, Kerslake towards the rear of the house by way of the back stairs, and Cox descending by the main staircase to begin unlocking the doors and windows at the front of the house.

It was at this time that John Alloway arrived for his last day's employment and he straightaway sought out Holcomb, who was busy in the stables, and asked him what work he wanted done. Holcomb sent him to work in the greenhouse and it was as the boy crossed the yard that the third member of the outdoor staff, Daniel Oliver, arrived.

At five-past-six Cox, approaching the drawing-room, was surprised to find the door open. Then on entering the room she was further surprised to see that the lower shutters of the centre window were open too—as was the window itself. The bottom sash had been raised about six inches. The fact that it was the centre window of the three was in itself a little surprising, as that window could only be opened with some effort, it having a rather stiff running action and tending to stick at the height at which it now stood. Cox couldn't understand it, but then, seeing that there were no signs of forcible entry and that nothing within the room appeared to have been disturbed, she assumed that the window had been opened in order to give the room an airing. Satisfied, she closed the window again and, without mentioning anything to Kerslake, went on with her work.

About 6.30 Mrs. Holcomb appeared at the house ready to start her day of scrubbing, and a little later, closer to seven o'clock, the assistant nursemaid Emily Doel arrived. She began her day, according to her usual custom, by lighting the fires to heat kettles of water for the children's baths, and it was at this time, seven, that Kerslake, preparing to scald the milk, lit the boiler-stove in the scullery.

While the kettles of water were heating Emily Doel went upstairs, took the bath from the lumber-room and carried it into the nursery. Elizabeth Gough was making her bed at the time and although she looked round on Emily Doel's entry she didn't speak to her. Eveline, the young assistant nursemaid saw, was already up and dressed, while of Savill there was no sign at all. Still, as she said later, it was "not her place to ask questions", and she did not. In the course of the next ten minutes she was in and out of the room several times carrying the kettles of water but at no time, even so, did the nurse say a single word to her.

After a while, her present particular task complete, Emily Doel left the nursery and returned downstairs. Immediately she had gone Elizabeth Gough went across the landing to the master bedroom and knocked on the door. A few minutes earlier Mrs. Kent, waking, had leaned across her husband and looked at his watch. It was 7.15. Mr. Kent, she noticed, though not sleeping, lay with his eyes closed. She got out of bed and put on her slippers and dressing-gown; it was at that moment that the knock came at the door. Mrs. Kent went to open it.

Elizabeth Gough, standing on the threshold, asked at once: "Are neither of the children awake, ma'am?"

Mrs. Kent looked at her in surprise. "What do you mean, *neither* of them?"

"Master Savill—isn't he with you?"

"With me? Certainly not!"

"Well," said the nurse, "he's not in his bed."

Panic rising, Mrs. Kent hurried at once into the nursery. There was Savill's cot, empty of the child, but presenting a most peculiar picture. The covers had been neatly turned back while on the pillow could be seen a clear, deep impression of the child's head—an impression much deeper than one would normally have expected to find.

As the height and structure of the cot made it impossible for the boy to have left it unaided Mrs. Kent then asked:

"Did you leave the chair next to the crib?"

"No, ma'am."

"When did you miss him?"

"At about five o'clock."

Mrs. Kent was astonished. "At *five o'clock*? You should have come to me at once and told me! Why didn't you?"

"I thought he was with you. I thought he must have woke up and cried out, and that you had heard him and come and taken him away."

Such pathetic self-justification was clearly not to be accepted for a moment. "You wicked girl!" Mrs. Kent cried out. "How dare you say such a thing! You know perfectly well he is too heavy for me to carry. Only yesterday I told you to put him down because he was too heavy for me. I have often told you that if there is anything wrong with the children you are to come to me at once." Mrs. Kent was bewildered. "Go upstairs to his sisters' room," she ordered the nurse, "and see if he's with them."

The nurse hurried off up the stairs to knock on the elder girls' door, and Mary Ann, answering the summons, undid the lock and opened the door. Immediately Gough asked whether Savill was with her. No, of course he wasn't, Mary Ann answered. Hearing the exchange Elizabeth, naturally curious, came to her sister's side, then, a moment later the adjacent bedroom door was opened and Constance stood there, half-dressed, listening to what passed. Though both Mary Ann and Elizabeth voiced their ignorance and concern over Savill's disappearance Constance, it would later be recalled, spoke not a word.

When Elizabeth Gough returned to the nursery she found her mistress still standing beside the empty cot. Mrs. Kent, on being told that Savill was not with his sisters left the room and went downstairs. There, seeing Cox, she was told that the drawing-room door, window and shutters had, that morning, all been found open.

It must strike one as extraordinary that with the growing panic and confusion that ensued following the discovery of his favourite son's disappearance, Mr. Kent should have stayed where he was—in bed. Mrs. Kent later said that she "was in confusion, going from room to room", yet her husband, lying awake through all that confusion, did nothing. All that frantic discussion between his wife and the nurse took place only a few feet from where he lay—yet through it all he did not stir.

On Mrs. Kent's return to the bedroom she told her husband: "Savill is missing. He is nowhere in the house."

It was at this point, Mrs. Kent later stated, that Mr. Kent was prompted to move, saying, "Then we must see where he is," and getting up from the bed went into the dressing-room. If this was indeed his reply, this rather laconic response, it is hardly what one would expect from a man who, in the circumstances, might be expected to be totally bewildered, panic-stricken and desperately afraid for his son's safety.

However, when at last he really did move he moved swiftly.

Dressing hurriedly he went quickly downstairs to Cox where she repeated her account of how she had found the state of the drawing-room. Following that he dashed out of the house. Holcomb, standing with Alloway and Oliver, saw him, wearing his overcoat, with his hat upon his head, come running round the corner of the house by the drawing-room window. Seeing the men there he stopped and shouted to Holcomb: "Have you seen anything of my little boy?"

"No, sir," Holcomb answered.

"He's lost!" Kent said. "He's been stolen and carried away!" He turned to Alloway. "Is there a policeman about?"

"There's Urch, sir."

"Go and fetch him." With this peremptory order Kent turned and ran back the way he had come.

Alloway at once sped away to P.C. Urch's house and gave the message that he was wanted at Road Hill House as soon as possible. The constable, who had been on duty till the small hours, was still in bed, but on receiving the summons he said he would be there at once and got up and began to dress.

Mr. Kent, meanwhile, had made a decision. Going back into the house he told his wife that he intended driving into Trowbridge to inform Superintendent Foley. Then he yelled for William to run and tell Holcomb to get the phaeton ready. William, who had begun his own search for the child, at once ran off to do his father's bidding. When he returned he was instructed to impress upon everyone that Mrs. Kent, who would remain in her room, was *on no account* to be disturbed. Then, although Alloway had already gone off to take word to P.C. Urch, William was also ordered to run into the village and "fetch the nearest policeman".

William, who must have missed Alloway only by seconds, didn't know where to go as he dashed blindly out of the gates. Thomas Benger, a small-holder who was grazing cows nearby, saw him as he ran across the green and heard him shout something as he went by. But Benger couldn't make out what the boy had said, and before he could ask him he had run on towards the village.

It was at the bakery where William stopped, and breathlessly he asked the baker, James Morgan, where the nearest policeman could be found. Morgan at once directed him to Urch's house and William ran off in that direction.

Urch, although he had already been alerted by Alloway's message, hadn't made much progress—for the simple reason that he was most uneasy about obeying the summons. Road Hill House was over the border into Wiltshire and Urch, being of the Somerset police force, had no jurisdiction there. On receiving the second summons, though, he realized that he would have to do something—and he did—he went straightaway to the bakery and asked James Morgan for his advice. The matter then was soon settled; Morgan told Urch that he would accompany him—in his capacity of parish constable —and together they set off for the house on the hill.

By this time word was beginning to travel around the village. William Nutt, the shoemaker and district clerk, was told at his front gate by a passing neighbour, Mr. Greenhill, that the child Savill Kent had been stolen—a story which Nutt viewed with some measure of doubt, telling Greenhill that he would "go and hear further about it", adding, "I cannot believe the child was stolen exactly." Then, making his way towards the crossroads "to see who was standing about", he saw Benger and, further off, Morgan and Urch as they came hurrying into view.

The men of the law were about forty yards from the gates of the house when Mr. Kent's phaeton appeared and turned up the hill in the direction of Trowbridge. Morgan, urging P.C. Urch to "make haste", called out to Mr. Kent who stopped his carriage and waited while the man ran up to him. Morgan asked what he and Urch were needed for, and Mr. Kent answered, "I have had my little boy stolen. I'm going to Trowbridge to fetch Superintendent Foley."

"You needn't go further than Southwick, sir," Morgan said. "The policeman there will forward a message on to the station, so you can return here straightaway."

"No," said Kent, "I shall go on."

Urch, still uncertain of his position, had been hanging back, but now as he approached, Kent asked that the two men should go to the house and make a search. Then, catching sight of Benger on the green, Kent called out to him: "My little boy is lost. I won't begrudge ten pounds to the man who finds him!" A moment later, whipping up his horse, he drove swiftly away.

As Urch and Morgan entered the grounds of Road Hill House, Nutt approached Benger across the green. Briefly they discussed what they had heard of the matter and Benger suggested that they go at once and begin a search for the missing boy. Nutt, though, refused, uneasy at the idea of trespassing on Mr. Kent's property—and he had reason to be hesitant considering that his brother Abraham had been prosecuted by Kent for that very offence. Benger, however, insisted that no one would be prosecuted "for looking for a lost child" and, persuaded, Nutt reluctantly agreed to help. So the two men crossed the road and passed through the gates.

"Mark my words," Nutt said as they crossed the lawn, "if the child is not in the house then we might as well look for a dead child as a living one."

Morgan and Urch, in the meantime, going to the back door of the house, were ushered into the kitchen and then into the drawing-room where Cox demonstrated how the centre window had been found open. The men then asked whether they might see the nursery. Cox went upstairs "to see if it was convenient" and, on returning, directed them up to the first floor landing where Elizabeth Gough was waiting for them at the top of the stairs. At P.C. Urch's request she took them to the nursery and pointed out to them the cot in the corner of the room. The two men saw with some surprise how tidy was its appearance, the sheet being so neatly folded back over the quilt—"almost as if", Morgan was to report later, "the bed had been freshly made".

He couldn't get over the cot's neatness. "Do you mean to say," he asked, "that this is where he was?"

"Yes," the nurse answered. Pointing out the deep indentation left on the pillow by the child's head she then drew back the covers so that there on the mattress they could plainly see the equally deep impression of his loins.

"What time did you miss the child?" Urch asked.

"At five o'clock."

"Did you make inquiries for him at once?"

"No, not until seven."

"Why not till then?"

"I thought Mrs. Kent had heard him cry and had come in and taken him away with her."

"Has she done that in the past?"

"No . . . not in my time—but I've heard she did it when the other nurse was here."

Morgan then asked her: "Did you find anything else missing—besides the child?"

She hesitated for a moment, and then said:

"A small blanket that was between the sheet and the quilt. It must have been drawn out from between them."

"Anything else?"

"No, nothing else."

While Morgan and Urch were questioning the nurse, outside in the grounds Nutt and Benger came to the end of their search.

They had begun by looking in the shrubbery at the front, then, keeping to the left of the lawn, had made their way around to the outbuildings at the back. With Benger continuing his searching by way of the rear of the house Nutt returned around the front, crossed the lawn and made his way towards the yew shrubbery at the edge of the grounds. It was near this shrubbery—in which stood the privy—that the two men met again. At Nutt's suggestion they moved towards the privy and there saw, just inside the open door, a small pool of blood.

For a moment the men just stared in horror, then, entering the privy, Nutt watched while Benger lifted the lid and peered down through the hole in the seat. There was something there. Putting

The Crime

his hand down, Benger's fingers touched some soft material. He straightened up.

"William, fetch a candle. As fast as you can."

"Oh, Benger," Nutt groaned, "it's as I predicted." Turning, he dashed away towards the house.

Near the back door he met Mary Holcomb who knew at once from his strained face and hurried steps that something had happened.

"Mary, quickly," Nutt told her, "get me a candle."

She stared at him, her own dread rising. "For God's sake, William, whatever's the matter?"

"Don't alarm yourself. I just want a candle—to see what we can see."

The elderly woman turned and went quickly into the house, Nutt following her. In the passage he saw the young lad William Kent and, in the kitchen, Mary Ann and Elizabeth, the latter holding the baby Eveline in her arms. Kerslake, lighting a candle and handing it to Nutt asked him, "What is it? What have you found?" but he just took the light and hurried out again, Mary Holcomb running after him.

Reaching the privy once more, Nutt went in and held the candle high. Benger reached down and lifted up a blood-stained blanket which he dropped on the seat at his side. Then he spoke.

"Look here, William . . . here's the poor little fellow."

Savill, still wearing his nightshirt, lay just beneath the seat, almost wedged between the splashboard and the back wall. He lay on his right side, his left hand and foot slightly raised.

Benger reached down once more and, grasping the child's cold body, lifted it out.

As he did so the boy's head fell grotesquely sideways. His throat had been cut from ear to ear, so deeply that the head was almost severed from the body.

Chapter 9

BEGINNING: THE SEARCH FOR A KILLER

William Nutt spread the blood-stained blanket on the floor and Benger gently laid upon it the mutilated body of the child.

Incongruously, in spite of the dreadful gash in the throat, the expression on the dead face mirrored no pain, no fear. The mouth was slightly open, the upper lip drawn back a little over the teeth, while the tip of the tongue protruded slightly. The flesh around the mouth was darkened but the eyes were peacefully closed. The dead boy's expression, Benger thought, was "quite pleasant".

Wrapping the body in the blanket, Benger placed it in the arms of Mary Holcomb and then the melancholy trio set off towards the house.

Urch and Morgan, after leaving the nurse, had commenced searching. On the lawn outside the drawing-room they examined the window for any signs of forcible entry, finding none; Urch also noting that there were no footprints in the dry grass. Back in the house Morgan left Urch to keep a watch while he himself set off across the yard with the intention of searching the outbuildings. It was then that he saw the little procession coming from the direction of the privy.

Inside the kitchen the watchers looked in horror as Benger took the little blanket-wrapped body and laid it on the table.

"He's been cruelly murdered," he said.

The room seemed to be full of people, servants, family and neighbours, and all staring aghast at the exposed body of the dead child. Nutt, turning to the nurse, remarked with a trace of bitterness: "You must have slept very soundly to have allowed someone to come in and take the child away without your knowing."

Elizabeth Gough answered sharply:

"You know nothing about it."

Moments later, both having briefly left the room, Mary Ann and Elizabeth returned to the kitchen and there saw at once their little brother's body lying on the table. They were both so overcome that Nutt, thinking they were about to fall, ran to them and took them both around the waist. Then, still supporting them, he led them out of the kitchen into the passage, away from the awful sight. Later, recalling the sisters' reactions he said, "I cannot describe their horror and amazement."

On studying the various accounts of the inquiries that followed it is often impossible to pinpoint with accuracy the times at which certain of the incidents took place on that day of horror and confusion. In respect of specific times the evidence is often contradictory and is obviously the result of certain witnesses just guessing at the hour rather than their actually knowing it. It is safe to say, however, that Savill's body was found not long before eight o'clock, and it was within minutes of its discovery that the Rev. Edward Peacock from the nearby vicarage, having been hurriedly summoned by Constance, came hurrying up the drive of Road Hill House. He was met with the word that the dead child was in the kitchen, and after seeing the body he went off at once to saddle his horse and ride after Mr. Kent with the bitter news.

In the meantime, Mr. Kent's carriage was making its way towards Trowbridge and at some time near the same moment that marked the discovery of his son's body had been stopping at the Southwick turnpike where Mrs. Ann Hall, the keeper, opened the gate to let him pass through. He paid his fee—and that for his return journey also—and then asked where the nearest policeman could be found. She told him that P.C. Heritage lived close by and gave him the necessary directions. As he started off again he said to her:

"I have had a child stolen and carried away in a blanket."

"When did you lose it?" the woman asked.

"This morning. If you see anyone coming you must stop them."

In another moment he had passed through the gate and gone on his way.

Two or three minutes later Mrs. Heritage, the wife of the local policeman, heard a voice calling and looking from her front window saw Mr. Kent beckon to a young boy who went over to his carriage. She watched as Mr. Kent gave the boy a halfpenny at which the boy turned and pointed out the policeman's house. At once Mrs. Heritage hurried outside.

Mr. Kent, without getting out of his carriage, asked if the police-man was at home. He was, Mrs. Heritage said, and he was in bed.

"You must call him up, then. I have had a child stolen out of my house last night—or rather we missed him at five o'clock this morning. A little boy of three years and ten months—supposed to have been taken out of the drawing-room window."

Mrs. Heritage then asked whether any clothes had been taken.

"No," Kent told her, "he was wrapped up in a blanket." He added quickly: "Tell your husband he must get up and make every inquiry. I'm going on to Trowbridge to inform Mr. Foley."

"What is your name and residence, sir?" the woman asked him.

"Kent. Road Hill House." Whipping up his horse, Mr. Kent drove on towards Trowbridge.

Back at the Southwick turnpike some time later Mrs. Hall hur-ried out to let through the Rev. Peacock. "This is a sad affair at Road, sir," she said to him, at which he replied: "The child has been found."

"Where?" she asked.

"In the garden." And he rode swiftly on.

The next time Mrs. Hall went out to open the turnpike gate was for Mr. Kent who was on his way back to Road. By that time he had seen Mr. Peacock who had given the news to him. Now Mrs. Hall called out to Mr. Kent, "Then the child is found, sir."

"Yes," said Kent, "—and *murdered!*"

Regarding Mr. Kent's drive towards Trowbridge that morning there is one particular question which to this day remains unanswered. And it is likely to be so for all time. That question is: Where and when did he meet the Rev. Peacock who went riding after him? Was Mr. Kent overtaken by the cleric as he drove *towards* Trow-bridge, or did he meet him on his way *back* from that town?

It was generally reported, and accepted, that Mr. Kent had not reached Trowbridge when he was overtaken by Mr. Peacock, in which case an explanation was needed as to how it should have taken him such a long time to go such a short distance. *The Journal* asked the question that was on the minds of so many observers:

. . . The Rev. Mr. Peacock . . . rode after him and caught him before entering Trowbridge. The distance is less than five miles:

how is it that Mr. Kent was so long on the road? Surely with even only ten minutes' start, driving as he should have driven, it would have been impossible so to gain on the trap as to overtake it in a four-mile ride? We should like to hear an explanation of this circumstance.

Much later Mr. Kent was to state that he was *returning* from Trowbridge when he met Mr. Peacock, but those reports at the time have it the other way and no one came forward with any denial; not even Mr. Peacock, who was a friend of Kent. A simple statement from the reverend would immediately have quelled the rumours that circulated but there is no record that he denied them.

Later on the police would be searching for blood-stained clothing, for the murder-weapon, and for Mr. Kent's dark-lantern which had mysteriously disappeared. It was wondered, therefore, whether he had broken his journey in order to dispose of some incriminating article. Certainly Mr. Kent was alone when he returned by the Southwick turnpike, so it can be accepted that Mr. Peacock was the one who actually reported the child's death. But had Mr. Kent already reported the child *missing*? Whatever the answer to the question, it seems clear that he had a definite purpose in dashing away from Road Hill House and was not simply acting without thought, as might at first be supposed. No, there was surely reason behind that seemingly frantic behaviour. Examine for a moment the pattern of that behaviour, from the time Savill's absence was first broadcast in the house:

Why, with panic mounting all around him, with his wife totally distraught and running about in bewilderment, had he continued to lie in bed, saying nothing, doing nothing?

His actions over the next few minutes appear equally odd. Having seen from the state of the drawing-room window and door that no one could possibly have *entered* by that way, and also learning that the rest of the locks in the house were secure he then dashes out into the yard and yells to Holcomb: "Master Savill is lost! *Someone has stolen him and carried him away!*" Clearly this was the one thing that had *not* happened.

Why did he leave the house to go dashing off without even taking the briefest glance into the nursery? *Why*, too, did he leave without speaking one word to the nurse—the girl who was employed with the sole object of caring for the children?

His behaviour at the gates was also strange. Why did he *insist* on driving on to Trowbridge—even though Morgan had told him that he need go no further than Southwick? By carrying out Morgan's suggestion he could have made sure that the police were informed and also that he himself could swiftly return to the house. But no, he would go on—which meant that he would be absent from the scene for an unnecessarily long time.

But why did he leave Road Hill House in the first place? His wife, eight months pregnant, was in a delicate condition, and everyone knew that at any moment there could be dire news about Savill. Surely then, in the circumstances, Mr. Kent's place was at his wife's side.

Why did he choose to leave just at the time when he was most needed at the house? Without him there was no one to direct the search. Mrs. Kent was certainly not capable of it and it was only by the merest chance that he had met the local policemen on his exit from the grounds. With his abrupt departure he left Road Hill House in an even greater state of chaos.

Why, if he did indeed deem it so urgent that the Trowbridge police be informed with such urgency, did he not send James Holcomb? Holcomb was a young man, intelligent, fit, and presumably, as groom, an able rider. He on horseback could have travelled so much faster than could Mr. Kent in his carriage.

Why did Mr. Kent himself make *no attempt at all* to search for his missing child? This, surely, would be the natural first action of a suddenly-bereft parent. . . .

As stated, it is difficult to escape the conclusion that Mr. Kent's hasty departure was a most deliberate move—a move from which he *would not* be dissuaded. And the reasons behind his actions are not difficult to find. Part of his purpose—if not the whole of it—was surely to add to the confusion that already reigned at Road Hill House and, further, to be away from that place when his son's body was found. His time on the road gave ample opportunity for this latter to happen, and with the body being discovered in his absence he was spared those first awful moments of confrontation; moments he would otherwise have had to endure; moments which, in similar circumstances, have been the downfall of the cleverest of men. By the time Mr. Kent returned to Road Hill House the worst was known and the first terrible shock had been sustained.

Only Mrs. Kent, we are told, had been kept in ignorance of the boy's death. She, according to her later testimony, first heard of it from her husband on his return to the house. During his absence she had remained in her room, seeing only the nursemaid who had joined her to dress her hair. While they were together they "spoke of the missing child", whereupon Gough had volunteered the opinion: "Oh, ma'am, it's revenge." It was only a little while before this exchange that she, the nurse, had seen Savill's body carried into the kitchen, yet somehow she managed to keep the news from her anxious mistress. As Mrs. Kent was to inform the court: "The nurse knew the child had been brought in dead, but she was not allowed to tell me."

Well, there were many things not being told that day—*and* in the days, weeks, months and years to come, and while salvation was dependent upon certain secrets those secrets must be kept.

P.C. Urch was soon despatched to his headquarters at Frome to make his report and ask for reinforcements, so for a while at Road Hill House the law's only representative was Morgan, the local baker-*cum*-parish constable. Not for long, though; soon the place would be overrun by the police of two counties, and all under the immediate direction of Superintendent Foley of Trowbridge.

In *The Case of Constance Kent* John Rhode writes:

> Of Superintendent Foley and his conduct of the first and vital investigations it is difficult to speak without impatience. He was a partially educated man who had risen to the rank of superintendent through no particular merit of his own, and the occurrence of a crime in the house of a man whom he regarded as far above him in station upset his faith in human nature and in the essential fitness of things. . . . He was entirely incapable of carrying out such an investigation as was required in the present case.

There is much truth in that, but Foley's situation—and his predicament—is better understood when viewed in its correct, contemporary, context.

If Gilbert wrote truthfully in 1879 that "a policeman's lot is not a happy one",[1] then such sentiments were even truer in 1860.

The recent Police Act (1856) compelling counties to establish police forces had not had time to be fully implemented and by 1860 those newly formed forces were still taking over from the old system, that of night-watchmen in the towns and parish constables in the counties. And there was nothing cohesive about the new police forces; there were about two hundred-and-forty of them in England and Wales and they were unlike each other in size, pay, pensions, hours of duty, style of uniform and type of recruit.

Most policemen in the counties were recruited from the ranks of farm labourers, the main requirements being literacy, tallness and a strong constitution, but due to the uncongenial work and low wages more than half the men recruited left after less than two years' service. The police in the South West were the worst off of the lot. In an area where "low wages and inefficient forces were the dominant characteristic"[2] the average pay for a police sergeant in 1860 was less than twenty shillings a week—well below the national average. The work was hardly enjoyable either; they were expected "to walk an average of twenty miles a day in all weathers at a steady pace",[3] the general boring nature of their days being only enlivened by occasional violent encounters with wandering navvies, gangs of poachers or able-bodied vagrants. And the only respite granted to a county policeman each year was *one week of unpaid leave*. Apart from that they worked every day, including Sundays. It was not till 1900 that they would be magnanimously given one or two days off each month.

Taking all this into account it can be seen therefore that the Road murder was not likely to be investigated by men who were the pick of the crop, and the only advantage that Foley had over his men was the fact that, having started as an ordinary parish constable, he had been in the business longer.

When John Rhode wrote that Mr. Kent was a man whom Foley "regarded as far above him in station" he was absolutely right, and the fact that Foley was in awe of Mr. Kent is hardly surprising.

Foley's ordinary constables earned hardly fifty pounds a year.

<hr>

[1] *The Pirates of Penzance*: W. S. Gilbert.
[2] *The Police: A Study in Manpower*: J. P. Martin and Gail Wilson.
[3] *Ibid.*

Superintendent John Foley himself earned less than eighty. Mr. Samuel Savill Kent, on the other hand, earned eight hundred.

After Savill's body had been brought in William was sent dashing off to Beckington to summon Dr. Parsons, and just before nine o'clock the surgeon arrived in his carriage, the boy sitting at his side. William, acting on the assumption that his stepmother had not yet been given the bad news, took Dr. Parsons round the back way into the house and there showed him into the library. Mr. Kent joined the surgeon there and after some little conversation took him to the laundry, to which room the child's body had recently been removed.

Entering alone, Dr. Parsons found the little body clothed in the nightgown and flannel shirt, both of which were stained with blood, and with "old soil" from the privy's splashboard. There was a good deal of soil on the blanket also; and a quantity of blood—most of the latter being on the inside of the blanket.

On looking at the body itself the surgeon saw first of all the great wound in the throat—a wound which "almost amounted to decapitation". He observed too, apart from the blood that had run over the child's face, that blackened appearance about the mouth that Benger had also noticed. Following that, Parsons discovered on the first finger of the left hand two small cuts. The body's very rigid state led him to believe that the boy had been dead for at least five hours.

Without authority he could make no more detailed examination, so word was despatched to Mr. George Sylvester, the County Coroner, for authorization for a *post-mortem* to be carried out. Dr. Parsons was then shown up to the nursery where he talked to Elizabeth Gough and where she showed him the victim's neatly made cot, the bedclothes placed, she said, "exactly as if his mother or I had done it."

Downstairs in the kitchen, the servants and some members of the family still congregated, finding, as people often do in times of crisis, comfort in the proximity of others. And the outsiders were still there too, and more of them. Word of the crime had spread like fire into the surrounding areas, and there were many who tried to find their way onto the premises, perhaps seeking to experience some *frisson* that might be found at the scene of such a grisly act.

Road Hill House would never be quite the same again, and very rapidly it was to become the centre of attraction for many miles around.

So it was to such a scene of coming-and-going that Superintendent John Foley arrived some time after nine o'clock, and immediately, accompanied by the police constables Heritage and Dallimore, went to view the body in the laundry.

After this, Foley was taken to the drawing-room to look at the window and shutters there, which told him quite clearly that no one had broken into the house from the outside. Then he went up to the nursery to examine the cot and question the nurse.

She told him how she had tucked the sheet and the quilt in under the sides of the mattress, so that the blanket, being between the two covers, and smaller, was not visible. Foley then asked her when she had first missed the child and she repeated her story of having awakened at five o'clock, of having knelt on her bed to cover up the baby Eveline and of seeing in that moment that Savill's cot was empty.

Was she not alarmed at such a discovery? Foley asked her. No, she told him, she had assumed that his mother had heard him crying and had come in and taken him away to her own room. After that, she said, she lay down again and went back to sleep until six o'clock, at which time she got up and went to her mistress's door. She knocked twice, she told Foley, but getting no answer returned to the nursery where she read a chapter of the Bible and then washed and dressed the baby Eveline. It was after that, she said, that she went again to Mrs. Kent's room and asked for Savill.

"When did you first realize that the child's blanket had been taken?" Foley asked.

"Not till he was brought in wrapped up in it."

"Only then?"

"Yes. Not till then—when he was brought in."

Earlier that morning though, *before* Savill's body had been found, she had told both Morgan and Urch that the blanket was missing from the cot.

Chapter 10

THE SEARCH CONTINUES

Leaving the nurse, Foley went to examine the knives in the hope that some telltale stain might provide him with a clue. All the the knives had been cleaned earlier that morning though, so, drawing a complete blank in this, Foley, with Heritage at his side, set off for the yew shrubbery to examine the privy. This was situated some seventy-nine paces from the drawing-room window, but only about twenty from the kitchen door.

According to Mr. Kent the privy was not generally used; he himself being the only one who occasionally availed himself of it. It had a very deep cesspool beneath—measuring some ten feet by seven feet—which also ran beneath the servants' privy situated nearby in the stable-yard. The seat was a "one-holer" and the only way in which it was at all remarkable was in the fact of its having that splashboard on which the child's body had been found lying. It was by Mr. Kent's orders that the splashboard had been fitted. It was just a piece of wood running the width of the privy seat, fitted just below the seat and slanting steeply down to within six or seven inches of the rear wall. Mr. Kent had had it fixed there as a safety measure to prevent the possibility of an accident befalling one of his small children—an accident that would surely have proved fatal. Had it not been for that splashboard, Savill would most certainly have fallen down into the vault below.

Now, inside the privy, Foley leaned over and peered down past the splashboard into the vault. There, apart from a good deal of blood-stained paper, he could see what appeared to be a piece of cloth lying on the soil's surface. At once he sent for a crook, then, attaching it to a stick he leaned down once more and hooked up a piece of blood-stained flannel.

It measured about fifteen inches by twelve and at the corners bore marks where strings had once been attached. It had been, at one time, thought Foley, a woman's chest-protector, or breast-flannel. The underside of the fabric was dirty from the soil of the water but its upper side appeared quite clean except for some marks of blood which, Foley assumed, had dripped onto it from the child's body. One thing was very clear to the superintendent, and that was that the article had not been there very long.

The vault of the privy held four or five feet of water, and now Foley, having what he believed to be an important piece of evidence —and hopeful of finding others—arranged for the vault to be emptied. For this purpose Thomas Fricker was sent for.

In the meantime Dr. Parsons, having carried out his own investigations in the privy, had returned to the house, leaving, all about, the general search continuing—one of the objects of which was the murder-weapon. In this direction one Stephen Millett, a local butcher-*cum*-parish constable, was adding his efforts along with the others. He had been among the first arrivals on the scene and had gone to investigate the privy even before Mr. Kent's return to the house. In the privy Millett had noted the small coagulated pool of blood on the floor, the drops that had fallen on the front of the seat, and the blood that had fallen into the vault's soil. On going outside again he had been met by Alloway who handed to him a piece of newspaper which he had just picked up some few feet from the privy's door. The folded piece of newsprint revealed, on being unfolded, a bloody mark as if a knife had been wiped upon it.

When he later saw Foley, Millett gave him the piece of paper and it was duly lodged, along with the breast-flannel, in the police wagonette that stood in the yard. These two finds marked, so far, the sum total of the material discoveries that might possibly lead to the apprehension of the guilty. As time went by it would begin to appear as if nothing else of significance was to be found.

One of the first tasks given to Urch and Heritage was to get rid of the casual onlookers who were still making their way into the grounds, and once these were gone men were posted around the premises to prevent the further entry of any thrill-seekers. Much more than this Urch and Heritage could not do—except wait for further orders. They were clearly out of their depth, finding in their experience little precedent for the performance of any duty beyond the role of police routine. They were convinced—as was Foley— that the crime had been committed by an inmate of the house and that therefore it would be only a matter of time before the culprit was found. Like many others, though, they were in for quite a number of surprises.

At about eleven o'clock two more men who had heard of the calamity arrived to offer their help, and after a brief consultation with the keepers of the gate they were allowed inside. They were Mr. Kent's legal adviser Mr. Rowland Rodway, and Dr. Joseph W. Stapleton[1] who was surgeon to the local factories under Mr. Kent's jurisdiction. They immediately sought out Superintendent Foley and found to their great surprise that the police in their investigations had only been given access to the nursery, the kitchen and the drawing-room; they had been given *complete* freedom to pursue their inquiries *outside* the house but no similar rights regarding the interior. Complete freedom for the police was of course an absolute necessity; it was essential that they conduct a thorough examination of the house *and* all its inhabitants. Foley, however, had allowed himself to become intimidated by his feelings of awe for Mr. Kent and had not insisted on what was clearly his duty. Mr. Kent, on the other hand, had been positive in his assertions that the criminal would be found *outside* the house, and kept insisting that that was where the investigation should be concentrated; he would entertain no suggestion to the contrary. Writes J. W. Stapleton:

From a very early period Mr. Kent, in his conversations with his friends and in his instructions to the police, avoided and combated every suggestion which directed suspicion to any member of his family or household. He invariably . . . alluded to persons who owed him an old grudge or had threatened him with vengeance, and related several incidents tending to carry out of the house the motive for the deed, and to fix it upon some stranger or discarded servant.

Incredibly Mr. Kent continually insisted that fencing off his property, prosecuting Abraham Nutt for trespass and stealing, and discharging an angry nursemaid were valid reasons for the perpetration of the murder—that it was an act of revenge. And he would have it no other way. It was only after a conversation with Stapleton and Rodway that Mr. Kent was persuaded to "surrender" to Superintendent Foley "himself, his family and his household" and the freedom of his house.

Not before time, either. After such a delay Foley must have been a little less sanguine of successfully searching for traces of the

[1] The author of *The Great Crime of 1860.*

killer; but somewhere there *was* a murder-weapon; somewhere, too, there was perhaps the killer's clothing, blood-stained. But where? Ample time had passed in which a hundred clues might have been destroyed, apart from the fact that one member of that household —Mr. Kent himself—had left the scene of the crime at a time when it was vital that he should have remained.

Even when Foley and his men did begin to search within the house they were given no peace by Mr. Kent, who kept insisting, still, that they were wasting their time. "His mind," says Stapleton, "seemed to wander irregularly, discursively and unsteadily over a wide field. He suggested a succession of suppositions all equally vague and improbable and unsupported by any testimony or by the evidence of a single fact." Dr. Stapleton was clearly convinced that his friend was shielding someone. And he was sure who that some-one was.

Foley, though obviously well out of his depth, did his rather poor best and began a search within the house. Dr. Parsons, who was awaiting the coroner's warrant for the *post-mortem*, accompanied the superintendent.

Ill-equipped as Foley was, both intellectually and as regards his professional support, there can be no doubt that his intentions were honourable, and he went to his task with conscientious enthusiasm. Unfortunately though, as he was soon to demonstrate, his lack of wise judgement was to prove a great disadvantage—to say the least.

He was astute, however, in his belief that the criminal must have been wearing night-clothes at the time of the crime, so for now the household's night-attire became the main object of his attention.

How thorough and methodical such examination of the inmates' linen was, though, is questionable. It appears to have been rather haphazard. Dr. Parsons, who assisted Foley in his task (but having his own ideas as to the direction in which the search should be made), could not later recall much of what had taken place. He could not remember examining any of the linen belonging to Mary Ann or Elizabeth, saying rather vaguely, "Foley examined some items; I examined others". He did, however, clearly recall examin-ing a nightdress belonging to Constance. Together he and Foley had gone into her room—in the girl's absence—and looked casually through the linen in her chest of drawers. They saw nothing there to excite suspicion. Then Dr. Parsons took up from the bed the

girl's nightdress that she had worn the previous night. It was perfectly free of any stain and Foley at once dismissed it from his mind.
Not so Dr. Parsons, however. On the contrary he was disturbed by
the fact of the garment being *so clean*, and he remarked to the
superintendent on its relatively little-used appearance. Foley, though,
intent on following his own train of thought, didn't take the hint.

Dr. Parsons was in the library with Mr. Kent and Dr. Stapleton
when the coroner's authorization for the *post-mortem* arrived. Dr.
Parsons asked Stapleton, himself a surgeon, if he would assist in the
examination and the two men made their way to the laundry to
begin the task.

While they were thus engaged the police continued with their
work of investigation, their numbers being swelled at about two
o'clock with the arrival from Frome of Sergeant James Watts. Inside
the grounds he paused for a moment to observe Fricker and his
helpers at work emptying the vault of the privy, then, going on into
the house sought out Superintendent Foley and offered his services.
He, like the other officers there, was at once set to making a search.
Unlike the others, though, Sergeant Watts was to make a discovery.

In the laundry the first thing Dr. Parsons did was to remove from
the body the stained blanket and clothing.

Now with the corpse naked the two surgeons discovered another
wound. It was on the left side of the chest. Just below the nipple a
deep stab had been made, delivered with such force that it had
pierced the night-shirt and the flannel vest. A sharp, pointed knife
had been used, Dr. Parsons thought, the blade of which had penetrated three-quarters of the way through the chest. The wound,
though, appeared to have bled very little, and the sides of the cut
had not retracted. The surgeon was convinced that the wound had
been inflicted after death.

When at last the examination was over the two surgeons returned
to Mr. Kent in the library. He came towards them weeping. To
console him, Dr. Parsons assured him that the child had died swiftly
and painlessly, adding: "He suffered much less than you will."

At that time the two surgeons concurred in what appeared to be,
quite obviously, the cause of death—looking no further than the
gash in the throat. Later, however, Dr. Parsons would give much
more thought to the matter; he would be increasingly disturbed by

his recollection of those *trickles* of blood over the child's face when he would have expected great quantities to have been splashed about, both over the child and the surrounding area. And then there was that blackened, bruised appearance about the child's mouth. . . .

Dr. Parsons became more and more convinced that he had been hasty in forming a conclusion as to the cause of death and the further he thought about it the more certain he became that those other, inescapable signs indicated a *different* cause of death—a cause he had not previously considered.

P.C. Dallimore's wife Eliza arrived from Trowbridge at about four o'clock. She had been summoned to Road Hill House as a "female searcher" and went into the kitchen with the announcement that she was there "to search the female servants". Obviously one rule was operating for the rich and another for the poor, for no member of the Kent family was similarly physically examined by anyone. This was not Mrs. Dallimore's concern, though; she was there to do the job for which she was being paid. She began her job by asking to be shown up to the nursery—for it was upon the nurse that Superintendent Foley's suspicions were becoming centred.

The nursery door made a noise as it was opened, Mrs. Dallimore noticed—"a creaking noise, as if the lock was out of order". The nurse, seeing her, at once demanded:

"What do you want with me?"

"You must undress yourself," Mrs. Dallimore said.

"I cannot."

The policeman's wife told her that it must be done and that that was the purpose of her being there. Then, following the nurse into the little dressing-room, she said:

"Well, nurse, this is a very shocking thing about the murder."

"Yes," said the nurse, "it is."

"Can you give me any account of it, do you think?"

"I got up at five o'clock and missed the child from the cot, and then I lay down again."

"Why did you lie down again after you missed him?"

"I thought he was with his mamma; he generally goes in there of a morning." A few moments later she added: "This is done through jealousy. The little boy goes into his mamma's room and tells everything."

Said Mrs. Dallimore, "No one would murder the child for doing such a thing as that. Who would do such a thing for that?"

"I really cannot tell."

After satisfying herself that nothing about the nurse's underclothing gave any cause for suspicion, Mrs. Dallimore left her to get dressed again and went away to examine the two Sarahs, Kerslake and Cox. Noting that "neither girl had put on a clean shift that day", she then set about examining the "nightdresses of the household". In Constance's room she looked at the nightdress lying on the bed and saw that it was completely free of any stain. The same with Elizabeth's. On examining Mary Ann's nightdress, though, she found some stains of blood upon it, and although quite certain that they were due to natural causes she nevertheless went to Superintendent Foley and informed him of the fact. Foley too was of the decided opinion that the stains were of no significance but even so he instructed Mrs. Dallimore to take possession of the garment. This she did and, her task complete, went to the kitchen for a while to relax and talk before returning home to Trowbridge. When she left she took Mary Ann's nightdress with her.

Also that afternoon Mrs. Silcox, the undertaker's mother, began *her* task—that of laying out the dead child. Elizabeth Gough had been instructed to help the old woman, but did not; as Mrs. Silcox later said: "She never came near the place." Some writers have commented upon Gough's unwillingness to help as being significant of her guilt in the crime, but surely her attitude is not to be wondered at; there must be few girls under twenty-three who wouldn't shrink from such a task—that of handling the badly mutilated corpse of a little child they had been fond of.

When Dr. Stapleton learned that afternoon (almost certainly from Mr. Kent who had insisted that Foley share all his findings with him) that Mary Ann's nightdress was found to have blood-stains upon it he attached no importance whatever to the fact. He did not believe for a moment that she could be remotely connected with the crime, and the only possible—and certain—result of the garment being exhibited would be acute embarrassment to the young woman.

There was, however, a second garment discovered that day; unlike Mary Ann's, though, *this* one had been *hidden*.

Chapter 11

THE SECOND GARMENT

On the afternoon following the crime, some time before five
o'clock (the times given in evidence ranged between four
and six), Sergeant Watts of Frome, accompanied by Urch,
Heritage and Dallimore, moved via the connecting door from the
kitchen to the scullery. Stopping by the boiler-stove in which the
fire had long since gone out—though "there were ashes and cinders
in it as if it had been recently used"[1]—Watts stooped and put his
hand up into the flue beyond the hot-plate. His fingers touched
something, and a moment later he had pulled out a hastily-made
parcel, held together by the twisting of one end of the brown-paper
wrapping. The parcel had been pushed back as far as possible and
"might not have been seen by anyone lighting a fire there"[2]
unless they had stooped and looked in. Had a fire been lit, then the
parcel would almost certainly have been burnt.

Watched by the three constables, and Fricker, the sergeant undid
the wrapping and took out a woman's garment, very dirty and
stained with blood.

The men looked at it. Fricker thought "the marks arose from
natural causes", as did the three constables who "were for putting
it back again".[3] However, Watts decided on the wiser course and,
quickly rolling it up, left the house and went into the stable across
the yard. Inside with the three other officers in attendance he once
more opened the wrapping. Giving the contents a more thorough
examination all four men were convinced that the stained garment
had no connection with the crime, but even so it would still have
to be shown to Foley. With this intention Watts, accompanied by
Dallimore, took the garment and went in search of the superintendent.

[1] Watts in evidence.
[2] Ibid.
[3] Fricker in evidence.

They were just outside the stable-door when Mr. Kent came up demanding to know what had been found. He had obviously heard that some discovery had been made and, quite understandably, was anxious to know about it. When told he at once said, "I must have it seen; Dr. Parsons must see it." Watts, though, politely refused and, saying that it was his duty to give it to Superintendent Foley, continued on his way. He found the superintendent in the rear part of the house and there in the presence of Dallimore handed the parcel over.

Foley, it must be remembered, was on the look-out for any garment bearing traces of the night's happenings, his search being mainly concentrated on the household's nightclothes. Looking at *this* garment, however, and seeing what appeared to be stains of menstrual blood and other bodily functions, he was quite satisfied that the discovery was of no significance whatsoever. "Can't you see," he said, putting it into Dallimore's hands, "it's just a nasty, dirty chemise."[4]

Was Foley right in assuming that the discovery had no importance? Many students of the crime believed then, as they do now, that it was vital evidence which, with the proper attention, might have yielded dramatic results. Unfortunately, at just about the time when it was needed most the chemise had, as far as was known, ceased to exist.

Concerning the chemise a great deal of fuss and confusion was to arise which in turn was to lead to much self-justification and re-crimination. The eruption of all this did not occur however until the end of November, exactly five months to the day after the crime took place, and by that time memories of exact days, hours and minutes had faded considerably. Even so, taking into account the sometimes conflicting evidence a clear story does emerge.

Dallimore, holding the chemise handed to him by Foley, expressed the opinion that it must belong to one of the younger servants, and named one of them (which one is not known, though it was not Elizabeth Gough), to which Foley replied, "Don't expose the girl". It was at this point that Sergeant Watts left the two men together. After some further discussion Foley decided that, just to be safe, the chemise should be shown to a "medical man" and, with these

[4] The garment was also to be frequently known by the rather outdated term, *shift*.

instructions, left the matter in Dallimore's hands. Dallimore at once took the chemise and showed it to Dr. Stapleton, after which he placed it in the police wagonette in the stable-yard.

When Dallimore asked the surgeon for a professional pronouncement on the garment he did not give any details of its discovery, and Dr. Stapleton, having only very recently learned that Mary Ann's nightdress had been found with blood-stains upon it, at once jumped to the conclusion that *what he was now being shown was the property of Mary Ann.*

In his book he writes:

. . . The marks upon it, and all the circumstances connected with them, and the history of the garment itself, furnished unequivocal evidence as to their nature, and refuted the possibility of their being associated with the murder.

Seeing such a dirty garment and believing it to belong to Mary Ann, Dr. Stapleton was understandably anxious that it should not be exhibited. His embarrassment is evident in his peremptory dismissal of it. "Put it away," he told the constable, "it has nothing to do with the crime."

That he was actually looking at the chemise, however, is borne out by the following statement (in which he writes of himself, as always, in the third person):

. . . Two hours afterwards he went into the stable-yard to get out his carriage, and there he found a policeman standing in charge of the police-cart, in which he said he had some things which the superintendent had retained in custody, and was going to take away to Trowbridge. The surgeon . . . went to the police-cart, and there observed *the same garment*[5] which he had seen two hours previously.

It has been quite firmly established that the chemise was left lying in the wagonette, and furthermore it was the *only* garment there. Mary Ann's nightdress, it will be recalled, was in the possession of Mrs. Dallimore, and she kept it with her all the time until she got home to Trowbridge. Dr. Stapleton, therefore, could *only have seen the chemise* lying in the wagonette—"*the same garment*" which,

[5] His italics.

according to his own insistence, "he had seen two hours previously". He was to persist in his mistaken belief that he had never seen the chemise but it is quite obvious that he had.

However, putting order into the confusion that had arisen does not, unfortunately, answer the all-important question, which is: Was that garment found in the boiler-stove connected with the murder? Some writers believe that it was, that it was evidence of the complicity of either Constance or Elizabeth Gough. In her book *Saint—With Red Hands?* Yseult Bridges says:

> That a blood-stained garment found the day after a murder in a place where it had obviously been concealed with the object of contriving its secret destruction should have no connection with the murder is not credible.

Mrs. Bridges believes that that blood-stained garment was proof of the complicity of Elizabeth Gough and Mr. Kent, and her theory has been widely accepted as fact. It is an ingenious theory and must be most seriously considered—particularly as the "Mr. Kent/ Elizabeth Gough intrigue" idea was favoured by so many at the time.

Below, then, is Yseult Bridges' theory of how the crime took place and how the chemise (or shift)—which she believes was the nurse's nightdress—came to be discovered in the boiler.[6]

Mrs. Bridges puts forward the belief that Mr. Kent was carrying on an affair with the nurse and went that night to the nursery where she was waiting for him in her nightdress. While the couple were amorously involved on the nurse's bed young Savill awoke and saw them. Mr. Kent, afraid that the child would cry out and arouse Mrs. Kent, snatched up the nurse's chest-flannel and held it over the boy's mouth. Kent was desperately afraid that the arousal of Mrs. Kent would lead to discovery of his intrigue with the nurse, and consequently a scandal which would bring about his downfall; he had just applied for his much-needed promotion and it was essential that his character should be regarded as unblemished.

After holding the flannel over the boy's mouth whilst listening for sounds of movement in the house, Mr. Kent took the gag away only to discover that his son was dead, suffocated.

[6] The quotations used in this précis of Yseult Bridges' theory are all taken from her book *Saint—With Red Hands?*

Now more desperate than ever, Kent quickly evolved a plan which, he hoped, would remove suspicion from any inmate of the house and place it upon an outsider; several cut-throat murders had occurred in the area over a number of years and the perpetrator had never been found; it was on this unknown killer that Mr. Kent intended to cast the onus of his son's death.

Outside in the garden Mr. Kent took a carving-knife and, putting his hands inside the blanket that wrapped the child, cut the dead boy's throat "with one powerful slash. Then perhaps his nerve failed him, for he had loved the child; and it was the nurse who lifted the body from the floor. Heavier in death than in life she had to brace its weight against her thighs, the blood from the wound oozing through the blanket and staining the front of her night-shift.

"Either they had forgotten the splashboard, or had thought that the body would pass it. When it would not, Mr. Kent, in a frantic endeavour to force it down, drove the knife deep into the body. The effort was unavailing. . . . Then the blanket was pulled away in the hope that without its impeding folds the body might yet go down, but only the breast-flannel fell into the vault below."

Back in the house they washed the knife and returned it to the drawer. "Then they washed themselves and took clean garments from the airing cupboard close by." Elizabeth Gough took off her blood-stained nightdress, and as "she folded the garment up in the piece of brown paper, some of the blood was transferred to the back of it, though less conspicuously. As Watts said, 'More blood was on the front than the back.' "[7] The nurse then thrust the hastily-made parcel "up the flue of the boiler-stove in the confident expectation that it would be consumed by the flames when Kerslake lit the stove in the morning". Unfortunately, though, that parcel survived to be discovered by Sergeant Watts, its survival due to the fact that "owing to the prevailing disorganization in the house Kerslake had omitted to relight the boiler-stove that morning".

This, in essence, is Yseult Bridges' theory which, as stated, has become widely accepted as fact. But it will not stand scrutiny. However, in view of its wide acceptance it is necessary that its implausibility should be demonstrated.

---

[7] Watts did not say this; he said just the opposite: "The stain was greater behind than before." (See p. 106). This forms part of his *signed* deposition still in existence at the Public Record Office, London.

First to the matter of the garment found in the boiler-hole, the facts concerning which have never, in my opinion, been conscientiously examined.

The garment was described as being plain, short in length, short-sleeved, made of a coarse material and having a falling flap at the back and front. Much of Mrs. Bridges' theory hangs upon her assertion that this garment was Elizabeth Gough's nightdress (or night-shift). But it was not. It was, as Foley named it, a chemise, an under-garment in such common use and of such a standard, accepted pattern in the mid-nineteenth century that the shape of it remained unaltered for many, many years.[8] Its very severe plainness characterized it as an article meant to be entirely concealed from view—totally distinguishing it from the nightdress which, being invariably full-length and long-sleeved and usually with frills or other decorations, was designed to be seen.

Even so, having established that the garment was not, as Mrs. Bridges would have it, "a copy of the latest fashionable whim" in nightdresses, but was instead just a common chemise, the questions still remain; among them: Did the blood-stains come from the child?

The answer is not difficult to find.

Over the course of the two days following the chemise's discovery it was examined by several persons. As a result there is, apart from a description of the cut of the garment, a very full and accurate description of the *condition* the garment was in.

Said Sergeant Watts when later questioned:

"The garment was nearly worn out. There were holes under the arms. It was in a very dirty state; the blood extended about sixteen inches from the bottom; there were no marks of blood above the waist. The marks of blood *and smears*[9] nearly covered the tail part. I should think, from the appearance, the blood had been caused from the inside. The stain was greater behind than before. There was no blood on the paper. . . . I should not think the marks had been there long, but should not think they had been made that day."

Said Mrs. Dallimore:

[8] For more information the reader is referred to *The History of Under-clothes*, by C. W. and P. Cunnington, pub. by Michael Joseph, 1951. This book contains a photograph of such a chemise and gives a description of it which also describes *exactly* the garment discovered by Sergeant Watts.

[9] My italics.

"It was of a coarse material. . . . It was dirty, ragged and mended, and appeared to have been worn out at the bottom by kneeling on it. . . . It appeared to have been dirty before the stains were on it, and to have been worn as long as possible afterwards. I believe the stains were from natural causes. . . ."

And P.C. Dallimore:

"It was very dirty. It was well-worn, and had been repaired near the arm, and appeared to have been worn a week or two longer than it should have been. . . . The stain in front was small as compared with the stain behind."

It is clear then that *all* those who saw it were quite convinced that the stains on the chemise had been caused by natural functions of the body and had no connection whatsoever with the boy's death. If further evidence were needed as to the garment's lack of involvement in the crime there is Sergeant Watts' statement that the stains were quite dry and that he didn't think they had been made that day. In addition, the total absence of stains on the wrapping-paper is further indication that the chemise was dry when it was wrapped up.

The above descriptions of the garment also negate the idea that Elizabeth Gough was wearing it when keeping a tryst with Mr. Kent that night. Bear in mind those descriptions of the nurse as having "*chic* and sophistication", of being "a smart girl", and a "superior person". Is it likely for one moment that the "superior, *chic*, sophisticated, smart" Elizabeth Gough would in such a garment have awaited a visit from her lover? In a filthy, very old, worn-out chemise with holes under the arms, darns at the knees, and "blood and smears" nearly covering the "tail part"? It is quite incredible. Incredible too is the assumption that Mr. Kent, a cultured man with excellent taste, could have found such a vision seductive!

Furthermore, not only did the nurse not wear the chemise that night but she never even owned it. Mrs. Dallimore said of it: "It appeared to be worn out at the bottom by kneeling on it." Elizabeth Gough, though, did no heavy work about the nursery or any other part of the house.

Having established then that the chemise was not Elizabeth Gough's we are yet left with the questions: To whom did it belong, and when and why was it placed in the boiler-stove?

I am quite certain that the chemise had no part in the crime, but was hidden in the boiler *as a direct result of it*.

First: *When* was it hidden?

Contrary to Yseult Bridges' statement that "owing to the prevailing disorganization in the house Kerslake had omitted to relight the boiler-stove that morning", the stove *was* lit, *and* at the usual time. Watts said he thought that the boiler had been recently used and he was right; Kerslake later testified that she had lit it at seven o'clock "to scald the milk", and let it out, as usual, at nine. The Trowbridge magistrates, in a later inquiry, were to make absolutely certain of this fact.

The proof is cast-iron then that the chemise was hidden in the boiler-stove *at some time well after nine o'clock*. Had it been placed there earlier, at the time of the crime or at any time before seven that morning, it would, of course, have been burnt.

But why was it hidden there at all?

As stated earlier, Mrs. Dallimore arrived at Road Hill House that Saturday afternoon with the announcement that she had come "to search the servants", and began her task by going to the nursery to examine the nurse.

Now, apart from the nurse there were four other female servants working in the house that day; they were Sarah Kerslake, Sarah Cox, the elderly Mrs. Holcomb, and the young assistant nurse—who did the heavy nursery work—Emily Doel. And one of those females panicked, afraid that the filthy, blood-stained chemise she wore beneath her dress would at any moment, by the demands of Mrs. Dallimore, be exposed.

It was not Kerslake or Cox, for Mrs. Dallimore testified that both those servants were wearing underwear that had not been put on clean that day. Nor was it Mrs. Holcomb, for she was well past the age of menstruation. Only Emily Doel is left for consideration —and she it must have been. She was not quite fifteen years old, she came from a very poor family, and she worked twelve hours a day at Road Hill House doing the scrubbing and other heavy tasks in the nursery and elsewhere.

As it turned out Emily Doel need not have worried, for the policeman's wife only searched the *resident* servants. At that time, though, the girl wasn't to know Mrs. Dallimore's intentions, and while Mrs. Dallimore was upstairs examining either Gough, Kerslake or Cox, the assistant nursemaid took action to protect herself from shame. In some private place, perhaps the servants' privy, she removed the dirty chemise and wrapped it up in paper. The wrapping had two purposes: she would not be seen *carrying* the garment, and also it would be protected from the soot in the boiler flue.

In the scullery, unobserved by anyone else, she pushed the parcel into the fire-hole of the boiler. It would be safe there, she believed, till Sarah Kerslake lit the fire the following morning—but long before that time she, Emily Doel, would have an opportunity to retrieve it.

The poor girl must have suffered much when she learned—either by being told or by making her own discovery—that her dirty, blood-stained chemise had been found by the police. How could she reclaim it after that?

It would be as well to briefly examine several other unacceptable points in Mrs. Bridges' widely accepted theory.

Surely Mr. Kent would not have been so foolish as to get into the nurse's bed with his wife in the next room! Mrs. Kent had given the strictest instructions that the nursery door was never to be locked, further telling the nurse never to be surprised to see her in the nursery at any hour of the day or night. Whether these instructions were prompted by the thoughts of a suspicious wife or an over-protective mother is a matter for question, but they surely indicate that the nursery was the last place in which Mr. Kent might safely conduct an illicit affair.

Secondly, the Yseult Bridges theory indicates that Gough was wearing the breast-flannel shortly before Savill's death. This could not have been so; there were no strings attached for tying, although it did have the marks of where strings had once been. It is conceivable that in the throes of passion *one* string could have come off, but to suggest that they *all* should, simultaneously, is really stretching credulity too far.

Also, why would Mr. Kent pick up the breast-flannel in order to press it over his son's mouth? Such an action would be quite superfluous. Surely in such an emergency one would react instinctively and use the quickest and most efficient means of stifling another's cries: i.e. a hand.

Mrs. Bridges writes of Mr. Kent and the nurse: "Either they

had forgotten the splashboard, or had thought that the body would pass it. . . ." Such a statement is not acceptable for a moment, though. It was Mr. Kent who had had the splashboard fitted, and it had been fitted there *for the sole purpose of preventing any child's body falling into the vault below.* Nor can one believe that after having gone to all the trouble of having it fitted he now, at the most vital moment, forgot that it was there.

Why was the knife used? It is suggested that it was resorted to in order to force the body down past the splashboard. But it is hard to believe that a man would needlessly inflict further mutilation on the body of his much loved son. And equally, why attempt *to push with a sharp-pointed knife?*—surely that would be the most inefficient means of such a manœuvre. One would use a blunt instrument. In the circumstances one would have expected Mr. Kent to have used his hand. Why did he not? The body was only just beneath the seat, well within his reach.

Why was the child wrapped in a blanket? If Savill was dead he could hardly come to harm from the night air.

It is clear that so many parts of Mrs. Bridges' theory will not stand examination. But even so, that does not mean that Mr. Kent and the nurse were not involved in the ghastly happenings of that unforgettable night. I am certain they were.

Chapter 12

STRANGE HAPPENINGS

Late that Saturday evening Foley and Mr. Kent had a meeting at which it was arranged that two constables would spend the night at Road Hill House. The original suggestion had come from Foley who, getting nowhere fast, believed that the culprit or culprits might choose the night hours for covering tracks and destroying clues, and with this in mind he thought it would be as well if one or two officers could "perambulate the premises". Mr. Kent, on receiving the suggestion, at once agreed, appearing to show the greatest willingness to co-operate.

So, Urch and Heritage were instructed to go home, get their suppers and return to the house at eleven o'clock when Mr. Kent would be waiting for them. The other inmates of the house were not to know of the policemen's presence there, the men were told, therefore they must go about their business quietly. On their arrival at the house they must tap upon the library window, Foley said, adding: "Mr. Kent will tell you what to do."

This last comment from Foley shows clearly that he had some plan of action in mind and was relying on Mr. Kent to see that it was put into effect. Foley's plan, however, stopped there, and when the two men were let into Road Hill House that night it was Mr. Kent alone who directed the proceedings.

He began by taking them into the library to explain "the purpose of their presence in the house", of which purpose Dr. Stapleton says:

It was suggested that, if there was anything to conceal, anything to destroy, the kitchen fire would be the place to effect such a design; and, on the supposition that the murderer or an accomplice was in the house, it was inferred that such an attempt would be made that night.

And *if* such an attempt should be made, it was suggested, then the two policemen, waiting in the kitchen, would be in the best possible position for the apprehension of the culprit.

Urch and Heritage, it seems, accepted this from Mr. Kent as the purpose of their presence there and, following him to the kitchen, saw that their proposed vigil was well-provided for: bread-and-cheese and beer had been laid out on the table.

Mr. Kent didn't remain with them long, and after telling Heritage that he wouldn't be required beyond two o'clock, left them to the comfort of the food, the drink and the fire and returned to the front of the house.

In the bedrooms above all was quiet. Up there only Mrs. Kent knew of the constables' presence in the house. She knew also that her husband did not intend sleeping that night and, anxious for company, had asked her stepdaughter Elizabeth to share her bed. Eveline's crib was also brought into her parents' room. The vacancy left by Elizabeth in the room she shared with her older sister was filled by Constance who forsook her own bed to spend the night with Mary Ann.

Elizabeth Gough was for once without her charges, and for some reason she stayed downstairs long after the other inmates—besides Mr. Kent—had gone to bed. Various newspapers were swift to discover this fact and they did not hesitate to ask why. When the nurse did at last go upstairs she did not stay alone in the nursery but slept instead in the room of the two Sarahs. Of the whole household only William's sleeping arrangements remained unaffected; but even here there was a slight difference; he locked his bedroom door.

Shortly after two o'clock Heritage, feeling the time had come for him to leave, got up and moved to the door. "It's time for me to go," he said to Urch, and then found to his surprise that the door was locked. Loudly he began to knock and Urch, startled at the sudden disturbance, cautioned him to be quiet, saying, "You're making enough noise to wake everybody in the house!"

"We're locked in!" Heritage told him, "—and I've got to get out!"

He continued to knock for almost twenty minutes until Mr. Kent, arriving close on the appointed time, unbolted the door and opened it.

"I didn't know we were to be locked in like that," Heritage said. But Mr. Kent merely replied:

"I've been walking about."

While Urch stayed in his comfortable chair near the kitchen range Heritage hurried past Mr. Kent and strode into the hall. Kent paused only for a moment—to lock the door again on the unsuspecting Urch—and then let Heritage out of the house.

Three hours later, at 5.30, Mr. Kent returned to the kitchen where he unbolted the door and told Urch:

"You'd better go; the servants will soon be up and about."

The constable, tireder but no wiser than when he had arrived, got up and left.

What was the reason for Urch and Heritage being locked in the kitchen that night? Various theories have been expounded, including Yseult Bridges' absurd claim that it all had to do with the chemise discovered in the boiler-stove during the afternoon.

Insisting that the chemise was Elizabeth Gough's nightdress and therefore a "vital clue which had fortuitously escaped the destruction planned for it and might at any moment . . . bring about the downfall" of Mr. Kent and the nurse, she presents a strange fantasy wherein Kent sets out to retrieve the garment. Her story is that Foley was persuaded by Kent to replace the chemise in the boiler-stove—in the belief that the guilty person would attempt to regain possession of it—and that later, while Urch and Heritage were distracted by the food and drink in the kitchen, Kent crept into the scullery next-door, took the chemise and subsequently burnt it.

It is all nonsense. For one thing the chemise was not even in the house that night. It had been taken to Trowbridge by Dallimore and would remain in his possession until Monday morning when, after he and his wife had thoroughly examined it, it would be brought back to Road.

But even if the chemise *had* been a "vital clue" implicating Mr. Kent or someone close to him he would hardly have used *those* means to retrieve it. For one thing a door that could not be locked connected the kitchen where sat the policemen and the scullery housing the boiler-stove.[1] The police, therefore, had free access to

---

[1] In *Victorian Murderesses* Mary S. Hartman dispenses with this connecting door altogether. She says: ". . . What happened was that the witless officers were trapped for several hours in the kitchen, *which had no access to the scullery*. . . ."! (My italics.)

the boiler-stove at all times, not to mention the fact that if they *had* been detailed to keep an eagle-eye on it they would surely have realized that sitting in another room to do so somehow defeated the object!

No, let there be no mistake, Mr. Kent's motive for locking up the policemen had nothing to do with the chemise.

What, then was his purpose?

It is most interesting to note that he not only locked the kitchen door but also that door connecting the rear passage with the front of the house, thereby completely sealing off the rear interior from the front. Urch and Heritage, therefore, could only move from the kitchen to the scullery and out into the passage—*and no further*—unless they wished to go outside, which they could easily do by means of the rear scullery door or the main back door. That, though, would only leave them in the yard wherein the Newfoundland guard dog was roaming, a move that would hardly seem to their advantage, to say the least.

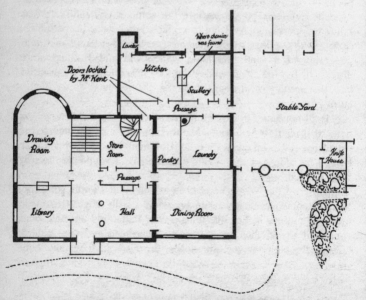

Plan of the ground floor of Road Hill House.

Mr. Kent's purpose, then, soon becomes clear. He was not so much locking them in the kitchen as *locking them out of the house.* Road Hill House has nineteen rooms and by his action that night Kent allowed the police the run of only *two* of them[2]—two rooms well apart from the main body of the house—two rooms where he could safely leave them, secure in the knowledge that *there* they could discover *nothing.*

Ever since his return from Trowbridge that morning Mr. Kent had suffered the police breathing down his neck and overrunning the house, while his repeatedly voiced assurances that they should be *outside* directing their searches had done little, if anything, to relieve the pressure on him. And, if Foley had had his way that same situation would have continued even into the night. But Foley, as we have seen, did not have his way; due to Kent's cunning manœuvres the two policemen sent to keep the planned vigilance were put safely under lock and key, able to witness nothing at all. Add to this the fact that *all* the household knew that Mr. Kent was to be awake and roaming the house that night and he could be quite certain that whatever he had to do he could do it freely, safe from all hindrance and observation.

If Mr. Kent wanted that freedom to allow for the destruction or disposal of any incriminating evidence—and to talk in private to Elizabeth Gough—then he engineered his opportunities perfectly.

When Foley heard of what had happened he was furious. But even greater than his anger was his embarrassment. He had detailed two men to go to the house to keep a watch and the men had ended up as virtual prisoners—and prisoners of a man who, by rights, should have been regarded as one of the possible suspects. Within twenty-four hours of being called to investigate the crime Foley had committed a terrible blunder, word of which, if it should get about, could only result in his being regarded as a fool and totally inadequate to the task. Foley's superior, Captain Meredith, when informed of the charade quite possibly entertained such a view; certainly he was very angry at the proceedings. The only hope, therefore, of preventing the Wiltshire investigators from losing face was to try to keep the matter quiet and pretend it had never hap-

[2] The laundry, wherein lay Savill's body, had also been locked for the night.

pened. This, as far as possible, they did. They had to; their very livelihoods depended upon the respect accorded them and there would be little of that respect remaining once word of the fiasco got abroad. The silence on the matter was not to last for very long, but while it did the police stayed free of the calumny that its later exposure would heap upon them.

When the news of the episode did break and questions were asked, Mr. Kent was to say that he had bolted the door so "that everything might appear as usual"—which would have been the case had any member of his household made any attempt to get into the back part of the house that night. No member of that household would ever have tried, though—not then; as already stated, the altered sleeping arrangements showed clearly that all the household knew of Mr. Kent's plans to stay awake and downstairs. This knowledge would have been enough to deter any would-be prowler from venturing from the safety of the bedroom. No, the house that night was *anything but "as usual"*.

There was one thing that emerged from Mr. Kent's request to the police to keep a watch in the kitchen. By doing so he openly acknowledged that the guilty person or persons would be found in his own house.

Chapter 13

BEFORE THE INQUEST

By the time Monday came the newspapers had had two days in which to glean information on the sensational case and report to their eager readers. As yet only the barest facts were known, but these facts were so shocking that even the most blasé individual was held rapt. It really was a most extraordinary crime, and it became more sensational by having been committed at the house of such a prominent local gentleman as Mr. Kent. In that handsome mansion on the hill, inhabited by the supposedly happy, wealthy Kent family, an innocent child had been brutally done to death and his butchered body thrust into the disgusting grave of a water-closet vault. To the stunned villagers and other interested people the event was almost unbelievable; even where murder was concerned this particularly ghastly crime seemed to go against the order of things.

The villagers did not accept for a moment that the killing was the work of an outsider; for a long time they had sensed that all was not well within the house on Road Hill, and they had their own ideas as to which of its inhabitants was guilty. Surely, they felt, it would only be a matter of time—with the inquest to be held that day—before all would be revealed and the suspicions confirmed.

That Monday morning crowds of people—villagers, reporters, and sightseers from further afield—converged on Road Hill House. In spite of the police guard the fence proved an easily surmountable barrier to those thrill-seekers who were bent on getting into the garden to gaze at the privy, while some of the more determined members of the press even managed to get into the house itself.

The interior of the house, too, presented a scene of constant coming and going. After the hastily empanelled jury had been sworn in at ten o'clock they had been brought to the house by their foreman, the Rev. Peacock, joining there the County Coroner, Mr. George Sylvester, and several other "interested persons". Once assembled the crowd of men trooped through the passages and rooms of the house; for many of those jury-members it was a once-in-a-lifetime experience, access to the hallowed precincts of such a fine mansion being entirely outside the routine of their everyday lives.

They gazed upon the mutilated body of the child where it lay in its coffin; they saw the drawing-room window and shutters opened in the manner in which Cox had discovered them two mornings before, and they crowded into the nursery and stood around the victim's cot—still in the neat state in which the nurse professed to have found it. Then, outside in the grounds they looked at the privy —around which the yew shrubbery was beginning to show the signs of the many feet that had so recently tramped that way.

Also on the premises, of course, were the policemen—and there were new faces amongst these, too. One of them was Captain Meredith from Devizes, Wiltshire's Chief Constable. After the happening of Saturday night with Heritage and Urch getting locked in the kitchen he had probably deemed it as well to come and see for himself what was going on.

There, too, was P.C. Dallimore. He had arrived earlier that morning from Trowbridge, bringing with him in the wagonette Mary Ann's nightdress and the chemise. This latter garment had been examined by him again that morning, and also by his wife.[1] He had looked in vain for any initials or other distinguishing marks which might have pointed to its owner, while Mrs. Dallimore had given it as her opinion that it probably belonged to Sarah Kerslake, as the cook had remarked to her "that she made her garments dirty because of the work she had to do".[2]

As soon as he had arrived at Road Hill House, Dallimore was again involved in a search of the premises, but then, as the hour of the inquest drew nearer he was called upon by Foley to leave his searching and fetch Mary Ann's nightdress from the wagonette. For his own professional protection Foley must have a medical opinion as to the stains on the garment. He was quite certain they were due to natural causes, but should they prove not to be then the night-dress might figure as important evidence at the forthcoming in-quest.

[1] Their comments on the garment are given on p. 107.
[2] Mrs. Dallimore in evidence, 30th November. See p. 247.

When Dallimore had brought the nightdress he and Foley sought out Dr. Stapleton and asked him to look at it, which he did. He did not, however, realize that he was looking at a *different* garment from the one he had previously seen—the *chemise*. Dr. Stapleton firmly believed that he had seen Mary Ann's nightdress twice on the preceding Saturday—once in the house, and then later when he had examined the items lying in the police wagonette. Now, this Monday morning when the police came to him bearing the nightdress he was convinced that he was about to see it for the *third time*; it is understandable, therefore, that the attention he paid it amounted to little more than the most cursory glance. Once more he wasted no time in dismissing the garment before him as having no bearing on the investigation.

Certainly Dr. Stapleton was very lax in his examinations of the garments shown to him, and so was Foley who failed to point out that there were *two separate garments*. Both Foley and Stapleton were to regret that laxity, for very soon the whereabouts of a *third* garment would bring into question the conduct of those men and a veritable panic would ensue. The seeds of that panic were, at that very moment, being sown.

Stapleton's all-too-brief examination of Mary Ann's nightdress must have taken place before ten o'clock for by that time it had been returned to her and was subsequently given to Sarah Cox to be packed in one of the laundry baskets with the rest of the family's washing. This left in Foley's possession the chemise—but no knowledge of to whom it belonged. The superintendent, totally satisfied in his own mind that it had no connection with the crime, told Dallimore to fetch it from the wagonette and put it back where it had been found. A few minutes later Dallimore, carrying the chemise, went into the scullery.

Sarah Kerslake was at work in the area of the kitchen and scullery and was later to recall Dallimore's presence there. She was not, however, nearby when he approached the boiler-stove. There the policeman, seeing that no one was near, stooped to put the parcel back into the flue over the hot-plate—only to find that he could not as the fire was still burning. Instead, he placed it on the floor at the side of the boiler. Later in the day, on returning to the scullery, he found that the parcel containing the chemise had gone. Which is hardly to be wondered at considering that Emily Doel had been in and out of the scullery many times in the course of her work.

Attending to the family's laundry was one of Sarah Cox's regular weekly tasks. And this week would be no exception. One innocent member of that family had been horribly murdered but life for the rest of the family must, as well as it could, go on.

On the landing outside Constance's room Cox stooped and picked up the soiled stockings the girl had thrown there. A nightdress was lying on the floor too, a fact which registered on Cox's mind as Constance usually left her soiled nightdresses to be collected from her room. The maid thought no more about it now, however—though later she would—and adding the nightdress to the rest of the clothing she made her way down to the lumber room on the first-floor landing below. There she sorted the various articles for the laundry and, when she had finished, informed Mary Ann that they were ready to be checked and entered in the laundry book.

Apart from the other items there Mary Ann and Sarah Cox checked three nightdresses—the one belonging to Mary Ann herself, another to Constance, and the third to Mrs. Kent. There was a fourth, but that belonged to Elizabeth and had been separately listed and parcelled by her. When Mary Ann's job was done she went back to her own room, leaving the maid to pack the clothes into the baskets.

Cox wasted no time in doing her work and, after one minor interruption, soon had it done. Then, leaving the two baskets covered—one with a tablecloth and the other with one of Mrs. Kent's dresses—she hurried away to get ready for the inquest. She had been called as a witness and the proceedings were due to begin at eleven.

Chapter 14

THE INQUEST

It should have been obvious to anyone that the largest room at the Red Lion Inn would not accommodate the jury, the coroner, the witnesses, the officials and the press—not to mention even a fraction of the crowd that pressed against the doors clamouring for admittance. It was later to be suggested that the venue was *deliberately* chosen with a view to restricting, substantially, the number of those who wished to witness the proceedings—and there may well have been truth in this—even so, the Red Lion Inn was soon seen to be totally impractical for its present desired purpose. Soon after the jury had reassembled on their return from Road Hill House, the coroner, George Sylvester—at the suggestion of the Chief Constable, adjourned the inquiry to the larger premises of the Temperance Hall which stood nearby. This place was the obvious choice from the start.

The official proceedings, therefore, only got under way after considerable delay and disruption; and there was to be no increase in efficiency as the inquiry progressed. On the contrary, it was to get worse.

Watched avidly by the spectators who had packed into the hall— mothers even holding aloft small children to afford them a better view—Mr. Sylvester took his place on the platform. He was surrounded by various "gentlemen interested in the case", one of whom was Dr. Stapleton. Surprisingly, Mr. Kent was not present, though his solicitor Mr. Rowland Rodway was there to watch the proceedings on the bereaved father's behalf. After the jury had taken their seats the first witness was called.

Much earlier that morning when Foley had accompanied Mr. Sylvester to the Red Lion Inn for the swearing-in of the jury he had asked the coroner which individuals he would require as witnesses once the inquest began. To Foley's astonishment he was told that the only ones who would be called from Road Hill House were the nurse and the housemaid.

Now, with the proceedings at last in progress, the first witness, housemaid Sarah Cox, was called and sworn. From the questions and answers that followed the listeners heard that, as usual, she had secured the door and shutters of the drawing-room on the past Friday night; they learned, too, that no one could have entered the house that way without using considerable force, the results of which would have been immediately discernible. Mr. Kent had been the last person to go to bed, she stated, as was his custom, and there had been no disagreement occurring amongst the family or the servants.

The next witness was the nurse Elizabeth Gough who, said *The Journal*, had a "prepossessing appearance". Her deposition was as follows:

"I am nursemaid at Mr. Kent's house. I have been there rather more than eight months. The deceased was a very good-tempered child, not troublesome. He slept in a cot by himself in the corner of my bedroom. Another child, a girl of two years of age, sleeps in a cot in the same room. I usually put the deceased to bed about eight o'clock, and I did so on Friday evening. He was then well and in good spirits. Mrs. Kent always comes into the room after prayers to see the children, and she did so that night. I went to bed about five minutes past eleven; the child was then lying on his side, with his face to the wall, his arm under his head. After I had been in my room a little while Mrs. Kent came up to bed and shut my door as she passed. I usually left the door open for her to shut when she came up, lest the little girl who was sleeping in her room should cry, and then I might hear her. I did not go to sleep till about twelve and heard nothing during the night. I woke about five o'clock; the nursery door was a little open, and I missed the deceased from his bed. The impression of the child was there as if he had been softly taken out; the clothes were smoothly put back as if his mother or myself had taken him out. He wore at night his nightdress and a little flannel shirt, but no piece of flannel.[1] When I saw the deceased was gone I thought his mother had come in and taken him out. The piece of flannel does not belong to the house; it was not worn by anyone in the house.

"I went to Mrs. Kent's room about a quarter- or twenty-minutes-

---

[1] She refers here to the piece of flannel found by Foley.

to-seven o'clock to ask for one of the children—supposing that she had both of them. I knocked twice at the door, but obtained no answer, and as Mrs. Kent was unwell I went away again and came again at a quarter-past-seven. Mrs. Kent was then in her dressing-gown and said that she had not seen the child. I then went to the Miss Kents' bedroom upstairs, but they had not got him either. I then went downstairs and searched all over the house and looked in the garden and kitchen-garden and all around the shrubbery. The housemaid had told me she had found the drawing-room door and window open. I looked for footmarks but did not see any except on the drawing-room carpet-covering; there were impressions of two hobnail boots. They were of a large foot.[2] There is a little piece of gravel the person would have to cross in going to where the child was found. I did not go there to look."

On being further examined Elizabeth Gough stated:

"There has been no disturbance or unfriendliness in the house. I can state positively that no one was in my bedroom or the dressing-room which opens out of it, as we had a sweep that morning and in the evening everything was put away; I pushed a stool and a box under my bed and went into the dressing-room. I put the things in order in my bedroom and lit the night-light. There were three small knives in my room but none of them were touched. I know of no one who could have had a dislike of the child. My room door has a latch on it and a bolt, but I was never allowed to bolt it, in order that Mrs. Kent might come in if the children cried. The door opens very noiselessly; it is bound round with lint to make it do so, that I might not wake the children. . . .

"I often wake in the night if it rains or blows. I heard nothing whatever that night. I was asleep the whole time. The deceased was a very heavy sleeper and would sleep especially sound that night as, due to the sweep being in, he had missed his usual sleep during the day."

The nurse was then asked whether she knew of any part of the family absenting themselves from home for several days, to which she answered, "I believe two of them did, but it was not during my time". Did she know the cause? she was asked. No, she replied, she did not.

[2] She must have seen these later for they were made by P.C. Urch.

Thomas Benger was next to be called and he described how, with William Nutt, he had found the child's body. Among the statements he made were the following:

"There was no blood on the walls, or the seat of the privy. I moved the lid off. . . . The blanket was on top, not wrapped round the child; he was lying on the splashboard inside the seat, which prevented him from descending into the vault. One hand and one leg were slightly thrown up. . . ." He ended his deposition with the information that he had assisted in emptying the vault, in which was found "five feet of water, but nothing of importance".

Superintendent Foley, who was not sworn, then came forward and produced the piece of flannel he had hooked up from the surface of the privy's soil. This article—still with the blood on it—was described by him as probably having been a "female breast flannel"; he said that marks could be seen where strings had once been attached. One thing that was certain, though, whatever the flannel's purpose had been it was not new; it was later to be described as "an old piece",[3] and "nearly worn out".

William Nutt was called next and after corroborating Benger's account of the finding of the body he was followed by Millett the butcher, who produced the pieces of newspaper picked up near the privy. The two pieces had been folded over together and appeared "as if something bloody had been wiped" on them. Holding up the pieces of paper—which, it was later established, had come from *The Times* of the 9th of July, 1857—he said, "They were folded as they are now; the blood on them was moist, and the larger piece stuck together".

Elizabeth Gough was then recalled and in the course of answering further questions said that William Kent had been home from school for his summer holidays for about a fortnight. She also went on to say no, she didn't get the impression that the Newfoundland guard dog appeared to have been drugged.

Stephen Millett, recalled, said that his work as a butcher acquainted him with the loss of blood "from animals when dying" and that he would have expected to have seen more blood at the scene than he had observed—which he reckoned to have been about three half-pints. Dr. Stapleton, clearly annoyed to hear a mere

[3] These two quotations are both from Inspector Whicher's reports of the 30th July and 8th August, 1860.

butcher giving medical evidence, took advantage of "the remarkable informality of the proceedings" to let the people know that qualified medical men were present. Quite out of place in the inquiry he interposed: "We *medical* men up here think that that is not enough. We think that three pints of blood from a child that size should be accounted for, and that has not been done."

Millett was then asked by a juryman whether he thought that it was not possible that the murder had been committed in the closet. The butcher answered that he thought it *was* possible, and, causing the greatest sensation, added:

"It's my impression that the child was held by his legs, with his head hanging down, and that his throat was cut while in that position."

Joshua Parsons the surgeon was next called and told of his findings at the *post-mortem*. After saying that he had found the body "in the laundry, the blanket and nightdress stained with marks of blood and soil", he went on to describe the victim's wounds.

"There were two small cuts on the left hand, evidently made by a sharp instrument after the body had been drained—there was little or no blood on them. The throat was cut to the bone by some sharp instrument, from left to right; all the membranes, blood-vessels, nerves and air-tubes were completely divided. There is no doubt that the cut was made by a single sharp, clean incision. I found afterwards a stab on the body, evidently made by some broad, sharp, long and strong instrument, as it penetrated the flannel shirt and nightdress, passing below the pericardium,[4] through the diaphragm, and wounded the outer wall of the stomach. It severed the cartilages of two ribs and extended three-quarters across the chest. I judge it was done by a sharp-pointed instrument; it could not have been done by a razor. It must have been, I think, a sharp-pointed, long, wide and strong knife." There was further sensation at this. Then the surgeon continued. "The wound was not less than four inches deep, and when it was inflicted the body must have been previously drained of blood.

"I examined the interior of the stomach to ascertain if the child had been drugged, but he had not. I found the internal parts healthy. Deceased was a child of remarkably fine development. I am satis-

---

[4] The sac round the heart.

fied that no drug had been given him. I am of the opinion that he had been dead at least five hours before I first examined him about nine o'clock in the morning. He was quite cold and I was surprised to find so much rigidity. My opinion is that there has not been produced today so large a quantity of blood as was likely to be caused by the wounds I have described. . . ." Dr. Parsons was leading up to that rather startling conclusion he had been drawn to make. He went on: "The severed arteries would have sent out with a gush at one jet a great quantity of blood, the veinous blood draining out afterwards. The blood flowing from a child that size would have been not less than three pints—whereas I do not think we have seen anything like a pint. I should also have said that there was a blackened appearance all round the mouth—such as we do not usually see in dead bodies. It was likely to be produced by the violent thrusting of a blanket into the mouth to prevent him crying out, or it could have been done with a hand."

These statements from Dr. Parsons were of vital importance yet for some reason—either obtuseness or a deliberate act—the coroner *ignored* them. Divertingly, he merely asked the surgeon whether he believed that the child might have been struck on the head before having his throat cut. Dr. Parsons answered this in the negative, adding, "If he had been I should have seen the mark."

At this point Superintendent Foley spoke up and said that he thought he could reconcile the apparent difference in the evidence respecting the quantity of blood found in the closet, as he had been the first to disturb the soil. "When I examined the vault," he said, "I found a large quantity of paper, as much as would cover this table" (which was about two yards square) "and every particle of that paper was saturated with blood. Below that was four or five feet of water. I have no doubt whatever that the murder was committed in the closet and that the child was brought there alive."

Dr. Parsons was then told that he might step down—which astonished him for he had not yet been asked for his opinion as to the cause of the child's death—and this of course is one of the primary purposes of an inquest. However, not to be silenced, he said aloud as he took his seat:

"It's my belief that the child had been smothered by the pressure of a soft substance over the mouth."

Dr. Parsons' statement, though, was made voluntarily and therefore was not added to his deposition—and consequently it was not regarded as evidence. Even so, it was clearly a most provocative statement and many there present must have thought that at last the inquiry was really beginning to get under way. To the great surprise of nearly everyone in the hall, however, it suddenly became clear that the inquest was *over*. No further witnesses were called and already the coroner had begun his summing-up and his address to the jury. It was evident to everybody there that someone in the house had been responsible for the crime, yet of all the nine persons who might be deemed capable of having committed it, only two had been examined.

The jury's dissatisfaction at this was very soon made apparent, and while they muttered and hastily conferred with each other the spectators also made known their feelings, many of them calling out, demanding to know why no members of the family had been summoned to appear. Mr. Peacock, the jury foreman, could no longer ignore the jury's insistent demands and eventually—and "most reluctantly"—he interrupted the coroner to say that several of the jurymen wanted to have other witnesses called, "and to have some of the family examined". The spectators showed their approval by applauding this, demonstrating sentiments obviously not shared by Mr. Peacock, who went on to say, "I myself do not see its utility, and for the sake of the family should wish to avoid it, as their feelings ought to be in some degree respected". This last brought sounds of hissing and cries of dissent from the spectators, which broke out anew when the coroner concurred with the fore-man's views.

But the jury was insistent, and with the spectators cheering their demands the coroner could do nothing but accede. Only very un-willingly, though. "I must say," he said, "I don't see what end is to be served by it. Anyone else will only confirm what we have already heard and say they know no more about it. However, if it is a wish of the majority of the jury it must be done." Backed up by a fresh burst of hand-clapping several jurymen at once exclaimed that "with the exception of their foreman, they were *unanimous* in their request".

After Dr. Parsons had quickly risen to state that Mrs. Kent's state of health would not permit her appearance as a witness the coroner addressed the jury: "If you are insistent in your determination to examine any part of the family I shall adjourn the inquest to the house."

This brought a fresh outcry of dissatisfaction from the spectators, for it meant they would be excluded from part of the inquiry—that part they were most anxious to witness. The coroner was not this time to be dissuaded, however, and he went on to ask the jury: "Which part of the family would you like to be examined?" This brought a chorus of voices. Some called for the examination of the two younger members, Constance and William, while others demanded, "Try them all! Show no respect to one more than another!" The specific calls for the examination of Constance and William were not, of course, based on anything more than suspicion; but that suspicion was there and it was strong. All the villagers were aware that Constance and William were not happy with their lot at Road Hill House—their attempt at escape four years earlier was proof of that—and now they read into the discontent and resentment a possible motive for the crime.

During further discussion in which the coroner, the jurymen and the spectators took part, Mr. Rodway hurried off to Road Hill House and came back with the information that Mr. Kent was quite willing for any members of his family to be examined. He could, of course, do little else but comply with the request. He was at liberty to refuse but considering the suspicion already directed towards the family this would have been a most unwise move.

The coroner, as soon as he had received word of Mr. Kent's magnanimous answer, ended all further discussion by getting up and leaving the hall. The jury, when informed that they could be *compelled* to follow him, could do nothing else but that, and accordingly they trailed in his wake as he strode off towards Road Hill House.

There in the kitchen Constance and William were brought before the assembly, and of the totally inadequate examination that followed one reporter was to write that it was of a most "cursory and superficial kind",[5] going on to say that the coroner "put several of his questions in a leading form". Those questions, and the answers they brought, resulted in the following statements—neither of which was written on parchment in the form of a deposition, but simply attached, as notes, to the other reports.

[5] *The Journal.*

First, from Constance:

"I am sixteen years of age. I knew nothing of this affair until after my brother was found. About half-past ten on Friday night I went to bed, and I knew nothing until seven o'clock. I generally sleep soundly. I did not leave my bed during the night. I do not know of anyone having a spite against the boy. There was no disagreement in the house, and I am not aware of anyone having a grudge against the deceased. The nurse was always kind and attentive to him. On Saturday morning I heard he was missed; I was then getting up."

And William's statement:

"I am brother to the deceased. I went to bed on Friday night at ten-thirty and got up at seven o'clock on Saturday morning. I did not get out of bed during the night. I have nothing to add about his death—I wish I had. The deceased was a great favourite of us all, not of one in particular. I did not see deceased after dinner-time[6] on Friday; I was out. I always shut my door at night, but I do not lock it usually; I did last night for fear."

William, it was said, gave his answers "clearly and well, his eyes being fixed on the coroner throughout". Constance, on the other hand, answered "in a subdued but audible tone, without betraying any special emotion, her eyes fixed on the ground".[7]

These brief examinations being over, Mr. Sylvester instructed the jury to return to the Temperance Hall where, once they were settled in their seats again, he began to address them.

He began by cautioning them to dismiss from their minds all preconceived opinions and suspicions (as John Rhode says: "A very necessary warning in view of the flood of rumour which overlay the countryside") and to rely solely upon the evidence that had been placed before them. This of course was laudable, except that the coroner had not made it possible for any real evidence to be given.

He then went on to remind the jury that the available evidence showed that no one had forcibly entered the house—though the culprit might or might not have left by the drawing-room window. He was inclined to believe, he said, that the fatal blows had been inflicted in the closet, and that it would have been possible for the

[6] Mid-day dinner.
[7] *The Journal.*

killer to have staunched the flow of blood with the blanket in which the child was wrapped.[8] With regard to the difference of opinion respecting the quantity of blood that was found he thought there was a great quantity of blood on the blanket and other articles, and Mr. Foley had accounted for the discrepancy by stating that he was the first to examine the vault of the closet where, before the soil was disturbed, a great quantity of blood had been visible.

"Gentlemen of the jury," he went on, "this is a most mysterious and atrocious murder, committed by some person or persons, but I fear it will not fall to your lot, under the present aspect of the case, to criminate any person in connection with it. The cause of death is apparent to you, but the mystery lies in this: what cause or motive could have induced the perpetrator of the deed to have murdered a child three years and ten months old in this way?"

He then gave various motives for child-murder—none of which could possibly apply in the case under examination—and then continued:

"Now it seems to me that someone might have secreted themselves in the house overnight and, having some malicious feelings towards any members of the family, for the purpose of wreaking their spleen or vengeance, may have taken this little boy out through the drawing-room to the closet, there murdered him and cast him in, with the object of concealing the body. It would, indeed, have been malicious to have wreaked vengeance in this manner on an innocent child of those tender years; what offence could he have offered anyone? But this is only supposition; we have no proof of it; the matter remains enveloped in the deepest mystery. It would have been a satisfaction to you and to me to have traced this crime to the perpetrator of it, but we cannot do that. You may have suspicions on your minds tending to implicate some member——" He broke off here, and hastily corrected himself: "—some *person* —but suspicion, you must remember, is not proof."

It was quite clear that, a moment before, the coroner had been about to say "*some member of the family*"—which was where the general suspicions were directed; the coroner knew it and everyone else knew it. The coroner was not about to admit it, though. He continued, drawing now to a close.

[8] The blanket was found lying on top of the body, not wrapped round it. See Benger's evidence, p. 124.

"I think, gentlemen, that you cannot but agree with me, and record it in your verdict, that this murder has been committed by some person or persons unknown." To which came the clear reply from one of the jurymen:

"It *is* unknown, but there is a strong suspicion which don't at all settle on my stomach."

This was greeted with cheers, and a chorus of approval, following which another member of the jury remarked that it was clear to him "that no one could have got in from outside".

The coroner was quick to reply.

"Whatever suspicions you may have in your mind must not influence you in giving your verdict. You must remember that suspicion is not proof. We have no direct evidence before us, circumstantial or otherwise, and you must, therefore, decide upon that which is before you, and that alone. I have no doubt but that sooner or later the mystery in which this crime is at present enveloped will be cleared away, and the author or authors of it brought to light. You must remember, gentlemen, that our duty is merely to inquire; we are not responsible for our inability to discover the author. But also recollect that although the action was concealed from the eyes of men, yet it was seen and recorded by One above; the eye of Providence saw the deed and can penetrate the mystery, and punishment will await the guilty."

Clearly, though, the jury were not content with the knowledge that the crime's perpetrator was known only to God, for after a brief conversation amongst themselves they requested of their foreman that the inquest be adjourned. This request, most proper under the circumstances, was not, however, approved by Mr. Peacock and he did not, as he should have done, press the point with the coroner. To the further bewilderment of the main body of the jury, they were not asked to make any verbal statement on their verdict. Instead, the coroner completed a printed *Form of Inquiry*, read it aloud, signed it, and then passed it to the jury for their signatures to be added. They did not do so without some protest, though, and one man, a certain Mr. West, rose quickly and, hand over his heart, told the coroner "in an impressive and excited manner" that he felt they had not done their duty. Many other members of the jury spoke up here, but their protests did them no good and they were left with no alternative but to take the document and—albeit reluctantly—affix their signatures to it. As one juror, a Mr. Marks, signed his name, he proclaimed that he had never before signed anything so much against his inclination.

So the verdict of *Wilful murder against some person or persons unknown* was duly elicited. The inquest was over.

Mr. Sylvester's exit from the Temperance Hall was marked by booing and shouts of derision, voices crying out that the jury had been packed, and demanding to know why *all* the Kent family had not been examined.

In all, from start to finish, the inquest had lasted only five hours.

As Yseult Bridges so rightly points out, the purpose of an inquest is to determine the cause of death and, as far as possible, who is likely to have caused that death. For this purpose, therefore, it is essential that *all* available evidence should be examined. Witnesses called are, on oath, bound to answer *any* questions relating to the case; it is necessary, then, that *everyone* connected with the case is brought forward for questioning. In this way the coroner and the jury are, ideally, presented with a complete picture; any available evidence can be thoroughly sifted and examined by them, enabling them finally—and hopefully—to make a specific charge against some person or persons.

Once an inquest is closed, justice can only be furthered by a specific charge being made against some particular person or persons, and once an individual has been charged *only the evidence relating to that specific charge against that particular person is permissible*. For this reason it is absolutely essential that the inquest is most thorough in its procedure and lays a solid ground on which a subsequent charge can be based.

That Mr. George Sylvester failed in his duty is only too clear. As far as possible he had to execute three tasks; one: to determine the cause of death; two: to determine the nature of the act that led to that death—whether it was murder or manslaughter; and three: to endeavour to lay a charge at the feet of some person or persons.

He failed in every instance.

As has been seen he did not even ask Dr. Parsons for his opinion as to the cause of death, and notwithstanding the surgeon's voluntarily-given opinion that the child had been "smothered by the pressure of a soft substance over the mouth" went on to pronounce, *himself*, on the cause of death, speaking of "the fatal blows inflicted" and telling the jury, "The cause of death is apparent to you"—making it perfectly clear that whatever Dr. Parsons' opinion might be, he—the coroner—accepted without question that the child had died as a result of the wound in the throat. Mr. Sylvester was also a surgeon and all except one person there accepted *his* opinion as to the cause of death. The only person who did not was Dr. Parsons—and he had carried out the *post-mortem*.

Sylvester's second failure was in never suggesting that the death could be anything but the result of murder. The word manslaughter was never uttered by him, and manslaughter was a definite possibility if Dr. Parsons' remarks on suffocation were properly considered.

Thirdly, the coroner made no attempt whatsoever to discover who might possibly be guilty of having committed the crime. Not only was no attempt made, it appears that he acted *determinedly to avoid* any possible charge being brought.

He was correct in stating that there was no evidence pointing to any particular person, but in that case it was his duty to have adjourned the inquest in the hope that such necessary evidence would sooner or later come to light. Mr. Sylvester prevented such evidence coming to light; even Constance and William would have been excluded from examination if he had had his way.

Those who had witnessed the proceedings were quick to claim that a cover-up was taking place, while the press was unanimous in its condemnation of the handling of the inquiry. *The Journal* expressed the general feelings of strong dissatisfaction, saying:

We must seriously object to the course pursued in appointing someone who was avowedly an intimate friend of the family as foreman of the jury. . . . It is our firm conviction that a man who was beyond suspicion of partiality was the only proper person to occupy a position of such responsibility. Again, seeing that the murder must have been committed by someone either resident or concealed in the house, all who slept under the roof that night should have been brought before the jury for examination. This was not done, from a desire to spare the feelings of the family, a very commendable wish in cases of minor importance, but wholly inapplicable to a case of such an intensely serious nature. We

think, also, that it would have been a wiser course had the jury
adjourned for a few days rather than so promptly have returned
their verdict. , . .

The comments from the public were less polite and less subtle,
and the echoes of the dissatisfaction were to reverberate for a long
time to come. Hardly surprisingly; the coroner, in his address to
the jury, had described the crime as the most mysterious and
atrocious murder he had ever heard of, yet he had dispensed with
the whole inquest into that crime in just a few hours, allowing for
no more than the most superficial inquiry.

If the coroner had conducted the inquest correctly and rightly
adjourned the proceedings in the hope of finding further evidence
he would not have had to wait long. Even as that drama was being
played out in the Temperance Hall another drama was taking place
in a different part of the village.

The stained chemise had been examined, as also had Mary Ann's
nightdress. Now, while the coroner bemoaned to the jury the sad
lack of evidence, a third garment was swiftly becoming the centre
of attention. The circumstances relating to *this* article were to have
very far-reaching effects and were eventually to put in peril the life
of one of Mr. Kent's daughters.

A chief participant in this other drama was Mrs. Esther Holly, a
local laundress.

At about twelve o'clock, just when the inquest was getting re-
started after its transfer from the Red Lion Inn, Mrs. Holly and
her daughter Martha were approaching the back door of Road Hill
House. Ever since the Kents' arrival in Road Mrs. Holly had done
their weekly washing, collecting it every Monday and returning it
every Friday. It was much-needed employment she wouldn't have
for much longer.

Admitting them to the house, Sarah Kerslake took the woman
and her seventeen-year-old daughter up to the lumber room on the
first floor and then helped them carry the two baskets back downstairs. Outside in the yard Martha took the smaller basket under
her arm and helped her mother with the larger, heavier one.
Together they set off for home, their steps rather more hurried than
usual.

The reason for their unaccustomed haste was Mrs. Holly's curiosity; she had heard word that a nightdress belonging to one of the young ladies of Road Hill House had been detained by the police (this, of course, was Mary Ann's, but Mrs. Holly didn't know this) and she was eager to see whether the laundry baskets would confirm or deny the rumour.

In the Hollys' kitchen in Union Cottages the woman and her daughter immediately sorted through the baskets in search of the nightdresses. And they found them at once. Not four, though, as were usually there, but three. Only three. It appeared that that rumour was right, one of the nightdresses *had* been detained. But whose? Although the laundry book had been omitted it was still the easiest matter to determine who those three nightdresses belonged to. From an intimate knowledge of the Kent family's washing, Mrs. Holly knew that the nightdresses of Mrs. Kent, Mary Ann and Elizabeth were embroidered with edged frills. Constance's nightdresses were different; they were plainly made of long-cloth and had correspondingly plain frills. The three nightdresses in the basket were clearly identifiable as belonging to Mrs. Kent and her two elder stepdaughters.

Constance's nightdress was missing.

Chapter 15

AFTER THE INQUEST

As soon as the inquest was over and Mr. Sylvester had departed, the attention of the spectators and the press was immediately switched from the Temperance Hall back to Road Hill House. It was there at the gates, later, that Captain Meredith made an appearance to announce to the reporters that, having taken into account the force needed to inflict the victim's wounds and, further, the extreme neatness of the cot from which the child had been removed, he was of the opinion that *two* persons must have been involved—a man and a woman. This information was, of course, quickly seized upon by the listeners, and the resulting speculation gave rise to endless rumours, some quite realistic and others as wide of the mark as they could possibly be.

Upstairs in their rooms, Mrs. Kent, Mary Ann, Elizabeth, Constance and William must have felt besieged. Looking from the windows they could only have been aware of the eager knots of watchers while, closer at hand, on the stairs and in the rooms and hallways of the house itself, there was an endless procession of feet as the various friends and professional associates of Mr. Kent, eight or nine policemen and the indoor servants went about their appointed or self-appointed duties.

One particular policeman, new on the scene and sent from Devizes to assist Foley, was Superintendent Wolfe who, in the course of his investigations, was taken over the house by Mr. Kent. Part of the object of this exercise was to discover any likely hiding-places where someone might conceivably have remained hidden.

Incredibly, Mr. Kent was even now insisting that someone had gained ingress and secreted himself in the house that Friday night, an idea totally at odds with the belief implied by his action in asking for two policemen to keep a watch in the kitchen on the night following. Foley must have seen how inconsistent such behaviour was. If anyone from outside *had* committed the crime and straightaway thereafter made his escape, it is hardly to be supposed that he would have made an attempt to get back into the house and the kitchen the following night in order to destroy any incriminating evidence!

Even so, Mr. Kent continued to waste the time of the investigators by taking and sending them on wild-goose-chases. On this particular occasion when Wolfe asked *where* could a person have hidden himself away, he was answered by Mr. Kent taking him to various lumber rooms, etc., rooms cluttered with boxes, trunks and children's toys. Apart from a space under the roof—where it was obvious that no one had been before—Superintendent Wolfe saw no place that might have been a likely hiding-place.

Continuing to assist Foley, Wolfe accompanied him later when the nurse was questioned again. She, however, was sticking to her second story—that of not having known that the blanket was missing until the dead child had been brought in wrapped up in it. There were many points in the nurse's story which Foley found difficult to accept.

It had been suggested to him that she might have had a lover whom she had invited into the nursery that night while the rest of the household was asleep. Perhaps, the suggestion went on, she and her lover had been discovered by the waking child and that child had then been put to death to ensure his silence on what he had witnessed. It was a possibility that Foley had to consider. But how did the lover get into the house? Through the nurse's window? This was situated just above the flat roof of the dining-room and the only way up to it would have been by means of a ladder. There was a ladder on the premises but it was quickly seen that it had not been disturbed for some considerable time. Foley then turned his attention to the ivy that grew on the wall but quickly dismissed this as a possibility when it was found that it would not bear the weight of a boy, let alone a man. Could it be, then, that the nurse had let in a lover through some downstairs entrance?—perhaps by the window, through which he had afterwards made his escape. . .?

For all his problems, Foley was getting no help at all from the nurse herself. She was even insisting, most strangely, that Mr. Kent had not spoken to her *once* on the subject of the child—neither when it was first found missing or afterwards when discovered dead.

Mr. Kent's behaviour, too, grew no less strange. Was it possible that *he* could be cast in the role of the nurse's lover? Such an idea was later to gain wide acceptance—as seen illustrated by Mrs. Bridges' theory—but when it came newly to Foley for his serious consideration it must have been shocking and disturbing—disturbing for one reason in that while he had no qualms about pursuing a charge of murder against a *servant* he felt very differently about pursuing a similar charge against a man of Mr. Kent's social position.

There is no doubt that Foley had much to perplex him.

He and Wolfe saw Mr. Kent coming from the library in the course of that day, and Foley, obviously with worrying questions on his mind, at once asked Kent whether he had known that a blanket was missing from the cot *before* he had left the house for Trowbridge.

"I did not," Kent replied.

Foley was much surprised and pressed the question. "You didn't know anything about it, sir?"

"No," Kent said emphatically, "certainly not."

Yet on the way to Trowbridge he had distinctly told both Mrs. Hall and then Mrs. Heritage that his child had been *"carried away in a blanket"*.

Of all the people there that day, Rowland Rodway, Mr. Kent's solicitor, was not the least disturbed at the way in which events were turning. Earlier that day, against his wishes, he had been persuaded to attend the inquest *instead* of Mr. Kent—to "watch the interests" of his client, and he was becoming more and more convinced that Mr. Kent was deliberately trying to thwart the ends of justice.

At a private meeting with Kent that afternoon Rodway politely remonstrated with him and pointed out to him that it was quite clear that the crime had been committed by an inmate of the house and that therefore the investigations should be encouraged in that area. The meeting ended with Rodway resigning his post, and leaving Mr. Kent to seek another, and more pliable, legal adviser.

Of his resignation, Mr. Rodway later wrote in a letter to *The Morning Post*:

. . . I suggested to him [Mr. Kent] what I considered to be the probable solution of this mystery; but I found that our views of the crime, and of the mode and direction of its investigation, widely differed; and as I could not adopt Mr. Kent's views, nor he mine, I abstained from further interference.

Mr. Rodway's rather transparent excuse didn't really fool anybody. *The Bath Herald*, commenting upon his letter, wrote that the solicitor was of the decided opinion

that Mr. Kent's ideas, both as to the nature of the crime and the mode and direction of investigations, were so wild and absurd that he could not, with any regard to conscience or self-respect, consent to act upon them; whereupon he threw up his brief and left Mr. Kent to find some more compliant counsellor. As Mr. Rodway will not tell us what those impracticable ideas were, we will ourselves inform the public. Mr. Kent seriously maintained that the murder was committed by some tramp, or possibly by a discarded servant; but, at all events, by no one connected with Road Hill House. The investigation might range far and wide, provided it kept clear of the only place where the criminal was likely to be found. Mr. Rodway refused to go on this wild-goose-chase, and he speedily ceased to be Mr. Kent's solicitor.

Two things are clear. First, Mr. Kent wasn't fooling many people, either. Secondly, whether Mr. Rodway was dismissed or whether he resigned that day, it is certain that, through his conscience, he talked himself out of a job.

In fact, Rodway's interview with Kent following the inquest was a continuation of one that had been initiated on the day of the murder. Years later Mr. Rodway wrote to the Home Secretary, Sir George Grey, telling him of that meeting. He wrote:

. . . After several hours' investigations and inquiry, I was myself so impressed with the belief that Constance Kent had done the deed, that before I left on that day I expressed my belief to Mr. Kent, and warned him that in his daughter's state of mind and feeling the deceased child might not be the only victim.

Chapter 16

CONSTANCE'S NIGHTDRESS

Tuesday morning, 3rd of July, saw Mrs. Holly going to Road Hill House to collect money that was owing to her. While she was there she mentioned nothing about there being only three nightdresses in the washing instead of the usual four; after all, it was none of her business. She did, though, ask Sarah Cox for the laundry book which, by some oversight, had not been forwarded with the washing.

Now, Mrs. Holly could neither read nor write so, even with the laundry book in her hand she was no wiser about the situation. Until she arrived home, that is. Once there, her daughter Martha took one look at the book and saw at once that *four* nightdresses should have been sent.

Mrs. Holly was naturally very much disturbed. A nightdress was rumoured to be missing, and now all present appearances made it look as if it had gone missing at *her hands*. Not knowing what to do about it she did nothing—except worry. So much so that when a group of policemen came knocking at her door to inquire for the "woman who did the Kents' washing" she, thinking they had come about the nightdress, panicked and gratuitously informed them that "the clothes were right with the book".

To her further surprise, though, she found they had merely come to show her the piece of flannel and ask whether she remembered ever having seen it before in the family's wash. This was a question she answered truthfully, saying she never had.

As soon as the police had made their departure Mrs. Holly's agitation increased—on top of everything else she had now lied to the police. The clothes were right with the book, she had told them —when it was perfectly clear that they were not. Obviously, something would have to be done. It was: Martha was immediately sent to Road Hill House to get the matter put right.

At the house Martha spoke to Sarah Cox and told her that, including Miss Elizabeth's, four nightdresses had been listed but only three sent, and that the nightdress missing was that belonging to Miss Constance. Martha then asked for another nightdress "to make the washing right with the book—as the police had been round and she was afraid they were coming back". "If another nightdress isn't sent," she said, "mother will have to tell them about it."

Cox of course told Martha that her mother must be mistaken—she was quite certain that Constance's nightdress had been packed in the basket—she had packed it herself (which indeed she had). Then, telling the girl to wait she hurried away and came back a couple of minutes later with both Mary Ann and Mrs. Kent. Mary Ann did not hesitate in confirming that Constance's nightdress had been packed with the rest of the laundry and Martha, in the face of all this, could do nothing but say that she would tell her mother so.

Mrs. Holly, on receiving the message, became even more worried and decided that there was nothing for it but to go herself to Road Hill House. She did—with the result that Mr. Kent came down to the door and, to her horror, accused her of stealing the nightdress. He further told her that if she did not return it within twenty-four hours he would have a search warrant taken out against her.

And Mr. Kent's threats were no idle ones. True to his word, the next day the police appeared at Mrs. Holly's house carrying a search warrant and, in an effort to find the missing nightdress went over the place from top to bottom. Failing to find it they then—under further pressure from Mr. Kent—directed their investigations to the lane next to Road Hill House and searched the cottages there, concentrating on the dwelling inhabited by the daughter of Mrs. Holly who was married to one of the Nutt brothers. It will be remembered that another member of the Nutt family, Abraham, had, years before, been prosecuted by Kent for trespassing and stealing apples; Mr. Kent was now suggesting to the police that the killing of his son could be an act of revenge for this—that Mrs. Holly had taken the nightdress (at her son-in-law's instigation) for the sole purpose of casting suspicion on one of Mr. Kent's daughters.

Kent cannot possibly have believed that there was any foundation for his furious accusations and must have known very well that Mrs. Holly had not stolen the nightdress. However, as shall be seen, it suited his scenario to play that particular charade and to play it to the hilt; the more forcefully he apportioned blame *outside* Road Hill House the better chance he had of diverting suspicion from inside it. Also, by his direct accusations of the Holly and Nutt families he helped further to thoroughly confuse the issue.

It could also be that Kent's behaviour was to some degree reactionary. Almost four days had passed since the killing, and in those four days not one single piece of evidence had appeared that would point to any member of his family. Then, just as he was beginning to breathe more easily the nightdress went missing. He panicked all over again; Constance had already come in for some measure of suspicion where the villagers were concerned and now here, suddenly, they were presented with ammunition for those suspicions.

That Mrs. Esther Holly, an honest, hard-working woman, was merely a pawn in the game of salvation goes without saying. Even so, at the time she did not come out of it well. Apart from the frightening experience of having hordes of policemen turning her home upside-down she also lost the job of doing the Kent family's washing—a job which had brought her a much-needed seven or eight shillings a week.

Foley was diligent in his search for the missing nightdress and all those at all concerned with it were questioned. They all stuck rigidly to their stories, though; Constance said that she had put it out for the wash, a statement which Cox confirmed; Mary Ann was adamant that it had been packed—as was Cox; while Mrs. Holly and Martha were equally insistent that they had never received it. All Foley had at the end of this line of investigation was what he had started with: the certain knowledge that Constance's nightdress was missing.

The almost fanatical thoroughness with which Foley sought the missing garment sprang largely from his own increasing desperation. He had let the chemise out of his hands without showing it to the magistrates and he now became afraid that people, learning of its discovery, might assume that it was in fact the missing nightdress—and he no longer had the stained chemise to prove that it was not.

When all Foley's efforts to find the nightdress resulted in nothing he let fall another veil of silence—this time over the discovery of the chemise. If no one but the policemen knew that it had ever been found then he would avoid the certain embarrassment that knowledge of its discovery would bring to him.

With the closing of the inquest permission was granted for the burial of Savill's body, and arrangements were made for this to take place on Friday, 6th of July. To avoid further painful publicity and the inevitable attraction of the thrill-seeking crowds—many members of which were showing overt hostility to Mr. Kent because of the proceedings so far—it was determined that the burial should not take place at Road but in the family grave at East Coulston; in the grounds of the tiny church that stood looking across the water towards Baynton House, the Kents' former residence.

Early on the Friday morning a closed carriage set off from Road Hill House. Within, sitting on either side of the coffin were Mr. Kent and his only remaining son, William. A second carriage following behind carried Mr. Rodway and the three medical men, Dr. Parsons, Dr. Stapleton and Savill's godfather, Dr. Mallam.

There at East Coulston that bright July morning the mourners congregated in the churchyard and stood, heads bowed, around the newly opened grave of the first Mrs. Kent, watching as into the grave of that most unhappy woman was laid that other, small coffin —the coffin in which lay the mutilated remains of her successor's son.

When the melancholy service was over the mourners got back into their various carriages and set off back to Road Hill House.

The four men in the second carriage, whilst driving back along the leafy, winding lanes towards Road, held a conversation in which they discussed who might be the most likely perpetrator of the awful crime. All four of them, each expressing his own view, found that they were in total agreement. Following this it was arranged that Dr. Parsons should communicate their beliefs to Mr. Kent. This Dr. Parsons did, later that day telling the bereaved father that it was the conviction of the four men that Constance was responsible for the killing.

Without mentioning it to Mr. Kent, Parsons and Mallam were also agreed on the most likely motive for the deed. They were well aware of how, over the years, the members of the first family had

CERTIFIED COPY OF AN ENTRY OF BIRTH

	REGISTRATION DISTRICT Westbury and b

1860. **DEATH** in the Sub-district of North Bradl

Columns :—	1	2	3	4	5
No.	When and where died	Name and surname	Sex	Age	Occupation
234	June 30th 1860 Road Parish of North Bradley	Francis Savill Kent	Male	3 years	Son of Samuel Savill Kent Sub-inspector of Factories

CERTIFIED to be a true copy of an entry in the certified copy of a Register of Deat

Given at the GENERAL REGISTER OFFICE, LONDON, under the Seal of the said Office, th

DA 658976

Savill's death certificate.

been treated; the motive for the killing, they felt, was clear. It was revenge.

But what did these worthy men who gave their unsolicited opinions to Mr. Kent think that he would do about it? Did they hope that, finding himself in agreement with them he would hand over his daughter to the authorities? If they had good reasons for thinking as they did—that Constance was guilty—did they not think for a moment that the same conclusion must have been reached by Kent himself? A successful prosecution of Constance would surely save him from the suspicion that was daily growing stronger against him, so there was much to be said for such a course. Yet how, it

Given at the GENERAL REGISTER OFFICE, LONDON.

Application Number......703H

...down

____ in the County of Wilts ____

6		8	9
use of death	Signature, description, and residence of informant.	When registered	Signature of registrar
Murder	Information received from George Sylvester	Third July 1860	Edward Singer Registrar
some			
or persons	Coroner for Wilts		
unknown	Inquest held 2nd July 1860		

District above mentioned.

... day of October 19 77

he General Register Office shall be received as evidence of the birth
s to have been given in the said Office shall be of any force or effect

...ticate as true, knowing it to be false, is liable to prosecution.

might be argued, could he give up his own daughter—possibly to
the hangman—notwithstanding that she might have killed his son?
That course might simply reaffirm the views of those many people
who believed that, were she guilty, her terrible action was a direct
result of some past mistreatment of herself, her brother and her
sisters.

Whatever Parsons, Stapleton, Mallam and Rodway hoped, or
expected Mr. Kent to do, they were disappointed. He did nothing—
except to continue to insist that no one within his house could
possibly be guilty of the crime.

On the grey Bath stone that lay over his son's grave Mr. Kent made clear for all to see the role he was playing. Beneath the words in memory of his first wife the following is written:

ALSO OF FRANCIS SAVILL KENT
THE DEARLY LOVED SON OF
SAMUEL SAVILL AND MARY DREWE KENT,
WHO WAS CRUELLY MURDERED AT ROAD
JUNE 30TH 1860
AGED 3 YEARS AND 10 MONTHS.
SHALL NOT GOD SEARCH THIS OUT?
FOR HE KNOWETH THE SECRETS OF THE HEART

Whatever Mr. Kent knew, he was telling no one.

Chapter 17

DESPERATE MEASURES

Superintendent Foley, under increasing pressure, was becoming desperate to prove himself able to apprehend the culprit. As he floundered, though, seemingly way out of reach of his goal's attainment the Trowbridge magistrates watched his efforts with growing dismay; he had come forward with no positive evidence at all—nothing but vague suspicions—and daily the hope of finding any evidence was growing paler. In view of this seemingly hopeless situation Mr. H. G. Ludlow, after a meeting with his fellow magistrates, wrote to the Home Secretary, Sir George Cornwall Lewis, asking for the assistance of a detective officer from Scotland Yard. On the same day, "to save time", he made a similar appeal, this time by telegraph, direct to Scotland Yard itself. Receiving his appeals, the Home Office and Scotland Yard communicated with one another and decided that the request should be vetoed, the Metropolitan Police saying that they did "not think it a case in which it was necessary that a detective officer should be sent", and the Permanent Under-Secretary, Mr. Waddington, making the comment that such a course "was quite irregular". "Now that the County Police is established," he added, "the assistance of London officers is seldom resorted to."

Even before they had received the negative answer to their request, though, the Trowbridge magistrates decided to begin their own inquiry into the grisly incident. This inquiry—which, they stated, would be strictly *in camera*—would take place at the Temperance Hall in Road, and would start on Monday, 9th of July.

The magistrates, having conferred at length with Foley, and being influenced by his particular beliefs, soon made it clear that the object of the inquiry was to be directed against the nurse. This was an aim that was strengthened by a certain visit paid by Mrs. Dallimore to Road Hill House on the very morning the inquiry began. Her purpose, at Foley's instigation, was to see whether the newly washed chest-flannel fitted any of the three servants, Cox, Kerslake or Gough.

After it had proved too small for either the housemaid or the cook, Mrs. Dallimore went to the nursery where she told the nurse she must take off her clothes and try on the piece of flannel.

"It's of no use," the nurse protested, "if it does fit me it's no reason to think I should have done the murder."

The flannel did fit.

"You see, Nurse," Mrs. Dallimore said, "it fits you exactly—which it didn't the other servants."

Elizabeth Gough protested again, adding, "It might fit *many* people."

Mrs. Dallimore had to agree. "Yes, that's true. It fits *me*—and it might fit many others—but they were not in the house." And Mrs. Dallimore was right, of course, though the value of the test was surely negated by the fact that Foley did not ask that Mrs. Kent or her three stepdaughters should be requested to try on the flannel.

Neither was any member of the Kent family made to attend at the Temperance Hall for examination by the magistrates. Mr. and Mrs. Kent and Constance were questioned, but those questions were put to them within the walls of Road Hill House, an arrangement doubtless brought about by Mr. Dunn, the solicitor who had replaced Mr. Rodway in the service of Mr. Kent. Mr. Dunn, of Frome —described as an astute man—continued his good work for Mr. Kent by managing to be present throughout the inquiry at the Temperance Hall and during its adjournments to the house—in spite of the fact that the said inquiry was supposed to be strictly secret.

Elizabeth Gough was called for examination on the first day of the inquiry—shortly after the episode with the chest-flannel—and was cross-examined for three hours before being allowed to return to Road Hill House. Other people examined that first day included Kerslake, Cox, Holcomb, Alloway, Dr. Parsons, and Mrs. Holly and her daughter Martha.

Next day, Tuesday, Elizabeth Gough was summoned again and, as before, waited for her call within the parlour of the local saddler, Stokes, a room from which she had a view of the comings and goings of the police officers and the eager crowds who thronged at the closed doors of the Temperance Hall. While she was there, said *The News of the World*, she "was apparently in the highest spirits, and talked in a very off-hand manner of how she should have enjoyed herself at the haymaking had not this 'business' occurred. She said she was so conscious of her innocence in the matter that she should not be afraid to go before a *hundred* judges and be examined". Her bravery was soon to be put to the test. After a long period of waiting she was called and closely questioned again, with the result that the magistrates—in conjunction with Foley—decided that in view of "certain discrepancies occurring in her evidence" it would be proper to keep her for a while in custody. This put an abrupt end to the nurse's high spirits and off-hand manner. Hearing the news she at once went into screaming hysterics and fell senseless to the ground.

When she had come to and recovered some of her composure she was told that she was not being charged with the crime, nor being put under arrest; she was merely to be lodged for a period at Trowbridge in the care of P.C. Dallimore and his wife.

It was later stated that the magistrates and the police had taken such a course *not* because they felt she was guilty, but because they believed she knew more than she admitted, and that whilst she was under scrutiny she might—in order to free herself from suspicion—be induced to reveal what she knew or suspected.

So in her house at Trowbridge Mrs. Dallimore tried hard to elicit some hint, some clue that might lead to the discovery of the criminal. "It's impossible for only one person to have done the murder," she said to the nurse. "You can see from the size of the child that they couldn't have tucked in the bed-clothes with him in their arms."

"I don't know," replied the nurse. "I didn't touch the cot; that was how I found it."

Following up the gossip that was so prevalent in the area, Mrs. Dallimore asked the nurse what she thought of the idea of Constance having done the killing.

"I don't think Miss Constance would do it," the nurse answered.

After a moment Mrs. Dallimore asked: "What about Master William doing it with Miss Constance?"

Many of the people who had named Constance also named the fifteen-year-old William (he had his fifteenth birthday that 10th of

July) as her partner in the crime. There was no evidence at all for such a view. The suspicion arose merely because of his close attachment to his sister and because of the nagging belief that more than one person *must* have been involved. Therefore if Constance were guilty—and assuming that she had probably been aided in the deed —then it was very likely that William had been her accomplice. This was the view shared by so many.

It was a view which was clearly *not* shared by Elizabeth Gough, though, and she answered scornfully Mrs. Dallimore's question as to belief in William's possible involvement:

"Oh," she said disparagingly, "Master William's more fit for a girl than a boy."

And the conversation continued. Mrs. Dallimore asked the nurse how she had slept on that night.

"I slept more soundly," the nurse answered. "I'd had more work to do during the day—cleaning the nursery."

Mrs. Dallimore was unimpressed, though, and said she just couldn't understand how the nurse didn't hear anyone coming into the room.

"I don't know," said Elizabeth Gough, "they might have put something under my nose to make me sleep."

Other questions followed.

"Do you think Mr. Kent could have done the murder?" Mrs. Dallimore asked.

"No. I couldn't think that for a moment. He's too fond of his children."

"You said you thought it was done by someone secreted in the house; and the door creaks—how could it have been opened by a *stranger* without making a noise?"

"A person accustomed to opening it could do it without making a noise."

There was another conversation which occurred late one evening while Mrs. Dallimore and the nurse sat before the fire. Elizabeth Gough, clearly very aware of her doubtful situation, suddenly said:

"Mrs. Dallimore—do you know there is a nightdress missing?"

This was the first that Mrs. Dallimore had heard of the missing nightdress. She said at once, "No—whose is it?"

"Miss Constance's. You may depend upon it—that nightdress will lead to the discovery of the murderer."

Earlier she had denied the possibility of Constance being involved in the crime. Now she was hinting at it. Her behaviour shows the strain she was under and her great desire to make stronger any evidence that pointed *away* from herself.

As the desperation of the Trowbridge magistrates increased, one of their members, Mr. William Stancomb, wrote to the Home Office on the 11th July asking for permission to issue a proclamation offering a reward for information leading to the arrest of the killer and a pardon for any accessory. On receipt of the request Mr. Waddington instructed his secretary: "Write the usual letter offering £100 and pardon, assuming that no one is now in custody charged with the crime."

Mr. Stancomb wrote again the following day and, on behalf of the magistrates, once more pleaded for a detective officer to be sent from Scotland Yard. This time the plea had the desired result. Mr. Waddington at once instructed his secretary: "Write to Sir Richard Mayne[1] to send down an intelligent officer who will put himself in communication with Mr. Stancomb. . . ."

At last things were moving. Perhaps now some positive progress would be made. Perhaps, after all, everything was not lost.

Mr. Samuel Kent also, through his solicitors, was in touch with the Home Office. On the day that Mr. Waddington received the magistrates' renewed request for Scotland Yard's help he received a similar appeal from the father of the dead child—made through Mr. Kent's family solicitors, Mosely, Taylor and Mosely. Part of the letter reads:

Without complaining of the conduct of the local authorities in the matter, Mr. Kent, in common with the public, cannot be satisfied unless a more rigorous and searching investigation be adopted by Government itself; with the view of detecting the perpetrator of the tragedy.

Mr. Kent's means are not large enough to bear the great expense attendant upon an investigation so thorough as he would wish to be conducted, and, as from the nature of the deed, suspicion is attached in the neighbourhood to every member of the

[1] Head of the Metropolitan Police.

family, public justice demands that the most perfect machinery should be employed to trace out the actual murderer.

We may observe that the Metropolitan Detective Officers, from their experience in such matters, are much fitter persons than the local constabulary to investigate a case of this description.

As Mr. Kent's solicitors we have to beg your best consideration of the case, and we entertain the earnest hope that you will, after such consideration, be of opinion that this is a fit case for Government interference, and render Mr. Kent and the public that assistance which justice and the circumstances of the case demand.

Mr. Kent's plea for help gives clear indication of his thoroughness when it came to his attempts to thwart the ends of justice. As will be seen, the last thing he wanted was for anyone to get to the bottom of the mystery, but it was essential for himself that he should be deemed more eager than most that justice should be done. His letter also puts the apparent stamp of innocence on himself and all the members of his family.

There is a certain bitter humour in Mr. Kent's remarks implying that the local constabulary were unfit to pursue the investigation, for those policemen's failures were due, in great part, to the machinations of Kent himself. Superintendent Foley—assisted by Supertendent Summers of Frome—had been searching desperately for some evidence which would resolve the seemingly unfathomable mystery and so save his swiftly crumbling reputation, and as Foley's self-confidence had sunk lower so Kent had sought to undermine it even further. At Mr. Kent's suggestion the grounds of the house were searched again and again—in addition to which Foley even had the nearby River Frome dragged. None of the measures yielded any clue. By continually offering suggestions as to the course the investigations should take, Kent managed to imply that Foley was incapable of thinking for himself, added to which he did a fairly thorough job of keeping the investigations *away* from the house.

Possibly Mr. Kent's cleverest move where Foley was concerned was his repeated suggestions—well before he made the request through his solicitors—that Foley should call in Scotland Yard. If such an idea had been in Foley's mind Mr. Kent's suggestion scotched it. Of course, it clearly implied that Foley was unequal to the task, and therefore was almost a guarantee that the superintendent would *not* admit defeat, but would continue to plod on in his desperate, haphazard fashion.

Samuel Gough, Elizabeth's father, came from Isleworth on the 13th of July to visit his daughter at Trowbridge where she was under surveillance at Dallimore's house. The following day he accompanied her to Road when she was called yet again by the magistrates but, with the inquiries proceeding *in camera* he was banned from entry to the Temperance Hall.

In the saddler's little house Elizabeth Gough once more waited to be summoned for questioning. Although outwardly she appeared composed she was, in reality, suffering the greatest distress and anxiety. This was made manifest when Ann Stokes, the saddler's sister, looked from the window and saw the magistrates and the police emerge from the hall and hurry purposefully away in the direction of Road Hill House. At this, and the obvious air of excitement among the crowd outside, she remarked,

"Something must be found out!"

Inspector Pitney, who was also there in the room, moved quickly to the door saying that he would go and find out what was happening. The next moment Ann Stokes' attention became completely focused on Elizabeth Gough. Later she described the nurse's behaviour:

"The nurse became very excited and walked to and fro in the room, pressing her hands to her sides and saying that she felt as if the blood had gone from one side to the other. She also said that she could not hold out much longer, and that she could not have held out so long but that Mrs. Kent had begged her to do so. Some time after that she remarked that she had pulled out some grey hairs from her head, which she had never done before; that no one knew how she suffered, and that if anything else occurred she thought she would die."

If the reason for the sudden adjournment of the inquiry *was* that "something had been found out", it was obviously not to the discredit of the nurse, for, with the inquiry's resumption she was called, questioned, and allowed to leave again. To the reporters who crowded round the door she announced that she would be returning to the Dallimores, but that first she would be going to Road Hill House to see Mrs. Kent.

Later on she gave Ann Stokes an account of her visit to Mrs. Kent that day. She had, she said, told her mistress that she could bear the situation no longer, that she must give up her employment with the Kents and, as soon as she was allowed to, leave Road and return to her home. Mrs. Kent, expecting the birth of her child at any time was, of course, most anxious for the nurse to stay—for how, at that time and at such short notice, could she find anyone to replace her? She at once pleaded with the nurse: "Oh, don't say that! You have done so well so far. Do keep it up. You must. For my sake."

And so Elizabeth Gough was persuaded.

In London, as the wheels of official machinery now moved more swiftly, so, in the West Country, Foley's first period in the role of chief investigator into the crime was as swiftly running out. It ended on Sunday, the 15th of July, with the arrival of Inspector Jonathan Whicher who had travelled from London to Trowbridge, taken a room at the Woolpack Inn, and at once got down to business.

With his appearance on the scene the prayers of the magistrates were answered. So, too, was that appeal sent at the behest of Mr. Kent—though he surely never expected it would be. Perhaps, however, he breathed a little more easily with the realization that, by the time Whicher arrived to get on the killer's trail, that trail was already two weeks old.

Chapter 18

THE MAN FROM SCOTLAND YARD

The detective today is a most firmly established part of the police force. But before Sir Robert Peel created the Metropolitan Police in 1829 this was not the case. In those earlier times unless a criminal was actually apprehended whilst committing a crime, or was "shopped" by reward-hungry cronies, he usually managed to escape justice, going scot-free to continue his career. All this was to change, however, and it was with the formation of Peel's police force that the arm of the law grew long; the officers actually set out in *pursuit* of their man, using detection to track him down and bring him to his just desserts. The success of Peel's revolutionary methods was such that in 1842 the Metropolitan Police created a special department to concentrate solely on the work of detection. The criminal would never feel as safe again.

The Detective Force was made up of two inspectors and of from eight to twelve sergeants. Inspector Jonathan Whicher, who had been part of the specialized branch since its inception eighteen years earlier was, in 1860, the most highly regarded of its members, and of those thought to be the most able in the matter of solving the Road mystery he was the natural choice. Charles Dickens, to whom Whicher was known, was so impressed with the detective and his work that he immortalized him as "Whichem" in *Household Words*, while Wilkie Collins, similarly fascinated, handed him down to posterity as Sergeant Cuff in *The Moonstone*. There is no doubt that Whicher was a very successful man.

Dickens' description of Whicher tells us that he was not exceptionally tall for a policeman, was somewhat thick-set "and marked with the small-pox". Also, he had "something of a reserved and thoughtful air, as if he were engaged in deep arithmetical calculations". Of his work we are told by Belton Cobb in his book, *Critical Years at the Yard*:

> His record of successes in criminal cases was supreme. It is said of him: "Whicher was, indeed, an excellent officer, quiet,

shrewd, and practically never in a hurry, generally successful, and ready to take on any case", while another man who worked under him calls him, "The prince of detectives . . . the best detective Scotland Yard ever possessed."

This, then, was Jonathan Whicher, forty-five years of age, in the prime of his life and at the pinnacle of his success. This was the man who was given the task of solving the mystery of the Kent murder; the man who, hailing from Camberwell, had never before heard of the village of Road. He would regret, a thousand times, that he ever did hear of it.

The news that the investigation of the crime was now to be undertaken by such an eminent man in the field of criminal detection was met on all sides by gratification and the voiced belief that the solution to the mystery would soon be found. Whicher might be late appearing on the scene but even so, like the eager onlookers, he must have been sanguine of success. After all, the crime was of a purely domestic nature and there were few suspects. He was to feel his hope and his efforts soon rewarded, too, believing success to be in the palm of his hand, so sure would he be of the results of his deductions.

Foley, of course, did not tell Whicher of the stained chemise found in the boiler-hole. That was an embarrassment to him and for his own sake he would continue, if possible, to keep its one-time existence a secret. For the rest, though, he passed on to the newcomer whatever information he felt he must, telling him of Constance's missing nightdress and also giving him those material discoveries, the piece of blood-stained newspaper and the chest-flannel.

That the help Foley gave was given grudgingly cannot be doubted. His resentment of Whicher's presence on the scene was strong indeed. It was total acknowledgement of his own total failure.

Whicher was aware of this, of course, and tried to combat it by including the superintendent in his work and sharing confidences; the peace that seemed to prevail, though, was uneasy at the best of times and Whicher knew full well that his investigations were likely to prove an uphill struggle.

When the magistrates resumed their inquiry on Monday, the day following Whicher's arrival, the inspector was present at the Temperance Hall, listening and taking notes. Mr. Dunn, Mr. Kent's solicitor, was also there, though several magistrates who "had not been in attendance throughout . . . were requested to withdraw".[1] The solicitor's power was further in evidence when the magistrates adjourned to Road Hill House to examine Mr. Kent and members of his family; at this time "Mr. Dunn objected to many of the questions put to them and these went unanswered".[2]

Among those whom Whicher saw interviewed that day was Elizabeth Gough who, at the end of her examination, was informed that she was at liberty to go where she pleased. To the reporters who waited for news at the door she said that it was her intention to return to Road Hill House as she had agreed to do "at Mrs. Kent's special request". And this she subsequently did, notwithstanding the fact that, as certain newspapers reported, "some members of that household" did not welcome her presence there.

When the members of the press were admitted to the Temperance Hall at the end of that final day's inquiry, they were officially told that the Home Secretary had placed Inspector Whicher in charge of the investigations. They were also informed that a reward of £200 was offered for the detection of the murderer; half of that sum to be provided by the government and the other half by Mr. Kent—further proof that, with this gesture, Mr. Kent didn't do things by halves.

After studying Foley's reports and making exhaustive inquiries of his own, Jonathan Whicher found his suspect. Constance.

One of the first things he had learned about her was that incident four summers earlier when, accompanied by William, she had dressed as a boy and run away from home. Knowledge of this episode must have singled her out as being at least most interesting and worthy of further attention. And this further attention brought results. Whicher's suspicions waxed stronger. The grounds for his growing suspicions are partly encapsulated in his roughly made notes—which have been preserved in the Metropolitan Police records of the case. Amongst these notes, jotted down in Whicher's clear hand, are the following (which I have numbered):

[1] *The Journal.*
[2] *The Advertiser.*

1. *Socks of boy formerly removed.*
2. *Finding, secreting Times newspaper with account of trial of Madeleine Smith.*
3. *Grounds for opinion of two medical men that C. Kent had homicidal propensities, and was of unsound mind.*
4. *Appearance and manner when told child was missing.*

The first note refers to an incident that took place some year or more earlier. Savill, it was said, not being well, was left carefully covered in his cot, and was in that state when the household retired for the night. The next morning, however, he was found with the bedclothes stripped off him and his bedsocks removed. Later on the socks were found; one was on the nursery table and the other beneath Mrs. Kent's own bed. As the other members of the family, except for Mrs. Kent and Constance, were away from home, suspicion fell upon the girl.

Whicher, learning of this, read into it a possible rehearsal for the crime to follow, or evidence of that motive he attributed to Constance, spite or revenge against her stepmother.

2. Whicher's note here refers to an incident told to him by Mr. Kent, an incident which, if it was significant for Whicher in his investigation is equally significant today in an examination of the crime and its startling sequel.

The episode concerned the trial of the twenty-one-year-old Madeleine Smith who in 1857 had been arrested and charged with the poisoning of her lover, Emile L'Angelier. Her trial had begun on the 30th of June (exactly three years to the day before the crime at Road), the case attracting nationwide fascination. During that time Constance had been home on holiday from school and showed great curiosity about the sensational murder trial that was taking place in Scotland; everyone was talking about it and the newspaper accounts were read avidly as each day's events were reported.

For the duration of the trial, according to Mr. Kent, he and Mrs. Kent had read with much interest *The Times*' daily reports of the proceedings. Constance, though, was denied access to them; she was only thirteen and it was not considered proper that she should read of the sensational, torrid love affair between the prosperous architect's daughter and the seed merchant's inpecunious clerk. Consequently all the papers containing the account of the trial were studiously kept away from her and placed in a drawer. Some days later, however, on going to the drawer, Mrs. Kent found the papers to be missing. Constance, owing to the curiosity she had displayed, was at once suspected. When questioned about the papers, though, she denied all knowledge of them, but on her bedroom being searched they were found secreted between her bedstead and mattress.

It must surely strike the reader as odd that Mr. Kent would relate such an incident which told *against* his daughter, but there, quite clearly he had his reasons. Not that Whicher seems to have seen any significance in *that*, however; he appears to have been impressed only with the fact that the story showed clearly Constance's ability to lie in the face of direct questioning, gave further evidence of her cunning and of her ability to make a plan and to put that plan into operation.

Perhaps he also thought that her very interest in the case was significant—in that it was a case of murder. If so, I'm sure he was mistaken. To me her interest appears perfectly natural and understandable. After all, she had reached the age of puberty, and growing sexual awareness was a positive new factor in her life; therefore such a scandalous love affair—everyone else's common gossip— would certainly be of great interest to her. Further to that her strong desire to read the newspaper accounts would be the predictable result of the determined efforts to keep them hidden from her. Her desire serves to mirror a facet of human nature: there are no books or films so sought after as those our moral guardians would ban as unfit.

To return to Whicher's list:

3. Whicher felt he was on strong ground with the medical men's opinions as to Constance's "homicidal propensities" and "unsound mind". In his report to Sir Richard Mayne on the 30th of July he says that he learned from Constance's father "that her mother and grandmother were of unsound mind and that her uncle, also on the mother's side, had been twice confined in a lunatic asylum". In the same report he states that Dr. Parsons and "another medical gentleman" (either Stapleton or Mallam) "well acquainted with Miss Constance are of the opinion that she is affected with homicidal madness". The former gentleman," says Whicher, "stated to me that *he would not sleep in a house where Miss Constance was without*

having his door secured,[3] and that any cunning displayed either before and after a crime is quite consistent with his idea as to the state of her mind."

4. Constance's "appearance and manner" when told Savill was missing seemed, to Whicher, highly significant. In the same report to Sir Richard Mayne he writes: "When the nurse ran upstairs and called up the elder Miss Kents and told them that the child had been stolen, Miss Constance *stood close by, but made no remark.*"

No part of any of the above could be regarded as *evidence* against Constance, but even so it was enough to convince Whicher of her guilt. His task then—and a difficult one—was to try to find positive evidence against her. The more he searched, though, the more certain he became that he was on the right track.

Whicher's list of "clues" raises a point briefly touched upon before—that much of the information pointing to Constance *came from Mr. Kent himself*, not the least damning of which was his assertion that Constance's mother had been insane and that insanity had been prevalent in the Windus family.

In taking such a drastic step Mr. Kent's desperation becomes manifest. Clearly he was desperate to achieve self-preservation even at the cost of branding with the taint of hereditary insanity *all* the four surviving children of the first marriage. Why? He had never before spoken *publicly* of insanity in the Windus family and doing it now he must have been aware of the possible consequences. In those days any hint of mental instability was a much greater stigma, therefore he knew full well that apart from the certain harm he was doing to Constance he was also jeopardizing William's chances in life; and likewise any hopes for Mary Ann and Elizabeth, though by that time their lives were already blighted.

Why then did Mr. Kent imply that Constance was mentally unstable and, by means of various revelations of her past, indicate that she might have been responsible for the crime? And not only to Inspector Whicher did he make known his feelings. As *The Devizes and Wilts Gazette* wrote on the 19th of July:

Mr. Kent has not hesitated to intimate—and that in the plainest manner—that *his own daughter* committed the murder! and it

[3] In the quotations from Whicher's reports the *italics* are his own.

has been alleged as a reason for supposing that the foul deed was committed by her, that she has been guilty of freaks during childhood which might lead to the supposition that she is subject to fits of temporary aberration of mind.

The explanation for Mr. Kent's behaviour is not at first apparent —which is partly because his behaviour appears to be so paradoxical; he had gone to great lengths to divert suspicion *away* from his house and now he was actually hinting at his daughter's guilt. Whilst shielding her with one hand he seemed to point at her with the other. Why? The answer, as shall be seen, is that as he saw that his efforts to protect her were likely to be ineffectual *he took measures to ensure that, were she successfully prosecuted, she would automatically be regarded as insane.* Further, the result of total belief in her insanity *must be, therefore, that no reliance would be placed on anything she said.*

In the course of Whicher's inquiries it came to his ears that to one of her schoolfellows Constance had expressed an aversion to returning home for the summer holidays and, more importantly, a dislike of her young half-brother. The detective investigated the rumour and, after informing the magistrates of the sum total of his findings, accompanied them to Road Hill House where once again Constance was examined. Although very little is generally known of what was said at the magistrates' secret inquiry the transcript of Constance's statement on that particular occasion has, fortunately, survived. Also, the examination seems to have been quite thorough and one can get a clear idea of what was in the minds of her questioners. In answer to the various questions she made the following statement:

"I am the third daughter of Mr. Kent. I have not been to Beckington with my brother since the 10th of June. I didn't walk part of the way with him. I remember now: I did go over to Beckington to pay a bill. My brother returned from Beckington with me. I left home to go to Beckington after lunch and was back to dinner. I called at Miss Biggs and Miss Williams. I didn't go to any shops.

"I went to bed at quarter past ten on the Friday night. I remember my sister coming in before I went to sleep. I don't remember what she said. I have had no Lucifer match-box in my room these holidays.[4] I was told by papa and mamma not to keep matches. I have seen a Church of England magazine in nurse's room. I was very fond of deceased. When I first heard of our loss I ran by my mother's wish to Mr. Peacock. I could carry the deceased the length of this room easily. I was generally considered pretty strong at school. Deceased used to be not very fond of me; he appeared fonder these holidays. The little boy was not fond of me because I teased him. I never struck him or pinched him.

"My eldest sister was present when my box was opened when I came from school. I have heard that the nurse had turned the cot to take the child out. If I wanted a light in the night I should have gone to the nursery. I did not say to any of my schoolfellows that I should rather not go home for the holidays. I have said I should not like to be always at home. My favourite at school is Louisa Hatherall who lives near Badminton. I was friendly with Miss Nicholls of Brighton.[5]

"I did not see my brother William after we went upstairs. William is my favourite of my brothers and sisters. We write to each other when I am at school.

"A window was left at the back of the house unfastened. My father told me of this this morning. It would require a ladder. There are several ladders in the stable. The dog wouldn't fly at me if he recognized me. He would bite me if he didn't know me. My father takes a lantern when he goes out to let the dog loose. I have a cat but I don't care anything for it. I am not considered very timid. I don't like being out in the dark.

"I once did cut off my hair and fling it down the same place where my little brother was found. I cut part of my hair and my brother cut the rest. I thought of the place to put it in. I and my brother William went to Bath by an indirect road. This was about four years ago. I didn't behave well and I went off because I was cross at being punished. I persuaded my brother William to go with me.

"I went to my aunt's in London last Christmas twelvemonth. I

---

[4] Although there is no mention of it elsewhere, it would seem logical to assume that spent Lucifer matches or a Lucifer matchbox were found at the scene of the crime.

[5] It is not known who Miss Nicholls was.

came down from London by myself. I think it was all ladies in the carriage with me.

"I heard of Madeleine Smith's affair, but was not allowed to read it. I may have taken a paper but I didn't intentionally take a paper with an account of this in it. I heard Madeleine Smith's friend was poisoned. I used to hear papa talk about it.

"I put my nightdress out of my room on Monday morning. Cox the housemaid took it. I don't think I have thrown out dirty linen before this these holidays.

"I have locked my door since because I thought it was safer. I slept with the nurse two or three times since the murder. I have never done so before. I believe the nursery door opens easily. The door falls to easily when opened. I have often tried the door. I like the cook best of the servants. I like the nurse very well. I have never taken a walk alone these holidays with the little boy that is dead. I think my father was quite well on the Friday. If he had been unwell I should have heard of it."

Investigating further, Whicher found in Constance's bedroom a list of the linen she had brought with her from school. Three night-dresses were listed on it. With this—and the information that one of those nightdresses had been "lost in the wash"—he questioned Sarah Cox who had packed the laundry baskets that day of the inquest. After hearing from her that she was quite certain that Constance's nightdress had been packed he then learned of that minor interruption that had occurred in the course of her work. It was, to him, highly significant.

Cox told the detective how she and Miss Mary Ann had checked off the items one by one and of how she had been left alone, as usual, to complete the packing of the two baskets. She was just getting to the end of that packing, she said, when Miss Constance had appeared in the lumber room doorway. As the maid looked up Constance had taken a step into the room and asked: "Sarah, would you look in my slip pocket and see if my purse is there . . ." going on to explain that she had somehow mislaid it.

Cox turned to the larger of the two baskets, pulled the clothes aside and searched in the pocket of the slip. No, she told the girl, the purse was not there. Constance nodded and then said:

"Would you get me a glass of water, please? There are people downstairs. . . ."

Cox got up at once and hurried down to the pantry on the floor below, Constance following her as far as the head of the winding back stairs. The maid found her there when she returned with the water a short while later. She handed the girl the water, and Constance drank it, thanked her, and returned up the back stairs towards her own room.

This information was just what Whicher was looking for—Constance had for a brief time been alone in the vicinity of the laundry baskets. Yet Foley had not found that out; the superintendent hadn't even made any effort to ascertain how many nightdresses the girl should have had, and had only examined that nightdress she was thought to have worn on the night of the killing. Whicher later wrote in his report:

> . . . I think the evidence against her would have been far more conclusive if the police had ascertained as soon as they arrived, *how many* night-gowns she ought to have had in her possession, for the medical gentleman to the family, from what he thought of her, at once stated his suspicions respecting her to Superintendent Foley, and accompanied him to her bedroom soon after the discovery of the murder to examine the night-gown *she was supposed* to have worn the night previous. They found a nightdress on the bed which they examined merely for marks of blood, but the medical gentleman informs me that he noticed the nightdress was *remarkably clean* and drew the attention of the superintendent to it; *he* appears, however, not to have noticed this remark. . . . Had the superintendent taken *the hint given* . . . as to it appearing very clean, and have interrogated her at once *as to how many* she had in her possession, I believe the blood-stained bed-gown would have been *missed at once and possibly found*. There would have been little difficulty in ascertaining the number of nightdresses she ought to have had in her possession as the list of linen was in a chest of drawers in her bedroom at the time; at least I found it there on my arrival. . . .

Whicher, of course, did not believe for a moment that Constance's nightdress had been lost in the wash. He was certain that she had taken it out of the basket. Briefly, his well-known theory is as follows:

Constance, after committing the murder, found that her night-dress was blood-stained and, taking it off, put on a clean one which she had taken from her drawer. This *second* nightdress she wore for the remainder of the night and laid on her bed the next morning; this was the one that Parsons and Foley inspected. Her first night-dress, with the blood-stains on it, she hid away until she found an opportunity to destroy it. But its destruction left her with only two nightdresses instead of the three she should have. She therefore evolved a plan to account for the loss of one garment. On the Monday morning she put out for the wash the second night-dress—which she had worn only for three nights. In her room she listened as Cox called to Mary Ann that the laundry was ready to be checked in the book and then waited until her sister had finished the task and returned—past Constance's door—to her own room. Constance now knew that Cox was alone with the laundry. This was the time to act and straightaway she went down to the lumber room and asked the maid to look for the "missing purse". "This, I believe," said Whicher, "was part of her stratagem to ascertain which basket her nightdress was in". Taking careful note of where her nightdress lay—right next to the slip in which Cox was searching —she then asked the housemaid to fetch her a glass of water. While Cox was downstairs it would have been the work of only a moment for Constance to have taken the nightdress from the basket and conceal it beneath her skirts. Upstairs in her room again she took the nightdress back into use, going on to wear it for the rest of the week. For the fact that her nightdress would subsequently be found missing from the wash, said Whicher, "the laundry would be blamed, and that would account for her being one short if inter-rogated on that point".

On Wednesday, the 18th of July, still pursuing what he firmly believed to be the truth, he searched Constance's room again, and then summoned her to it. When she entered he indicated the clothes-list and asked: "Is this the list of your clothes?"

"Yes."

"In whose hand-writing is it?"

"Mine."

He pointed to the list. "Here are three nightdresses. Where are they?"

"I have two; the other was lost in the wash the week after the murder."

When he asked to see the remaining two she took them from a drawer. Both were unwashed; as Mrs. Holly had lost her job as the family's laundress no washing had been done since the 2nd of July. Whicher took the two nightdresses then pointed to a nightdress and night-cap that lay folded on the bed.

"Whose are those?"

"My sister's."

He left the room.

Whatever else he might have thought of her, Whicher must surely have admired what he saw as Constance's cleverness and cunning: she had been so successful that while he was quite certain that he had the right answer he still had no real evidence to prove his theory.

And now the magistrates were anxious to learn of his progress.

So it was that on Friday the 20th of July they met at the Temperance Hall for the purpose, as the detective later reported, "of hearing the result of my inquiries as far as I had gone, and to take my opinion as to the best course to pursue". He went on: "After due consideration of the evidence I stated I should be able to lay before them on a future occasion [a case] against Mr. Kent's third daughter, Constance. . . ."

It was Whicher's hope that after putting that case before them, he would be free to return to London. The magistrates, though, had other ideas. In Whicher's words:

The magistrates decided upon taking my information and issuing a warrant for her arrest, which they desired me to execute, having previously sworn me as a Constable of the County of Wilts. I pointed out the unpleasant position such a course would place me in with the county police—especially as they held opinions opposed to mine as to who was the guilty party, but they (the magistrates) declined to alter their determination, stating that they considered and wished the inquiries to be entirely in my hands. . . .

During the three hours that Whicher and the magistrates were in discussion an expectant crowd gathered outside the Temperance Hall. When the doors of the hall were opened at two o'clock Whicher appeared and, accompanied by Captain Meredith, set off towards the Kents' residence.

It is ironic that by this time the public's suspicions had switched from Constance and, like the theories of the local police, were now centred upon Mr. Kent and the nurse. The excited crowd hurrying along in the wake of the London detective believed now that they were about to witness the arrest of those two people, and on a level with their excitement was their determination not to miss any part of the spectacle.

Inside Road Hill House Whicher was shown into the drawing-room and Constance was sent for. On her appearance he formally said:

"I am a police officer and I hold a warrant for your apprehension, charging you with the murder of your brother, Francis Savill Kent, which I will read to you." He then read to her the words of the warrant and she began to cry, saying, "I am innocent! I am innocent!" over and over. Afterwards, in her bedroom, Whicher stood silently by while she put on her bonnet and mantle and then, when she was dressed, escorted her down the stairs to the front door.

The crowd waiting outside were not disappointed in their hopes for sensational developments. They were shocked, and "a murmur of ''Tis Miss Constance!' was speedily heard in various quarters in mingled tones of commiseration and pity".[6] Whicher, out of consideration for the young girl, offered her his arm. For a moment she hesitated then reluctantly laid her fingers upon it. So, followed by the crowd and closely surrounded by the police and the reporters, the detective and the girl made their way to the Temperance Hall.

The proceedings inside did not take long. As Constance sat silently, hands clasped—and unsupported by the presence of any member of her family—Whicher told the bench of her arrest, adding: "I now pray the bench for a remand of the prisoner, to enable me to collect evidence to show the *animus* she entertained towards the deceased, and to search for the missing nightdress, which, if still in existence, may possibly be found."

[6] *The Advertiser.*

The magistrates, while granting the remand, stipulated that it would only be for seven days—which was little time for the detective to compose any solid case against her. He pressed for a longer period, hoping—in the event of no damning evidence being found—that a protracted confinement would induce her to confess. The magistrates, however, felt they could not—when the evidence against her was so slight—ethically concede to his wishes. Whicher must be content with a week.

When the brief hearing was over Whicher accompanied her in a carriage to Devizes Gaol, during which journey she remained in "a kind of sullen silence, not displaying the slightest emotion".[7]

[7] Whicher's report of the 22nd July.

Chapter 19

"THIS YOUNG LADY"

THE CASE AGAINST CONSTANCE KENT:
27th OF JULY

When Whicher had deposited Constance at Devizes Gaol he returned at once to Trowbridge and sent a message by *The Electric and International Telegraph Company* to Sir Richard Mayne at Scotland Yard:

> I have this day apprehended on a warrant Constance Kent, the third daughter, who is remanded for a week. The magistrates have left the case entirely in my hands to get up the evidence. I am awkwardly situated and want assistance. Pray send down Sergeant Williamson or Tanner.

Whicher's appeal for help was of the utmost necessity. He was indeed awkwardly situated and of this difficulty he wrote again a few days later.

> I am very unpleasantly situated as regards acting with the County Police, in consequence of the natural jealousy entertained in this matter by them, especially as our opinions differ; they suspecting Mr. Kent and the nurse; and should it appear in the end that my opinions are correct, they would be considered at fault, but I have studiously endeavoured to act in concert with them as far as possible.

The prompt appearance on the scene of Sergeant Frederick Williamson[1] in response to Whicher's appeal must have encouraged the detective and with the newcomer's help he continued with his monumental task. During that week the two men pursued every available avenue in the hope of finding evidence to prove the charge against the schoolgirl lodged in Devizes Gaol, their work even including repeated experiments with the Kents' Newfoundland dog—experiments proving the animal to be friendly and of such a placid nature that he would permit anyone to approach. Other areas of

[1] Full name Adolphus Frederick Williamson. He was later to become Superintendent of Scotland Yard's Detective Department.

investigation, however, yielded no such positive results, and the notice that Whicher affixed to the door of the Temperance Hall, offering a £5 reward for "a lady's nightdress, supposed to have been thrown into the river, burnt, or sold in the neighbourhood", got no reaction at all. This desperate search for the missing nightdress—and the murder weapon—occupied Whicher right up to the very day set for the hearing—as shown by his expenses form in an entry dated the 27th of July: "Paid workmen for taking down water closet and opening a drain . . . 6s. 6d." He found nothing.

After that there was no more time. He was due at the Temperance Hall. He had investigated the case to the best of his ability and now, incredibly, only aided by the Clerk of the Court, he would have to prosecute it.

Constance suffered no great physical hardship during her week's incarceration in Devizes Gaol. She was kindly treated there and her father, by payment of the required fee, was able to ensure that she was granted whatever comforts could be obtained; consequently she was provided with good food, a table and chair for writing, and a comfortable bed. On the Sunday evening, July 22nd, Mr. Dunn and Mr. Kent went to the gaol to visit her, the solicitor having an interview with the girl but her father, in accordance with the rules, not being admitted to her cell. Mr. Kent must bide his time until Friday, the day of the hearing.

The proceedings that day were due to begin at 11 a.m. and by that time all the officials were seated in the hall. Mr. Kent, making his first public appearance since the crime sat, as he was to remain almost throughout the hearing, leaning forward, his elbow on the table and one hand shielding his face. Next to him sat his solicitor Mr. Dunn, while next to that gentleman sat Mr. Peter Edlin of Bristol who, at Mr. Dunn's instruction, had undertaken to defend the prisoner. Mr. Rowland Rodway was also there—surprisingly—and it was understood that he had been hired by "friends of Samuel Kent to act on behalf of the second family".[2]

The police were well represented. Wiltshire's Chief Constable was there as well as the superintendents from Trowbridge, Devizes, Warminster and Frome. Whicher and Williamson were of course

[2] All quotations, unless otherwise indicated, are from various organs of the local press.

present and, completing the body representing law and order, the Trowbridge magistrates. Behind the magistrates' bench certain seats had been reserved for a limited number of privileged spectators while the first three rows of seats facing it were taken up by members of the press.

At half-past eleven Constance entered by a side door accompanied by Mr. Alexander the gaoler. Seeing her father she went forward "with faltering step" and kissed him and then moved to the seat that was indicated to her. As soon as she had sat down "the crowd came in with a tremendous rush, occupying every available inch". However, this "surging, noisy mass of spectators who had fought their way into the room" were hampered in their attempts to obtain any close examination of the prisoner for she kept her veil down throughout the proceedings.

When at last those proceedings began in earnest Inspector Whicher must have become acutely aware of the great problem before him. At that time in our history there was no office of Public Prosecutor and this situation was to work seriously against Jonathan Whicher and the furtherance of his case. He should, of course, have been able to put all his evidence (such as it was) and his witnesses into the hands of a competent lawyer who would have undertaken the case for the prosecution, but this he could not do. He was later to write of the "difficulty the magistrates appeared to be placed in owing to the peculiar nature of the case as Mr. Kent, who should have been the prosecutor, naturally found counsel for the defence of his daughter". *"There was,"* wrote Whicher, underlining the words, *"no professional man to conduct the case for the prosecution."*

The first witness called was Elizabeth Gough who repeated much of her former evidence. In addition, questioned regarding her visit to the elder sisters' room to see if Savill was with them on the morning of the crime, she said:

"While I was talking to them I saw the prisoner; she was standing at the door of her room nearly dressed. I spoke in a loud voice and she was near enough to hear all that passed. She made no remark to my recollection. I observed nothing unusual in her manner at the time." The nurse also said of Constance: "I have never heard her say anything unkind to the deceased; I have never seen her conduct herself otherwise than kindly towards him."

After William Nutt had described how he had found the body his place was taken by the third witness, Emma Moody, one of Constance's schoolfellows. Responding to questions from the clerk she gave the following information:

"I live at Warminster with my mother. I know the prisoner; I was at school with her at Beckington. I went home for the holidays when she did, on the 17th or 18th of June."

The magistrates' clerk then asked her: "Have you ever heard the prisoner make use of any expression of ill-feeling towards the deceased?"

"I believe there was a dislike through jealousy."

Mr. Edlin quickly interjected: "That is not an answer to the question. What did the prisoner say?"

The question was repeated and the girl answered:

"I have heard her say that she disliked the two younger children; that she pinched them and liked to tease them—but I believe more for fun than anything else; she was laughing when she said it. It was not this child more than the others. I believe it was through jealousy, and because the parents showed great partiality. I have remonstrated with her on what she said. I was walking with her towards her home one day during the last half-year; we were talking about the holidays; I said, 'Won't it be nice to go home for the holidays soon?' She said, 'It may be to your home, but mine's different.' She led me to infer, though I don't remember her precise words, that she did not dislike the child, but it was through the partiality shown by the parents. She gave me as a reason for not liking her home that the second family were treated better than the first. She told me so several times. We were talking about dress on one occasion, and she said, 'Mamma will not let me have anything I like. If I wanted a brown dress she would get me a black, or just the contrary.' I don't remember any other conversation with her about the deceased child; she has only slightly referred to him."

When Emma Moody had answered Whicher's questions in the course of his investigations she had told him a little more than she was now telling the court and the clerk pressed her, asking if she could remember any other conversation she had had with the prisoner regarding the deceased child. This was not to Mr. Edlin's liking, however, and he objected, on the grounds that the clerk's manner of examination was "most unusual and improper".

"I have only endeavoured to elicit facts," protested the clerk, going on to say: "I have been putting questions according to the rule of evidence, and if I do not get an answer I must put the question again." Said Mr. Edlin, "Then you have asked it again and again, and therefore your business is at an end." Here Mr. Ludlow, Chief Magistrate, stepped in and allowed the question to be put: Did the witness recall any conversation with the prisoner with regard to the feelings she entertained towards the deceased? Replied Emma Moody—much to Whicher's disappointment: "I do not remember anything more."

Under cross-examination she said that twice she had been interviewed by Mr. Whicher, and also that Constance, at the end of the school term, had carried off the second prize for good conduct. Asked why Mr. Whicher had called upon her she said: "To show me a piece of flannel which had been found near the body of the child. The second occasion was to serve the summons upon me." At this, Whicher, making a desperate effort to elicit from her everything that she had told him earlier, said to her:

"And I impressed upon you the importance of telling the truth and nothing but the truth."

"We take that for granted," said Mr. Edlin.

Whicher: "I would rather have it from the witness."

An altercation followed in which Mr. Edlin remonstrated with the clerk, the chairman and with Whicher—a battle won by Mr. Edlin, for the witness was told to step down.

The examination of Emma Moody illustrates to a degree the difficulties suffered by the prosecution. The bench were on Whicher's side but even so, against the practised eloquence of Mr. Edlin they were having little success. He took complete advantage of the fact that not one of his opponents had the experience or the training to equip him for the niceties of the situation. He continually interrupted and notwithstanding interventions from the chairman managed to direct and orchestrate the proceedings according to his own desires. This situation, however, greatly pleased the spectators. They clearly demonstrated throughout—by numerous bursts of applause—that their sympathies were with Constance; they had set themselves up as the champions of the unhappy sixteen-year-old girl who sat there charged with the dreadful crime and from her accusers, therefore, they became increasingly alienated. So far, Mr. Edlin was scoring all the points.

Dr. Parsons was called next. He repeated much of his former evidence, in the course of which saying: "My impression was that the blackened appearance around the mouth was produced by forcible pressure during life." Regarding the wound in the chest he said:

"I found the stab in the chest had not penetrated the heart, but had pushed it out of place, penetrating the diaphragm and slightly wounding the outer coat of the stomach on the right side of it. I consider that it must have been made with a long, pointed knife. The wound was from an inch to an inch-and-a-half in width, and there was a slight transverse notch on one side of the wound, as though the knife had been withdrawn in a contrary direction. . . ." He added later, "It would require very great force to inflict such a blow as that through the nightdress and flannel shirt, to that depth. In reference to the heart being pushed aside, the force used by the knife would have caused the flexible ribs to be pushed forward, so pushing the heart out of its place. . . ."

Of the throat wound he *now* said: "I think the incision in the throat, as far as I can judge, was the immediate cause of death." Clearly, although sure of the suffocation, he could not be sure that it had proved fatal.

Regarding the business of the nightdress the surgeon said:

"I accompanied Mr. Foley in a search through the house, and in the course thereof went into Constance Kent's room. I examined the linen in her drawers, and the night-cap and night-dress which were on the bed, and the whole of the bedding. The nightdress was perfectly free of any stains. I could not say whether it had on it the dirt resulting from a week's wear or not, but it was *very clean*. I am not certain as to whether I examined the nightdresses of Mrs. Kent or either of the Misses Kent or not, as Mr. Foley examined some and I the others. There was nothing about Constance Kent's nightdress that attracted my attention other than that it was *very clean*. I made a remark to Foley upon it."

Cross-examined on the subject he said: "In my judgement the night-gown *might*"—he stressed the word—"have been worn a week, or nearly so, by a young lady sleeping alone . . ." and a little later: "I examined the linen in her chest of drawers, and I believe I saw a clean night-gown there."

To the detriment of Whicher's case no effort was made to pursue further the fact of the *cleanness* of Constance's nightdress. Those listening in the court seemed satisfied as to her innocence by the fact that her nightdress was quite free of any blood-stain. The fact that Dr. Parsons had found her nightdress—supposed to have been worn almost a week—to be *remarkably clean* seems not to have touched them with any significance whatsoever.

And throughout all the questions and answers upon which her fate might well depend the prisoner sat, neatly attired in black, the crêpe veil over her face. Said *The Journal*, "She sat with her head bent forward, and during the examination neither moved nor spoke.[3] The events of the past month had evidently told severely upon her, for in her thin, pale face we should scarcely have recognized the robust, deep-complexioned girl of five weeks ago. The same singularly forbidding cast of countenance, however, characterized her features." One who studied keenly her features through her veil that day was the artist on the staff of *The Bath Chronicle*, and his sketch of her—omitting the veil from her face—shows that bent-forward head, a set mouth, and a gaze—avoiding all other eyes in the hall—directed continuously, and unseeing, at her lap.

After Dr. Parsons had left the stand the next witness Constance saw was her friend fifteen-year-old Louisa Hatherall from Oldbury, Gloucestershire. She told the court:

"I was at school with the prisoner at Beckington till last June. I have heard her speak of her home and say there was partiality shown by the parents for the younger children. She spoke of her brother William being obliged to wheel the perambulator for the younger children, and that he disliked doing it. She also spoke of her father comparing the elder son to the younger, saying what a much finer boy the younger would be."

Asked if the prisoner had ever said anything in particular about the deceased, the girl said she had not. Mr. Edlin declined to put any questions to the girl and the next witness was brought forward. This was Sarah Cox.

The housemaid told of picking up Constance's nightdress from the landing and packing it in the laundry-basket and of how, later, Constance had come to the lumber room door asking if her purse

---

[3] A *prisoner* could not give evidence until the passing of the Criminal Evidence Act in 1898.

was in her slip pocket. Cox then related how she was asked to fetch the glass of water. "I did so," she said, "and she followed me to the top of the back stairs, close behind me; I found her there when I returned with the water, and I was not gone near a minute, for I went very quickly. She drank the water and then went up the back stairs to her own room." Asked whether she had heard any sound from the prisoner's room on the night in question, Cox said: "Between my room and Miss Constance's there is only a paper wall; I can hear very plain; on the night of the murder I did not wake at all."

Under cross-examination by Mr. Edlin, Sarah Cox said:

Constance Kent as she sat before the magistrates in the Temperance Hall. (From a sketch appearing in *The Bath Chronicle.*)

Constance Kent about 1856

ABOVE LEFT: Cliff
Cottage, Sidmouth. *From
a drawing made in 1826*
BELOW LEFT: Walton
Manor, Walton-in-
Gordano, Clevedon
ABOVE RIGHT: Mary Ann
Kent, *née* Windus, first
wife of Samuel S. Kent.
*From a miniature painted
in 1828 by William
Hudson*
RIGHT: Edward Windus
Kent about 1853. *From a
daguerreotype*

ABOVE: Baynton House, Coulston

BELOW: Road Hill House as it appears today

ABOVE: Road Hill House, rear view

BELOW: The main street in the village of Road. On the left is the Red Lion Inn where the inquest opened

INSET: Samuel Savill Kent, and Acland, aged three years two months, in September 1863
BELOW: Mary Drewe Kent, *née* Pratt, second wife of Samuel S. Kent. *Photographed in September 1863*

Constance Kent. *From a photograph taken about 1862*

SACRED TO THE MEMORY OF
MARY ANN,
THE WIFE OF S. SAVILL KENT ESQ
OF BAYNTON HOUSE,
WHO DIED MAY 5TH 1852,
AGED 44 YEARS

ALSO OF FRANCIS SAVILL KENT
THE DEARLY LOVED SON OF
SAMUEL SAVILL AND MARY
DREWE KENT, WHO WAS
CRUELLY MURDERED AT ROAD
JUNE 30TH 1860
AGED 3 YEARS AND 10 MONTHS
SHALL NOT GOD SEARCH THIS OUT FOR HE
KNOWETH THE SECRETS OF THE HEART

Taken from a wax-rubbing of the gravestone in St. Thomas à Becket's churchyard, Coulston

RIGHT: No. 2, Queen's Square, Brighton, the centre of St. Mary's Convent. *Photograph by courtesy of John Farquharson Ltd*

BELOW: St. Paul's Church, West Street, Brighton

I, Constance Emilie Kent, alone and unaided on the night of the 29th of June 1860, murdered at Road Hill House, Wiltshire, one Francis Savile Kent

Before the deed none knew of my intention, nor after of my guilt; no one assisted me in the crime; nor in my evasion of discovery

ABOVE: Constance's confession in her own handwriting. This is the paper she handed to Sir Thomas Henry at Bow Street

RIGHT: Part of Constance's statement made at Bow Street, taken down by the Chief Clerk and signed by Constance and Sir Thomas Henry. Constance's signature gives clear indication of her trembling hand

"in the crime, nor in my evasion of its crime Id not wish to add any thing to the above statement.

Constance Emily Kent,

Taken at the Police Court aforesaid the day and hour first mentioned before me

Thomas Henry

THE PENNY
ILLUSTRATED PAPER

WITH THE NEWS OF THE WEEK.

REGISTERED AT THE GENERAL POST OFFICE FOR TRANSMISSION ABROAD

No. 189.   LONDON, SATURDAY, MAY 13, 1865.   Vol. VIII.

THE HIDDEN MILLION; or, THE NABOB'S REVENGE, a novel and exciting Serial Tale, will shortly be commenced in a new and improved Series of this Journal, printed on better paper, with the first number of which will be issued a COLOURED SUPPLEMENT, GRATIS.

MISS GRACE GIVING HER EVIDENCE.   MISS CONSTANCE KENT.

Constance's appearance before the Trowbridge magistrates was
front page news

Arthur Douglas Wagner. *Photograph by courtesy of Sir Anthony Wagner, KCB, KCVO, and the Sussex Archaeological Society*

The effigy of Constance Kent exhibited at Madame Tussaud's. When first shown in September 1872, the following comment appeared in the press: The female miscreant, Constance Kent, or rather her most veritable effigy, now occupies a place in the dock of the 'Chamber of Horrors', in Madame Tussaud's celebrated gallery. The effigy represents a short, or rather what is termed a dowdy sort of personage, and exhibits in the features and expression nothing from which the perpetration of the Road murder could be suspected. It is a good likeness, very faithfully modelled from the original, and is the most attractive effigy at present in the whole of the valuable collection. *Photograph: Radio Times Hulton Picture Library*

View of Millbank Prison, from the Thames in 1884

Part of Constance's mosaic pavement before the altar in the chapel
at the Bishop's Palace at Chichester. *Photograph by courtesy of
'The West Sussex Gazette'*

PRINTED AT H.M. CONVICT PRISON,
MILLBANK. 4—80.

PETITION.

Date. 23ᵈ July 1884

Register No. *n 5*

Present Age. *40*

Name, *Constance Emilia Kent*

Confined in *Fulham* Prison.

49113

Convicted.		Crime.	Sentence.	Remarks.
When	Where			27
19 July 1865	Salisbury Summer apzas	Murder on her own Confession	Reprieved P.S for Life	Conduct V. Good L.Scale Lady Superintendent

The Petitioner not to write on this margin.

To the Right Honourable *Sir William Vernon Harcourt* Her Majesty's Principal Secretary of State for the Home Department.

The Petition of *Constance E. Kent*, a prisoner in the *n 5*

HUMBLY SHEWETH—

Petitioner most earnestly prays that some hope of liberty, however distant, may be given to her

She pleads that she has Entered her 20th year of imprisonment and states that friends are willing to receive her

Charles Edward Crellin
Chaplain
23/7/84

that she has entered upon the 20ᵗʰ year of a long and ingenious imprisonment, without one single ray of hope to brighten a life which, since earliest recollection has been passed in confinement, either of school, convent, or prison, while before her now only lies, a gloomy future of approaching age, offers a youth spent in dreary waiting, and heart-sickening disappointment, in complete isolation from all that can make life worth living, amid uncongenial surroundings, from which mind and body alike shrink—

That her miserable fate is well deserved she most humbly owns, with deepest contrition for the past, knowing that she is wholly undeserving of the mercy she feign would crave, yet, let it not be accounted presumption in your most humble petitioner that she now prays with heaven all humility, for one word, one single ray of hope, however small, however distant—

Can humble petitioner her friends most willing to receive her as their last proposal to send her to South Africa fully proves—

Your humble petitioner almost in despair, implores for hope, one glimmer of hope for pity's sake, and may the mercy of Heaven nerve you, your clemency your humble petitioner will as in duty bound ever pray.

Constance E. Kent.

OPPOSITE: Constance's petition
made in July, 1884
ABOVE: Fulham Prison,
Constance's home from 1877
to 1885. *Photograph by
courtesy of Hammersmith
Public Libraries*

RIGHT: Constance's cell in
Fulham Prison; cell No. 29.
*Photograph by courtesy of
Hammersmith Public Libraries*

BELOW: William Saville-Kent in
Brisbane, about 1888

00 years old: once he nursed lepers

ABOVE: The nurses' home on the corner of Elgin and West Streets, Maitland, New South Wales. *Photograph by Stephen Knight*
LEFT: Ruth Emilie Kaye, photographed by *The Sunday Sun and Guardian* on the occasion of her 100th birthday. *Photograph by courtesy of the Mitchell Library, Sydney, N.S.W.*

"On Saturday, 30th of June, I took down a clean night-gown of Miss Constance's to be aired, and another the following Saturday . . . the dirty one I put in the basket on the Monday would, with the two I aired, make three; I am clear that these were Miss Constance's nightdresses; I observed no mark or stain on the one I put in the basket; it appeared to me to be as dirty as one would expect in a nightdress worn nearly a week; I am perfectly clear as to the airing of the two night-gowns. . . .

"During the time I have been in Mr. Kent's service I have never heard or seen from Miss Constance anything unkind or unsisterly in her conduct towards the deceased. She was romping with him the day before the murder. She went to see him with the other members of the family when they did; she appeared as upset as they were, and cried as they did; she kissed him." After giving an account of the dispute with Mrs. Holly over the missing nightdress she concluded her evidence by saying that she had observed in Constance's behaviour after the murder "nothing except ordinary grief".

After Sarah Cox had stepped down the last witness, Mrs. Esther Holly, was called.

In the course of her testimony she told of how she and her daughter Martha had collected the two baskets of washing and, having heard a rumour of a missing nightdress, had examined the baskets' contents as soon as they had got home. "We found one missing," she said; "it was Miss Constance's." She then told of Mr. Kent's threats of a search warrant if the nightdress was not returned within twenty-four hours and of the subsequent police-search of her house. Asked whether she had ever lost anything in the wash before, she said: "Two things: one an old duster, the other an old towel."

Mrs. Holly was the last witness called for the prosecution and with no witnesses being called for the defence Mr. Edlin rose to address the bench. He already knew that most of the spectators were on the side of the forlorn veiled girl who had sat so composedly throughout the proceedings of that long summer's day; soon, as her champion, he would receive further proof of their sympathy. Now he said to the magistrates:

"I think the duty which I have to perform here today in this most important case is an exceedingly clear and simple one, and I think, gentlemen, that the duty devolving upon you is not less clear. My duty is to ask that this young lady be instantly liberated and re-stored to her friends." There was a burst of applause here which was swiftly quelled. Mr. Edlin continued, "—and I apprehend that it will be, as I have said, not only your duty but your *pleasure* to say 'aye' to that at once.

"There is not one tittle of evidence against this young lady; not one word upon which a finger can be laid to show that she is guilty, nor can the finger of infamy in respect of this matter be pointed against her. I ask you to consider the effect of dragging this young lady from home at such a time, if she is really innocent, as I believe she is. I know that an atrocious murder has been committed, but I am afraid that it has been followed by a judicial murder of a scarcely less atrocious character. I ask you, if this young lady is truly innocent, what will be the consequences of this procedure against her? If this murder be never discovered—and we know how dark are the paths of crime—it will never, never be forgotten that this young lady was dragged from her home and sent, like a common felon, to Devizes Gaol. I say, therefore, that this step ought to have been taken only after the most mature consideration, and after something like *tangible evidence*, and not upon the fact that a paltry bed-gown was missing—as to which Inspector Whicher knew that it was in the house and that Mr. Foley examined it with the medical man the day after the murder. . . .

"I say that to drag this young lady from her home in such a way and at such a time, when her heart was already harrowed by the death of her dear little brother, and when, more than at any other time, she needed the affectionate sympathy of her family, is quite sufficient to excite in her favour the sympathy of every man in this country—and not only that, but that of every man of unbiased mind in this land who has heard—and there are few who have not —of this horrible murder. The steps you have taken will be such as to ruin her life—her prospects are already blighted. Every hope is gone with regard to this young girl. If she is innocent, as I believe, it is really terrible to contemplate the result to her, and it must be particularly so to gentlemen of feeling like yourselves.

"*And where is the evidence?* The sole fact—and I am ashamed in this land of liberty and justice to refer to it—is the suspicion of Mr. Whicher—a man eager in pursuit of the murderer and *anxious for the reward which has been offered*. And it is upon his suspicion, unsupported by the slightest evidence whatever, that this step has been taken. . . .

"The prosecution's own witnesses have cleared up the point about the bed-gowns; but because the washerwoman says that a certain bed-gown was not sent to her you are asked to jump to the conclusion that it was not carried away in the clothes basket. But there can be no doubt in the mind of any person that *the right number of bed-gowns has been fully accounted for*—" then directing himself to Jonathan Whicher: "—and that this little peg upon which you seek to hang this fearful crime has fallen to the ground. It rested on the *ipse dixit* of the washerwoman only, and against that you have the testimony of several other witnesses." Mr. Edlin turned his attention back to the bench again.

"I do not mean to find fault with Mr. Whicher unnecessarily, but I think in the present instance his professional eagerness in the pursuit of the criminal has led him to take a most unprecedented course to prove a motive, and I cannot help alluding to the meanness—I may say *discredit*—and I was about to say the *disgrace*, but I do not wish to say anything that shall leave unfavourable impressions hereafter—but I will say the ineffable discredit with which he has hunted up two schoolfellows and brought them here to give the evidence we have heard. Let the responsibility and disgrace of such a proceeding rest upon those who have brought the witnesses here!

"But what does the evidence amount to? Nothing whatever. There is not a single word pointing to any *animus* on the part of the young lady towards her little brother. Was there anything strange in that, in the unlimited confidence of school-children, she should speak of her stepmother, and say that the younger children were preferred by her? Where is the stepmother who will not prefer her own children to those of the former wife? But because the conduct of the stepmother formed a subject of conversation between these schoolfellows you are asked, therefore, to find in it a motive which would induce this young lady to imbrue her hands in the blood of this dear little boy. Every fact in the case, on the contrary, not only rebuts the presumption of guilt on her part, but is consistent with the purest innocence. . . . A more unjust, a more improper case . . . was never brought before any court of justice in any place, as far as I know, upon a charge of this serious nature. . . .

"If, upon reading the evidence, you think that guilt is brought home, if not conclusively, at all events in a *prima facie* manner, to Miss Constance, your duty will be to let the matter come before you for further investigation. But if you regard all the consequences, and consider that for nearly a whole fortnight Mr. Whicher has been engaged in the investigation and has not succeeded in finding any one fact authorizing you to say that this young lady is guilty ... I am sure you will order her discharge. ...

"What Dr. Parsons said is well worthy of your attention in guiding you to a conclusion. ... The boy, he says, was unusually heavy for his age, and he expressly states that it must have required a blow of great force to have pierced through the nightdress and flannel and penetrated to the depth of the wound found on the body. Is it likely that the weak hand of this young girl, as she held the child with the other arm, can have inflicted that dreadful blow? Is it likely that hers was the arm which nearly severed the head from the body? It is perfectly incredible.

"And then with regard to her manner on the following morning, which we have seen exhibited nothing which distinguished her from her sisters and the other members of the family sharing the common grief. And we have the important testimony of Dr. Parsons as to the state in which he found her nightdress, *free from any stain or mark indicating participation in the hideous deed*; and as to the fact, too, that according to his belief, there was a clean nightdress in the drawer which, together with the one returned from the wash that week and afterwards brought up, would complete the proper number, according to her own list, in her own handwriting, preserved in her chest of drawers. It is true that Dr. Parsons expresses only his *belief* that he saw the clean nightdress in the drawer, but he says that Superintendent Foley also examined her linen on that morning—he is here in court, and although he has not been called on this inquiry it is known to you that such also is his belief. And really this is tantamount to satisfactory proof that it was there, because, had it not been there the circumstance must inevitably have attracted their attention at the time. ...

"It were idle to dwell upon what the washerwoman has told us, or to hold it as entitled to any weight. She admits that she told a falsehood to the policemen,[4] and the story of her having searched

---

[4] Her remark to the police when they came inquiring about the chest-flannel that "the washing was right with the book". See p. 140.

the basket on the Monday . . . for that which she says was missing . . . but which no one else had ever heard was missing . . . is so improbable, so utterly inconsistent and irreconcilable with the other undisputed facts in the case, that it ought not to weigh with you for one single moment. . . ."

Mr. Edlin's eloquent speech was coming to an end. . . .

"There are no facts to justify this charge," he said, "there is no proof of motive. . . . It would, indeed, astonish any judge to be told, on reading the examination taken last Friday and today, that this young lady had been, thereupon, sent to gaol charged with having murdered her brother . . . I call upon you in the interests not of humanity only, but of clear and simple justice, to detain her not one moment longer in custody, but to liberate her, and restore her to that home from which she ought never to have been taken."

When Mr. Edlin took his seat following the closing of his speech the magistrates retired to consider what should be their judgement. When they reappeared they announced that Constance Kent would be released upon her father entering into a bond of £200 for her to appear again if called upon to do so.

The crowd of spectators greeted the announcement with "loud and vociferous enthusiasm"—clearly they were unaware of the implications of the announcement: Constance had not been cleared of the charge; it had only failed through lack of evidence and she could be re-arrested upon it at any time. This reality didn't strike them, though, and as she left the hall with her father the crowd gave her "a tremendous ovation".

If Constance was less than happy at the result that still cast doubt upon her innocence, Whicher must have been in the depths of despair. Later when he left the hall many members of the crowd shouted imprecations after him. He had failed, totally, in his aim to prove what he fully believed to be the truth. He had stood there while Mr. Edlin had insulted and degraded him, making him appear a blundering, avaricious fool in front of the gullible spectators. The disgrace was to remain with him for a long time. It was to change his whole life.

Chapter 20

REPERCUSSIONS

The release of Constance Kent prompted a flood of articles from journalists all over the country. Nearly all were in her favour, totally, seeing her severally as a martyr, a pawn or a victim. Not surprisingly, therefore, her traducer, Whicher, came in for much scorn, abuse and general calumny. He was seen as the arch villain of that particular drama, a blundering man who had cruelly accused a poor young schoolgirl of the vilest of crimes and had, in consequence, subjected her to the most appalling humiliation and suffering. When passions were running at their highest letters appeared in the press demanding the detective's resignation, a demand which was also made in the House of Commons. All of this, of course, delighted the Wiltshire constabulary who from the start had been highly resentful of Whicher's interference; now, having been to an extent exonerated, Captain Meredith could afford to smugly state that the girl's arrest had "been contrary to his advice and wishes".

The Annual Register, reporting at the end of that year, made full use of hindsight and exemplified the feelings of those who believed fully in Constance's innocence:

> The grounds on which this accusation were made were so frivolous and the evidence by which it was attempted to be supported so childish, that the proceedings can only be described as absurd and cruel. The ground of the arrest was that one of the young lady's nightdresses was missing. . . . The only other evidence to support the charge was singularly empty and vexatious. Whicher produced two of the poor girl's schoolfellows, who deposed to some silly expressions of jealousy by the young lady . . . respecting the greater attention received by the children of the second family. . . . Notwithstanding the utter emptiness of the evidence the magistrates only discharged the accused on her father entering into recognisance of £200 for her appearance if called upon.

Even those writers who tried to remain objective in their approach were disturbed by the case being brought when there was clearly so little evidence, circumstantial or otherwise. In *The Road Murder*, a monograph written in 1860, its anonymous author, writing under the pseudonym of "Barrister-at-Law", wrote:

> The detectives were rash and cruel in arresting Constance Kent before they had even a skeleton of a case made out against her. A nightdress is missing, and upon the strength of that one circumstance she is charged with the most dreadful of all felonies. Literally there is not a particle more, even of circumstantial evidence. We are not assuming her innocence any more than we are begging the question of her guilt. We deal with the matter as one of proof, and would any barrister in England have taken it upon himself, at the instigation of Mr. Whicher, to arraign that young girl as a murderer?

Not *all* journalists were so swift to condemn Whicher and to see Constance as the innocent victim, however. A week after her release *The Journal* wrote:

> . . . We cannot sympathise with the great outcry which has been so unanimously raised both by the press and the public as to the terrible and unjust punishment which has fallen on Constance Kent in her apprehension and lodgement in Devizes Gaol. . . . We cannot but approve most heartily the course adopted by Mr. Whicher and sanctioned by the bench. So far from Constance Kent's apprehension being a punishment, we regard it as a course fraught with *advantage* to her own position.
>
> Previous to Mr. Whicher's arrival, the greatest suspicion lay in the public mind with regard to her. On all hands her guilt or innocence was freely debated, and of this her arrest was *not a cause but a consequence*. Had she continued at liberty that suspicion would still have clung to her, would have been increased. . . . Now, however, she is freed from this disability; she has this advantage, she can say to all the world: "I have been arrested, I have been discharged. The most intelligent detective officer in the kingdom and his assistants have, after a fortnight's inquiry, failed to substantiate a single fact proving my complicity

in the crime." Surely this is preferable to a lingering continuous suspicion. . . .

Regarding all those accusations that Whicher had "exceeded his duties", *The Journal* was later to write:

> The responsibility also was not his alone: it was shared by the bench of magistrates who granted the warrant for her arrest, and remanded her for a week; and . . . he ought not to be exposed to the merciless censure to which he has been subject. . . . The difficulties he has had to contend with have been great. Arriving at the scene a fortnight after the crime was committed, when ample time had been allowed for the destruction of the evidences of guilt, we fear he was met with some degree of coldness and jealousy on the part of some of those who should have been his coadjutors, and has not had afforded to him that cordial assistance which he had a right to expect.

The last sentence quoted above bears out John Rhode's statement that *The Journal* had "access to information denied to the remainder of the press". It is also worth noting that *The Journal*, unlike the national papers, had reporters *on the spot* throughout the entire investigation. However, in spite of their more privileged situation the view they held was a minority view; the majority went along with the opinions expounded by Mr. Edlin, Constance's defence counsel. Who was right?

It cannot be denied that Mr. Peter Edlin's work that day was masterly. His eloquence seems to have blinded almost everyone to the significance of the few, *though positive*, factors that made up Whicher's case. From the very start, as *The Journal* said, Mr. Edlin

> succeeded in establishing his supremacy over the whole court; his will appeared to be law; his dictum was calmly submitted to, and it was not until Mr. Ludlow took the examinations-in-chief into his own hands that even a comparative freedom from interruption was experienced. It is greatly to be regretted that the magistrates had not secured the services of some professional gentleman whose peculiar abilities might have better fitted him to cope with Mr. Edlin than did Mr. Clark. . . .

This latter sentiment was, of course, fervently echoed by Whicher, whose comments are quoted in the previous chapter. *The Journal* and Whicher were right: had there been a professional counsel for the prosecution Mr. Edlin would not have so easily succeeded in destroying Whicher's case. But he did, and he did it by his eloquence and verbal sleight of hand.

Let us examine, briefly, his work that day.

First of all, he played on the emotions of the people gathered there. Constance's very appearance told in her favour and the spectators were quick to be moved by it. Says *The Journal*: "When the poor creature who was accused of so dread a crime fell into her father's arms and kissed him, a sensation was produced which had a most marked effect on the feelings of the crowd during the whole day." Mr. Edlin naturally took advantage of this "effect" and throughout his closing speech always referred to her in emotional terms: "this young lady"; "this young girl"—and to the victim in words equally guaranteed to stir the heart: "this dear little boy"; "her dear little brother". He spoke of Constance being "dragged from her home and sent like a common felon, a common vagrant to Devizes Gaol"—when in fact she received anything but the *common* treatment there, for she was "supplied with bedding and food of her own choice".[1]

But apart from Mr. Edlin's calculated tugs at the heart-strings, what of his more positive defence of the prisoner?

He was to say, "There is not one tittle of evidence" against her. This was blatantly untrue. It was believed by everyone that the crime had been committed by someone wearing night-clothes; and one of Constance's nightdresses was missing. As evidence it was purely circumstantial, but then, so is most of the evidence used in a court of law.

Sarah Cox, in her evidence, said she had taken a clean nightdress from Constance's room on two consecutive Saturdays for the purpose of airing them, but, as *The Journal* said, because a nightdress was "taken downstairs to be aired, it does not follow that it must have been worn on the succeeding night". And that writer was correct: Cox, quite unwittingly, could have taken *the same clean nightdress to be aired on those two consecutive Saturdays.* Yet Mr. Edlin managed to persuade most of his listeners that Cox's statement amounted to proof that all three nightdresses had "been fully accounted for". Said *The Journal*:

[1] *The Journal.*

By a species of most ingenious bamboozling, Mr. Edlin seconded what may have been a cunning trick, and thus demonstrated to all surface-thinkers that all three of Constance's bed-gowns were really inspected the day after the murder by the police. The mode in which two may be made into three was not on Friday shown, but it is worked out in the minds of the police with great clearness.

But what *did* become of that nightdress which was found to be missing from the laundry-basket? It is a question that has considerably bothered those people who—right to the present day—would champion the cause of Constance's innocence. Yseult Bridges presents the incredible suggestion that *Mrs. Kent* was responsible for its loss; she suggests that as soon as Cox left the lumber room in order to get ready for the inquest Mrs. Kent came from her own bedroom and took the nightdress from the basket. Mrs. Kent's motive?—the shielding of her husband and the nurse by throwing suspicion "towards Constance Kent, whom she hated". Such a supposition would be quite laughably melodramatic were it not for its distasteful implication—and one *entirely* without foundation—that Mrs. Kent actually *plotted* to deliver her stepdaughter into the hands of the hangman! Such a ludicrous theory illustrates the desperation of those writers who, at some point in their narrative, are forced to produce an alibi for the accused girl.

Mr. Edlin's solution to the question of the missing nightdress was less subtle but equally incredible. He simply said that belief in its loss rested solely on the word of Esther Holly, implying that she had lied. By why would she? She had maintained an untarnished reputation for twenty years. She had nothing to gain by stealing the nightdress; in fact she had everything to lose. And she *did* lose by its loss. She lost her best employer and by ninety-five per cent of the English newspaper-reading public was deemed simply a liar and a thief. The way in which Mr. Edlin set out to destroy the reputation of this woman is saddening and surprising. He used her naïve admission that she had lied to the police—"The washing is right with the book"—to show that her word was worthless—yet she had told that lie purely *in order to shield the Kent family from suspicion until she had had a chance to check with them and try to put the matter right.* She had no possible motive for stealing the nightdress, and it was preposterous and cruel of Mr. Edlin to suggest that she did it.

He was equally cruel, as we have seen, to Jonathan Whicher. Not only did he speak of "ineffable meanness", "disgrace" and "discredit" when referring to him, but he actually accused him of being "anxious for the reward" which was offered. He must have known that Whicher's position did not entitle him to claim that reward. If anyone was guilty of "ineffable meanness" that day it was surely Mr. Peter Edlin. But there, he had achieved what he had set out to do—secure the release of Constance Kent; to him the reputations of the detective and the washerwoman were expendable; where his job was concerned there was obviously no room for the niceties of ethics.

Following Constance's examination and release at the Temperance Hall, Whicher had an interview with Mr. Ludlow, the Chairman of the Bench. At this meeting he told the magistrate that he saw no hope of finding further evidence against the girl, therefore there was no point in prolonging his stay in Road. The only piece of evidence that might ever be found, he said, was the nightdress, and that, he feared, was destroyed.

When the interview was over he and Williamson made their preparations to return to London, and it was there on the following Monday that Whicher sat at his desk to write a detailed report on the case; he must convince Sir Richard Mayne that his failure was *not* due to mishandling of the affair.

However, where it was one thing to convince Sir Richard—a man who had known Whicher for many years and held him in the highest esteem—it was another matter when it came to the rest of the population. As shown earlier, the greater part of the English public fully believed that the detective had had no case against Constance Kent, and that her arrest had been a cruel, precipitate measure born of desperation and incompetence, and over the week following his return to London the newspapers—through their editorials and readers' letters—made this view abundantly clear.

It was all the adverse criticism that made it necessary for Whicher to write again on the case to Sir Richard Mayne. This report, like his earlier one of the 30th of July, shows that he had *no doubt* as to his complete conviction in his beliefs. Over a total of twenty-three foolscap pages he carefully set out his case. Notwithstanding the letters that daily arrived at the offices of Scotland Yard, each with its own "solution" to the mystery, Jonathan Whicher was convinced that *his* answer was the one.

First, as to *how* he believed the crime took place: (The italics are his own.)

. . . It is quite certain that no person *came in* by the drawing-room window, and I am decidedly of opinion that no person had gone out at that window, which was shut down to within a few inches of the ground and the folding shutters were closed on the inside. . . . I am clearly of opinion that the child was not taken out at that window, but down a back staircase leading . . . to the kitchen door, *which door is within twenty paces of the privy* where the body was found. . . . The distance from the window alluded to is seventy-nine paces, and the guilty party would have had to pass in front of the house immediately under the windows where the family were sleeping. . . .

If Miss Constance is the guilty party I believe her original intention was to have *thrown the child down the privy* . . . I am therefore of the opinion that the child was suffocated, or partially so, in the house after being taken from the bedroom, then carried out and thrust in that state through the hole in the privy seat, thinking it would fall down and sink into the soft soil beneath, where it would have disappeared; but finding the body would not pass down between the splashboard and the wall the knife was resorted to in order to make death certain. . . . I am of opinion that the original intention of the murderer or murderess was not to have shed blood. . . .

As to *who* had committed the crime he did not waver in his belief that it was Constance. The factors that make up his case against her are listed below. I have numbered them:

1. I cannot find the least motive that anyone else could have had for the act except Miss Constance . . . arising from jealousy or spite entertained towards the younger branches of the family by the second wife in consequence of the partiality shown them by the parents, and thus working on a mind somewhat affected, might have prompted her to commit the crime.

2. As regards the state of her mind, it appears that her mother, uncle and grandmother were of unsound mind, and the present medical adviser of the family and another gentleman well acquainted with Miss Constance are of opinion that she is affected with homicidal madness.

3. The murder was no doubt committed by some person who slept in the house that night. The murder took place soon after her return from school, *viz.* the fourteenth night. She was the only person who slept in a room *alone*, except her brother William.

4. Miss Constance had made remarks to her schoolfellows expressing her jealousy as to the partiality shown to the children of the second marriage before she went home for the holidays.

5. When the nurse ran upstairs and called up the elder Miss Kents and told them that the child had been stolen Miss Constance *stood close by, but made no remark.*

6. There is every reason to believe that the person who committed the murder did it in their nightdress. Miss Constance, previous to the murder, had three nightdresses, *one of which is missing.*

7. There is the circumstance of the place where the murder was committed being the same in which she threw her hair and clothes when she absconded from her home disguised as a boy some time back.

8. There was some doubt as to her physical capacity to commit the act, but I find that she is a very powerful young girl, and I am informed by her schoolfellows that romping she was dreaded by all the others, frequently displaying her strength of which she was in the habit of boasting; and as to her moral capacity, she appears to possess a very strong mind. [In an earlier report Whicher wrote on the question of Constance's physical capabilities: "Her schoolfellows state that she was very fond of wrestling with them and displaying her strength, and sometimes wishing to play at *Heenan and Sayers.*"[2]]

[2] Prizefighters Tom Sayers of England and John Carmel Heenan of the U.S.A. were the superstars of the hour. In April of that year, 1860, they had fought for the World Heavyweight Championship, going forty-two rounds before the fight was stopped by the audience invading the ring. The result was declared a draw.

Ending his list, Whicher says: "These are the circumstances which induced the magistrates to grant the warrant for her arrest, and these facts and suspicious circumstances still exist against her."

Taking into consideration all those facts and suspicious circumstances it might appear that Whicher's case was not so weak as many would have one believe. Obviously, though, due to the absence of an able man who could have effectively presented the prosecution's case that case hadn't stood much of a chance. Whicher refers to this lack when writing of that *"proof of animus"* he had so desperately wanted to show. He wrote:

> As regards the evidence of the witness Emma Moody, her schoolfellow, I am of opinion that had there been a professional man to have examined her, she would have proved the *animus* beyond doubt, for she stated to me in the presence of her mother, before the warrant was granted for the arrest of Miss Constance, that she had frequently heard Miss Constance *express her aversion to the deceased* in consequence of the partiality shown him by the parents, and that on one occasion she [Emma Moody] remonstrated with her on the subject, telling her how wrong it was to dislike the child on that account as it was not his fault; to which Miss Constance replied, "Well, perhaps it is, but how would you like it if you were in my place."

The fact that Whicher so quickly saw Constance as being the likely killer does not mean that he did not examine other possibilities. He did, and in accordance with the various rumours, opinions of the local police and other suppositions he had made investigations to see whether cases could be made out against Mr. Kent, Elizabeth Gough, William Nutt (the shoemaker who had found the body), or William Kent.

Mr. Kent and the nurse were quite soon eliminated from Whicher's list of possible suspects, as too was William Nutt; the rumours that had put Nutt under the inspector's eagle eye were to the effect that the shoemaker and the nurse could have been carrying on an amorous affair in the nursery, and that the child's wounds could have been inflicted with a shoemaker's knife. Whicher soon dismissed this idea, saying of Elizabeth Gough that

> she in the first place was not acquainted with him, and in the next place I do not suppose she would condescend to speak to

him in any way, much [less] as an admirer, as she is rather a
superior girl for her station in looks and demeanour, while on the
other hand Nutt is a slovenly, dirty man, weakly, asthmatical, and
lame.

As regards William Kent having been involved in the crime,
Whicher had serious thought on this. In his reports he turns to the
question several times. At one point he states:

> Supposing Miss Constance to be the guilty party and to have
> had an accomplice, that accomplice in my opinion would be her
> brother William, aged fifteen. Judging from the close intimacy
> between the two, I think it possible he knows something of the
> matter from her since its commission if he did not actually assist
> in the deed, as he appears in a very dejected state; but under the
> peculiar circumstances I could not ask the father or any member
> of the family to endeavour to elicit anything from him.

In another instance Whicher speaks again of William's dejected
state, "both before and after his sister's arrest", and of "the sympathy existing between the two"; which leads him, he says, to be
"strongly impressed" with the opinion that the boy participated in
the crime.

Supposing that Constance was guilty it is hardly likely, however,
that William would have played any part in it. He had in the past
—for example, on their running away from home—proved himself
a most inefficient, unheroic partner, and as such would surely have
been the last one to have the courage to participate in such a
terrible crime—even taking into account that he could be quite
pliant under his sister's influence. Whether or not he did "know
something of the matter", though, is something else.

Still, for all his suspicions, Whicher was not overly concerned
with the boy William; his efforts had been concentrated on securing
a committal of Constance, and in this he had failed. He had not
been completely discredited, though, and certainly not in the eyes
of those Trowbridge magistrates at whose request he had originally
gone to the village of Road. Writing of his *last* interview there with
Mr. Ludlow, the Chairman of the Bench—the interview that took
place immediately following Constance's release at the Temperance
Hall—Whicher said: "He expressed himself perfectly convinced

that Miss Constance was the guilty party, although we had failed
to obtain sufficient evidence for a committal. . . ."

That Mr. Ludlow was confirmed in his opinion is borne out by
a letter he wrote on the 24th of August from his home in Westbury
to Scotland Yard's superintendent. This was prompted by an article
in the press in favour of Whicher. Mr. Ludlow wrote—and the
italics are his:

> Mr. Ludlow presents his compliments to Sir Richard Mayne,
> and on reading in The Times that Mr. Inspector Whicher has
> been enough blamed, Mr. Ludlow feels much pleasure in hearing
> testimony to his good judgement and ability in the case. *I fully
> agree* with Mr. Whicher as to the perpetrator of this most
> mysterious murder and that he was fully justified in acting as he
> did.

Only four days later, on the 28th, the magistrates as a body
wrote to the Home Secretary:

> . . . As some disparaging observations have lately been made
> in the House of Commons with regard to Inspector Whicher's
> conduct in this case we think it only just towards him to state it
> to be our opinion that he acted very prudently and with great
> ability in the investigation.

The Journal, also, still refused to take the common—hysterically
emotional—view in which Constance was seen as Little Red Riding
Hood and Whicher as the Big Bad Wolf. Adding a much-needed
objective voice to the general sentimental chorus it said:

> We could not for a moment assert or insinuate her guilt; by
> all means let her have the full benefit of the want of proof; but
> we do protest against so uncalled-for a hue and cry as has been
> raised on her behalf. . . . Mr. Edlin was perfectly correct in say-
> ing that nothing had been adduced which was not compatible
> with the purest innocence; but the reverse is true also: nothing
> was brought forward incompatible with her guilt.

In their attempts to speak up for Whicher, though, *The Journal*
and *The Times* stood almost alone in the rush to denigrate him.

In *The Advertiser* meanwhile there appeared a paragraph about
Mr. Kent that said:

It is stated on good authority that soon after the apprehension of Miss Constance, he applied, under the idea that she might be convicted, to her trustees to ascertain if the property to which she was entitled through her late mother might be secured so as not to be confiscated to the Crown.

If that newspaper's informant spoke truly then Mr. Kent was by no means confident of his daughter's release. And obviously he had his reasons.

But there for the time being—on the surface, anyway—the question of Constance Kent's guilt rested. And life went on. On Monday the 30th of July, exactly a month after the death of her first son, Mrs. Kent's second son, Acland Savill, was born. Elizabeth Gough —who two days later was twenty-three years old—assisted at the birth. The occupants of Road Hill House once again numbered twelve. By this time, of course, Constance was back in her home; as Mr. Edlin would have it, in that home from which "she ought never to have been taken"; in truth, though, it was the home to which for most of her older life she had been denied access.

Chapter 21

MR. SLACK'S INQUIRY

Superintendent Foley witnessed the failure of the case against Constance Kent with satisfaction. Scotland Yard's best detective had been sent to take the investigation out of Foley's hands and offer up a satisfactory solution to the mystery—and that detective had miserably failed. Now with Whicher gone Foley had a chance to repair his own reputation, and with the murder inquiries reluctantly placed in his own incompetent hands once more he was determined to succeed where the man from London had not. Whicher had hardly shaken the dust of Road from his heels when Foley set to work.

Now *anyone* who viewed with any objectivity the results of Whicher's inquiries must have seen that even though no case was *proved* against Constance there still remained certain undisputed factors that indicated a *possible* guilt on her part. Even Foley, obtuse as he was, realized this; as also—in spite of his former protests—did Captain Meredith. It was this realization that inspired them with the idea of carrying on where Whicher had left off—of trying to find positive, irrefutable proof against her. The murder weapon would never now be found, this they knew—but on the other hand *the nightdress might still be in existence.* This, if it could be discovered, would result in the greatest glory not only for Foley, but for the whole of the Wiltshire constabulary; it would show the country that Whicher had just not been thorough enough and that the Wiltshire police had had to finish the job *for* him. That, from the country bumpkins, would be one in the eye for the city slickers.

There was also, of course, the matter of the lost chemise. Should questions ever be raised about that then Constance's nightdress, if it could be found, would successfully negate them.

With these ideas in mind Captain Meredith, on the 31st of July, wrote an astonishing letter to the Home Secretary saying:

I have received information that an article of dress which may throw some light upon the late mysterious murder of Francis Savill Kent at Road in the County of Wilts on the 29th ultimo is supposed to have been concealed in the coffin and interred with the Body of the Murdered Child.

I have therefore to request that you will be pleased to grant authority to the Ministers and Churchwardens of the Parish of Coulston in the said County to disinter the Body of the above named Child to enable me to have the Coffin searched for the article missed.

Permission was granted at once and on the 2nd of August the heavy gravestone was lifted up and the coffin opened. The following day a much subdued Captain Meredith wrote back to the Home Office to say that the dead child's coffin contained nothing "which would throw any light upon this very mysterious murder".

Obviously the Wiltshire police were determined to leave no stone unturned!

The day before the opening of Savill's coffin Captain Meredith and Superintendent Wolfe had gone to Road Hill House and, in the presence of Mr. Dunn, questioned Elizabeth Gough and proceeded to carry out an interesting experiment. She had always insisted that she had seen Savill's cot was empty whilst kneeling on her own bed in order to tend to the baby Eveline. Now Captain Meredith placed a dark blanket in Savill's cot while Wolfe knelt on the nurse's bed in the position she had indicated. Try as he might, though, from his particular vantage point Wolfe could see no part of the blanket; the sides of the cot were too high, and the structure of the canework sides, at that angle, made it impossible to see through.

If nothing else, the experiment proved that at least part of the nurse's evidence had no basis in truth.

With Constance believed to be innocent by so many it naturally followed that the guilt for the crime must be laid at someone else's door, and where the house's inmates were concerned the suspicion was directed at—either individually or as a couple—Mr. Kent and the nurse. With regard to Elizabeth Gough, the following quotation from *The Journal* gives a good example of the rumours that were circulating with regard to her involvement in the crime.

An elaborate theory has been woven out of the nursemaid's supposed attachment to some military friend at the depot at her native place, Isleworth. It is presumed that this fabulous individual, on coming to pay her his addresses at Mr. Kent's house, chose the night as the time, and a ladder, the flat leads and the nursery window as the mode of entrance, and then being perceived by the child, who is imagined to have awaked, to be where he ought not to have been, and being afraid of disclosure, he placed a hand over the boy's mouth to prevent him crying out, so that he fainted away, being weakened by a calomel pill taken the night previously. Thinking the child dead, and alarmed at what he had done, the "friend" was then let out of the nursery window to complete what he had begun. A very ingenious fiction, this, but purely fictitious, and we can only account for the hold it has taken on some people's minds by the fact that it is the most humane method of accounting for the death.

The letters that continued to arrive at the offices of the newspapers, the Wiltshire police, Scotland Yard and the Home Office put forward similar theories, though in most instances either Mr. Kent or William Nutt were cast in the role of Elizabeth Gough's lover. Mr. Waddington, Permanent Under-Secretary of State, after receiving yet another such typical "solution" to the mystery, noted: "This seems to be the favourite notion now."

Other rumours voiced again the old idea that the criminal was someone who had secreted himself in the house; the object attributed to this intruder varied, being either revenge on the family, a rendezvous with the nurse, or burglary. One amateur sleuth put forward the theory to Scotland Yard that Savill had awakened in the night (because of the laxative pill he had taken) and on the way to the lavatory had disturbed and *recognized* a robber—in this case William Nutt. While yet another unsolicited answer to the mystery suggested that Mrs. Kent had murdered her son in a fit of puerperal insanity.

However, in all those letters still in existence giving solutions to the great question Constance's name is conspicuous by its almost total absence: clear indication that Mr. Peter Edlin's efforts, her release and the subsequent hue and cry raised on her behalf had had the effect of almost completely eliminating her as a possible suspect—at least as far as England's would-be detectives were concerned.

One of these was Sir John E. Eardley Wilmot of Bath who developed a most passionate interest in the matter for the reason, as he wrote to his friend Peter Edlin, that he firmly believed Constance to be "innocent and unjustly dealt with", and adding: "Why Whicher followed that poor girl and hunted her to prison must always be as great a mystery as the murder itself."

Sir John was also known to Mr. Waddington, the Under-Secretary, and wrote to him at the Home Office suggesting that an official inquiry should be instituted and that he, Sir John, should be appointed Commissioner. In his letter he wrote:

"I possess an accurate knowledge of the facts of this mysterious case, as also of the premises and locality, and . . . have a strong suspicion that I know the track in which the search should be made. . . ." And adding further: "When Mr. Kent heard that I had taken a deep interest in the discovery of the guilty party he sent word to me, *a total stranger*, that he should be glad to show me every part of his premises and give me every facility to endeavour to trace the crime. Was this the act of a guilty man. . .?"

It would indeed appear as if Mr. Kent was trying to be helpful, but then of course one must realize that Sir John had made it clear to him that he did not suspect any member of the Kent family. However, Sir John took up the invitation and went to Road Hill House where, in the company of Mr. Dunn ("extremely courteous and obliging"), he made a full examination of the premises.

It was as a result of his investigations that he made the interesting point (as also had Whicher) to the Home Office that Mr. Kent would not have selected the privy as a hiding-place for the child's body as it was by Mr. Kent's directions that the splashboard was fitted there in the first place. Mr. Kent, said Sir John, was the only member of the family to use that privy, therefore, whereas he would be familiar with its structure, others might not be.

Notwithstanding Mr. Kent's insistence that he should be glad to give to Sir John "every facility to endeavour to trace the crime" his guest was not much aided when it came to making an examination of the *persons* concerned. As he later wrote to Edlin, "I did not see Miss C.K.", adding, "I rather thought it a peculiarity that the father did not offer to bring her into the room where we were the day we were at Road. But I did not ask it as I considered that part of the inquiry as extinct and at an end."

Sir John, in fact, did not see "any of the family except Mr. Kent, and the nursemaid and housemaid", the latter whom he described as "a noble creature, the picture of openness and straightforwardness". Even so, he obviously learned enough to confirm him in his ideas as to the direction in which his suspicions lay. It was his opinion, he stated, that "no woman or girl could have cut the throat in the *clean* way it was done" and that it must have been made "by a male adult". In short, he believed that the killer was an unknown lover of Elizabeth Gough. To the Home Office he wrote: "From my observations of her demeanour and general appearance, I may tell you confidentially that I am convinced she knows all about it. . . ."

For all his evident enthusiasm, however, Sir John's plea to be appointed Special Commissioner to look into the case elicited from the Home Secretary a polite declinature. The Under-Secretary, though, was impressed with Sir John's theory and the subsequent Home Office correspondence shows that the nurse-and-lover idea was rapidly gaining ground, in high places.

And if there was truth in the belief that Elizabeth Gough had entertained a lover that night, then who was it likely to be? The obvious choice was, of course, Mr. Kent, and even among those who scoffed at the notion there were many who could not escape the idea that he was more involved than he would have them believe. Sir John Eardley Wilmot exemplified this feeling of doubt, writing to Mr. Edlin on the 7th of August regarding Mr. Kent: "I am convinced of *his* innocence—he no more did it than you or I"; and then less than two weeks later asking Edlin, "Are you quite and thoroughly convinced in your own mind of the *entire innocence* of Mr. Kent? It is clear that *one* in the house at least knew all about it."

Well, Sir John was certainly right in that respect, but everyone knew that anyway.

On the 27th of August, her employment with the Kent family being terminated, Elizabeth Gough's father arrived in Road to take her home with him to Isleworth. Before leaving Wiltshire, however, she had an interview with Superintendent Foley at which she assured him that she would be immediately ready to return to answer further questions at any time.

It must have been with great relief that she sat on the train that carried her eastwards, away from the scene of so much drama. But she had not seen the last of it. She was not to know, but even as the wheels of the train drew her closer to her home, so the wheels of officialdom-in-the-pursuit-of-justice were turning to bring her back again. The very next day the magistrates wrote to the Home Office saying that the Wiltshire police were "prepared with further evidence" which, it was believed, was sufficient to justify the apprehension of "one of the inmates of Mr. Kent's house at the time of the commission of the murder".

The letter went on to the effect that when Constance had been examined she had had the benefit of a solicitor *and counsel*, while the Crown on the other hand had not been represented. In such a situation, the magistrates said, justice "could not properly be administered", and to avoid a repetition of any similar, one-sided affair they were anxious "that a solicitor for the prosecution should be appointed" by the government. In reply to this request Mr. Waddington wrote:

> . . . The proper course will be for the Chief Constable to employ a local solicitor of respectability and experience who can retain Counsel to conduct the examination of the witnesses if it is thought necessary. In a case of such great difficulty and importance Sir George Lewis will recommend to the Treasury the payment of such extra expenses as may be properly involved.

In other words, if after having got up the case it was thought necessary to employ professional aid for the prosecution of that case then the government would pay the bill.

The Wiltshire magistrates and police, however, *did not as yet have a case to prosecute*, notwithstanding the fact that they had already informed the Home Office that they *had*, that they were "prepared with further evidence". They were not. Their aim was to bring a charge against Elizabeth Gough, but without sufficient supporting evidence the task seemed almost an impossible one. Their answer to the problem was to use the Home Office's offer of help *for the purpose of finding that evidence.* So, intentionally mis-interpreting the Under-Secretary's words, they secured the services of a certain Mr. Slack of Bath—a "local solicitor of respectability and experience"—for the purpose of *getting up a case* against the unsuspecting suspect! Such unprecedented proceedings just go to show that the magistrates, given a second chance to secure a con-viction, were not trusting anything to fate.

So it was that the Home Secretary found that he had unwittingly authorized a most unconstitutional investigation. But by that time it was too late; Mr. Slack's infamous inquiry was well under way.

Just before the time of Mr. Slack's appointment an extraordinary document, the *Bath Memorial*, had been received by the Home Office. This petition, signed by the Mayor and forty-five other eminent inhabitants of the City of Bath requested the Home Sec-retary to grant a Special Commission for the investigation of the crime, on the grounds that the ordinary means of finding the crimi-nal had entirely failed. It pointed out that "the condition of the doors, windows and fastenings of the house prove that . . . the murderer was an inmate of the house or was secreted there for the purpose, and that accomplices before and accessories after the fact are to be sought in that mansion. . . . Mr. Kent's household are therefore collectively responsible for that murder and the innocence of no one of them is to be assumed. . . ." It further pointed out that Mr. Kent and the members of his family had never been publicly examined—which was clear indication of the direction in which lay the suspicions of those Bath inhabitants.

The Home Office rejected this plea for a Special Commission on the grounds that it would be "highly unconstitutional, and an entire departure from the principles upon which this country has long been governed". A second petition, from the inhabitants of Road, and towns in its vicinity, fared no better.

The setting up of Mr. Slack's inquiry—which was, of course, to be unwittingly financed by government funds—was in direct opposi-tion to the laudable sentiments expressed by the Home Secretary, and it is hardly surprising, therefore, that the press and the public in general, not knowing the true circumstances, should view such "conflicting" proceedings with disgust. In their eyes the Home Sec-retary had openly vetoed the request for a Special Commission while at the same time, and most hypocritically and clandestinely, instituting a more limited inquiry. Fuel was added to this particular fire by the fact that Mr. Slack began his inquiries without divulging the authority under which he was working. In this, of course, he was acting according to the instructions of the Wiltshire magistrates. They wanted his "authority" to be kept secret, not from the public, but *from the Home Office itself*; they were very much afraid that if the Home Secretary should learn of the unconstitutional proceedings "he" had sanctioned they, the magistrates, would be censured for exceeding the powers he had granted them—and which indeed they had. The public and the press, however, knew nothing of the real situation behind Mr. Slack's inquiry (indeed, it has only *now* come to light) and they would continue to regard it with anger and disgust; as *The Bath Express* wrote of the Home Secretary, Sir George Lewis: "Every possible fault has been committed by him in the miserably small, undignified and almost secret proceedings which he has now resorted to . . ." and, "Englishmen are not yet converted to the doctrine of secret tribunals."

The "authority" behind Mr. Slack's inquiry was still a closely guarded secret when Mr. Kent first heard of it on the 4th of September. This was from Superintendent Foley who had appeared at Road Hill House with the surprising notification that Mr. Kent's servants would be required for examination the next day at Mr. Slack's Bath office. Mr. Kent—understandably quite bewildered—said that before agreeing he would have to consult his solicitor.

Just prior to Foley's arrival, Mr. Kent had been writing a letter to the Under-Secretary at the Home Office. After giving his own address as "Road Hill Hill" (evidence of a somewhat fraught state of mind?) he asked if Mr. Waddington would afford him "an interview on Friday or Saturday". Continuing with his usual game of bluff he goes on:

> . . . I am very anxious to afford the Government every aid in my power in pursuing any further investigation into the matter and it has occurred to me that an interview between us and my solicitor might assist you in determining what shape any further investigation should assume.

Mr. Waddington, though, was not unduly impressed with Mr. Kent's "anxiety to help" and consequently declined, saying that any representation he wished to make to Sir George Lewis should be made in writing.

In the meantime, following Foley's appearance with the summons from Mr. Slack, Mr. Kent contacted his own solicitor, Mr. Dunn, who at once wrote to Mr. Slack asking by what authority he demanded to examine Mr. Kent's servants. Mr. Slack replied cryptically that he was "regularly instructed by a proper authority" and added, causing further dismay, that Mr. Kent and his whole family would also be required for examination on the 9th of September. Mr. Kent, through his solicitor, refused to obey the summons, which refusal brought forth from Mr. Slack the statement that he was working under the authority of the Home Office. This made no difference, though; Mr. Kent still declined to submit.

Nothing at that time, it seemed to Mr. Kent, was going his way. Not only was he being pressed to answer questions at a most unusual inquiry, but his own request for an interview with the Home Secretary had been quite curtly denied. He wrote to Mr. Horatio Waddington again on the 7th of September, politely complaining:

. . . I have to regret that you could not see it right to afford me an interview . . . as I was most anxious personally to assure you of my earnest desire that every facility should be afforded for a public and searching examination of myself and my whole household. . . .

And *then* going on to say:

I would only add that I have received a request from Mr. Slack, a solicitor of Bath, to attend with my wife and family for separate examination in his private office, and he asserts that he has the sanction of the Home Office for doing so. I am sure you will see that in declining to comply with this request I am in no way acting in opposition to the assurance I have given you.

Mr. Waddington replied to the effect that the Home Secretary had recommended to the magistrates that a local solicitor should be employed to conduct the prosecution, and he supposed, though he had "received no intimation to that effect, that Mr. Slack was the person selected for that purpose". He then added:

In deciding as to the propriety of attending with your family, to be examined by that gentleman in any preliminary inquiry which he may think it right to make, you must be guided entirely by your own discretion and the advice of your solicitor.

No, Mr. Waddington was not taken in by Mr. Kent's insistence on his readiness to help. And neither was Sir George Lewis, the Home Secretary. A letter arriving along with that last letter from Mr. Kent—from an anonymous writer signing himself "Justice"—suggested that Mr. Kent was the child's murderer and asked pertinent questions regarding the "suspicious behaviour" of Mr. Kent and the nurse. Sir George's written comment on the letter says: "This anonymous writer is not far from the mark:"

That Mr. Kent was impressed by the coolness of Mr. Waddington's reply is evidenced by the fact that he *did* submit himself and his household to examination by Mr. Slack—albeit most reluctantly—but insisted that such examination *of his family* should take place not at Bath but at Road Hill House—and in the presence of his solicitor, Mr. Dunn.

The Bath Express was loud in its condemnation of the situation that had evolved—and particularly with regard to Mr. Kent's "defensive position". It said:

> How . . . can we avoid the inference that other persons, and those strangers, have showed more eagerness and exhibited more activity in endeavouring to discover the murderer than the father of the murdered child himself? Acting as a lawyer, Mr. Dunn was justified in advising his client not to answer Mr. Slack's summons. But Mr. Kent was the parent, and in his parental instinct he ought to have spurned any legal punctilio, and ought to have expressed his willingness to appear anywhere, he and all his household, to answer the most rigorous inquiries which either human sagacity or suspicion could frame. Instead of which, he has had a counsel and an attorney at his elbow to assist him in evading inquiries and restricting examination, not in promoting them. . . .

Feeling against Mr. Kent was running very high now and he suffered increasing distress. His threat to take out a libel action against *The Bath Chronicle* did nothing to still the rumours that circulated throughout Road and the surrounding areas; the rumours only increased. He was seen by many—perhaps owing to the pressure created by Mr. Slack's investigation—as a very frightened man. On the 15th of September *The Journal* wrote:

> . . . There is no truth whatever in the statement that Mr: Kent has attempted suicide. His position, however, whether innocent or guilty, is so intensely painful, that the report has a greater appearance of probability than have many of its predecessors.

For several weeks now Mr. Kent had had to read in the newspapers report after report on the killing at Road—many of them hinting very strongly at his complicity in the deed. Added to this a stream of anonymous letters and insensitive sightseers contributed further to his unhappiness. *Keene's Bath Journal* made comment upon this.

> . . . Whatever views may be entertained as to the culpability of certain of the inmates of Road Hill House, we must discountenance the system of persecution and annoyance to which all the residents are subject. Not content with sending letters containing threats and gross insults, there are those who most improperly trespass on the premises out of curiosity and cruelty. This, at all events, is most unjustifiable. On Sunday afternoon last, for instance, a party of six persons, dressed like gentlemen, rode into the grounds of the house, laughing, smoking, and joking, and, halting in front of the house, made the affair the subject of ribald jest. Seeing one of the young ladies at the window, they shouted, "There is Constance," and it was only on Mr. Kent making his appearance that they rode away.

Such an incident was by no means uncommon; when the spectators didn't ride into the grounds on horseback they went on foot or drove through in carriages.

Although Mr. Slack's inquiry was conducted in the "strictest secrecy" still some newspapers managed to keep their readers *au fait* with what was happening. Mr. Slack, it appeared, had undertaken his task with earnestness. A succession of individuals was summoned to his office for questioning, among them certain past servants of Road Hill House. One of these was Emma Sparks, one-time nursemaid to the Kent children. Said *The Journal*: "She appears to be less favourably impressed with regard to the household harmony than have other witnesses."[1]

When Mr. Slack was not asking his questions in Bath he was asking them at Road Hill House. By Thursday, the 20th of September, he had examined there every member of the Kent family but Constance—even making an attempt to examine the five-year-old Mary Amelia. Mrs. Kent's examination, it is said, lasted four hours. Mr. Dunn was present during all the inquiries made at Road Hill House, remaining throughout "an all but passive listener". He did speak up, however, to refuse to allow any of the family to sign their statements, though those given by other persons and "taken at Bath were severally read over and signed". Mr. Dunn was also responsible for the fact that Constance had not yet been examined; he objected "on the ground that she still stood charged with the murder, and was now only out on bail". She herself, though, it was reported, "expressed a wish, as she had frequently done before, that her statement should be received".

On Saturday, the 22nd, she spent the whole day being examined, during which, said *The Frome Times* (who somehow managed to have a reporter on the spot), "we saw her, at the request of Mr. Slack, making an effort to open the heavy drawing-room window and, to appearances, helplessly fail."

Meanwhile, outside in the grounds of Road Hill House one or two members of the police force, under Foley's instructions, "carefully dug up the piece of garden which Constance had been accustomed to regard as her own".

This last piece of information is most interesting. Obviously Foley had not given up the idea that Constance *could* have been involved in the crime. What was he looking for?—her nightdress? —the murder weapon?—and what of Mr. Kent's dark lantern which had never been seen since the night of the murder? Whatever the superintendent was looking for, nothing was found.

The idea that Constance might be the object of Mr. Slack's inquiry exercised several minds, one of which was Mr. Peter Edlin who thought there was a strong possibility that he would be called upon to defend her a second time. And his task, he feared, might not be as easy as it had been that previous July.

[1] All quotations here are, unless otherwise stated, from *The Journal*.

In preparation for such an eventuality he had asked an acquaintance, a certain Mr. Henry Pullen of Warminster, to inquire into the character of Constance's erstwhile schoolfellow Emma Moody—having heard that she was something *less* than respectable—with a view to discrediting the value of any evidence she might be called upon to give. Mr. Pullen was most thorough in his investigation and his resulting report to Mr. Edlin is such a gem that it just has to be quoted. From Warminster on the 11th of September he wrote:

My dear Sir, Since I last wrote to you I hear some alteration may take place in my business appointments at Bristol which may prevent the pleasure of my seeing you, but if I *do go* I expect it may be the latter part of the day on Thursday or Friday. In case however I should be frustrated I will at once report progress.

There is no mistake about the so-called young *lady* being a *thoro' bad 'un* in every sense of the word. Her general character is notorious although perhaps merely a select few can particularise individual feelings. Under the guise of modest affectation she would not stop at *any*thing however immoral or indecent.

In fact she was so proverbially known to be a loose low girl that the Misses Haskew and Cruse (a respectable ladies' seminary close by me) politely refused her remaining with them as a pupil and it is believed she was actually dismissed by them, the reason given being on account of her *lying* propensities and inculcating deceit and falsehood amongst her schoolfellows. Moreover she is a stupid simple *Fool*—but nevertheless possessing a certain amount of cunning likely to mislead. Her cognomen is "Crackedbrained Miss Moody" and she is generally known in the Town by this appellation.

Her mother (who is a complete softy and has no moral control *whatever*—over any of her daughters) is subject continually to their ill-conduct. They sometimes *beat* her and even in their violent conduct have been known to throw a knife at her.

One of the girls is now on her bed with a spinal complaint.

The one in question was I believe sent to Beckington School on account of her great intimacy with young Chambers of the "Wynne Inn" here (a loose fish!) whom she termed "her man", and notwithstanding the mother has forbidden her intercourse with him I have ascertained as a fact that within the last fortnight she actually bribed a low vagabond of a woman named Eliza Snow to go to Chambers and arrange an appointment with him. This is mild though in comparison with her moral conduct as she is constantly outside her house *whistling*, playing the fool and larking with all *male* passers-by.

There is a Miss Holdman or Oldan (Holden) at Bath who used to be a teacher and parlour boarder at Beckington and who knew Miss Moody and Constance Kent *well*. She says the reason she gave evidence against Constance Kent is that in consequence of Moody being a fool and made sport of at school and Constance being full of fun and a sharp girl she has been in the habit of ridiculing and chaffing Moody tremendously who not having the ability to return it was only too glad to have the opportunity of displaying a grudge against Constance.

I think however you may be assured by me (from good authority) that she will *not* be again called as a witness.

Very truly yours,
Henry Pullen.

As it turned out, however, Mr. Edlin saw it as unlikely that he would be called upon to make use of such a fine example of character-assassination as Constance emerged from Mr. Slack's examination with the belief in her innocence stronger than before, the solicitor himself openly expressing his faith in her guiltlessness. Even *The Journal*, which had previously—and right from the start —appeared most suspicious of her, was now moved to write in her favour, saying:

In one fact we are happy to be able to express our confident belief, namely, that Mr. Slack is entirely satisfied in his own mind that the murder was not committed by Miss Constance Kent. This conclusion we have arrived at by information from several quarters, and one fact may be adduced to bear it out. The purse for which Miss Constance went to the lumber room on the day of the inquest, asking the maid if it was in her pocket, which was regarded by Mr. Whicher as so suspicious a circumstance, was subsequently found behind her chest of drawers. We are the more gratified in stating this partial exoneration, as we have from the very first regarded the published facts as bearing most suspiciously against her. She not being guilty, there is no question whatever—all admit it—that she is the victim of the vilest plot that ever imagination conceived.

This about-face from *The Journal* was very unexpected. Surely they could not have been led to change their very strong beliefs merely on the fact that Constance's "missing" purse had been found behind her chest of drawers. What evidence did anyone have that Constance herself had not *placed* it there to support her story? Clearly, though, *The Journal* had changed their minds—seeing the girl now—as did the rest of the public—in the role of scapegoat and heroine. Why? Could it be that *The Journal*—possibly through information that had leaked from the Slack examinations—had now formed a most decided opinion with regard to some other person's guilt?

With one notable exception every individual who might possibly have been involved with Road Hill House or the crime had been examined by Mr. Slack. That exception was Elizabeth Gough. Not one question had been put to her and she had remained with her family quite ignorant of the fact that the Wiltshire authorities were sparing no effort in building a case against her. On the 19th of September Sir Richard Mayne had received notification from the Wiltshire constabulary office that it intended shortly to issue a warrant for the nursemaid's arrest. From that time onward a watch was kept on her at her father's house on South Street, and on the 28th, Superintendent Wolfe travelled there with a warrant for her arrest. That same day he brought her back with him to Devizes where she was formally charged with the murder of Francis Savill Kent.

The news of the arrest caused a sensation throughout the country. The nurse's apprehension only confirmed what so many had suspected all along. Now, at last, it was believed, the mystery would be solved.

Chapter 22

THE CASE AGAINST ELIZABETH GOUGH:
1st–4th OF OCTOBER, TROWBRIDGE

Elizabeth Gough was charged with the wilful murder of Francis
Savill Kent but there was not one member of the police force
who believed her to be guilty of the crime. She was arrested
in the sole hope that, believed to be an accessory, she would implicate Mr. Kent and so lead to his successful prosecution.

The apprehension of the nurse illustrates perfectly the inadequacy
of the Wiltshire police and the incredibly hit-and-miss methods
which from the start had coloured their inquiries. Foley had started
off by suspecting the nurse and Mr. Kent, and then his suspicions,
affected by Whicher's findings, had switched to Constance. With the
collapse of the case against her, however, attention had once more
become centred on the police's original suspects. In view of all this
it is hard to avoid the conclusion that the police were acting less
from a total conviction than from a desperate need to acquit themselves of that very negative onus placed upon them. By arresting
Elizabeth Gough they were pacifying the public's demand for action
and there was also the chance, the hope, that even though the evidence against the nurse was slight, it still *might* get results.

The hearing against Constance, where she alone had had the
benefit of a professional advocate, had taken one day; that against
Elizabeth Gough, where both sides were represented, took four days
—though it was said that "a stipendiary magistrate from London
would have disposed of the affair in twelve hours".[1]

The inquiry began on Monday, the 1st of October, with the bench
under the chairmanship of Sir John Awdry. Mr. T. W. Saunders,[2]
instructed by Mr. Slack, conducted the case for the prosecution
while the prisoner's defence lay in the capable hands of Mr. Ribton,

[1] *The Road Murder*—"Barrister-at-Law".
[2] Not to be confused with Mr. T. B. Saunders who later conducted his
own inquiry into the case. See following chapter.

a barrister well known for his work at the Old Bailey. This gentleman was instructed by the solicitors Farrell and Briggs, a firm hired "at his own cost" by a wealthy Isleworth brewer. For some unstated reason Mr. Peter Edlin was also present—instructed again by Mr. Dunn. He had no business in this case, so why was he there? Obviously, as he had done so well on Constance's behalf it was believed that his expertise might prove a valuable asset in the present inquiry; he was there to protect the interests of Mr. Kent—who was well aware of the major reason behind the nurse's arrest.

On that Monday morning the townsfolk of Trowbridge and visitors from far afield excitedly crowded the approaches to the court, anxious to catch a glimpse of the prisoner or of members of the Kent family who, it was understood, were to be examined. Elizabeth Gough, accompanied by Superintendent Wolfe, was brought from Devizes in a fly—which not being recognized by the sightseers enabled her to get into the court-house unhindered. Mr. and Mrs. Kent and Constance also managed to get in almost unobserved—therefore luckily missing the "unpleasant demonstrations from those congregated in the locality, who hissed and groaned at the occupants of the other cabs as they drove up to the door".[3]

By eleven o'clock, when the magistrates took their seats on the bench, the courtroom was packed with eager spectators and a large number of reporters from the surrounding areas and from London. At 11.20 Elizabeth Gough was brought in. "She was attired in black, wore a thick crêpe veil and was accommodated with a seat in the dock, Mr. Superintendent Wolfe sitting beside her. She appeared to have been crying, and was thinner and more pale and careworn. . . ."

And so the four days' inquiry began, during which Elizabeth Gough "appeared to feel acutely her painful position, and to watch with feverish anxiety the various questions of the learned counsel. . . . She also made frequent notes, which she handed to her solicitor . . . and which were invariably passed on to the learned counsel for the defence."

Much of the evidence given during that first week in October was, of course, a repetition of that heard previously. Therefore I shall confine the account of the proceedings only to that which is relevant and/or new.

[3] The immediate quotations here are from *The Bristol Daily Post*.

After the charge had been read out Mr. Saunders got under way with his speech pointing out the case against the prisoner, and very soon after beginning he referred to the previous examination when Constance had stood charged with the crime. "I may say here," he said, "and I am glad to have the opportunity of saying so, that I believe from first to last there was not the slightest ground for justifying that proceeding against her. I believe at this moment that the young lady ought to go forth to the world as clear from suspicion as any gentleman I have now the honour of addressing." He then went on to draw attention to "the facts" in the case against Elizabeth Gough.

The murder, he said, was committed some time after half-past-eleven on the night in question. "Strange to say, although Mr. and Mrs. Kent were sleeping in a room adjoining . . . separated only by a passage . . . and although Mrs. Kent was in that condition that causes a lady to be exceedingly ill at ease during the night, yet she did not hear anything during the whole of that night to awake her attention. Nevertheless the boy was murdered close to her own door, was carried downstairs and out of the house; bolts were undone, locks were undone, shutters were undone, and the window was lifted up. It is one of the mysteries of this case that all this took place without alarming any one of the inmates of the house."

He then related how the nurse had knocked at Mrs. Kent's bedroom door inquiring for Savill, of how the drawing-room window and shutters had been found opened and of how, later, the child's body was discovered. "The surgeon who was called in found that the throat was cut in such a way as almost to sever the head from the body, and was of opinion that the gash was inflicted after death. We all know that the arteries give a pulsating motion, and if they are severed while the heart is beating there must be spurts of blood. Instead of this there was only a trickling of blood from the wound, which he concluded was produced by blood casually streaming out after life had ceased to exist. There were certain signs which lead us to believe that suffocation was resorted to before the gash was inflicted. This opens a wide field for speculation. Was the wound inflicted for the purpose of killing the child, or was it for the purpose of misleading those who would be disposed to think that someone in the house had done it? *My conclusion is that the child's throat was cut as a blind, for the purpose of drawing suspicion away from*

the proper quarter. There was also a stab in the child which penetrated some four or five inches, *and that stab was inflicted after
death.* The question is, therefore, who committed the murder?''

Mr. Saunders then posed the question as to whether anyone
might have broken into the house, but showed that they could not
have done, and could only have entered the building with the con-
nivance of one of its inmates. Nevertheless, he said, "it is utterly
impossible to believe that one person committed this murder. The
child was a very heavy boy for his years, and it is idle to suppose
that one person took him from his cot, took the blanket and
wrapped it around him and then left the sheet and counterpane so
smoothly arranged as to present the appearance of never having
been interfered with. In taking the blanket from between the
counterpane and the sheet a very great disturbance must have taken
place, and he or she who took the child could not also have
arranged the clothes . . . and could not have a *motive* for arranging
the clothes." There must have been a second person in the room,
said Mr. Saunders, to have removed the child and to rearrange the
bedclothes afterwards. "If there were two persons, does not the
conclusion irresistibly force itself upon your mind that one must
have been the nurse?" Was it within the bounds of probability, he
asked, that the nurse had remained sleeping whilst a stranger had
entered?—the door, he pointed out, "unless opened carefully, made
a creaking noise". Was it therefore probable that the deed had been
committed only a few feet from where she lay? He answered his
own question. "The suggestion is absurd."

Relating the nurse's story of how she had awakened first at five
o'clock, then slept again until she re-awakened and knocked "two
or three times" on Mrs. Kent's door—without receiving an answer
—he said that Mr. and Mrs. Kent would deny such knocking had
taken place or they would have heard it. Furthermore, the nurse
knew that Mrs. Kent's state of pregnancy made it impossible for her
to have lifted and carried away the heavy child.

He then drew attention to the nurse's knowledge of the missing
blanket. There was "no doubt that the prisoner had the knowledge
that the blanket was gone", for she had said as much to Urch and
Morgan. "Could she," asked Mr. Saunders, "know of it any other
way than by being conscious of how the blanket was taken away?"
Mr. Saunders believed she could not and that, regretting her admis-

sion to the police, she had changed her story: "She felt the pressure of that knowledge, and when the child was afterwards discovered, covered with the blanket, she declared that that was the first she knew that the blanket had gone with the child."

There was also the matter of the piece of flannel, which had fitted the nurse exactly, and was made of similar material to that of the prisoner's petticoat. As regards her statement of kneeling on her bed and seeing that the victim's cot was empty, it was found, said the learned gentleman, "by actual experiment, that it seemed impossible, from the position she described, that she could have seen the boy in his crib or could have missed him from it".

Mr. Saunders concluded his speech by saying that "the magistrates could come to no other conclusion than that the case was fraught with suspicion of the gravest character against the prisoner, and the interest of public justice imperatively demanded she should be sent for trial before another tribunal".

Mr. Ribton (defence) then submitted to the magistrates that there was no necessity to call witnesses as there was no new evidence against the prisoner, beyond that which the magistrates had heard at her previous examination. His suggestion was denied, however, and the first witness was called. This was Mr. Kent.

Samuel Kent had tried hard to escape this public examination for which he had been summoned—as he had managed to avoid any similar examination in the past. On this occasion Dr. Parsons certified to Sir John Awdry, Chairman of the Bench, that he had visited and examined Mr. Kent "and found him in such a state of agitation and mental incoherence that it was impossible for him at that time to give reliable or coherent testimony". The other surgeon, Dr. Stapleton, concurred, saying that Mr. Kent was suffering from "moral and intellectual palsy" which "had overtaken and prostrated his faculties, and which could neither be simulated nor concealed"!

Those efforts on behalf of Mr. Kent failed, though, and his presence was insisted upon. As one of the reasons for the charge against the nurse was the public examination of Mr. Kent the magistrates were determined that, having got this far, they would allow nothing to stand in its way—and certainly no doctor's certification of "mental incoherence"!

So, Mr. Kent took his place in that packed courtroom, at last preparing to undergo his first public examination. He had not been present whilst Mr. Saunders was making his opening speech for the prosecution, so he had heard none of those comments that surely implied his implication in the crime: If two people were involved in the murder, and the nurse was one of those two, then Samuel Kent, surely, must have been the other. No one believed for a moment that she had admitted to the house some lover from without. This now was the reasoning of those hot in pursuit of a solution and a conviction, and Mr. Kent was perfectly aware that his position was fraught with danger.

After answering various questions regarding his family and his household Mr. Kent, in evidence, made the following statements:

"I slept very heavily . . . I heard no noise in the night; I was asleep all the time. I awoke about half-past-seven by the nurse knocking at the door. Mrs. Kent was then dressing. I shortly after went to Trowbridge in search of the police. As I returned home I met Mr. Peacock about a mile out of Trowbridge who told me he was sorry to be the bearer of bad news, but that my little boy had been found with his throat cut." He began to weep here. After a moment he went on: "After I came back I made a thorough examination of the premises; I did not see anything to lead me to believe that violence had been used to enter the house, and the house could only be entered from without by the use of violence."

Regarding Urch and Heritage going to the house on the night following the crime, Mr. Kent said, "On the Saturday night Mr. Foley sent two policemen to my house"—at which Mr. Saunders at once asked: "What was their object in coming there?" This question was objected to by Mr. Ribton, however, on the grounds that Mr. Kent could have no knowledge of the police's object, except what they had actually told him; the question was not pressed and went unanswered. To further questions Mr. Kent replied:

"I took the policemen into the kitchen; one of them was to leave at half-past-two; the other I let out at about five o'clock in the morning. I provided them with refreshment. I was in the library during part of the night, but left the house once or twice."

Mr. Saunders: "For what reason?"

This brought a swift objection from Mr. Ribton who said he

could not see "what the conduct of Mr. Kent, in reference to the police, while in his house, had to do with the charge against the girl at the bar for murder"; he could not see "how anything done or said by Mr. Kent could be evidence against the nurse". (It is easy to see that the questions put to Mr. Kent at this time were coloured by the deep suspicion in which he was held. And Mr. Ribton's objections uphold this interpretation; he did not want his client, the nurse, to be convicted through evidence that Mr. Kent, possibly her partner in crime, might give.) After further discussion the debated question was allowed to be put, and Mr. Kent said that he had "left the house to see if the lights were out". He continued, "I went out several times with the same object. The officers at that time were in the kitchen; they could have left the kitchen and the house if they had unbolted the doors."[4]

The Chairman: "They could have let themselves *out*, but could *not go into* the house?"

Mr. Kent: "Yes—if the passage door was not locked; I am not clear whether I locked that door or not;[5] I locked the officers into the kitchen. . . ."

Mr. Saunders asked, "What reason had you for locking the door?"—but this question was objected to and had to be re-phrased: "Had anything occurred to induce you to bolt the kitchen door?"

Mr. Kent: "I bolted the door that the house might appear as usual, and that no one might know there were policemen in the house.[6] My dog is a full-grown Newfoundland, which I keep for the protection of my premises, and let it loose at night. I let it loose that Friday about ten or a little after ten. It barks and makes a noise at the approach of strangers. . . . On the Friday night I did not hear it bark for I was asleep the whole night."

Mr. Saunders asked rhetorically, "The dog would not bark at an inmate of the house," to which Mr. Ribton, not about to miss a trick, quickly remarked: "If Mr. Saunders is going to give evidence

---

[4] The two doors leading to the yard. See diagram on p. 114.

[5] He later admitted that he *had* locked the passage door, such information being given by Mr. Rodway in a letter written to the editor of *The Morning Post*.

[6] But all the household *knew* that the house was *not* "as usual"; see pp. 112, 116.

he should go into the box." Even so, the question was allowed, drawing from Mr. Kent the answer that he believed the dog did *not* bark at the house's inmates.

Questioned further, Mr. Kent said: "Before going to Trowbridge I looked around the garden and in the drawing-room, and ordered my men to continue the search . . . I thought the child was stolen, and that was why I went to Trowbridge; the nearest police station was there . . . I had not been in the nursery before I went to Trowbridge; I got off as soon as possible."

On the subject of the layout of the house, Mr. Kent said that to get from his dressing-room into the nursery he would have to go through his own bedroom and then across the landing: i.e. the door connecting his dressing-room with the landing was not in use. (This statement supports Dr. Stapleton's comments in his book and in view of later developments is of considerable significance.)

Right from the start of the investigations Mr. Kent had insisted that the child had been stolen by someone from *outside* who had gained access to the house. Now, floundering, he contradicted his earlier claims; under cross-examination he said:

"I might have said to several that no one could have got into the house from the outside; I did not state it to the police; they were at my house every day." And then he contradicted even *that* statement: "I *may* have mentioned it to the police. My mind is so disturbed that there are many things I am not so clear about as I could wish . . . I may have expressed an opinion that no one could have got into the house from the outside—I don't recollect. *I did entertain that opinion.*" Regarding his dashing off to Trowbridge, he said: "I thought I could give the alarm quicker myself than if I sent any servant." Then, regarding Urch and Heritage's stay overnight at the house: "The police came on Saturday by arrangement with Mr. Foley. I did not require it. It was not arranged by me that they were to come; in the afterpart of the day Mr. Foley communicated to me that they would be sent. . . ."

At this point Mr. Ribton remarked that a plan of the premises would be useful, and one of the magistrates handed over a plan of the house taken from *The Bath Chronicle*. Mr. Kent, on seeing it, remarked, "That, I think, is not correct."

In an undertone Mr. Saunders made some remark to Mr. Ribton, following which the latter asked Mr. Kent:

"Have you refused to allow a person to go over the premises to get a more correct plan?"

After hedging for some moments Mr. Kent said: "There was a request sent to me, through Mr. Dunn, my solicitor."

Mr. Ribton repeated his question. *"Did you refuse?"*

"I did . . . through Mr. Dunn."

Mr. Dunn himself broke in at this. "That is not correct. I have had no application made to me."

Mr. Ribton spoke again to Mr. Kent who, it seemed, had lied. "You refused to allow a correct plan to be taken?"

"Yes." This admission from the man who had all along insisted that he was most eager to assist the investigation in any way he could.

Cross-examination continued. Asked whether he had questioned the nurse regarding the loss of the child, Mr. Kent replied, astonishingly: "No. I inquired of the other servants, but not of the nurse." Asked whether *anyone* had inquired of her, he answered, "Mrs. Kent inquired of her—but not in my presence." *Why*, it was asked, did *he* not interrogate her? to which he replied, "Mrs. Kent did so on the morning of the murder—and told me. *I* did not put any questions to her."

From this one is expected to believe that a man whose favourite child has been "stolen" and murdered did not ask one single question of the person who had the responsibility for that child's safety. And Mr. Kent must have realized how incredible such a statement sounded, for he contradicted it the very next moment.

"I think the nurse did tell me how the bed was left, in the course of the day," he now said; and then: "I may have asked her a few questions. I believe I did."

Mr. Ribton: *"Then why did you tell me you did not?"*

Mr. Kent did his best to extricate himself from this difficulty. "Mrs. Kent gave me the account she had received from the nurse. I cannot positively say whether I questioned the girl or not."

Elizabeth Gough, it should be noted, did not ever waver from her story that Mr. Kent had not once spoken to her about the child or alluded to the matter in her presence. And up until now Mr. Kent had been equally adamant that such was the case. Then could it be, perhaps, that in spite of such a situation sounding incredible there was actually *truth* in it?—that Mr. Kent had *not* spoken to the nurse on the matter?

Next came up the subject of the blanket—another subject which, for Mr. Kent, was fraught with dangers.

"Before I started for Trowbridge I knew there was a blanket missing," he now told the court. "When I went to wish Mrs. Kent goodbye, previous to starting out, she told me so, and seemed pleased with the idea, as it would keep the child warm. I told the turnpike woman of the circumstance. *I never have, that I am aware of, denied knowing anything about the blanket."*

This was certainly a lie, for on the Monday following the crime when asked by Foley and Wolfe whether he had known that the blanket was missing before starting out for Trowbridge he had replied twice in the negative—and most firmly: "I did not," and "Certainly not." Also, his present statement about Mrs. Kent seeming "pleased with the idea of the blanket as it would keep the child warm", has the ring of a lie embellished with sentimental elaboration—particularly when his memory appeared so vague about everything else.

Mrs. Kent was the next witness called. She was dressed in black and wore a thick veil. She had just proceeded with: "I am the wife of the last witness——" when Mr. Ribton asked if she would please lift her veil, whereupon Mr. Peter Edlin—whose success with Constance's case had obviously gone right to his head—submitted that if she spoke audibly the bench would not require her to do such a thing, and then suggested that Mr. Ribton should await his turn to examine the witness before making such requests. Mr. Ribton quite rightly objected to Mr. Edlin's interference here, and was backed up by the bench who stated that Mr. Edlin had "no position in the case". The bench had been badly burnt once already by the eloquence of that learned gentleman and they were not willing to let it happen again. So, with Mr. Edlin for once put firmly in his place, Mrs. Kent was again requested to raise her veil—which she did, and then continued with her deposition.

After relating how she had retired to bed that Friday night at about eleven o'clock—closing the nursery door as she went past, she went on: "Mr. Kent came to bed about half-past-eleven . . . he did not leave the room again until half-past-seven the next morning . . . I can't tell how soon I went to sleep . . . I was very restless; I awoke frequently during the night—several times. I slept very lightly. From my bedroom I can hear noise from the nursery . . . I can hear children cry. I did not hear them cry that night. Early in the morning I heard a noise, as if the drawing-room shutters were being opened. It was just light, like the light of a dull morning. I did not call my husband's attention to it as he was asleep. I can't say that I was alarmed at it, because I concluded it might be the servants. I did not hear the dog bark in the night; it is accustomed to bark at strangers; it does not bark in the day at anyone in the house. . . . I first rose in the bed at a quarter-past-seven; I looked at my husband's watch. I did not hear a knocking on the door that morning. While I was dressing the nurse came to the door. . . ."

Mrs. Kent then went on to tell how she had learned that the child was missing and how she had berated the nurse for not informing her immediately the discovery was made. She said: "When I told him [Mr. Kent] that the window was open he got up immediately and, having dressed himself, went downstairs. We were in a state of bewilderment, going from room to room." She then made a statement showing clearly that either she and Mr. Kent, or the nurse, was lying—or all three of them: "Before my husband left," she said, *"I was aware the blanket had been taken with the child. I knew it because the nurse told me so."* Yet Elizabeth Gough had long been adhering to her story that she had not known that the blanket was missing until the child was found.

Continuing to answer questions, Mrs. Kent said that after her husband had left for Trowbridge the nurse had come to do her hair. "We spoke of the missing child, and she said, 'Oh, ma'am, it's revenge.' The nurse," she added, "told me she was a light sleeper."

Under cross-examination, Mrs. Kent said that she had never, during Elizabeth Gough's employment, "taken the child . . . never when the nurse was in bed asleep . . . I cannot say whether I slept for a continuous period that night; the nurse knew I had had bad nights. She told me she had knocked at about a quarter-to-seven. . . ." At this Mr. Saunders asked her:

"When the nurse told you later that she had knocked two or three times at a quarter-to-seven, did you say to her, 'I expect I did not hear as I have had a bad night and therefore slept soundly in the morning'?"

"No," said Mrs. Kent, "I did not say that."

According to the nurse, though, Mrs. Kent *did* say that. Someone was lying here, too.

Mrs. Kent again went on to insist that the nurse had told her *before* Mr. Kent had left for Trowbridge that the blanket was missing: "I told Mr. Kent of it when he came to my door to say he was just going to Trowbridge. . . ." And a few moments later: "I was much afraid that the child would catch cold until I heard that the blanket had also been taken. . . ."

Regarding the nurse's behaviour after the child's death, Mrs. Kent said: "I can't tell whether she was much distressed that morning; I was too much occupied with my own and my husband's feelings. . . . This girl, to the best of my belief, was particularly kind to the child, and seemed very fond of him. He was very fond of her. . . . After he was brought in she frequently spoke of him with sorrow and affection. He was a nice, playful, good-tempered, chatty boy, and a general favourite. I don't know of anyone who entertained revengeful feelings against my family or my little boy." Mrs. Kent also said that she first learned of the child's death after her husband's return from Trowbridge; that he informed her of it. "They knew of it in the house before," she said, but were "not allowed to tell me."

Mrs. Kent having concluded her evidence asked if she might make a statement. Mr. Ribton objected, but Mr. Edlin, who had been quiet for too long for his own comfort, expressed a hope that "the magistrates would hear her". Some discussion ensued, after which the magistrates upheld Mr. Ribton's objection and told Mrs. Kent that any statement she wished to make should be made to her legal advisers. Mr. Edlin, anxious to regain his lost ground, now remarked, "I should not have interposed, but the lady voluntarily stated that she wished to make a statement," at which Mr. Ribton commented: "My friend is like a troubled spirit wandering about without a resting-place." There was much laughter at this, and Mr. Edlin—who had once held those same spectators in the palm of his hand—pathetically offered:

"I only once or twice interposed, and then in the most courteous manner."

After this Mrs. Kent was allowed to step down. Throughout her examination the nurse had taken "particular interest in her statements, and frequently looked at her".

Sarah Cox, who was next called, repeated her former evidence and also gave the information that she had not heard the dog bark during the night. At the close of her examination the case was adjourned until the following morning. Although Elizabeth Gough had "appeared to be very collected throughout the day . . . her face,

Elizabeth Gough as she appeared before the magistrates at Trowbridge. (From a sketch appearing in *The Bath Chronicle.*)

nevertheless, bore an anxious, careworn appearance". Accompanied by Superintendent Wolfe she was quickly conveyed back to Devizes Gaol.

Mr. and Mrs. Kent, as they left the courthouse and made for their carriage, were hooted by the "rabble" who waited outside.

The next day, Tuesday, showed a visible abatement in the excitement, though there were still crowds struggling for admission to the tiny court. The small area available for the public was taken possession of as soon as the door was opened, and those lucky enough to find seats scarcely stirred during the rest of the day's proceedings, "so unwilling were they to give up their advantageous positions".

Sarah Kerslake was called first, followed by James Holcomb. After him came Emily Doel who related the information that she had gone in and out of the nursery with the children's bath-water, and that the nurse did not say anything about the child being gone.

Mary Ann and then Elizabeth followed, giving evidence as to their time of going to bed on the night of the crime and of the nurse coming to their room the next morning to inquire whether Savill was with them. After Elizabeth, Constance came forward. She said of her half-brother:

"I last saw him in the evening when he went to bed. He was a merry, good-tempered lad, fond of romping. I was accustomed to play with him often; I had played with him that day. He appeared to be fond of me, and I was fond of him. . . ." She was then questioned at length about her three nightdresses—this of course was the first opportunity there had been for such questions at a public examination—after which Mr. Ribton asked whether she had heard "that morning anything of the missing blanket till the child was found"?

Constance: "I did from the nurse."

Mr. Ribton: "When did she tell you?"

"I don't know the time—whether it was before or after the child was found."

"Just recollect. Was it not after the child was found that you heard there was a blanket missing?"

"I'm not certain which it was." Constance then went on to state that she had heard the nurse go to her sisters' room that morning "to ask if they had the child with them or had taken it away".

Mr. Ribton: "How came you to hear it?"

"I was dressing. I heard her knock at the door, and went to my door to listen and hear what it was." She continued, "My door is quite close to my sisters'. I don't know what I was doing at the door. I was nearly dressed."

After Constance had left the box there was some little discussion over the fact that William should have been called to give evidence. He was, it was learned, away at school, and it was then decided that he would be called on the morrow—which made it clear to everyone that there was no hope of concluding the examination on the present day.

James Morgan came next, and then P.C. Urch. They gave evidence of being called to the house on the morning of the crime, of seeing Mr. Kent as he came driving out of the gate and then, later, of examining the cot from which the child had been taken. Morgan said he asked the nurse: "Have you lost anything from the nursery besides the child?" and that "she hesitated and then said there was a blanket taken from the cot". He also described how the nurse had turned back the bed-covers and shown them the deep impression left by the child's body.

Urch, after giving more or less the same information regarding the visit, was also questioned about the incident when he and Heritage were locked in the kitchen. He said: "We were to go there to do as Mr. Kent ordered us, and he told us to remain in the kitchen. We had some ale. Heritage was knocking about twenty minutes before he was let out. I don't think it was longer . . . I was in the chair."

"You were in the *chair*," said Mr. Ribton. "The chairman of the company, then."

There was much laughter at this, then Urch, resuming his evidence, said: "When Mr. Kent came to the door, Heritage said he was not aware we were to be locked in in that kind of way. Mr. Kent only answered, 'I've been walking about,'—that was all. . . . I didn't know that I was locked in afterwards. . . ."

Mr. Ribton: "You felt very comfortable and you remained in the chair?"

Urch said, over the laughter, "Yes."

William Nutt the shoemaker gave evidence then of the finding of the body, and this was confirmed by Benger. After that Foley was recalled. By the time he had reached Road Hill House that Saturday morning, he said, the child had been found. He then told how the nurse had said to him that she had not missed the blanket till the child was brought in wrapped in it. He described the appearance of the cot, more of his conversation with the nurse and then his discovery of the piece of flannel in the privy's vault. Mr. Ribton objected to this as evidence, saying that there was nothing to show that the flannel was connected with the crime, and that the prosecution "might just as well produce the whole contents of the privy". The chairman of the bench, Sir John Awdry, upheld the objection, saying that even if the flannel proved to have belonged to the prisoner it only showed that the crime was connected with her room, and the loss of the child already made this clear.

Cross-examined, Foley said:

"Mr. Kent told me that he did not know there was a blanket taken away until he returned from Trowbridge. He said so in the presence of Mr. Wolfe. I asked him twice. I have heard since that he said that he knew before he left Road that a blanket was taken away, but that does not alter my evidence." Regarding the strange adventure that had befallen Urch and Heritage he said: "I sent the police to Mr. Kent's house, but I did not desire him to lock them up. I was very much surprised when I heard of it. I didn't order them to be locked up, for what good would that be?" There was laughter at this, and Foley, encouraged, went on to quip:

"They were, I understood, to have the whole range of the house; but they only had the kitchen range."

The nurse, the superintendent went on, "said she was sure it was not Miss Constance" who had killed the child, and that "it must have been somebody concealed in the house". Then he added: "I said to her, 'That story won't do'."

The sweep who had been at the house early on the morning of the 29th of June was called, but had nothing of importance to contribute. Heritage then was called and confirmed Urch's story of their being locked in. After Heritage came Superintendent Wolfe.

He described how Mr. Kent had taken him on a tour of the house, pointing out places where someone might have secreted himself overnight but, said Wolfe, he had seen nothing that he had considered to be in any way a likely hiding-place. On the subject of his talks with the nurse he said she had told him, "The first time I missed the blanket was after the child was found; I went and looked at the crib when I went to do Mrs. Kent's hair." She told him this several times, Wolfe said, and, "Then she went on to describe how she had found the clothes on the morning of the murder—that they were folded back towards the foot of the bed."

At this point a model of the cot was brought into the court and the superintendent explained to the magistrates how the bedclothes were said to have been found. He said, "She told me that she awoke about five o'clock in the morning and, seeing that the baby lying at her side was partly uncovered, she raised herself up on her knees to cover her over, and in doing so she looked across to the little boy's cot and missed him." Wolfe, who was described as "a tall man", said, "I have tried the experiment of kneeling on the nursemaid's bed. Mr. Dunn was present and put a dark-coloured garment in the cot—which I could not see. The sides of the cot are of thick canework, and in looking over the cot I could only see about four inches inside. I could not see through the cane; it appeared solid at that angle."

Under cross-examination, Wolfe said: "The nurse never showed the least disinclination to answer any questions put to her. Once she said, 'I only wish I knew about the murder; I would soon tell you; do you suppose I could have kept it secret for seven weeks? I know nothing about who came into my room that night, or who went out I can't say. I did believe, and do now, that somebody must have been secreted in the house that night, or that they got in. How is it we hear very often of people secreting themselves in houses, sometimes for robbery?' She also said, 'The nightlight was quite burnt out in the ordinary way. It did not burn quite six hours. It was lighted just before eleven and was out when I awoke at five. If I had known anything I should have told Mr. Foley on the Saturday morning. What advantage would it be to me to keep anything?' In reply to a question I put to her on the 7th of August she said, 'Mr. Kent has never alluded to the matter to me since it occurred from first to last. The young ladies have, and so has Miss Constance; and Master William has often cried over it.' "

After Wolfe had confirmed Foley's statement that Mr. Kent had twice denied knowledge of the missing blanket before setting out for Trowbridge, the case was adjourned till the following day.

William, who had been brought from his school near Gloucester, was the first to give evidence on the third day of Elizabeth Gough's examination, however he had nothing to tell apart from the information that he had gone to bed at ten-thirty on the night of the murder, had slept alone and had awakened at seven the next morning.

Although at one time William had been suspected by many as having possibly been an accomplice in the crime he was, by this stage in the affair, almost unanimously regarded as quite free of guilt. His examination that day reflected the general opinion. When Mr. Ribton came to cross-examine, he said:

"I have only one question. When you speak of your brother you mean your half-brother? Your mother is dead, is not that so?"

"Yes, sir."

Daniel Oliver, describing himself as a jobbing-gardener, was called next, and he was followed by John Alloway, Mr. Kent's erstwhile odd-job boy. It was his job to clean the knives, he said, though on that morning James Holcomb had done it—he, Alloway, not having finished cleaning the boots. Alloway had, however, "turned the knives out on the bench", though he had not noticed any stain of blood on any of them or that any knife was missing.

After Alloway came Dr. Parsons, whose examination took some considerable time. In the course of it, as was to be expected, he, too, repeated much of his former evidence. Certain parts of his testimony, however, must be quoted here.

"There was not a large quantity of blood on the blanket itself.... The first wound I observed was upon the throat; it appeared to be one cut.... A considerable quantity of blood had flowed from the left angle of the wound down to the arm and elbow.... I observed black marks near the mouth. It had been pressed for a considerable time—say from five to ten minutes, and by a soft substance....

"At the time my impression was that the throat had not been cut where the body was found, because *I found no jets of blood such as would have proceeded from arteries being cut. I should have expected to find marks of jets of blood upon the child if the throat had been cut whilst the child was alive, but I did not find any such appearance.* It has since occurred to me that *the circulation of the blood had been stopped by pressure upon the mouth before the throat had been cut.* In that case life would have been almost extinct before the throat was cut....

"I think the stab in the side was inflicted after death, because there was no retraction of the parts, and no blood was flowing....

"The pillow had the marks of the depression of the child's head upon it, and also the depression where he had slept, but the sheet and counterpane were perfectly smooth.... I could not have folded it down so without considerable trouble. It was very neatly folded, as if by a practised hand."

Asked whether he had an opinion as to the cause of death, he said:

"Certainly. *My opinion is that the child died by suffocation, and then the wound in the throat and then the stab in the chest.* I cannot say that the wounds had *nothing* to do with the child's death. It might not have been *quite dead* when the cut in the throat was made. . . . It may have been suffocated to the extent of stopping the action of the heart. My opinion is that there had been heavy pressure upon the mouth, but whether to the extent of causing death I cannot say. I have not always been of opinion that the child had first been suffocated. . . . I have formed that opinion from a more mature reflection. . . . I speak *positively* as to the pressure on the mouth, but I speak doubtfully as to whether the pressure was the cause of death. I should say the pressure had been made by considerable violence."

So Dr. Parsons was sticking to his guns, quite certain that the child had first been suffocated but being brave enough to admit that he didn't know whether that suffocation had been fatal or only *near*-fatal.

The suffocation theory gave support to the popular notion that Kent was the guilty one, and for this reason Dr. Stapleton—who had assisted at the *post-mortem*—would not countenance such a theory. After all, the sole purpose of his book was to vindicate Kent, his friend; therefore he could hardly lend support to any theory that tended to incriminate him. And the more Dr. Parsons insisted that suffocation had *at least contributed* to the child's death the more Dr. Stapleton denied it. "The suffocation theory is untenable," he would declaim, "for that he died by the knife is a scientific and inevitable conclusion." However, he could produce no evidence to support his claim and when called upon to account for the total absence of the signs of spraying or spurting as would result from the severing of living arteries he was unable to do so. Not that he didn't *try. He* accounted for the absence of spraying blood by saying that at the moment of death the terrified child's heart had *"stood still"*!—adding, further, that after death the sides of the throat wound had been pressed together so that *the blood had drained from the body into the head!* In his book Stapleton labours his point so long, so loudly, and with such monotonous regularity that one also begins to wonder whether he was somehow affected by the fact that no one ever *sought* his opinion regarding the child's death—he must needs always proffer it, unsolicited. There must be something in the fact that of all the many people involved in the affair he was one of the *least* involved, while of all of them he was the one to make the greatest fuss; for witness see his book; throughout it he is like a resentful reserve player who fears—and with reason—that he will never be asked to join in the game.

Dr. Parsons was followed by Captain Meredith, and after he had stepped down a minor sensation ensued when the five-year-old Mary Amelia was carried in in the arms of Elizabeth, her appearance eliciting from the spectators those breathed *aah*'s and *ooh*'s that the British public reserves exclusively for children and animals. Mr. Saunders, looking at the little girl, said he could not think what she was going to depose, but he wished her to be examined as he understood that when taken before Mr. Slack for questioning Mr. Dunn had objected. However, said Mr. Saunders, as the child had slept in her parents' room on the night of the crime there was interest in what she might be able to say that was relevant.

The chairman of the bench, making an attempt to swear-in this new witness, asked her whether she knew her catechism. The only result of this was Mary Amelia showing the greatest alarm and turning away to cling even tighter to her sister.

"Do you think she knows the nature of an oath?" asked Sir John Awdry.

"I don't believe she does," Elizabeth answered.

Some discussion took place then as to the reason the child had not been examined in Mr. Slack's office, and Mr. Edlin said it was because Mr. Slack had found her "too young and too much agitated to give an answer to any inquiry put to her". This was remiss of Mr. Edlin—to speak for Mr. Slack when Mr. Slack was there to speak for himself, and Mr. Slack let Mr. Edlin know it.

"The reason this little girl was not interrogated by me was for quite a different reason from that given by Mr. Edlin," Slack said. "The fact is, Mr. Dunn—Mr. Kent's solicitor—evinced a desire that I should *not* interrogate her. I wished to see whether she was capable of answering or not; I asked her if she knew where she would go if she died after telling a falsehood, and she replied that she would go to hell if she did that."

"That, in ordinary cases," said the chairman, "would cause her evidence to be admissible."

"I then began to examine her," Mr. Slack went on, "but Mr. Dunn peremptorily *refused* to allow her to be examined."

This caused a great stir in the court, and Mr. Edlin, desperate to have at least one last word, said, "I am sorry Mr. Dunn is not present, or we would have his explanation." Following which, the little girl was taken out of the court, with the understanding that if her evidence was thought necessary she should be examined later.

Eliza Dallimore came next. During her appearance there she stated that she had examined the nightdress on the bed belonging to Constance, "but found nothing upon it. . . . It appeared to have been worn some nights, perhaps for a week". She told also how she had taken the piece of flannel and tried it on the nurse: "It fitted her exactly, and was a good fit. . . . It did not fit the other servants."

There was another incident she related with regard to Elizabeth Gough which, for a few moments, generated rapt attention. On the afternoon following the murder, Mrs. Dallimore said, she and the nurse had been sitting at the kitchen table when Fricker came in. The nurse, turning at the sound of his step, said: "What have you been doing, Fricker?" to which he replied that he had been open-ing the water-closet. "And did you find anything?" the girl asked him. "No," he said. Mrs. Dallimore, now relating the episode, went on:

"The nurse said then, 'You won't.' "

It was this last statement, being misunderstood, which caused the brief stir. Had the nurse said, *"Then you won't"*? But no; Mrs. Dallimore made it clear the next second; the nurse, she told the examiners, had merely said, *"You won't."* The stir of interest died.

It was revived again when she made reference to a repetition of the experiment with the cot. This had taken place that very morning at Road Hill House. With Superintendent Wolfe conducting the moves, Mrs. Kent had placed baby Eveline in Savill's cot while Mrs. Dallimore had knelt on the nurse's bed. Now Mrs. Dallimore told Mr. Saunders:

"I looked across from the bedstead to the cot to see if I could see the child, but I could see nothing but a little portion of the end of the pillow. I could see nothing of the child." Then she added, "The child was afterwards taken out."

"Of course," said Mr. Ribton, "—the child was not left there, was it?"

The laughter at this put Mrs. Dallimore quite firmly on the defensive. Feeling that the defence counsel was trying to make her the object of ridicule she began to answer with some flippancy, several times going so far as to reprimand the learned gentleman. Against Mr. Ribton, though, she couldn't win.

Speaking of the nurse, Mr. Ribton said he had been told that she had never worn a flannel in her life, then, turning to Mrs. Dallimore, asked: "It is usually old ladies who wear flannels, is it not?"

Mrs. Dallimore: "And many young persons wear them—I wear one myself." This brought loud laughter, for Mrs. Dallimore "was not of the age generally called 'young'."

"I am certainly not going to ask you your age," Mr. Ribton said while the laughter continued. "Do young healthy women wear them—young, healthy women, remember?"—at which the witness, not giving way, came back with: "Yes, sir; why, *I wear one myself*."

Even louder laughter at this. As it died away, Mrs. Dallimore, more put-out than ever, said: "I don't think so serious a matter should be turned to ridicule. It gives me the horrors to think about it."

Mr. Ribton: "You are very irritable, are you not?"

"Yes, sir. Perhaps you are, too."

"Then don't give *us* the horrors."

Over the period of question-and-answer that followed Mrs. Dallimore gave the information that she had not searched among the prisoner's other clothes to see whether she might have a chest-flannel there; neither had the prisoner—at the time when she had been physically examined—worn such a garment—though she *had* been wearing a flannel petticoat.

The policeman's wife was instructed to step down. She did so. Her encounter with the prisoner's defence counsel had taken the form of a minor battle which, seeing that she was about to come off the loser, she had tried to fight with obtuseness and near-insolence. And she had still lost.

Mr. Kent was recalled then, and following his testimony regarding a former nursemaid[7] who had left his employ "vowing vengeance against the children"—which, she had apparently stated, were "horrid children", particularly "the little boy"—the court was adjourned till the next day.

Thursday the 4th of October saw the courtroom as packed as before, and Elizabeth Gough on her arrival "looking far more anxious".

Mrs. Dallimore was recalled by the prosecution to relate conversations that had taken place with the prisoner when the latter had been staying in the Dallimores' house at Trowbridge, but with the subsequent encounter with the defence counsel—who even used threats to shake her reserve—she emerged from the examination with the validity of her testimony in some question. And neither was this helped by the appearance of P.C. Dallimore who followed his wife into the witness box. In testifying to those same conversations that had taken place between himself, his wife and the prisoner he corroborated his wife's evidence—and Mr. Ribton at once drew attention to this.

"You have come to corroborate your wife, and we will see how far you do so. You will no doubt have a curtain-lecture tonight; I fancy it won't be the first."

There was laughter at this, and Dallimore quickly remarked, "Perhaps I ain't the only one."

The constable's testimony ended the case for the prosecution and, as no witnesses had been called for the defence, Mr. Ribton addressed the court on the prisoner's behalf. The main points of his speech were as follows:

It was *not* impossible that some person had secreted himself in the house, committed the murder through malice directed towards Mr. Kent and then escaped undetected. If there was any suspicion against the prisoner there was equal suspicion against Mr. Kent, and an even stronger case against Constance. Mr. Ribton pointed out that Mr. Slack's inquiry had been promoted with a view to eliciting information, yet Mr. Kent and his family had consistently been protected at these inquiries by Mr. Dunn who had frequently

[7] One Annie Paul.

objected to certain questions put forward. Where, asked the defence counsel, had there been similar protection for the others called by Mr. Slack? And as for the prisoner, *she* had not been examined by Mr. Slack *at all*. Yet she had expressed herself ready at any time to answer further questions. The only inference from that proceeding, was that Mr. Slack's inquiry was for the sole purpose of building a case against the nurse; she herself had been given no opportunity to resolve any questions that remained against her.

He dismissed, totally, the evidence of Mrs. Dallimore, saying he had seldom seen "anything so disgraceful in a witness". "Her conduct had rendered her testimony in other respects utterly and entirely valueless." And what of those three things urged against the nurse? Her conflicting statements about the blanket might simply be the result of agitation on her part; the "good fit" of the flannel proved nothing; even if it had belonged to the nurse it would merely prove that the murderer had been in her bedroom—and everyone knew that, anyway. As for the possibility of her being able to see into the child's cot from a kneeling position on her bed—it would be ridiculous to interpret too literally the phrase "kneeling up".

Before the magistrates returned to give their decision their chairman, Sir John Awdry, appeared to ask whether any relatives of the nurse were present—this for the purpose of "ascertaining if the accused could readily obtain bail, if necessary". Whilst the prisoner "appeared greatly agitated" Mr. Ribton said that two uncles of the nurse were present in the courtroom. A few minutes later, with all the magistrates assembled once more, Sir John, seeing the anxious looks of the prisoner, announced that it was not proposed to commit the nurse for trial. The spectators applauded at this, following which the chairman said there was insufficient evidence to cause them to brand her with such a stigma as committal to prison would cause. "Yet," he said, "I do not say there is no material evidence before us which may, hereafter, perhaps with additions, be in some way or another acted upon; and therefore the magistrates' decision is this: that though they will not commit her for trial they will bind her to appear if she may be required to appear again. As she has friends here they must have thought that sureties in a moderate sum may be required for her. . . . The amount we thought of was £100 . . . either in a single sum or two of £50 each."

Elizabeth Gough's actual release was still a few minutes away, however. Mr. Dunn, in attempting to justify his interference during Mr. Slack's examinations, got himself into deeper water by eliciting from Sir John Awdry the comment that he, Mr. Dunn, *had* objected to certain questions being asked. Mr. Dunn felt naturally moved to protect his reputation, and said: "I objected to certain questions because I thought they did not tend to the interests of one person in the house." At this admission Sir John remarked that therefore Mr. Kent had been *very ill-advised*; surely the wishes of the family in such a "painful and harassing" situation "would be that the very fullest and searching inquiry should be instituted".

Mr. Dunn: "I am sure you will allow me to say, after that remark, that everything I have done, and everything I have advised Mr. Kent to do has been to the best of his interests; and I must say that the questions I objected to were such as never should have been put in Mr. Kent's house. . . ."

Said Mr. Ribton: "I do not wish to say anything disrespectful to Mr. Dunn, but I must say that Mr. Kent might have been better advised."

Mr. Edlin, of course, had to have his say, and speak up on behalf of Mr. Kent; after all, that's what he was being paid for. Now he said:

"That having been said in my presence, I must be allowed to say one word. There are witnesses present who are aware of the anxiety shown by Mr. Kent to afford *every facility* to the magistrates, to the police and by every mode of investigation. It would be detrimental to his interests if it were thought that he has in *any way* or at *any time* withheld information. It would convey what is not the truth. Therefore, Sir John, I trust that you will allow me—and I beg it to go forth—to say that Mr. Kent *has not offered any obstacle* to the most full and searching inquiry."

Sir John Awdry: "I don't wish to say anything unkind, but it having come under our notice that in the first instance policemen were locked up in the kitchen, and that until lately he refused a plan of the premises to be taken, it is impossible to say that he has been well advised on that point."

Mr. Edlin: "One other word upon that: in reference to Mr.

Kent and the plan spoken of. We did not know against whom it was proposed to take proceedings. Had the information been given us as to the parties it was required for, no obstacle would have been offered."

At this rather shocking—and naïve—admission that a full investigation *had* been hampered—and at Mr. Kent's behest—Sir John said: "It would have been wiser, *without knowing what use was to be made of the plan*, to have allowed every publicity." Mr. Peter Edlin was later to become Sir Peter Edlin, Q.C., and knowing that, it must be wished that in his future work he demonstrated better judgement than he showed in connection with the Road affair. One might also hope that, following that last exchange, he possessed sufficient sensitivity to feel considerably subdued.

One thing that did follow that exchange—to which Elizabeth Gough and the spectators had listened intently—was the discharge of the prisoner. Her uncle, Mr. Arthur Spackman of Blackheath, "became bail for the whole sum of £100" and, free again, the young nursemaid returned home by the night train to London.

The applause inside the court and the general approbation outside that had greeted the news of Elizabeth Gough's release were testimonies to the wave of sympathy that had been generated on her behalf. Not so for Mr. Kent, however. He came out of the proceedings very badly, and that last loaded conversation between the chairman and the lawyers gave further ammunition to those who were already disposed to think ill of him.

That Sunday, the 7th of October, when Mr. Kent and his family left the house for the very short walk to Christ Church on the hill they were greeted by a vindictive mob who shook fists in Mr. Kent's face and shouted, "Murderer!" at him, and, "Who killed his own son!" Mrs. Kent, it is reported, was so much affected that, almost fainting, she had to be helped into the sanctuary of the church porch.

Chapter 23

A MOST UNORTHODOX INQUIRY

The release of Elizabeth Gough naturally kept the journalists and their editors busy, and all were agreed that the mystery's solution lay with some person or persons who had slept that night in Road Hill House. Members of the public, too, continued to offer criticism, hints, information and assistance. To *The Times* one correspondent, signing himself "Commonsense", wrote at length on the matter, making some pertinent observations. Parts of his letter are as follows:

We know that parents have murdered their children, and sisters their brothers since the world began, and will do so again before the world ends, and it remains to be seen whether a crime of that atrocity has now been committed. Great stress has been laid on the fact that Mrs. Kent is supposed to have been a light sleeper, and that she was in a peculiar state of health that rendered her morbidly watchful; but, as there is no doubt that some person removed the boy from the room next to hers without being heard by her, it is clear that she slept sound enough on the night of the murder not to hear what was done; therefore her alleged wakeful position proves nothing. Moreover, all sick-nurses know how apt invalids are to protest that they have not closed their eyes, when they have unconsciously slept soundly for hours. . . . She [Mrs. Kent] stated that [her husband] had not left her side for more than a quarter of an hour during the night. How did she know that?

No traces of the murder have been discovered on the premises . . . ought we not, therefore, to think which of the inmates of the house had the best opportunity of disposing of such evidence of the crime before the police arrived—before any search took place—before there was any suspicion of murder at all? Mr. Kent is stated to have left the house in his carriage to seek a policeman who lived at a distance. . . . Is the precise road he took known—has it been searched thoroughly?

The nurse's conduct, to say the least, appears suspicious; it was undoubtedly grossly negligent, yet Mr. Kent has shown no *animus* against her. He did not even dismiss her from his service after the event, while he had no scruple in casting suspicion against a discharged nurse who has been shown to have had nothing to do with the matter. . . . Between Mr. Kent and the nurse there is clearly no ill-will.

Why did Mr. Kent lock up the policemen?

It is very possible that some or all of these questions may have been already answered satisfactorily by Mr. Kent, but it does not appear from the published evidence that they have been; they are in everybody's mind and in everybody's mouth, and it is for the interest of Mr. Kent if he is innocent, and for the interest of justice if he is guilty, that they shall be publicly met and dealt with.

The Morning Star wrote giving voice to the growing demand that the original coroner's inquest be quashed and a new inquiry held, on the grounds that the coroner's inquisition "was conducted in a shamefully bungling fashion". Said that journal:

. . . A coroner's inquest, three magisterial inquiries and a private inquisition . . . have been brought to a close leaving us very little wiser than we were before. . . . The criminal still continues to elude the grasp of justice. Of the two individuals who have been accused, one comes forth from the ordeal pure and stainless, and against the other there exist no proofs sufficiently conclusive to serve as a safe basis for the verdict of a jury. . . .

Sir John Eardley Wilmot, still convinced that the crime was committed by "a paramour from without", wrote again to the Home Secretary offering his services "for the purpose of elucidating the truth". Mr. Slack's inquiry, he wrote, "has materially added to the difficulties of the case, but they have rendered detection of the real offender far from impossible". Mr. Waddington, after politely declining the offer, commented:

"Does he wish to be employed as a detective or what?"

With the fact emerging at the nurse's examination that two policemen had been locked up in Mr. Kent's house on the night after the crime fascination with the mystery grew even stronger. It also tended to divert suspicion away from Constance and place it more firmly upon the heads of Mr. Kent and the nursemaid; it was *very* strong against Mr. Kent and, notwithstanding the fact that the nurse had been released, she was viewed as the only possible accomplice Mr. Kent could have had. With the confirmation of the rumour about Urch and Heritage being locked in, the plot appeared to thicken and the magistrates called a meeting where they questioned the two officers involved in the incident. The police, though, it seemed, were as much in the dark as were the magistrates, and after the inquiry the magistrates, none the wiser, discussed what, if any, their next course of action should be.

It was at this meeting that one of their number, Mr. Thomas Bush Saunders, a retired barrister from Bradford-on-Avon, made a speech in which he said he had been informed that a great deal of evidence, which had not yet been publicly given, could yet be adduced to throw light upon the mysterious crime; he would not call the crime "murder", as it was quite possible that it might turn out to be a case of manslaughter instead. Concluding his speech, he moved that a special committee of magistrates should be appointed for the purpose of inquiring into the circumstances of the death.

This motion did not meet with the approval of the Trowbridge magistrates. Mr. Saunders, however, was not to be daunted. His mind was made up, he said, and if those gentlemen would not agree, then he would pursue the course without them. Not that he would be alone, he informed them, as he had been promised support by his brother magistrates on the Bradford bench, and also that of Captain Meredith and the local police. It was with *this* backing that he contacted the Home Office and, soon after, in the last week of October, followed it with a visit to London to request the Home Secretary for official sanction for his proposed scheme.

Not surprisingly he didn't get it. Neither, though, did the Home Secretary forbid him to pursue such a course; he could hardly do that since as far as any witnesses were concerned their attendance at the proposed inquiry would be purely a matter of their own choice; no one could be forced to testify and no evidence could be taken on oath. Even so, while stating that it was his "duty to afford every assistance in his power" for the discovery of the criminal, Sir George Lewis nevertheless tried to dissuade Mr. Saunders from carrying out his plan. Mr. Saunders, however, was not to be dissuaded, and at the Temperance Hall just after noon on Saturday, 3rd of November, his extraordinary inquiry commenced.

And *so* extraordinary were those proceedings, and so much ridicule and scorn did they attract, that the Wiltshire magistrates felt compelled to make it known that they had no part in it, writing hurriedly to the Home Secretary that Mr. Saunders' inquiry "now being conducted at Road" was not sanctioned by *them*. Replied Sir George Lewis: "I strongly urged him to take no step until he had something more to go on than the hearsay evidence he related to me—but he persisted."

Mr. Saunders' purpose in holding the inquiry was, as he had stated, to gather relevant information that so far had not come to light. With this laudable object in view he invited all those who had knowledge to impart to come forward; at the same time, in accordance with the results of his own inquiries he sent specific requests to certain individuals asking for their attendance. Regarding those inquiries of his own he said in his opening speech:

"As some of you are aware, I have been many a day, and many a night too, travelling your neighbourhood, trying all I could to discover something more; and I think I shall be able to show that there yet remains a great deal to be made public, with which the public—and perhaps the police too—are not acquainted."

The police of Wiltshire, on that first day, were well represented. Sitting beside Mr. Saunders on the platform was the ubiquitous Captain Meredith, while superintendents Foley and Wolfe were also present together with a strong body of other members of the force. It all looked very proper and, no doubt, very impressive.

Apart from the police there were few others there that day to hear Mr. Saunders' opening address—this was due to lack of publicity—but word soon spread and the numbers swelled. Many of those who came, though, did so purely in the hope of being entertained, seeing the whole proceedings as a diversion from the common cares of a dull November day. That they subsequently viewed the inquiry much as one would a live theatre show is understandable: Mr. Saunders' inquiry was soon to be regarded as nothing more than a farce. Spectators laughed and joked amongst themselves and others gave testimony when it was quite clear that they had nothing to say and were just intent on being the centre of attention. Sometimes there were no witnesses at all, in which case Mr. Saunders would talk at length about letters he had received—but which he "had better not read aloud", and *most interesting* meetings he had had—which he "had better not discuss"; and on several occasions while the handful of spectators waited for the day's proceedings to begin Mr. Saunders himself would be absent. The inquiry lasted until the 12th of November and it is not surprising that it ended as it did—not as the result of a conscious decision, but simply dying—a slow death.

Yseult Bridges claims that Mr. Saunders' inquiry failed because it was "obstructed—by putting pressure on witnesses to keep them away, by encouraging a noisy *claque* to heckle and cause confusion, and by the copious use of ridicule". This is nonsense. Mr. Saunders was his own obstruction. A glance at the transcript of the inquiry shows that all the ridicule he suffered was brought about totally by his own conduct and was, if not all deserved, then at least to be expected. The interior of the Temperance Hall must often-times have resembled a school-room in which the unruly pupils know that their incompetent teacher has lost control over them.

Not that the proceedings were always chaotic by any means. There were many times, particularly when the inquiry was new, when Mr. Saunders gained their attention and made the most of an interested audience. When no witnesses were available he generally passed these times by just sitting and talking at them at length, mercurially skipping from one subject to another, seemingly with no clear purpose in view. The general tenor of these edifying addresses finds fair illustration in incident after incident; for example, on one occasion Mr. Saunders, wishing to refer to a particular date, took from his pocket a small almanac which, he informed his audience, was called *The Bradford-on-Avon Almanac and Annual Advertiser for 1860*—"a very useful little book". He had made this same comment, he said, when first seeing the almanac. He went on: "I did not mention that fact with a view to any benefit from it; I was going to purchase it, only the gentleman presented it to me, and I said, 'All contributions thankfully received.' " Mr. Saunders then observed in a "disconnected" manner:

"It has my private initials on it." Opening the book he then began to refer to certain dates within, remarking to the assembly that if those dates were wrong he hoped someone would tell him. "There was an instance," he said, "in Ireland when an almanac was fabricated for the purpose of saving a man's life. . . ."

And so he would go on . . . and on. . . .

The Bristol Daily Post commented upon one particular day's proceedings:

> The audience, or at least nine-tenths of it, was composed of women and children, and did not appear to comprise many respectable persons. As may be gathered from the report which we have given of the proceedings, the evidence, if evidence it may be called, was adduced in a most singular and undignified manner, question and answer being bandied about from magistrate and witness to the crowd in the court, without anything approaching either regularity or decency. On several occasions those present were at no pains to conceal the laughter which the proceedings were calculated to give rise to, and all throughout they seemed to consider that the whole affair was got up for their special amusement, rather than for the elucidation of a mysterious and terrible crime.

When it is realized that the above report refers to only the *second* day of the inquiry it will also be understood that with such a bad start the situation was not likely to improve. In actuality that situation just went from bad to worse.

Notwithstanding the fact that much of Mr. Saunders' time was spent telling stories that were totally irrelevant to the case, and likewise much of that information given by many of the witnesses was also useless, it would still be surprising if, throughout all those hours of inquiry, nothing at all of interest was adduced. And certain things were. Ann Stokes, in whose house the nurse had waited to be called for examination by the magistrates, described the girl's behaviour on those occasions—which Inspector Pitney confirmed—and further to that both Mrs. Heritage and Mrs. Hall testified that on the morning of the crime Mr. Kent had told each of them that his child had been taken away in a blanket. It was also established that a certain Mr. Quance, a local man, had broadcast to the area that at about five o'clock on the morning of the crime he had seen

Mr. Kent, shirtsleeved, in a field close to Road Hill House.[1] All this, of course, strengthened the suspicions held against Mr. Kent and the nurse, while existing belief in Constance's innocence took a further boost with the testimony of a local reporter, one George Groser, who said that on the morning of the inquest he had been in the hall of Road Hill House and had seen Constance coming down the main staircase. On seeing him, however, he said, she had stopped, turned around and gone back upstairs. This, to her champions, served to support her story that she had started out *herself* to fetch water but, as she had told Cox, did not do so as there were "people downstairs".

A great deal of the more interesting information imparted at Mr. Saunders' inquiry had already been given earlier, in private, to the Bath solicitor Mr. Slack. Now, however, as it was heard in public—and freely reported in the newspapers—it became, of course, nationally known. Mr. Slack's dossier which had remained conspicuously closed throughout the examination of Elizabeth Gough never was made public, therefore we must be grateful to Mr. Saunders who, if he did nothing else, at least provided the means whereby certain pieces of most valuable evidence have passed into the general knowledge.

There were other interesting points raised in the "farrago of nonsense in which the greater part of the sittings were wasted", but by far the most important, as far as the Trowbridge magistrates were concerned, was the fact that, in the late afternoon after the crime a stained garment had been found secreted in the boiler-hole in the scullery of Road Hill House. This, needless to say, was the chemise, all knowledge of which had, until now, stayed hidden. Somehow, though, word of it had reached the receptive ears of Mr. Saunders and in the Temperance Hall on Thursday, November the 8th, he asked P.C. Urch:

"Were you present when Sergeant Watts, in Road Hill House, found a certain thing?"

Urch: "I was."

"What was it?"

"Some woman's night-shift."

[1] When Quance was later questioned by the police on the matter he retreated, saying that he would not *swear* that it had been Mr. Kent.

"Some woman's shift," said Mr. Saunders. "I don't want to mislead you; was it a *night*-shift, then, or a *night-or-day*-shift?"

"It was a *shift*. It might have been worn night *and* day; it was such as is worn at all times."

So, news of the chemise (or shift) was out at last. Foley's almost perfectly kept secret. The result was to be a great deal of embarrassment, much self-justification and, more importantly, much confusion that would, for a while, mislead the criminal-seekers—that same confusion that has managed to mislead writers even in recent times.

The magistrates, on learning of the chemise's discovery and subsequent loss, were naturally most anxious about the matter. Could it be, they wondered, that that stained garment found in the boiler-hole was, in fact, Constance Kent's missing nightdress? Mr. W. Stancomb, on behalf of his brother magistrates, immediately set out to make inquiries.

While Mr. Stancomb was asking *his* questions there were other questions being asked that related to a different aspect of the case.

Following Elizabeth Gough's release Sir John Awdry had received a letter stating that a girl of the same name and fitting the description of the discharged prisoner had been employed for a period over the years 1858 and 1859 by a certain Mr. Hawtrey of Eton. The letter described her as "an artful girl" and said she had been discharged from Mr. Hawtrey's household owing to her "misconduct". Elizabeth Gough's past employment had recently become the subject of considerable talk, and the letter received by Sir John Awdry was not the only one on the matter; even Mr. Saunders hinted, in the course of one his days at the Temperance Hall, at having received a similar missive. The one that concerns us here, however, is that one sent to Sir John.

This particular letter was, after some unavoidable delay, passed to the police and on the 23rd of November Captain Meredith wrote to the Metropolitan Police Office asking for a check to be made to ascertain whether the Elizabeth Gough discharged from Mr. Hawtrey's house was the same Elizabeth Gough who had so lately been in Mr. Kent's employ. Whicher wrote back at once to the effect that Mr. Hawtrey had already been to the bakery at Isleworth and, on meeting Elizabeth Gough there, found that she was "not the same one".

This really was a most curious incident and it is a great pity that the matter was dropped so quickly without any further inquiries being made. Certain questions immediately come to mind: Why did *Mr. Hawtrey* not inform the authorities that a girl of the same name and answering the same description had been discharged from his house for misconduct?—surely that would have been the natural thing to do, *supposing that he himself had nothing to hide.* As it was the police learned of it from a letter written by a neighbour or acquaintance of the Eton gentleman. Also, what was that "misconduct" for which Mr. Hawtrey's employee was discharged? —and was she discharged at the instigation of Mr. Hawtrey *or of his wife*? Should it have been that the misconduct involved Mr. Hawtrey himself—or perhaps a grown son—then he would be the last person to want his erstwhile servant identified; that would only bring upon himself and his family a scandal which all England would soon know about! It does appear, from Mr. Hawtrey's behaviour, as if he had something to conceal.

If someone other than he—perhaps a neighbour—had been asked to go and see Elizabeth Gough, the result of the visit might have been quite different. For, make no mistake, the similarity between the two girls did not rest solely upon their bearing the same name —not a particularly common combination, anyway. No, they were the same age and were said to look alike, so much so that "each Elizabeth Gough had lost a front tooth, and they were corresponding teeth"![2]

Also, if they *were* one and the same person it might account for the strange fact that Elizabeth Gough came to the Kents as a nursemaid, when previously she had held the much higher position of lady's maid.

If Elizabeth Gough suffered some traumatic moments when confronted by Mr. Hawtrey in the bakery that day, it is a certainty that at Road Hill House the atmosphere was far from serene. Constance, it had been decided, must go away, and to a different country. In England she could only be the object of curiosity and

[2] J. W. Stapleton.

endless discussion, apart from which her continued presence amongst her family was the source of too much discomfort. There was a third reason for her removal from the house and from her homeland: whilst remaining she could never hope to feel safe from those official pursuers of justice who had not wavered in their belief in her guilt. And so arrangements for her departure were made.

Not long before she left she wrote to Mr. Edlin to thank him for a gift he had made to her. Her letter, dated the 23rd of November, reads:

> Dear Mr. Edlin,
>
> I write to thank you for the pretty pair of mittens and the scarf which I received yesterday; they will no doubt prove very useful and will remind me whenever I look at them of how much I am indebted to the giver. Fortunately they were not left in the train; Mr. Dunn found them in the courthouse and gave them to Papa when he went into Frome.
>
> I like them exceedingly and shall always value them very much.
>
> > With many thanks,
> > > Believe me,
> > > > Yours truly,
> > > > > Constance E. Kent.

Not only for her pretty mittens and the scarf was Constance "indebted to the giver".

Soon afterwards she left England for France where, in Dinan, she had been enrolled as a pupil at a fashionable finishing school—without the use of her first name, however; now she was just Emily Kent.

And what of her thoughts as she crossed the English Channel that day? Were they fixed upon her future—whatever and wherever that might be? What of her family?—had they watched her departure with feelings of regret or relief? Perhaps both. Did she wonder when and where she might see them again? She and her stepmother were never more to meet—but Constance was not to know that—and the thought would hardly have occurred to her. No, she would probably have had only one thing on her mind—putting the past behind her.

Chapter 24

FINAL EFFORTS

While Mr. Thomas Bush Saunders' bizarre inquiry was in progress other wheels were in motion seeking a more positive means of finding the solution to the mystery. Something had to be done, that much was certain. Two young women had been charged with the crime and had been released on bail, *both* still remaining under the cloud of a murder charge—and for the same murder. At least two men had made false confessions—one, a certain John Edmund Gagg, a thirty-year-old bricklayer from London, had given himself up on the 10th of August saying he had committed the murder for money—but "never got any for it"—and shortly afterwards asking: "Do you think they can try Miss Constance again?" A searching inquiry before the magistrates, however, soon established that he could not possibly be guilty and he was promptly released, his discharge putting an abrupt end to the great wave of excitement which his arrest had caused.

Now in the opinion of many the only course left open was to have the original inquest quashed and a new one held; and this time to ensure that it was properly conducted. Mr. Saunders, on learning of the magistrates' new plan decided, on the 15th of November, to "suspend" his inquiry—pending the outcome of the magistrates' application. In truth he must have been thankful for an excuse that allowed him to put an end to the proceedings with even the smallest show of dignity; for certain it was that he could not have continued much longer; his audiences now had shrunk to a mere handful and he counted himself lucky if he had *one* policeman in attendance there. Further to that, in just a week or so the Bradford magistrates were to make it known through the newspapers that they *never had* sanctioned his inquiry in the first place. On the Thursday, that last day of his inquiry, he was most insistent that he was merely *suspending* the proceedings; it was not, he said, the end. But he must have known it was.

The Justices who considered the Attorney-General's well-constructed application for a new inquest decided that, out of fairness to the coroner, it would not be right to grant the request—arguing that such a move would be likely to have a disastrous effect upon his career. They did, however, agree to pass a rule putting the onus on that coroner, Mr. George Sylvester, calling on him *to show why the original inquest should not be quashed*. By such means he would be given an opportunity to defend himself against his accusers. Should he fail then there was little doubt that a new inquiry must be held—and not conducted by Mr. Sylvester, either, but by a Special Commissioner.

Unfortunately there was to be no swift resolving of the question; the rule was granted only on the last day of the term and therefore there would be no chance to see it argued until the beginning of the next one, the Hilary Term, which commenced on the 11th of January, 1861. Till then there was nothing to be done but wait patiently and hope for the best.

In the meantime the magistrates were not being idle. Mr. Stancomb had finished his inquiries regarding the discovery of the chemise and, on the 30th of November, exactly five months from the day of the crime, a public meeting was held so that the whole matter could be brought into the open, discussed and disposed of. Mr. Stancomb's inquiries had convinced him and his brother magistrates that the garment had had no part in the crime but it was necessary also to satisfy the public of this. There were many who, on learning of the discovery of the chemise, believed it had been Constance's missing nightdress—a belief shared by Whicher who wrote to the magistrates:

Sir,

In reference to the recent disclosure relative to the local police having found on the day of the murder a blood-stained garment secreted in the boiler-hole in the kitchen of Mr. Kent's house, which circumstances, it appears, was not made known by them to the magistrates, I beg to state also that it was never mentioned to me by any member of the police during the fortnight I was engaged with them at Road assisting in the inquiry and in daily communication with Superintendent Foley and his associates who, it appears, were present when the garment was found. . . . I beg to state that I was no party to it for, as before stated, the fact was never made known to me.

That Whicher believed the garment to have been Constance's nightdress he made perfectly clear in another letter he wrote at the time—to the Chief of the Bath Police. That it was *not* the missing nightdress, however, was made evident by the inquiry when all those who might be remotely connected with its discovery were questioned at length before the public. Among those examined were Sarah Kerslake—who testified to having lit the boiler at the usual time of seven o'clock that morning, so *proving* that the chemise must have been lodged there *after* the fire had gone out—and those persons who had seen and examined the garment. These included Watts, Foley, Dallimore, Mrs. Dallimore and Fricker—and each of them made known his personal belief that the stains on the garment had been due to natural causes. The fact that Fricker voiced the same opinion is important. He was a totally disinterested party and had no reason to perjure himself on behalf of any "cover-up". The same could be said of Sergeant Watts; he was from a different police force and owed no allegiance to Foley or his men—particularly when, in this case, it could well have cost him his job. Watts, having no reason at all to speak anything but the truth, said he was of the belief that "the blood had been caused from the inside", and ended his statement: "The stain was greater behind than before."

When Foley was asked whether he was *certain* that a medical man had seen the chemise he said: "I wouldn't actually swear that any medical man saw it. I understood that Mr. Stapleton had seen it, but I can't state positively whether he did or not." Stapleton, however, whose conduct in the matter of the chemise and the nightdress had been called into question, denied having seen it—though he could do little else in the circumstances. The only garment he had seen, he said, was the nightdress belonging to Mary Ann—which he had seen on three separate occasions. He had seen it the first time, he told the magistrates, when it was shown to him by "a policeman" on the afternoon of the crime, and the second time, just two hours later, when it lay in the wagonette in the stable-yard. His third view of it, he said, was on the Monday morning—at which time Dr. Parsons had *also* seen it.

Dr. Stapleton's story didn't hold up, however, for it was clearly established that the only garment lying in the wagonette had been the chemise—Mrs. Dallimore having Mary Ann's nightdress in her keeping. As Foley told the magistrates: "Mr. Stapleton didn't see the nightdress till Monday, and if he saw the one in the yard in the cart it must be the one in question;" (the chemise). Further to that, Dr. Parsons firmly denied having seen *any garment with a stain on it—at any time*.

Stapleton also fell down when it came to describing the garment he said he had examined. While from the policemen, Fricker and Mrs. Dallimore one gets a perfect picture of the chemise's cut, material and condition, one hears from Stapleton only: "On no garment that I saw was there anything that could be associated with the death of the child. . . . I can say nothing of the shape, make or texture of the garment shown me on the first occasion. There were stains on it; I can't say whether it was a nightdress. . . ." Hardly the statements of an observant man.

Sir John Awdry (presiding over the inquiry), referring to Foley's stated reason for not showing the chemise to the magistrates, said: "By 'Don't expose the girl,' did you refer to a matter of decency, or had you any other motive?"

Foley: "Solely and wholly out of decency, nothing else. I did not believe it had anything whatever to do with the child's death; I considered it would be an indecent and improper thing to expose it publicly; I have seen many filthy garments, but never saw a filthier one than that in question. I am satisfied that a married man and an experienced man would see that it in no way related to the crime."

Mr. Ludlow: "You made up your minds to whom it belonged but, not wishing to expose the girl's dirty habits, you did not show it?"

Foley: "I am sorry I did not show it to you. I know it was neglect on my part, but I am satisfied it in no way related to the murder."

Mr. Ludlow: "You should have shown it to the magistrates, who would have referred it to a medical man, who would have reported upon it, and the matter would have been dropped."

Foley: "I had but one object in view, and that was to bring justice to the guilty party."

There can be no doubt, notwithstanding Foley's inadequacy, that this was indeed his aim. Therefore *if he had believed* the chemise to be implicated it is not conceivable that he would not have made the fullest use of it to gain for himself that glory and satisfaction he sought.

The magistrates—who were nothing if not diligent—accepted Foley's word and were not hard on him. They told him that he had "made a mistake in not keeping the garment and showing it to the magistrates", and thought he had not "used his usual astuteness and judgement". His conduct, however, they said, "had not been such as to shake the confidence the magistrates had in him".

Superintendent Foley got off lightly, and with his going there was an end to his inglorious part in the affair.

The case of *The Queen* v. *Sylvester* came up for hearing at the Court of Queen's Bench, Westminster, on the 30th of January, 1861, and dependent upon its outcome would be the question—vital to so many—of whether the original Road inquest should be quashed and a new one instituted. Sir Fitzroy Kelly, defending, said that the seventy-two-year-old Mr. Sylvester—who "had presided at 2,400 inquisitions and had never before had the slightest complaint made against him"—would deny that he had mishandled the inquest and misdirected the jury, and this erroneous belief was due solely to misquotations and misrepresentations made by certain members of the press. And as it transpired, Mr. Sylvester's denial was effective, for even though there were depositions presented from twelve jury-men—*and* eight others—clearly showing that the coroner *had* misdirected them as to their finding of the verdict the charge was allowed to fall to the ground.

After a very lengthy debate the case eventually came to rest on whether the coroner's failure to examine Mr. Kent amounted to legal misconduct, and to this question the Lord Chief Justice replied, saying, "Supposing it did, what end is to be answered by issuing a new inquisition?" Mr. Justice Wightman added his support here by citing a case where the Court had refused to rule for a new inquest even though the verdict at the original inquest had been, "Died by the visitation of God."(!)

At the end of the hearing Lord Chief Justice Cockburn said:

". . . The only ground on which the application rests is the allegation of misconduct on the part of the coroner, in the single instance of his not accepting the offer spontaneously made by the solicitor of Mr. Kent, and not examining Mr. Kent. I do think the coroner would have exercised a sounder discretion if he had accepted the offer; but it is not for a mere error in judgement that this court will set aside an inquisition found by a coroner's jury and issue a commission *ad melius inquirendum*

"If there *had* been judicial misconduct of a nature to justify the court in setting aside the inquisition it would still be a question whether that should be done . . . when it was seen what the object was—*viz.* to examine those among whom the guilt of the crime necessarily rested. That was not an object which the law would sanction."

And so the rule was discharged—and with it went justice's last hope of discovering *all* the relevant facts that would lead to the answer.

The newspapers were unanimous in decrying the outcome of the hearing, and *The Times*, concluding a bitter attack on the whole farcical proceedings, said:

> What actually passed at the Road inquest is now—thanks to the lawyers—as inscrutable as the murder itself, and will probably remain so to the end of time.

A few individuals, however, still refused to give up—Mr. Hughes, Chief of the Bath Police, for one, though he was unable to find any additional information of any value. The persistent Sir John Eardley Wilmot was another, and in May he wrote twice to the Home Office, once again suggesting an increase in the reward offered and once again offering his services. Commented Mr. Waddington: "This gentleman has a monomania upon the subject; a strange infatuation as it seems to me."

For the general populace, however, when the new inquisition was refused, hope died. And it was not so surprising considering how events had turned out and that the main protagonists were going their separate ways—Constance to France, Elizabeth Gough to Isleworth and Mr. Kent and the remainder of his family—soon—to the Somerset coast.

Samuel Kent could not possibly have remained in the vicinity of Road. He had become the target of increasingly virulent attacks, making his position there quite unbearable. In November a Plymouth newspaper had written: "It is perfectly well known that neither Mr. nor Mrs. Kent were models of virtue before their marriage . . ."—which indeed was correct, but was nonetheless distressing for all that. Even more disturbing, however, was the fact that that newspaper hinted at possible suspicious circumstances regarding the first Mrs. Kent's sudden death—which hints prompted Dr. George Shorland, who had attended her, to write that she had died of "an obstruction of the bowels". Not that this stopped the gossip, of course, and it was even rumoured in some quarters that Kent had been responsible for the earlier deaths of his very young children, Henry, Ellen, John and Julia. The feeling against him in Road itself is perhaps best illustrated by an incident that took place one Sunday when Mr. Kent wanted to remain after the morning service to take Communion at Christ Church. The Rev. Mr. Peacock, it is reported in *The Bristol Times*, gave his consent—but only after receiving from Kent "his solemn assurance of his innocence of the murder of his son". However, Mr. Kent's presence there was not to be borne by the other members of the congregation and, to a man, they got up and "immediately quitted the building".

It cannot be wondered at, therefore, that Samuel Kent should decide to seek new pastures, and in the March of 1861 the contents of Road Hill House were put up for sale, attracting enormous crowds. One of the main objects of interest was the dead child's cot but this, owing to the fear that it might find its way to Madame Tussaud's, was not available to any would-be purchaser. An object that *could* be seen, *could* be inspected, however, was the privy— and it became the centre of attention. Regarding this *The Journal* commented:

> Superintendent Foley was often requested to gratify the eager curiosity of the visitors by showing it. The spots of blood are still there; and it was strange to see young and fashionably dressed ladies seeking to learn every particular, and view every spot connected with the murder.

Mr. Kent, though, was no longer concerned about the thrill-seekers at Road Hill House. He was doing his best to put all that behind him. On leaving Road he and his family took temporary lodgings and then, later that spring, moved into Camden Villa, a large house in Weston-super-Mare. It was a hasty retreat and they wouldn't stay there long, but it would do for the time being; it would do until Mr. Kent's work-transfer was made a reality. This would take place early that autumn when his efforts on behalf of the Factory Commission would be henceforth centred on Wrexham, North Wales; not only had the dreadful calamity dashed all his hopes of promotion, but—and at his age and stage of his career— it had also driven him from that work-centre he had known for so long.

It was during their brief stay at Weston-super-Mare that, on the 19th of July, Mr. and Mrs. Kent saw the birth of their third daughter, Florence Savill.

By this time a year had passed since the killing, a year full of upheaval for all of the Kent family. For a few of their number life would in time resume a kind of normality—but that normality in itself would be different. For others the life they had known was completely over. Things would never be the same again.

Yet for all the rumours and the destructive suspicion that caused, and would continue to cause, so much suffering, still nothing certain was known. The mystery remained as much a mystery as ever. Those vital questions remained unanswered, leading, inevitably, to the inescapable conclusion that Mr. Kent, his daughter Constance, and the nursemaid Elizabeth Gough all knew far more about that night's work than they had ever hinted at.

Part Three

THE ANSWERS

Shall not God search this out?
For He knoweth the secrets of the heart.

Samuel S. Kent:
words inscribed on Savill's gravestone.

Chapter 25

EXILE

When Constance arrived in Dinan, Brittany, that autumn of 1860, she bore the name of Emily Kent, and it was under that name that she began her studies at the finishing school her father had chosen for her. But if she imagined for a moment that a different name and a different country would free her from the past she was mistaken. Even Dinan was too close to home and Mlle de la Tour's little establishment soon proved to be no place for a girl who had so notoriously figured in one of the most sensational crimes of the age. That crime had created a stir even in France and it was not long before her true identity became known. In the school itself, where there were many other English pupils, the history of the Road murder became a common topic and Constance herself the object of much unwelcome and unpleasant attention.

She bore the persecution as long as she could and, when it was past bearing, wrote and asked her father to take her away. So, as far off as she was, Constance had not ceased to be a problem to him.

On his part Mr. Kent was still doing all he could to thwart the endeavours of anyone who continued to persist in investigating the mystery and tried hard to mislead Sir John Eardley Wilmot who, even now, was showing an unflagging interest in the matter. That Mr. Kent was successful in this attempt is borne out by a letter written by Sir John to the Home Office. Following an interview with the Home Secretary, Sir John wrote on the 31st of October, 1861:

> After a long and close observation of Mr. Kent and his family and a handling of the question in all its implications, I am more than ever confirmed in my opinion that neither Mr. Kent nor any member of his family had anything whatever to do with the murder. Within the last few days I have received a letter from Mr. Kent, now living at Llangollen, conveying to me several minute but important facts relative to the offence in question.

Mr. Kent and his family have suffered great calamity in consequence of the murder of the child Savill Kent being still undiscovered. . . .

Mr. Kent had indeed suffered a great calamity, but he himself was by no means innocent of its cause. Sir John, though, was not to know this, and he once again vainly pressed for the renewal of efforts to find the murderer. *He* could yet do it, he wrote, and in only a fortnight, if he could have the assistance of "an able detective officer (anyone except Mr. Whicher) at the Government expense". Sir John might have been misled, but one has to admire his tenacity.

In that same letter he refers to Constance's troubles, saying:

. . . Mr. Kent has forwarded me letters showing that he is obliged to remove his daughter Constance from a school in France where she was being educated, persecution having followed her so closely wherever she has gone since that dreadful occurrence.

This situation of course had only brought Mr. Kent added difficulties. Where *now* could Constance go? She couldn't return to England, that much was certain—even greater attention and notoriety would await her there; although the Wiltshire police had dropped their inquiries the Bath police, under their chief, Mr. Hughes (encouraged, no doubt, by Jonathan Whicher), had become increasingly interested, had taken up the investigation and were giving out hints that they had evidence of the girl's guilt. Constance could not, therefore, hope to resume any normal life in England—not in the near future, anyway. The same problems, too, would apply in Wales, besides which, any prospect of a close proximity with her father and stepmother was totally out of the question.

Still, Mr. Kent couldn't leave her at the finishing-school; she had to go *somewhere*; he must needs take *some* action. He did. Less than a year after Constance had entered that establishment her father took her away and enrolled her as a pupil at the Convent de la Sagesse.

In distance it was a short move—just from one part of the town to another—and although it sprang from necessity nevertheless it was a step on the road that would lead, in time, to her spiritual salvation. Constance might not have found there that complete peace that she so desperately sought, but she did find a brief respite.

In the convent, perched high above the eleventh century walls of the little picturesque French town with its narrow streets, its tiny shops and huddled houses, Constance was less unhappy than she had been of late. She was free now of the persecution that had dogged her, finding in the convent a retreat and, when she needed it, seclusion from the outside world. There within the convent's grounds she could walk alone through the high gardens on the top of the steep cliff, at the edge of which, by the boundary wall, she might stop and look down on the waters of the River Rance below. Perhaps, in search of greater calm, she would sometimes stand and look at the nearby ancient parish church of St. Saveur—almost a cathedral in its status—and, entering, gaze upon the strange monument marking the resting place of the heart of Bertrand de Guesclin. Perhaps, too, looking at the altar there, she would wonder why she could no longer pray. . . .

Constance remained at the convent in Dinan for almost two years, during which time she helped the nuns in their work of caring for those in need—and in doing so helped to fulfil a certain need within herself.

The murder of Savill had changed her, forever. And that change in her is seen in her life at the convent school. Her stepbrother's death had subdued her to the point where this strong-willed, sensitive, determined girl almost faded into the background.

An Englishwoman, resident in Dinan at this time was later to write to *The Devizes Gazette*:

> I never saw her, but everyone I know did, and all describe her as . . . only remarkable for one particular trait, viz., *her extreme tenderness and kindness to very young children*. In the whole school in which she was a pupil she was the one who would probably be the least remarked if all were seen together.

Did that tenderness, that kindness, have their roots in guilt? Was Constance trying to atone, and by atoning, forget?

With the resilience of human nature there must have been occasions when she believed it would be possible, in time, to forget; times when, by thrusting the memory into the recesses of her mind, she could delude herself into moments of near-forgetfulness. The complete change in her situation, a different language, a different country, a different life, must all have helped towards this illusion. And even more—perhaps it was not only possible to forget, but possible to believe that the whole thing had never happened. Perhaps it was all a mistake.

But no, it was not a mistake. Her stepbrother's little, mutilated body lay in a grave in the quiet of an English countryside, and for Constance Kent there could be no quiet and no forgetting.

It is reported that, in the early summer of 1863, following Constance's nineteenth birthday, she was visited in Dinan by Mary Ann and Elizabeth, and later by her father and William. It is impossible to know whether there was any purpose behind these visits other than a mutual wish for a brief reunion, though the voyages were probably connected with the question of the girl's future: what was to become of her?

Since she had been in Dinan inquiries into the crime had ceased altogether and with the advent of other happenings—the American Civil War, the Prussian invasion of Denmark, Lancashire's cotton famine—it had receded far into the background. However, while the public may have lost consciousness of the Road affair that was not—nor could it ever have been—the situation for the Kent family. Constance could never go home again, even had she wanted to. Her schooldays, though, would soon be over. Something had to be decided with regard to her future.

The immediate problem was solved in July when an Englishwoman, a friend of Constance's, wrote on her behalf to the Reverend Arthur Wagner, Perpetual Curate of St. Paul's Church, Brighton. A few years earlier he had founded a convent and hospital affiliated to his church and now, on receiving the communication from France, agreed to take Constance as a paying guest into the religious home. Although he was informed who she really was it was agreed that she should be accepted under the name by which she now chose to be known: *Emilie*—she had adopted the French spelling of her name—and that no one but he and the Lady Superior would know her real identity.

So Constance gave up one place of exile for another. On the 10th of August, 1863, she arrived back in England and took the train for Brighton. There in that cheerful, banal, prosperous town she set off for number 2 Queen's Square, where Mr. Wagner, Miss Gream, and her fate, awaited her.

In order to fully understand part of Constance's story it is necessary to be aware of the vastly different religious atmosphere that then existed; also to attempt to see the Rev. Arthur Douglas Wagner through the eyes of those who lived in the mid-nineteenth century. One of Dr. Pusey's most ardent disciples, he was to become one of the leaders of what was disparagingly known as the "Puseyite" section of the Church of England, a movement which, with so much emphasis on trappings and ritual—ranging from the wearing of surplices and crucifixes to the use of the private confessional—approached the appearance of Catholicism, anathema to so many. It was *not* Roman, but in presenting the forms and privileges of the Roman Church it became branded as such. This revolutionary movement, *within* the established Church of England, attracted daily tirades in the newspapers, and the doings of the so-called Puseyites were the object of much hatred and scorn.

In our present world where even the oddest new religions are greeted with varying degrees of tolerance, it is difficult to see what, at *that* time, all the fuss was about. Therefore, at this remove in time although, as stated, it is as well to understand the popular view of the Rev. Arthur Wagner, it would be a mistake simply to *accept* his contemporaries' judgement of him. And judge him they did. One did not remain neutral with regard to Mr. Wagner and those who shared his convictions; one was either for him or against him, and most were against him—and with a passion.

Constance, entering St. Mary's Home that August, was destined to become for a while the focus of that religious fervour, and many people were to regard her as a mere pawn in the Puseyites' fight for recognition. It is not too much to say that the churchmen of England used her as a battleground.

This though, was still some two years hence. In the meantime Constance settled in at St. Mary's, spending her days working as a probationer at the affiliated hospital.

The nuns and novices at the Home, governed by the Superior, Miss Katharine Anne Gream, led strictured lives bound by the rituals of the order: penitence, prayer, fasting, and enforced silence. Constance, being only a paying guest at the Home, was not subject to these stringencies but, nevertheless, in that atmosphere she could not fail to be impressed by what she saw as a great closeness to God; a great oneness with Him and with all the peace that that state implied. She had entered the Home with no more religious conviction than when she had left Road; still feeling apart from God, still unable to pray. The influence of St. Mary's changed all that, though, and as the months passed she found herself increasingly moved by the passionately spiritual atmosphere that prevailed.

As she had never been confirmed in her religion the Rev. Arthur Wagner prepared her for Confirmation and when this took place—probably early in 1864—it was, for her, a revelation.

The story of Constance Kent shows clearly that whatever she set out to do she tried to do wholeheartedly; the token gesture was never enough where she was concerned; for her it was always all or nothing. Her embracing of religion was no exception. Her belief, when it returned to her, was greater than before; it was total and overwhelming. It is not easy to conceive of the power that worked in her, but it was there, and it was dynamic. It must have been for her as if she had never known God before, and now, suddenly finding Him, she must reach out and, with all her being, embrace Him and that salvation that he offered.

It was a turning point in her life. From now on there was only one course, leading towards one single goal. Redemption. And somehow, in some way, she would achieve her aim.

On the 6th of February, 1865, Constance was twenty-one years old and, attaining her majority, inherited that sum of £1,000 left in trust by her mother. Constance wasted no time; if her redemption could be bought then she would buy it. She went to the Bank of England, withdrew most of her inheritance in cash and, returning to St. Mary's, begged the Rev. Wagner to take it and use it in the various charities in which he was involved. He refused to accept it.

So, Constance was frustrated in her intentions. She must needs do something more.

At the start of Holy Week, a time when the spiritual passions were burning their most fierce, Constance Kent knelt in the confessional and, to the receptive ear of Father Wagner, poured out her story.

Having witnessed her desperate, transparent attempt to gain salvation, the Rev. Wagner must have strongly suspected what was the burden that weighed her down. Even he, though, could not have dreamed of the tale she was to tell. Even he, prepared as he was, for the worst, must have have been stunned by what she told.

Chapter 26

BOW STREET: 25th OF APRIL

Constance's baring of her soul in the confessional eased her torment but it did not end it. That ease she felt, though, was enough to carry her on; it was the breaking of the dam and it would be only a matter of time before she was swept along on the flood of her contrition.

And that time was to be short. Within hours she had told the Rev. Wagner that it was her intention to publicly confess her guilt and to surrender herself to justice. Then, to support her words she wrote a note authorizing him to inform the Home Secretary of her determination. Mr. Wagner could do nothing but acquiesce, and in truth he believed her proposed course to be the proper one, telling her "she was right to obey her conscience and make amends if she could; her life if spared could only be one long penance; and he exclaimed: 'What an awful wreck you have made of your life.' "[1]

It is not known when and by what means Mr. Wagner acquainted the Home Secretary with Constance's intentions, but it must be assumed that he did so soon after she requested him to. The Home Secretary, however, took no immediate action, leaving it to the girl to be responsible for her own fate. And she would be.

At the same time she had asked Mr. Wagner to speak to the Home Secretary Constance had also asked him to inform Miss Gream of her guilt and of her plan. This, also, he did.

On Wednesday of that same week, Holy Week, Constance had an interview with Miss Gream. The purpose of the meeting was ostensibly to discuss "religious matters", but it wasn't long before the Superior made reference to what Mr. Wagner had so recently told her—that the girl sitting before her had announced her intention of giving herself up for the Road murder. Now Miss Gream said:

"Mr. Wagner has told me about you. . . ."

[1] The Sydney Document.

Yes, Constance answered, she fully realized that. . . .

The Superior told her how sorry she was about it all, and then went on to ask: "Do you realize what such a step might involve?"

"Yes," said the girl, and added, "It is quite my own wish."

When they met again later that week their conversation was confined solely to matters of religion. The week following, however, soon after Easter Day, that more pressing subject arose once more —and how could it not?—it was in the forefront of the Superior's mind, while Constance herself was consumed by it. On this occasion, though, the conversation went beyond the girl's intentions. They actually spoke of the murder itself.

With all this, though, Constance was not, as yet, quite prepared for that final, irrevocable step, a *public* confession. Less than a week later, however, she was.

When she did eventually come to her decision she must have reached it suddenly; there can have been no planning days in advance; she must simply have felt that she could wait no longer; *now* was the time.

On the evening of Monday, the 24th of April, she completed her preparations.

First, taking the greater part of her inheritance she went to St. Paul's Church where, making sure that she was unobserved, she stuffed into the alms-box bank notes totalling almost £800. There would be no going back; she would burn her bridges. Then, returning to St. Mary's, she spent the evening at her writing-table. First, a letter to her father, telling him of her firm intention to give herself up. After that, a long, long letter to Sir John Eardley Wilmot, with whom she had kept up a correspondence and who had for so long been championing her "innocence". Writing to him now she fully confessed to her guilt in the crime and said that when she had returned home from school that summer of 1860 it was with the intention of committing it. She then went on to tell him exactly *why* she had done the killing.[2]

Next day, Tuesday, accompanied by Miss Gream and Mr. Wagner, she set off by train from Brighton to London. On their arrival

[2] Parts of this letter are quoted in chapter thirty. Further reference to it will be found in Inspector Williamson's report of the 24th July, 1865. See Appendix.

in the capital Mr. Wagner left his two female companions and went to the Home Office. There he informed the authorities that Constance Kent was on her way to Bow Street.

This was the second startling piece of news the Home Office had received that day, and already the London streets were abuzz with the other sensational tidings—those telling of the assassination of President Abraham Lincoln. The word concerning Constance Kent, however, required action—and immediately, and at once a messenger was sent riding off to inform Sir Richard Mayne at the offices of the Metropolitan Police and then on to the magistrates' court in Bow Street. Constance Kent was on her way to surrender herself for the murder at Road.

Mr. Wagner was later to be strongly criticized over the fact that Constance went to a London court to give herself up. Why, asked his critics—as do some today—did he not take her straight to Wiltshire for the purpose—for that was where the crime had taken place? Also, why did the reverend not communicate well in advance the girl's intentions to her father where he lived in Wales?

The answers to the questions are not difficult to find. It was Constance's own wish to go before a London magistrate, and Bow Street Magistrates' Court was the highest. She did not elect to go to Wiltshire as that, with all the travelling, would have meant considerable delay; Constance had no time to lose; once she had decided to act upon her initial decision that act must be carried out as quickly as possible; as Macbeth put it, "If it were done when 't is done, then 't were well it were done quickly." As for informing her father earlier of her intentions, this was a course Constance could not possibly countenance. Had he had notice of her plans he would have done all in his power to stop her. Constance knew this, and she was not to be stopped. Her letter to him was carefully timed; he would receive it in the morning following her arrival in the city. By that time it would be too late for him to do anything; his daughter would have committed herself; the machinery of the law would be irreversibly in motion.

· Shortly before four o'clock and only minutes after receiving the news of her impending arrival the officers of the court at Bow Street ushered the young woman and her two companions into the private office of Sir Thomas Henry, the Chief Magistrate. He too had had little time to prepare; word of her intention having only just reached him whilst he was sitting in court towards the end of the Petty Sessions that afternoon.

Now Constance Kent, "dressed in deep mourning and wearing a heavy veil", stepped forward and said in a low voice that she had come to give herself up. As she spoke she held out to the elderly man a small, flimsy sheet of cheap notepaper. Sir Thomas took it and looked at the words she had so carefully written there:

> *I, Constance Emilie Kent, alone and unaided on the night of the 29th of June, 1860, murdered at Road Hill House, Wiltshire, one Francis Savill Kent. Before the deed none knew of my intention, nor after of my guilt; no one assisted me in the crime, nor in my evasion of discovery.*

Sir Thomas raised his eyes from the paper to the young woman before him, Miss Gream close at her side.

"Am I to understand, Miss Kent, that you have given yourself up of your own free act and will on this charge?"

"Yes, sir."

"Anything you may say here will be written down, and may be used against you. Do you understand that?"

In the same low voice, she answered: "Yes, sir."

"Is this paper, now produced before me, in your own handwriting, and written of your own free will?"

"It is, sir."

"Then let the charge be entered in her own words."

Taking details of the girl's full name and address Inspector Avery wrote out the charge, the words of which were then solemnly read aloud:

"Constance Emilie Kent, 2 Queen's Square, Brighton, charged upon her own confession with having, alone and unaided, on the night of the 29th of June, 1860, murdered at Road Hill House, Wiltshire, one Francis Savill Kent."

Sir Thomas then handed the girl's written confession to the chief clerk, Mr. Burnaby, who prepared to copy down the words of her statement. Seeing the somewhat unusual spelling of her second name he asked her whether she was accustomed to spell it *Emilie* or *Emily*.

"It is quite indifferent," she answered. "I sometimes spell it one way; sometimes the other."

"I see on this paper—which you say is in your own handwriting —it is spelt *Emilie*. . . ."

"Yes, sir."

Sir Thomas Henry, indicating the notepaper bearing her confession, asked her:

"Have you any objection to signing that? I must remind you that this is the most serious offence that can be committed, and that anything you say or write may be used against you at your trial. I do not wish you to sign it unless you wish."

"I will do so if necessary."

"No, it is not absolutely necessary. There is no occasion for you to sign it unless you wish. I will have that paper attached to the depositions, and I will again ask you if you have made it by your own desire, and without any inducement from any quarter whatever to give yourself up."

"Yes."

Sir Thomas then turned his attention to the Rev. Wagner who, after being sworn, stated:

"I am a clerk in holy orders and perpetual curate of St. Paul's Church, Brighton, which is a chapel-of-ease to the parish church. I have known Constance Kent for nearly two years—since the summer of 1863."

Said Constance: "In August."

"About twenty-one months, then," Sir Thomas said.

Wagner nodded. "Yes. As far as I can remember an English family wrote to me, asking for her admission to St. Mary's Home, or Hospital, in consequence of her having no home, or of some difficulty respecting her. St. Mary's Home, or rather Hospital as it is now called, is attached to St. Mary's Church. She came about that time as a visitor, and has been there up to the present day."

As the chief clerk wrote down the words of the reverend's deposition the door was quietly opened and Superintendent Durkin entered the room. At his side was Inspector Williamson, that same man who as a sergeant, five years earlier, had aided Jonathan Whicher in his pursuit of this same girl. Now she sat before the two officers, in custody by dint of her own act of surrender.

Sir Thomas Henry continued with his inquiry.

"Now, Mr. Wagner," he said, "it is my duty to ask you if any inducement has been made to the prisoner in any way to make this confession."

"None whatever has been made by me," Mr. Wagner stated emphatically. "The confession is entirely her own voluntary act, to the best of my belief. It was about a fortnight ago, as far as I can recollect, that the circumstance first came to my knowledge. It was entirely her own proposition that she should be taken before a London magistrate. It was her own proposition to leave the Home and come to London for the purpose of giving herself up. The nature of the confession she made to me was the same, in substance, as the statement in her own handwriting. I can't remember the words, but that was the substance."

Said Sir Thomas, reading her confession: "That 'I, Constance Emilie Kent, alone and unaided, on the night of the 29th of June, 1860, murdered at Road Hill House, Wiltshire, one Francis Savill Kent'?—was that the substance?"

"It was."

"Did she make that known to you?"

"She did."

There followed some discussion here between Sir Thomas and Inspector Williamson as to the exact situation of Road Hill House —whether it was in Somerset or Wiltshire—when Mr. Wagner, obviously with something weighing on his mind, broke in to say that when he had been speaking of Miss Kent's confession he wished it to be clearly understood that he had not been referring to any *private* confession she had made to him, but to an open, public confession.

No importance was attached to Mr. Wagner's highly significant words, however; Sir Thomas brushed them aside, saying: "I will not go into that point here. It may be gone into at the trial, and perhaps very fully." He turned to Constance. "I hope you understand that whatever you say must be entirely your own free and voluntary statement, and that no inducement that may have been held out to you is to have any effect upon your mind."

Constance: "No inducement ever has."

"I was most anxious that you should most seriously consider that."

Mr. Wagner then said, "I wish to mention that many are in the habit of coming to confess to me as a religious exercise, but I never hold out any inducement."

"Yes, I think you ought to mention that," said Sir Thomas. "Did you in the first instance induce her to make the confession?"

"No. I did not seek her out, or in any way ask her to come to confession. She herself wished to do so. I never recommended it. I have been simply passive. I felt that she was doing right and, therefore, I did not dissuade her. She thought of it herself, without my suggesting it to her."

"That must be added to the deposition," said Sir Thomas. Then, picking up Constance's written confession he turned his attention once more to the girl.

"This is the paper you wish to hand in as your statement, is it?"

"Yes, sir."

Replacing the paper on the chief clerk's desk the man went on, "Now, understand that it is not too late, even now. I wish to tell you again that this is a very serious charge, and that whatever you write or say may be used against you. You are not bound to make any statement unless you wish."

She did not answer. In the silence that followed Mr. Burnaby held up her confession. "*Is* this your handwriting?" he asked.

With "slight emphasis" Constance replied: "Yes, it is."

Sir Thomas then asked Mr. Wagner if he knew Miss Kent's handwriting. Mr. Wagner answered:

"I never saw her write, so I cannot tell, though I have no doubt that that paper was written by her."

The chief clerk then read aloud the words of the confession which he had now finished copying onto the official blue *Statement of the Accused* form. "Do you wish to add anything to that statement?" asked Sir Thomas.

"No, sir."

She was then asked to sign the statement, which she did—reverting to the baptismal spelling of her second name: *Emily.* Her signature on the document shows so plainly her state of mind at that moment. Her writing has no natural flow, and the formation of the letters gives clear indication of her violently trembling hand and the great stress she was suffering. . . .

When she had laid down the pen Sir Thomas turned to the police officers.

"The offence was committed in Wiltshire, and the trial must be in that county. It will therefore be necessary to send her to be examined before the magistrates in that county." He gave instructions to Inspector Williamson. "You had better take the prisoner before them. I will send with you the warrant, Mr. Wagner's deposition, and the prisoner's own voluntary statement. The magistrates there will exercise their own discretion as to what further evidence they will go into." He ended by asking the inspector what had become of Inspector Whicher who had been engaged in the former inquiry in 1860. Williamson replied that Whicher had been "superannuated some two years back".

When Williamson had the warrant safely in his pocket he escorted Constance Kent out of the building to a waiting carriage. They were joined now by Sergeant Thomas. Before them walked Superintendent Durkin, while behind came Mr. Wagner and Miss Gream. As Mr. Durkin helped the two women into the carriage "a knot of four or five idle boys stopped to stare at the peculiar dress of the Lady Superior". She alone it was, and not Constance, who caused comment. Indeed, "so quietly had the whole proceedings been conducted that it was not even suspected that the gentle-looking young lady, so carefully tended, was Constance Kent, late of Road Hill House".

At Paddington Station Mr. Wagner took leave of Constance Kent and went about his own business. She, with Miss Gream at her side, was escorted by Inspector Williamson and Sergeant Thomas to the Chippenham-bound train.

In the carriage the four sat silently throughout the many hours' journey, arriving at Chippenham just after one o'clock the next morning. There they were met by a waiting post-chaise which carried them through the dark of that late April night, travelling in silence along the deserted country roads that wound amid the night-shadowed green of the Wiltshire hills, the loneliness relieved only by the small villages they passed through: Beanacre, Melksham, Semington. Then, at two o'clock, they arrived at Trowbridge Police Station where Constance was told that she would be brought before the magistrates later that same day. Miss Gream begged to be allowed to remain with her during the night, but Mr. Harris, the inspector on duty there, refused her request, saying that a room for the Lady Superior would be available at the nearby Woolpack Inn. Then Constance, tended by the superintendent's kindly wife, was led away.

Since the night of the crime Constance had experienced little ease wherever she had been, but perhaps in the rather raw comfort afforded by Trowbridge Gaol she might, with that relief which her act had brought her, have at last found some rest. After all, she had done what she had set out to do; she had confessed and given herself up. Was she, though, *fully* aware of the possible consequences of that action?

Chapter 27

TROWBRIDGE POLICE COURT: 26th OF APRIL

When word spread swiftly through Trowbridge that Constance Kent had confessed to the Road murder, was at present lodged in the local gaol and would be appearing before the magistrates that same morning, the excited townspeople hurried to the police court and crowded at its doors, anxious to be among that small number which its limited space could admit. The London newspapers had carried a full report of her startling appearance before Sir Thomas Henry at Bow Street, and now everyone was eager to witness any further proceedings; failing that, they hoped at least to catch some glimpse of the girl who, almost five years earlier, had been the object of so much keen attention.

The case was due to be heard at eleven o'clock, but that hour came and went with the crowd still waiting outside the closed doors. Eleven-thirty passed . . . eleven-forty-five. And still nothing happened—and nor would it until the star witness, the Rev. Arthur Wagner, had arrived. He eventually made his appearance soon after twelve, having just alighted from the London train; so, with his presence there at last, the proceedings could be got under way.

When the doors were opened "the rush to enter the court was tremendous. Every precaution was taken by the police to keep order, but children screamed, women and strong men fought their way in, and in ten minutes every inch of standing and sitting room was occupied."[1]

Apart from the anonymous faces of the reporters and the spectators, there could also be seen there that day the more familiar figures of those men who had earlier been involved in the aftermath of the murder: there was Mr. Rowland Rodway, Captain Meredith, Mr. Dunn and Mr. Joseph Whitaker Stapleton; this latter gentleman's book on the case, *The Great Crime of 1860*, had been published in 1861 with considerable success. Throughout his book the

[1] *The Advertiser.*

surgeon had hinted strongly at Constance Kent's guilt and now, by her own confession, the girl was proclaiming to all that he had probably been right all along.

To complete the picture presented by the courthouse interior that day I will use the words of one who was present and whose subsequent account appeared in *The Trowbridge Chronicle*:

> . . . There was a full bench of magistrates, and on the bench were several ladies. A seat near the chairman was occupied by a gentleman whom, from the extreme High Church cut of his garments I at once concluded was the Rev. Mr. Wagner . . . and the conclusion was a correct one. The rev. gentleman, who has certainly nothing of the leanness of the ascetic about his physique, sat with half-closed eyes, his hands resting on the top of his umbrella, and his chin resting on his hands. . . . When Constance Kent was called, all eyes were turned in the direction of the door through which it was expected she would enter, and presently there she appeared, dressed in black from top to toe. Black bonnet, relieved by a very slight trimming of a more cheerful hue, black cloth cloak, black dress, and black veil. . . .

So Constance, with Miss Gream at her side, came to take her place before the eager crowd.

Betraying no emotion, the girl walked steadily to the dock with "all eyes turned in pity towards her". Reaching the dock she sat down, never once raising her head, never once looking up. Beside her, at an angle, sat the Lady Superior. After a moment the girl was asked to stand while the charge was read to her. Wrote the same witness:

> She promptly obeyed the call, and, although her head was slightly bent, there was not a tremor observable in her features, and the natural ruby of her cheeks was not blenched by any fear of the position in which she had voluntarily placed herself. A vast change has taken place in her appearance since she last appeared before the magistrates charged with the murder of her halfbrother. Then she was a slim girl, now she is a fully developed woman, of considerable personal attractions, so far as I could judge from the partial view of her face that could be obtained through the loose meshes of her veil. She is fully of the average female stature, strong and healthy looking, with nothing certainly in her

manner and appearance that would lead one to suppose that her mind was diseased.

After the formal charge was read to the girl the clerk of the court read aloud the deposition made the previous day by the Rev. Wagner, that deposition ending with the words:

". . . I have never said anything to Constance Kent to persuade her to confess, nor have I said anything to dissuade her from doing so. I have been perfectly passive in the matter, feeling that she was doing the right thing. It is entirely her own free act. She thought of it herself without my suggesting it to her."

Mr. Ludlow, the Chief Magistrate, then asked Mr. Wagner:

"Is that true?"

"Yes."

The magistrate then turned to the girl.

"Have you any question to ask this witness?"

"No, sir." She was barely audible.

After Mr. Wagner had returned to his seat the clerk picked up the paper bearing Constance's signed statement. "I will now read over the statement which you made to the magistrate at Bow Street," he said. "It is this. . . ." And he began to read:

"I wish to hand in of my own free will a piece of paper with the following written on it: 'I, Constance Emilie Kent, alone and unaided on the night of the 29th of June, 1860, murdered——' "

. . . And suddenly the girl's composure deserted her. Hands clenched to her face she bent forward sobbing. The bench and the spectators gazed at her in pity, several of them turning away a moment later in an attempt to hide their own feelings. Then the clerk, having faltered to a halt, collected himself and continued to read:

" '—at Road Hill House one Francis Savill Kent. Before the deed none knew of my intention——' " The clerk was forced to stop again; the prisoner was sobbing uncontrollably now while at her side the Superior—who was trying to support her through the ordeal— also broke down and began to weep. " '—nor after of my guilt . . .' " read the clerk—and at this point one of the ladies on the bench handed to the weeping girl a smelling-box and Constance took it and used it. The clerk was coming to an end: " '—no one assisted me in the crime, nor in my evasion of discovery.' "

In the silence that followed the girl and her companion brought themselves under control. Mr. Ludlow waited for a moment and then asked whether she wished to add anything to her written statement. She shook her head. "No," she whispered.

Inspector Williamson then gave evidence of her arrest and identified the paper "written in a female hand". The girl's confession was read out once more, and this time at the sound of her murdered brother's name she lost all control. As the packed courtroom watched she sank back into her seat, her body shaking with the sobbing she could not suppress. A glass of water was offered to her but she refused it, and sat there while the tears streamed from her eyes and her companion tried to soothe her. It was a scene that few would forget.

When Inspector Williamson had concluded his evidence the girl, now recovered, was asked whether she had any question to put to him. In a low voice she answered, "No, sir."

"Have you any reason to give why the magistrates should not remand you?" asked Mr. Ludlow.

She shook her head.

"Then you will be remanded till tomorrow week at eleven o'clock in the forenoon, when you will again be brought before this court. Until that time you will be taken care of in the County gaol at Devizes."

So, for the moment it was over. In the company of the police officers and Miss Gream, the prisoner—"with a firm step"—left the court. A little later she was conveyed in a closed carriage to Devizes gaol.

Rumour had spread about the court that day that Mr. Kent was in the town and was shortly to appear in the courthouse. But that rumour had soon proved ill-founded. He was still at his home in Llangollen.

There were to be conflicting reports as to how he had learned that morning of his daughter's confession. Some journals said that the first he knew of it was from a newspaper he had purchased at the Cambrian railway station. Other papers, like *The Standard*, insisted that the news came to him first in Constance's letter—which he received just a few hours before her appearance before the magistrates at Trowbridge. Wrote the reporter for that paper:

. . . Mr. Kent, upon the receipt of his daughter's letter, well remembering the sad trials he had undergone, gave himself up for a time to unbounded grief. In her letter she expressed no wish either to see him or any other member of her family. This at first sight would appear as if terms of relationship had ceased; but I am informed that since her absence from home—nearly four years and a half—a correspondence of the most kindly nature has been kept up.

Still, however it was that Mr. Kent learned the shocking news there can be no question of his reaction to it. He must have been totally stunned.

Those—and there were many—who wanted a weapon to use against Mr. Wagner and his followers found one in Constance Kent's confession. They seized on that pathetic scrap of buff-coloured note-paper and wielded it as a rod across the backs of those loathed Puseyites, suggesting that the young woman had been brain-washed into confessing in order to bring the hated movement into greater prominence. Later those feelings would promote a veritable storm; now, though, at the start of it all, the criticism was rather carefully couched. Said *The Standard*:

. . . We attach no judicial importance to her confession drawn up at St. Mary's Home, a religious house attached to St. Paul's church, at Brighton, and we think it would have been far wiser and better, and more legal, had a private gentleman not escorted the young girl from Brighton to Bow Street, in order that she might confess herself a murderess. . . .

The same paper remarked: "It will be a very remarkable thing if this proves to have been the undictated language of a deliberate and independent young murderess," and added: "It bears the impress of a too zealous persuasion."

The Express appeared at first willing to give Mr. Wagner the benefit of the doubt:

. . . Supposing that Constance Kent, her conscience burdened with long-concealed guilt, sought Mr. Wagner out and voluntarily confessed her crime to him, his conduct would seem to have been kind, and discreet, and wholly free from blame. Still further light, however, is wanted on this matter. . . .

And then the article stated: "Out of the atmosphere of religious houses, girls of the age of Constance Kent have been known to accuse themselves wrongfully of terrible crimes." Which was no doubt true; nevertheless, throughout all the articles and letters regarding Constance's journey from Brighton to Bow Street the condemnation of Mr. Wagner himself—for his convictions—shines clearly through. Moreover, the journalists' transparent lack of objectivity spilled over into their general reporting on the subject so that the reverend was rarely described unless in the most negative terms. And similarly for Miss Gream; as a devout follower of Mr. Wagner she became, for the press, an object of ridicule, and they wrote smugly of her "most abject expression", and her "strange apparel".

So, many members of the public were suspicious of the authenticity of Constance's confession because of the "soil in which it had germinated"—and for one other, and most important, reason. That was the very preciseness of her statement. This preciseness had taken everyone by surprise. *The Standard* said it was "drawn up in the form and language of an affidavit. It could not have been written undictated by herself. It is a specimen of clear and accurate composition. . . ." While *The London Review* said:

No one who knows anything of women, or the way in which women write, will ever believe that the document handed to Sir Thomas Henry was the spontaneous and unaided composition of a girl of twenty-one. Nothing more comprehensive, terse and exact in language could have been drawn up by the best criminal pleader at the Bar. A confession springing directly from her heart and shaping itself in her own words would have been at once more vague and more detailed. . . .

And in part that journal was correct: the wording of the confession *was* comprehensive, terse and exact. Also, "a confession springing directly from her heart and shaping itself in her own words" *would* have been at once "more vague and more detailed". But that journalist did not know Constance Kent. She had had much time to draft and to perfect the wording of that very precise statement. In those fifty-two words she said exactly what she wanted to say.

In her cell in Devizes gaol Constance made it clear that she intended to plead guilty and that she wanted no legal aid. Instructed by her father, however, Mr. Rowland Rodway visited her to offer his services and arrange with her the preparation of a defence. At first she refused to see him, although later she was persuaded to. Even so, she only reiterated her intentions: she would plead guilty; she would not require his representation. Throughout the meeting, it was said, she appeared "to manifest the greatest indifference to her position". From her determination Mr. Rodway could not shake her.

Soon after six o'clock on the evening of Monday, the 1st of May, Mr. Kent arrived at Devizes station where he was met by Mr. Rodway. Together they went at once to the gaol and, producing a magistrates' order, were ushered inside. There, after a brief discussion, they agreed that Mr. Rodway should go first into the girl's cell —for the purpose of breaking the news that her father was there to see her.

The Standard wrote of the encounter that followed:

. . . With this object Mr. Rodway went to her cell. He found her writing. She rose upon his entering, and received him kindly. He observed no alteration in her. She looked well, was self-composed, and otherwise appeared completely resigned to her fate. After the exchange of a few words Mr. Rodway told her that her father had come to see her. The moment she heard this her calmness deserted her. She burst into a paroxysm of tears, and was sinking down upon the little mattress in the corner of the cell when her unhappy father rushed in, and catching her in his arms affectionately pressed her to his breast. The interview lasted some considerable time, but what transpired is only known to themselves and their solicitor.

Mr. Kent upon taking leave of his child was deeply affected, indeed the confession she has made appears to have completely stunned him. He walks and talks, as it were, mechanically. Constance, on the other hand, after the first shock, regained her self-composure, and while, as I am informed, she affectionately embraced her father, she persisted that the course she had adopted was due to him and her God.

Upon leaving the gaol Mr. Kent, appearing "completely overwhelmed", moved dazedly towards Mr. Rodway's carriage. Then together he and the solicitor drove off to the latter's house. Constance, now, had agreed to be legally represented. The two men must needs discuss her defence.

Chapter 28

TROWBRIDGE POLICE COURT: 5th OF MAY

At eleven o'clock on the morning of the 5th of May Constance Kent sat waiting to be called to the dock once more. Beyond her cell the courtroom was packed to the point of suffocation, while in other rooms waited those individuals who had been called as witnesses, some of whom she had not seen for almost five years.

Those five years that had elapsed since the murder had not only seen a change in the girl who was now a prisoner; there had been changes for some of the witnesses, too. Sarah Cox for one. She, the Kents' former housemaid, was now Mrs. George Rogers, having married that farmer of Steeple Ashton in the early summer of 1863. A major change for Jonathan Whicher, too, that detective officer who had come from London to investigate the Road mystery—and who had failed to secure a conviction of his suspect. He, having retired from the police force, was now living quietly in Salisbury, Wiltshire. It had mattered not that his colleagues and Sir Richard Mayne had totally believed in him; he was a servant of the public and that public had found him wanting, seeing him as a mean, incompetent, bungling man. Held in such low esteem it had been impossible for him to make further progress. Although the Metropolitan Police had received their usual quota of requests for the help of "an efficient officer" those requests too often *excluded* Jonathan Whicher. In the end his career had virtually come to a standstill, leaving him no alternative but retirement.

Did Whicher feel any bitterness as he sat waiting for his call to take the stand? Did he perhaps recall certain words he had uttered following his inglorious failure in 1860—words now quoted by Lord Folkestone in a letter to *The Times*:

The last words he said to a friend of mine at the time were "Mark my words, sir, nothing will now be known about the murder till Miss Constance Kent confesses."

Well, Constance Kent had confessed. But that confession had come too late to save Whicher's career. . . .

And what of that other officer—Superintendent John Foley—who had also failed in his efforts to search out the culprit? Foley had died the previous June of dropsy in the chest; he was totally beyond blame or praise now and would never know whether, in his deductions, he had been right or wrong.

A few minutes after eleven o'clock Constance Kent was brought into the courtroom accompanied by Inspector Gibson of Melksham and Mrs. Alexander, the wife of the gaoler. After a few words to the girl relating to the charge Mr. Ludlow, Chief Magistrate, addressed himself to Mr. Rodway. The solicitor then arose and said that he appeared at Mr. Kent's request on behalf of the prisoner. "I take this opportunity of saying," he said, "that it is not my intention to cross-examine any of the witnesses who may be brought forward today, or to present anything in the shape of a defence, as the circumstances will be gone into on a future occasion. The prisoner's confession has taken away the discretionary powers of the magistrates and left them no alternative but to send the case before another tribunal. I will therefore confine myself to watching the case, and will reserve the defence for the trial which must inevitably follow this examination."

The first witness to be called was Elizabeth Gough. She had been denied "social" employment since the tragedy at Road Hill House and had attempted to earn her living as an occasional seamstress. Rumour had gone around Trowbridge that she had married a sheep-farmer and emigrated to Australia, but this story was soon disproved, for here she was, taking her place before the assembly. "Very neatly dressed" and giving her evidence in "a modest and respectful manner", she repeated the account she had previously given. When she had last appeared in Trowbridge *she* had been the accused; she it was who had stood in the dock while Constance Kent had given evidence against *her*. And now she stood in that same courtroom—but this time as a witness, with Constance standing accused of the crime.

Thomas Benger, who had found the body, was called next, and he was followed by the surgeon, Joshua Parsons. This gentleman, proving increasingly unreliable as a witness, ignored his former evidence and now discounted the possibility that suffocation had caused the child's death. Now he stated categorically:

"In my opinion the incision in the throat was the cause of death," and then added that possibly "the circulation of the child was in a great degree stopped by suffocation before that was done". He went on: "The cut in the throat must have been done with a sharp instrument—either a knife or razor would have done it. The wound in the chest could only have been inflicted by a long, sharp knife."

When he was asked "Could the throat have been cut after the circulation had ceased?" he at once replied:

"I did not say the circulation had *ceased*. I said it was stopped in a great degree."

Dr. Parsons also repeated his former evidence to the effect that on examining Constance's nightdress some hours after the crime he had found it to be extremely clean and had made a remark to that effect to Mr. Foley.

Sarah Rogers (née Cox) was the next witness. Her evidence was the same as before, with the addition of one significant detail. On the subject of Constance's missing nightdress she said that when collecting the clothes for the laundry on the morning of the inquest she had found the girl's nightdress and stockings lying on the landing. Asked: "Was that where her nightdress was usually put?" she answered: "Sometimes I found her clothes there, but I never recollect finding one of her nightdresses there before."

"Where did you usually find her nightdress?"

"In her room."

After she had repeated her evidence regarding Constance's request for water while she, the maid, had been busy packing the laundry baskets, she stepped down and made way for Mrs. Esther Holly. The laundress had nothing new to add, however, and only repeated her original testimony. It was the same with the next witness, her daughter Martha—now married to Abraham Nutt. After corroborating her mother's testimony she was replaced in the box by Sergeant Watts who testified to finding the stained chemise in the boiler-hole.

"Was there much blood on it?" he was asked.

"Yes, a good bit. . . . The marks and smears nearly covered the tail part."

After the sergeant came Mr. Whicher. And here he was being

called to give the *same evidence* which in 1860 had met with such opprobrium and ridicule. And this time no one scoffed at his words. After describing how he had made every effort to find Constance's missing nightdress he was asked by the chairman:

"Did you ever hear of any bloody garment having been found?" (meaning the chemise) to which Whicher replied:

"No such communication was ever made to me by any member of the police force. I never heard a word of it until some three months after, when I read an account of it in the newspapers. You will recollect that I immediately wrote to you stating that it was quite new to me, and that I never heard a word about a stained nightdress being found."

Miss Gream, left, gives evidence before the Trowbridge magistrates. Constance, veiled, sits facing her. (From *The Penny Illustrated Paper.*)

The chairman: "I think it right to say that it never came to the knowledge of the magistrates until November."

So, most curiously, five years after those same magistrates had satisfied themselves as to the chemise's origins it was now referred to as a *nightdress*, and the mistaken belief that it had belonged to Constance was fostered all over again.

Miss Gream was the next witness and after being sworn she went on, unbidden, to make a statement:

"I desire to say that from the first when the prisoner came to reside at the Home I have stood in the position of a mother to her, and she as a daughter to me. I therefore wish to ask you not to press me with questions which would tend to betray the confidence that exists between mother and daughter."

The chairman: "The proper questions in a court of justice must be put to you, and no more; and those you will have to answer."

In reply to the first questions the Superior stated that the prisoner had arrived at the Home on the 10th of August, 1863, under the name of Emilie Kent; before that time she, the witness, had not known her.

The clerk: "Has she at any time said anything to you about the Road murder?"

After a long pause Miss Gream answered: "I spoke to her first about it on the Wednesday in Holy Week. She never said anything to me about it previous to expressing a wish to give herself up."

"Did you say anything to her to induce her to make a confession to you?"

"No. I had known previously that she had spoken of it."

The chairman: "Are you quite certain that previously to that you never said anything to induce her to make any statement?"

"Quite certain."

The clerk: "What did she first say?"

"I cannot remember. I said to her that I knew of it and was sorry for it, and I asked her if she fully realized what it involved."

"What did you refer to by 'it'?"

"To her wish to give herself up. . . ."

"Be kind enough to give us, as near as you remember, the exact words."

"The conversation was nearly wholly on religious subjects and

did not refer, as far as I can recollect, in any way to the act. I sent
for her, having been told of it."

"And then you said, 'I know of it'?"

"I don't suppose I said I knew of it. I can't exactly remember. I
meant her to understand that I had been told what she wished me
to know. . . . I think it most likely I said, 'Mr. Wagner has told me
about you'."

"What reply did she make?"

"She said she fully realized it. . . ."

The brief example, quoted above, gives an indication of the tenor
of Miss Gream's testimony, and from there it went from bad to
worse. There is not room in this book for a word-for-word account
of what passed during her appearance on the stand that day—and
in any case the reader's patience would run out faster than the
space provided. In her testimony she switched back and forth in
time seemingly at random, and seemed totally incapable of referring
to anything by its correct name; hence the word "it" was variously
meant to refer to the murder, to Constance's wish to give herself
up, and was also a euphemism for "sin." Her vagueness was probably due in part to the fact that she had just taken the oath and
was at pains not to stray from the truth in the slightest way. Nevertheless, it is hardly surprising that at one point the clerk, totally
confused, said to her, "We do not wish to press you unduly, but I
am bound to take the depositions in such a way that the judge can
understand them."

There can be no doubt that the Lady Superior meant well, but
her appearance on the stand resulted in a long, tedious period of
question-and-answer that annoyed the press and the public and
totally bemused everybody.

The essence of her testimony—when sorted out and put in order
—was to the effect that on Wednesday in Holy Week, having been
told by Mr. Wagner of Constance Kent's stated intention to give
herself up for the murder, she had sent for the girl to come to her
room. There she told Constance that she knew what she planned
to do and then asked the girl if she fully realized what such a step
involved. Constance had replied that she did realize, but that nevertheless it was her wish to surrender herself.

The following week, said Miss Gream, they had spoken of the
matter again, at which time she, the Superior, had referred to the

murder itself, saying to the girl: "All sins are aggravated by circumstances in God's sight." The Superior also said to the court: "She told me that she left the house by the drawing-room window, and that she used a razor for the purpose."

This statement produced a great sensation in the court, and even the witness seemed for a moment to be overcome by the implications of the revelations she was making. At the same time the prisoner was seen to tightly close her eyes "as if the reminiscences of the dreadful scene were overpowering her".[1]

Miss Gream, questioned as to what else she had said to the prisoner, replied, "I asked her whether the child cried out for mercy." Constance, she said, answered that the child had remained asleep.

The clerk: "Did she say where she got the razor from?"

"From her father's dressing-case."

"Did she say anything else?"

"She spoke of the nightdress that was lost. I think she said that she had taken it out of the basket again."

"Did she assign any motive to the crime?"

"I think she said it was not dislike to the child, but revenge on the stepmother." (Further sensation at this.)

"Did she say what she did with the razor?"

"No."

At the end of her testimony Miss Gream was asked again whether she had in any way induced the prisoner to confess or to surrender herself. She replied most firmly: *"Never, never."*

The last witness to be called was Mr. Wagner. After he was sworn he asked to be allowed to make a statement which he had "committed to writing" and which he "considered essential should be read". Said the chairman:

"We had better hear nothing till you have given your evidence."

The clerk of the court then read Mr. Wagner's deposition which was to the effect that the prisoner had confessed to the murder and that he had never in any way tried to induce or persuade her to confess or to give herself up. That, the reverend now affirmed, was the truth.

The clerk then said: "You say you have known the prisoner for twenty-one months. Had you known her previous to that time?"

[1] *The Daily Telegraph.*

Mr. Wagner: "I had not."

"Did she come to you in the name of Constance Kent?"

"No; she came to me in the name of *Emilie* Kent, in order that she might not be known." He added quickly: "Perhaps the court will allow me to read the statement now?"

But just as quickly the chairman interposed: "Not now."

"Then perhaps you will allow me to say," said Mr. Wagner, "that all communications which have been made to me by Miss Kent during the last seventeen or eighteen months have been made to me under the seal of confession, and therefore I shall decline to divulge anything which may have passed between us which may criminate her. I am quite willing to say when she authorized me to speak to the Home Secretary, but I must decline answering any question which would be a breach of the confessional." This was Mr. Wagner's prepared statement; he'd made it after all.

And that statement caused something of an uproar in the court. From the initial gasps of shock the spectators went on to show their disapproval of his words by muttering and loud hissing. "Order! Order!" called Superintendent Harris. "This is no place for hissing. It is uncalled for."

As calm was restored Mr. Ludlow said to the reverend: "You must answer the questions put to you in a court of justice. You have sworn to tell the truth before God. Upon the responsibility of that oath you have to answer." But Mr. Wagner replied:

"My duty to God forbids me to answer any question which shall in any way divulge anything that has been said in the secrecy of the confessional." A further outburst of angry hissing broke out at this. When it was quelled, the chairman, backing off from the challenge, said, "I think we had better proceed with the evidence in the regular way." Mr. Wagner was then asked:

"When did she first allude to the murder?"

"She authorized me to speak to Sir George Grey between three and four weeks ago."

"Had you said anything to induce her to do so?"

"I had not."

"While in conversation with her what did she say?"

"I do not recollect exactly, but she requested me to communicate with the Home Secretary that she was guilty of the Road murder and that she was willing to give herself up to justice or do anything that he told her to do."

"Who spoke first about it?"

"She did."

"What led to her telling you?"

"—I cannot answer that question."

". . . I mean, what conversation was there previous to her telling you?"

"I cannot tell you more than I have already without a breach of the confessional."² (More hisses.)

"Did she give you any reason for telling you?"

"I don't recollect that she did. She spoke to me first. I never suggested to her that she should make a public confession; it is entirely her own voluntary act."

"Without any inducement being offered to her she spoke to you first on the subject of giving herself up?"

"She did."

Constance was now asked whether she wished to put any questions to the reverend. As with the previous witnesses she declined. Mr. Wagner's testimony was over.

Mr. Ludlow then requested the prisoner to stand up, which she did "in a mechanical sort of way". Without raising her face towards the bench she continued to look down vacantly in the dock while the chairman formally announced that she was committed for trial at the next Wiltshire Assizes, which were to be held at Salisbury.²

It was now past six o'clock; the proceedings had lasted over seven hours. When the prisoner was taken from the court to be conveyed back to Devizes she bore the same expression of composure that had marked the greater part of her ordeal that day, "as if it was a matter of perfect indifference to her what else was said or done".

² They were to begin on the 19th of July.

Chapter 29

OUTCRY

While Constance Kent sat in the confinement of her cell at Devizes, Mr. Wagner had to face growing storms of abuse from the press and the public. He was seen in many different guises, none flattering; he was viewed as a monster who had delivered a poor deluded girl to within the grasp of the hangman; as a man who was the cause of that poor creature's "delusions"; and as one who had flouted British law for the glorification of his own ends. There were also those who tried to hoist him with his own petard, claiming that though *he* had used the seal of the confessional as reason for his silence in the courtroom, he had nevertheless himself broken that vow of silence by repeating the girl's confession to Miss Gream and the Home Secretary.

The greatest uproar, though, was that against his having been allowed, in a case of such importance, to have "arrogantly" refused to answer certain questions put to him in a court of law. As *The Brighton Gazette* said:

> . . . It is not enough to convict a person of a crime; that the Court of Justice should know the truth, it must be acquainted with the *whole* truth, and that is only to be obtained from the Rev. A. Wagner, who shields himself by saying, "My duty to God forbids me to answer any question which will in any way divulge anything that has been said to me in the secrecy of the Confessional"! The statement is positively astonishing, the consequences terrible. . . . Is the Confessional of the Anglican Church sealed against the law of the land?

When the same question was raised in the House of Lords, the Lord Chancellor replied to it in the negative, saying:

> . . . There can be no doubt that in a suit of criminal proceedings a clergyman of the Church of England is not privileged to decline to answer a question put to him for the purpose of justice. . . .

He is compelled to answer such a question, and the law of England does not allow even a Roman Catholic in dealing with a Roman Catholic to refuse to give evidence. . . . It is a matter of regret that the magistrates did not insist upon an answer.

In the House of Commons the Home Secretary's answer to a similar question was more guarded. He was not aware, he said, that the Wiltshire magistrates "had allowed any person to refuse to give evidence", and added that, "at the trial all necessary evidence would, no doubt, be forthcoming".

Perhaps Sir George Grey was uncertain of his ground; in which case he should not have been. As Yseult Bridges says:

. . . In point of fact . . . this very question had recently been put to the test twice. In the first case an Anglican clergyman had yielded and given evidence under the threat of commitment for Contempt of Court, while in the second a Roman Catholic priest had actually been sent to prison on that count.

One wonders, therefore, what would have been the Rev. Wagner's reaction to a threat of commitment for Contempt of Court. Would he have yielded to his examiners? He might yet be put to the test. Perhaps, as the Home Secretary had said, at the trial that was to be held "all necessary evidence would, no doubt, be forthcoming".

That, however, remained to be seen, and in the meantime the righteous public ranted and raved over what had already taken place, directing their anger at the cause of all the mischief—in their eyes—those hated Puseyites. Public meetings were held by bodies such as the Protestant Association, where members called for official legislation to prevent "such persons as the Reverend A. D. Wagner from officiating as a clergyman of the Church of England", and demanding that "a stop be put to the conduct of affairs at St. Paul's". And as the reverend found himself more deeply caught "at the centre of a whirling storm of execration" a police guard had to be mounted to protect his vicarage and St. Mary's; he had already suffered riots from angry mobs who had broken some of the convent's windows and torn down from the doors of St. Paul's the notice announcing the hours of confession.

There was one thing, however, against which the reverend positively reacted, and that was the charge that he had betrayed Constance Kent's confession. In a letter to *The Times* he wrote:

As I have been most unjustly charged by a portion of the press with committing the grave offence of betraying Miss Kent's sacramental confession, you, I am sure, will allow me to contradict that assertion in the most public manner possible. It was at Miss Kent's own request, and by her authority, that I communicated to two persons only the fact of her guilt. Those two were Sir George Grey and Miss Gream, and the following document, written by Miss Kent herself and given me a few days before Easter, proves that I have acted in all I have done in accordance with her instructions. The note, which is entirely her own composition, is as follows: "Sir, it is by my particular request that the bearer now informs you of my guilt, which it is my desire to have publicly made known. Constance E. Kent to Sir G. Grey." I may add that the written paper which Miss Kent gave to Sir Thomas Henry at Bow Street was also, to the best of my belief, her own composition. I never saw it, nor was I aware of her having written any paper at all until she herself produced it in Court.

His letter appeased very few, but in spite of all the verbal abuse he stood firm. And that abuse did not remain merely verbal either; he was soon made the victim of a cowardly and brutal physical assault for which the two culprits were convicted and gaoled. It is interesting to note here that quite in keeping with his character—often so much maligned—Mr. Wagner quickly and quietly sought out the wives and families of his assailants and maintained them at his own cost until the men were free once more.

Chapter 30

THE TRIAL

Murder, where newspapers are concerned, is good business, and as that July in 1865 drew nearer the editors must have been rubbing their hands in gleeful anticipation; that month would see not *one* sensational murder case tried, but *two*: Constance Kent at Salisbury and Dr. Edward Pritchard at Edinburgh. Both cases were remarkable for various reasons and both were destined to go into the chronicles of the truly "classic" crimes. It was there, though, that any similarity between the two cases ended; beyond that about all that the twenty-one-year-old English girl and the forty-year-old Scotsman had in common was the singular self-possession with which they awaited their trials.

F. Tennyson Jesse says that "the interest of a murderer lies, to the observer, in the motive . . ."[1] and that being the case there was promised much to fascinate the public in those two forthcoming murder trials.[2] Pritchard's motive for poisoning his wife and mother-in-law was probably gain, but the case was by no means as cut-and-dried as that—indeed, his motive remains, to this day, somewhat obscure. On the other hand that motive assigned to Constance Kent, revenge, though accepted generally as the correct motive, was none the less fascinating for its being recognized. Revenge is, in fact, one of the rarer motives for murder, infinitely less common than that commonest of all motives, gain, and infinitely more interesting when the one accused of being driven by it was a young woman who, after "keeping her secret for five years", had practically stepped from a convent with her confession in her hands.

That revenge, so Miss Gream had told the court, had been against the girl's stepmother, and with the publication of her words the inquisitive eyes were once more turned on the Kent family: what

[1] *Comments on Cain.*
[2] Edward William Pritchard was found guilty. He was hanged on the 29th of July, 1865.

had the stepmother, Mrs. Kent, done that was so dreadful that her stepdaughter should seek such brutal means of reprisal?—that a sixteen-year-old girl should cut her little stepbrother's throat with such thoroughness and such deliberation?

The question gave rise to further rumours, the wildest of which were exemplified by a Scottish newspaper which, after stating that Mr. Kent had taken the former Mary Pratt from a mill where she was working, "partially educated" her and then introduced her as governess into the household, went on to say, in all seriousness, that once the governess had become his wife she had used Constance as the lowliest servant, regularly beating her with a horsewhip!

Constance in her cell became increasingly aware of the damage being caused by her stated motive, "revenge on the stepmother", and anxious to avert any further pain being suffered by her family attempted to remove that onus of maltreatment which the public so mistakenly inferred. On the 15th of May she wrote regarding the matter to Mr. Rodway:

Sir,

It has been stated that my feelings of revenge were excited in consequence of cruel treatment. This is entirely false. I have received the greatest kindness from both the persons accused of subjecting me to it. I have never had any ill-will towards either of them on account of their behaviour to me, which has been very kind. I shall be obliged if you will make use of this statement in order that the public may be undeceived on this point.

I remain, Sir,
Yours truly,
Constance E. Kent.

It is interesting to note that in her letter to Mr. Rodway she does not deny that revenge was her motive; she simply denies that cruel treatment of herself was the motive for that revenge. And this indeed was the truth; she had not really been cruelly treated by her father and stepmother. The latter's treatment of her had been strict, oftentimes harsh, but it was not for this that Constance had developed such an all-consuming hatred. No, her desire for revenge had been excited by something more insidious than the boxing of her ears, banishment to the cellars or prolonged denial of access to her home. Her motive was as she had set down in her letter to Sir John

Eardley Wilmot, that letter posted from Brighton on the day she had left to give herself up. In it she had written:

The murder I committed to avenge my mother whose place had been usurped by my stepmother. The latter had been living in the family ever since my birth. She treated me with all the kindness and affection of a mother (for my own mother never loved or cared for me) and I loved her as much as though she had been.

When no more than three years old I began to observe that my mother held quite a secondary place both as a wife and as mistress of the house. *She* it was who really ruled. Many conversations on the subject, which I was considered too young to understand, I heard and remembered in after years. At that time I always took part against my mother, whom being spoken of with contempt I too despised. As I grew older and understood that my father loved *her* and treated my mother with indifference my opinion began to alter. I felt a secret dislike to *her* when she spoke scornfully or disparagingly of my mother.

Mamma died. From that time my love turned to the most bitter hatred. Even after her death *she* continued to speak of her with scorn. At such times my hate grew so intense that I could not remain in the room. I vowed a deadly vengeance, renounced all belief in religion and devoted myself body and soul to the Evil Spirit, invoking his aid in my scheme of revenge. At first I thought of murdering *her* but that seemed to me too short a pang. I would have her feel my revenge. She had robbed my mother of the affection which was her due, so I would rob *her* of what she most loved. From that time I became a demon always seeking to do evil and to lead others into it, ever trying to find an occasion to accomplish my evil design. I found it.

Having given a true account of her motive Constance had then continued:

Nearly five years have since passed away during which time I have either been in a wild feverish state of mind only happy in doing evil, or else so very wretched that I often could have put an end to myself had means been near at the moment. I felt hatred towards everyone, and a wish to make them as wretched as myself.

At last a change came. My conscience tormented me with remorse. Miserable, wretched, suspicious, I felt as though Hell were in me. Then I resolved to confess.

I am now ready to make what restitution is in my power. A life for a life is all that I can give, as the Evil done can never be repaired.

I had no mercy, let none ask it for me, though indeed all must regard me with too much horror.

Forgiveness from those I have so deeply injured I dare not ask. I hated, so is their hatred my just retribution.

It is known that Constance's letter to Sir John also contained an account of how the crime was committed. Unfortunately, though, only the foregoing part—that telling of her motive and deep remorse—has survived, and that due to a copy of it being sent to Mr. Peter Edlin, who was to help in Constance's defence. Sir John Eardley Wilmot, forwarding the copy, said that her narrative "would form the corner stone for her defence" and therefore until the trial must remain strictly secret. He went on to add:

> It points to an insane delusion of 13 years growth, indeed almost coeval with C.K.'s birth, when you consider that she was actually conceived by her mother while in a state of morbid and palpable insanity. This monomania broke out at the age so critical in girls, *viz.* 16, and led to the horrid crime with which she now stands scarred.
>
> From that time to the present reason has asserted its sway gradually until *now* she is perfectly *sane*! No jury could ever find C.K. otherwise than *insane* at the time of the murder. Hundreds of doctors examining her *now* would not shake one iota of your defence and you would get your verdict. . . .

So, while to some interested persons Constance's motive was established, the question of her state of mind—both at the time of the crime and at the present—was a matter that needed to be formally pronounced upon. First of all, what was the state of her mind *now*? Seeking an answer Mr. Rodway obtained permission from the Lord Chancellor to have an "expert" give his opinion and Dr. J. C. Bucknill of Rugby was duly directed to make the required examination. When it was completed he advised her counsel that she was, in his opinion, quite sane, and that no plea of present insanity could be urged in her defence.

The members of Constance's counsel were in no way disturbed by this pronouncement, however, for their hopes rested on a successful plea of the girl having been insane at the time of the murder. Such hopes of this move, though, were dashed by Constance herself. As Mr. Rodway later wrote to the Home Secretary:

> A plea of insanity at the time of the deed might, it is believed, have been set up with success, but she, fearing that such a plea might affect prejudicially her brother's chances in life, earnestly entreated that it should not be urged on her behalf. . . .

Constance also insisted that there would be no truth in such a plea, but her main reason for rejecting it was for the sake of William. Her self-sacrifice here did her great credit; it denied her a possible escape route from Mr. Calcraft, the hangman, if she should be found guilty, and guilty, she insisted, would be her plea. A London newspaper wrote:

> The public are naturally anxious to know what will be the duty of the presiding judge . . . should she resolutely adhere to her plea of guilty. Judges, under ordinary circumstances, are usually very reluctant to receive such a plea from a murderer. . . . They usually remonstrate with the accused, and advise him to allow the trial to proceed. But if he appears to understand the nature of the plea, and insists upon it being received, the judges are bound to accept it, and to pass the usual sentence, having in such cases no discretion. Therefore, should Constance Kent, on the occasion of her trial, still plead guilty, and should her mind be deemed sound, the duty of the presiding judge will be clear: he will have to act as he would were a verdict of guilty returned by a jury.

Constance's counsel for defence was Mr. J. D. Coleridge, Q.C., whom she reluctantly accepted, and then only to aid her in her intended plea. He subsequently advised her: "If you plead Not Guilty, then whatever I can do shall be done for your acquittal. If you plead Guilty, anything I can do to set others right shall be said. But I advise you against any intermediate course."

Constance wrote in return:

Sir,

I announced my determination yesterday to Mr. Rodway to plead guilty, and then if the judge should consider that a trial would conduce to clear those who are unjustly suspected, I would consent to leave the case in the hands of my counsel for that purpose.

If the case is not gone into it will not be believed that my confession is a true one, and I am persuaded that nothing will tend to clear the innocent so completely as my conviction.

Yours truly,

Constance Kent.

All her writings at this time, and her whole attitude, exhibit an unshakable determination to follow the course on which she was set: conviction. The help she accepted was only, as far as she was concerned, to make certain the achievement of that goal, and nothing that anyone said or did could move her from her resolve. This is shown clearly in Mr. Rodway's letter to the Home Secretary on the 2nd of August:

. . . On the day before the trial I informed her that her counsel were of opinion that if she would plead not guilty her acquittal was almost certain, notwithstanding the confession. I suggested to her to take this course and, in the case of acquittal, instead of suffering the enforced penalty of the law, to impose upon herself such penance or penalty as she might conceive due to her guilt. She, however, adhered to her plea of guilty as being her plain duty and the only course which would satisfy her conscience; but after pleading guilty, she said, she was willing to place herself in the hands of the court if the court thought it necessary to try the case for the purpose of more completely establishing her guilt and vindicating those who were innocent.

Constance Kent's determination in this particular resolve was further illustration of her own special strength. That strength and determination that was earlier evinced in her dressing up in boy's clothes to escape to freedom was now seen in the quiet determination with which she moved aside all obstacles in her path to the gallows.

The question of her life or death was to be presented at Salisbury Crown Court on Friday, the 21st of July, and on the Tuesday before this Constance was brought from Devizes and lodged in a cell in the county gaol at Salisbury, there to await the day that would bring pronouncement on her fate.

If she was reasonably sure what the outcome of her trial would be, others were not, and the question led to continuing debate. Said *The Morning Star*: "You could scarcely go into any out-of-the-way nook and corner of this usually quiet cathedral city without hearing the wildest and most improbable speculations floating about respecting this extraordinary case." The same journal reports that interest was so intense that not one eighth of the applications for admission to the very small Criminal Assize Court could be entertained, going on to describe that venue: "This place is one of the most inconvenient and ugly buildings set apart for the accommodation of those appointed to administer the law that can be found in this kingdom."

On the morning of Thursday, the 20th of July, while the police erected barriers to "keep back the immense crowd which was expected to press into the court for the trial", Mr. Justice Willes, inside, was delivering an address to the Grand Jury which had just been sworn in. To this body of twenty-four county magistrates under their chairman, the M.P. Lord Henry Thynne, he commented at length upon the case soon to come before them, that of Constance Emilie Kent—"of no occupation and well educated"—in the course of his address showing clearly that he had neither closely scrutinized the depositions of the witnesses nor studied the evidence to any degree of thoroughness. For one thing he referred to both Constance's missing nightdress and the garment found in the boiler-hole as *night-shirts*—quickly establishing that they were one and the same item, and further to that gave out that Miss Gream had been holding conversations with the prisoner on the subject of the murder for over two years! This of course was quite incorrect, as Mr. Wagner was later to make known by means of the press. The aims of Mr. Justice Willes, however, were honourable, and he made it known that he hoped the case would "be tried in the ordinary way before a jury, and with the advantages of the prisoner being represented by counsel, who can urge anything that can be said in her behalf".

As the jury was being dismissed, Constance's counsel, Mr. Coleridge, was having a meeting with her sister and brother, Mary Ann and William. Following that he continued, with the help of Mr. Rodway, to try to persuade the prisoner to alter her intended plea. She refused. In case she should at the last moment change her mind, though, he had to be totally ready; he would have to prepare for the girl's defence. He was later to write in his diary: ". . . sat up till near three, getting up my speech which, after all, I shall not deliver."

He knew, if few others did, how resolved was his client.

Next morning, Friday, the 21st, the gathering crowds swept aside the barriers and pressed up to the doors of the little Crown Court, grappling and pushing for admission, so that at 8.30 police reinforcements had to be called in.

Inside the court thirty-one witnesses were waiting, including, from the Kent family, Mr. and Mrs. Kent, Mary Ann and William, who had spent the night at the White Hart Hotel. Miss Gream and Mr. Wagner had stayed at the house of one of the latter's relatives, while the other witnesses had been accommodated at the White Lion. Among those other faces so familiar to Constance was her old school-friend, Louisa Hatherall—now bearing her married name of Louisa Long. Emma Moody had also been subpoenaed, and £4.00 had been set aside to cover the expenses of her journey from Ireland where she was now living, but illness had prevented her from making the trip. As it turned out, though, not one of those thirty-one witnesses was to see the prisoner in court that day.

While they sat in various rooms waiting to be called, and while the eager crowd outside thronged at the doors, there in the courtroom proper the trial was just about to begin.

In their places sat the counsel for the prosecution, Mr. Karslake, Q.C., and Mr. Lopes, and, for the defence, Mr. Coleridge, Mr. Edlin and Mr. Ravenhill. At 8.45 the judge entered and at once word was sent to bring forth the prisoner who had just been brought over from the county gaol in the prison van. On her arrival at the courthouse, said *The Morning Herald*, she had alighted "in the custody of the governor of the gaol and, accompanied by a female warder, was taken to the room appropriated for the reception of prisoners. Here she remained perfectly calm till requested to enter the court, when she displayed some little emotion. Nevertheless she entered the dock with a firm step."

Veiled, she was dressed in deep mourning, with black kid gauntlet gloves, a plain black cloak, and a bonnet which was in keeping with the rest of her apparel, the sombreness of which was relieved only by a small white collar. Going first of all to the back of the dock she was requested by Mr. Rodway to put up the veil that obscured her face. This she did, but as she turned around it fell again and she was once more asked to raise it. Now with her veil lifted again, and secured, she could be clearly seen by all those pairs of eyes that were focused upon her. Bearing out William Roughead's assertion that "none of us would show to advantage in the dock; it is a trying situation in which nobody looks their best",[3] *The Morning Herald* wrote of Constance: "Her personal appearance is anything but attractive. Her features are heavy, her eyes small, and her figure tending to plumpness." And from *The Frome Times*: "Her eyes looked very red, as if from long weeping; and, indeed, it was stated that she had cried more through Thursday night than she had been seen to do from the first." Clearly then, she was not about to impress anyone there that day with any powers of physical attraction—but there, she never had done.

The clerk, addressing the prisoner, said:

"Constance Emilie Kent, you are indicted for the wilful murder of Francis Savill Kent, at North Bradley, on the 29th or 30th of June, 1860. How say you, are you guilty or not guilty?"

In a voice that could only just be heard, the girl answered.

"Guilty."

Intense silence followed the utterance of that single word that must surely damn her; the word that Mr. Justice Willes did not want to hear. After a moment the judge himself spoke, asking her:

"Are you aware that you are charged with having wilfully, intentionally, and with malice, killed your brother?"

Keeping her head down the girl answered, her voice as low as before:

"Yes."

Another pause.

"And you plead guilty to that . . .?"

[3] *Classic Crimes.*

This question was met only with silence, and after waiting for some moments the judge prompted her.

"What is your answer?"

And still the girl said nothing.

In the taut, tense atmosphere that prevailed every eye was on the prisoner in the dock. Perhaps she would change her plea; or perhaps she would continue to refuse to answer—in which case the judge was empowered to record a plea of *not guilty* on her behalf. He spoke again:

"I must remind you that you are charged with having wilfully, intentionally, and with malice, killed and murdered your brother. Are you guilty or not guilty?"

And now she answered readily:

"Guilty."

". . . Then let the plea be recorded."

In "the profound silence that ensued" Mr. Coleridge arose and said:

"I desire to say two things before your Lordship pronounces sentence. First, solemnly in the presence of Almighty God, as a person who values her own soul, the prisoner wishes me to say that the guilt is hers alone, and that her father and others, who have so long suffered most unjust and cruel suspicions, are wholly and absolutely innocent. And secondly, that she was not driven to this act, as has been asserted, by unkind treatment at home, as she met with nothing there but tender and forebearing love; and I hope I may add, not improperly, that it gives me a melancholy pleasure to be the organ of these statements for her because, on my honour, I believe them to be true."

The clerk, then addressing the prisoner, said: "You have confessed yourself guilty of the murder of Francis Savill Kent. Have you anything to say why sentence of death should not be passed upon you?"

"No."

The black cap was placed upon the judge's head.

"Constance Emilie Kent," he said, "you have pleaded guilty to an indictment charging you with the wilful murder of your brother, Francis Savill Kent, on the 30th of June, 1860. It is my duty to receive the plea which you have deliberately put forward, and it is a satisfaction to me to know that it was not pleaded until after having had the advice of your counsel, who would have freed you from this dreadful charge if you could have been freed thereof. I can entertain no doubt, after having read the evidence with the depositions, and considering that this is your third confession of your crime, that your plea is one of a really guilty person. The murder was committed under circumstances of great deliberation and cruelty. You appear to have allowed feelings of jealousy and anger to have worked in your breast—" ("Not jealousy," the girl muttered) "—until at last they assumed over you the power of the Evil One." Here the judge, whose fortitude had been gradually giving way, broke down, and he bowed his head and wept. Constance herself had remained outwardly unmoved until this moment but now, with the judge's reserve gone, her own, too, was swept away. She gave an hysterical sob and, as if she would run from the scene, half turned in the dock. A moment later, regaining her control, she stilled her sobbing and faced the court again, eyes downcast. The judge went on:

"Whether Her Majesty, with whom alone the prerogative of mercy rests, may be advised to consider the fact of your youth——" again his words ceased and only the sound of his weeping could be heard, "—at the time when the murder was committed, and the fact that you were convicted chiefly upon your own confession, which removes suspicion from others, is a question which it would be presumptuous for me to answer here. . . . It well behoves you to live what is left of your life as one who is about to die, and to seek a more enduring mercy, by sincere and deep contrition, and by a reliance upon the only redemption, propitiation, and satisfaction for the sins of the whole world." He paused, and then:

"It remains for me to discharge the duty which the law imposes upon the court, and without alternative, and that is, to pass upon you the sentence which the law adjudges for wilful murder—that you be taken from the place where you now stand to the place whence you came; thence to a place of execution, and that you be hanged by the neck until your body be dead; and that after death your body be buried within the precincts of the gaol in which you shall have been last confined. And may God have mercy on your **soul.**"

Chapter 31

AFTER THE TRIAL

A fter the judge had finished his mournful duty," said *The Morning Herald*, "a breathless silence ensued, the prisoner standing in front of the dock with her head bent down, and motionless as a statue."

The murder trial, one of the shortest on record, was over, when to most onlookers it had hardly begun. Even the judge, it seemed, could barely grasp the fact. He hesitated in his chair, as if by doing so he could somehow rewrite that finale that was already a reality: the young woman who stood before him had been condemned to death, and the whole thing had taken just a few minutes from start to finish.

After some moments the judge got up and moved away, and at this the governor of the gaol took his cue and, also rising, touched the prisoner on the shoulder, signifying that they, too, must leave. At his touch "the wretched girl started, as if in a dream", then, raising her hands to let down her veil once more, she turned and, "with a firm step", left the dock.

Surely she, too, as she was conveyed back to her cell, must have wondered at the brevity and the efficiency of the proceedings that had so swiftly culminated in her sentence of death. Yet for all her wonder at it she must have been satisfied; her confession had been accepted; it had not been questioned.

She spent that night, said *The Advertiser*, "very tranquilly", and "told the governor of the gaol that she had never slept so well for the last five years". Truly, then, the course of her fate had brought her a new calm.

There were others, however, who were not at all satisfied with the trial's outcome, and Constance Kent's conviction served to point out the inadequacies of the law in such a way that no one could escape them. Her trial left a scar on the face of British justice. It is not enough that justice is done; it must be *seen* to be done, and in the case of Constance Kent this had not happened. How could it have?—if her counsel was right in destroying the only possible motive attributable to her then she had killed *without any motive*. Further to that there was no new evidence and that which already existed had formerly been the subject of ridicule. In essence Constance was convicted solely on her confession. And this was not enough.

That trial at Salisbury, so brief and so unsatisfactory, still left many questions unanswered, and those questions have remained right up to the present time. *Could* the girl have carried out the murder alone and unaided, as she claimed? Also, why had her father lied? Why, too, had the nurse lied? There *were* answers to these questions, and the public wanted them.

There was one man, however, who was completely satisfied with the outcome of the trial. Dr. Stapleton. He, it would appear on the surface, had been proved to be right, and he was quick to take up his pen to inform the newspapers and the medical journals of the "fact". Having all along denied the suffocation theory he was most eager to take Constance at her word—that she and she alone had done the deed, and with a razor. As stated earlier, though, he had only denied the suffocation theory as it was seen to point to Mr. Kent and Elizabeth Gough as the culprits, and in a letter to *The Times* soon after the trial he made this perfectly clear. He wrote: "The finger of suspicion was first pointed at the nurse and father of the murdered child by . . . a conjecture that he had suffered partial or complete suffocation." And then later: "Now, by Constance Kent's confession, the suggestion of suffocation, which placed Elizabeth Gough in mortal peril, is completely refuted."

It is difficult to see how Constance's confession, which told practically nothing, "completely refuted" the suggestion of suffocation, but there, that is what Dr. Stapleton would have one believe. Such a belief, though, does not take into account the bruising around the child's mouth and, more importantly, the *total absence* of sprayed blood at the scene of the crime. Regarding the latter *The Frome Times* reported that among the witnesses to be called at the girl's trial there were "several local medical gentlemen" who were ready to explain such a phenomenon, and that these men, "if called, would have stated that the murdered boy was carried alive to the closet, that his throat was cut there, but it was done so suddenly that *the heart ceased its pulsations with the plunge of the knife*, and this accounted for the absence of any blood at the spot of the murder". This, of course, as the lowliest medical student will verify, is a physiological impossibility. Clearly it was an "explanation" put forward by men who, firmly believing Constance to be guilty, were quite ready to adapt their opinions to support her inadequate confession.

Those medical men, including Dr. Stapleton, did not have the truth, though. And they *must* have known this. But what, then, *was* the truth? What was the real story? Everyone wanted to know. Perhaps, though, the questioners told each other, all would be satisfactorily explained in time; it was rumoured that the girl had made a *complete* confession; this, no doubt, would eventually solve the mystery.

On leaving the courtroom Mr. Justice Willes had wasted no time but had at once written to the Home Secretary that Constance Emilie Kent had been arraigned before him that day on a charge of murder to which she had persisted in pleading guilty. He then went on:

. . . I have no reason to think that the plea was other than the genuine confession of a really guilty person, in her sound mind. There was no alternative but to pass sentence upon her, and I sentenced her to death.

The murder itself was a very terrible one indeed. But when it was committed the prisoner was only sixteen. Further, she has now been detected and convicted upon her own confession, though corroborated by independent evidence. Lastly, the confession which she has made has removed suspicion from two innocent persons.

I beg to submit this consideration to your better judgement and plead for the mercy of the Crown to the extent of commuting the capital sentence.

Judge Willes' voice was not the only one raised in support of Constance Kent being allowed to live—but it was the most influential.

That same day in her cell Constance saw her father, brother and sister, Mary Ann, for about twenty minutes. The meeting, it is said, was "painful" and "of a most affecting character". Mrs. Kent at this time remained "in another part of the town". She and her step-daughter had long ago had their last meeting.

Later that day while Mr. Kent and his family were returning to The Tower, their home in Llangollen, North Wales, Constance saw, on separate occasions, Mr. Wagner and the Superior. The girl appeared, it was reported, "much pleased with these visits, especially that of Miss Gream".

When Mr. Rodway saw her he asked what she wanted done with the £800 she had placed in the church's alms-box. Mr. Wagner, who had immediately guessed its source, had placed it for safe-keeping in the London and County Bank, and now Constance told her solicitor that she would like it to be sent to her father, to be used "for the good of the family".

Mr. Coleridge, writing in his diary for that day, the 21st of July, penned the words: "Poor Constance Kent pleaded guilty. I said a few words and *there* an end. It was very solemn."

Well, solemn it undoubtedly was, but as for its being the end, that was a matter which was still to be decided. Not only did the Home Secretary receive several letters on the girl's behalf from people who had never met her, but those closer to her were making determined efforts to save her life. In this respect Mr. Rodway wrote from Trowbridge on the 23rd of July to Dr. Bucknill who had arranged, the following day, to visit London. Wrote Mr. Rodway:

My dear Sir,

Constance Kent

You will have seen in the papers the result of this case.

After conferring with my counsel I had an interview with her at Salisbury. I assured her on their authority that if she chose to plead Not Guilty her acquittal (notwithstanding her confession) would be almost certain. I submitted to her that in the event of acquittal she might impose upon herself what penance or punish-ment she pleased, such as banishment, or devoting her future life to the service of the sick, instead of suffering the enforced punishment of the law. But although she shrinks from punish-ment yet she nobly and magnanimously resisted all my sugges-tions, and determined to accept the consequence of her act, saying that no other course would satisfy her conscience and be consistent with her plain duty.

This poor girl, once so deluded, is now so fit to live and be a useful member of society. She has borne herself with so much resignation in prison, and shown so much good and right feeling, that my deepest sympathies have been moved in her favour. Had she been my own daughter I could have accepted her penitence and magnanimity as an atonement for her guilt, and great as her guilt has been, I could have taken her back again to my home and heart. . . .

If before you leave London you would see the Home Secretary or Mr. Waddington and communicate your opinion of her present state, and the probability of her character—at the time of her emerging from girlhood into womanhood—having been warped by influences, which would to some extent lessen the criminality of the act . . . you would confer a great favour on her family and friends. She is particularly anxious that insanity, hereditary or otherwise, should not be urged in extenuation, because she says it would not be true, and it might affect her brother's prospects in life. You will know how to deal with this sad case at the Home Office, and to your judgement and humanity—of which you have given such elevated proof—I confide the expression of the interests and hopes of this poor girl and her wretched family.

It is intended that a petition shall shortly be forwarded for commutation of the sentence, of which please inform the Home Office.

Believe me, my dear Sir,

Yours very faithfully,

R. Rodway.

On the day that Dr. Bucknill received this letter he met Mr. Waddington and put forward the case for commutation of the girl's sentence. Later that day he followed up the interview with a letter in which he wrote of "the position of self-sacrifice in which this unhappy young woman has placed herself, and the restraint that she imposes upon those who would wish to plead in her behalf. . . ."

There were many working to save the girl's life. In Llangollen both Mr. and Mrs. Kent signed a petition to the Queen, while Sir John Eardley Wilmot—that "great taker up of causes"—was entrusted with the task of presenting it to the Home Office.

Mr. Wagner, meanwhile, had applied for an interview with the Home Secretary and, on his request being politely declined, wrote from Brighton on the 25th of July:

I regret that I cannot *speak* to you on the subject of Miss Kent, as of course I could have *said* much more in an informal way than I can dare commit to paper; but I am very grateful for the opportunity which you have so kindly given me of even *writing* to you a few lines about her.

One point which I wish to assure you of is this. I have myself the fullest conviction of Miss Kent's real repentance for her sin. I know for certain that when she authorized me, last April, to inform you of her guilt, she did so, fully anticipating that the extreme sentence of the law would be carried out upon her, and without any thought of sparing herself. She felt it a duty she owed to God, to make at the cost of her life, what reparation she could to her father and others, for the unjust suspicions under which they have so long laboured.

And even since she has been in gaol, I know from the private letters she has written to Miss Gream that she has had great temptations to resist—temptations, I mean, offered her by the lawyers, who told her she would almost certainly be acquitted if only she would plead not guilty, but she has had the courage given her to remain firm to her original purpose, and take no course which might throw any doubt upon her father's innocence. All this, I would most respectfully submit, is greatly to her honour, and I feel sure will be taken into merciful consideration by those who have the decision of her future in their hands. . . .

Mr. Wagner then went on to suggest that if the girl could be pardoned completely he was willing to take her back to St. Mary's,

. . . where she might lead a life of seclusion and penitence, and of almost as much self-denial as in a prison, but where she would not be cut off from those means of grace to which she has been accustomed, and which certainly, under God, have been beneficial to her soul (for may I say, I hope, without breach of confidence, that two years ago, when she first came to St. Mary's Hospital she . . . was very ignorant of religion altogether).

I have no anxiety to see her spared any amount of *earthly*

punishment, but I am very anxious about her soul—anxious that she should persevere in her present state, and die in a state of Grace. . . .

Her pleading guilty the other day was, I know, entirely the dictate of her conscience, and without any hope of obtaining mercy by so doing. . . .

On the 25th of July Sir George Grey, the Home Secretary, after consulting the Cabinet, announced that Constance Kent's death sentence was to be commuted to penal servitude for life, saying in the course of his announcement:

. . . Had the prisoner been tried and convicted in 1860 her youth would probably, I may say almost certainly, have prevented her execution. It would be wrong to make a difference now in the course to be adopted because, at the time of her conviction, she is twenty-one. It is also a material fact that the conviction would not have been obtained except on her own confession. . . .

When Mr. Dorning, governor of Salisbury Gaol, carried the tidings to the prisoner in his care she, it was reported, "heard unmoved the news that her life had been spared". There can be no doubt, however, of her true emotions, for she did, most earnestly, want to live.

Mr. Rodway was swift to write to the Home Secretary expressing his relief and gratitude, in the course of his letter saying that a petition had already been prepared for the signature of Constance's sisters and brother, "their friends and others interested in the fate of the condemned girl, [but] as the sentence had already been commuted, no attempt was made to get it signed, although half the country would willingly have joined in its prayer for a recommendation to mercy".

Regarding that other petition, the one signed by Mr. and Mrs. Kent and entrusted to the care of Sir John Eardley Wilmot, it seems that Sir John was fated to be unsuccessful in his attempts to be of real use in the affair of the Road murder; now he wrote to Mr. Rodway saying: "I did not send the petition to the Home Office as Miss Kent was respited before I could present it."

Although Constance Kent's life had been spared the matter was

by no means over. The proceedings had left many questions unanswered and until these answers were forthcoming the doubts
would remain. Clearly, what was required from the girl was a complete statement showing *how* she had committed the murder and
also—as most of the population was in ignorance of her motive—
why. Then, at the end of August a letter appeared in the press,
written by Dr. Bucknill, by which means, it seemed, all minds
would be set at rest. Part of the doctor's letter is as follows (the
numbers and italics therein are my own; they have been inserted
to draw attention to particular statements which will later be examined):

Sir,

   I am requested by Miss Constance Kent to communicate to you
the following details of her crime, which she has confessed to
Mr. Rodway, her solicitor, and to myself, and which she now
desires to be made public.

   Constance Kent first gave an account of the circumstances of
her crime to Mr. Rodway, and she afterwards acknowledged to
me the correctness of that account when I recapitulated it to her.
The explanation of her motive she gave to me when, with the
permission of the Lord Chancellor, I examined her for the purpose of ascertaining whether there were any grounds for supposing that she was labouring under mental disease. Both Mr.
Rodway and I are convinced of the truthfulness and good faith
of what she said to us.

   Constance Kent says that the manner in which she committed
her crime was as follows:

   A few days before the crime *she obtained possession of a razor
from a green case in her father's wardrobe* (1) and secreted it.
This was the sole instrument she used (2). She also secreted a
candle with matches by placing them in a corner of the closet in
the garden, where the murder was committed. On the night of
the murder she undressed herself and went to bed because she
expected that her sisters would visit her room. She lay awake
watching until she thought that the household were all asleep,
and soon after midnight she left her bedroom and went downstairs and opened the drawing-room door and shutters. She then
went up into the nursery, withdrew the blanket from between the

sheet and the counterpane and placed it on the side of the cot. *She took the child from his bed and carried him downstairs* (3) through the drawing-room.

She had on her night-clothes and in the drawing-room *she put on her goloshes. Having the child on one arm she raised the drawing-room window with the other hand, went round the house and into the closet, lighted the candle and placed it on the seat of the closet, the child being wrapped in the blanket and still sleeping* (4). *While the child was in this position she inflicted the wound in the throat* (5). *She said she thought the blood would never come, and that the child was not killed* (6), so *she thrust the razor into the left side* (7) and put the body *with the blanket round it* into the vault (8). The light burned out.

The piece of flannel which she had with her was torn from an old flannel garment placed in the waste-bag and which she had taken some time before and sewn it to use in washing herself.

She went back to her room, examined her dress and *found only two spots of blood on it* (9). These she washed out in the basin, and threw the water, which was but little discoloured, into the foot-pan in which she had washed her feet overnight. She took another of her nightdresses and got into bed. In the morning her nightdress had become dry where it had been washed. She folded it up and put it into the drawer. *Her three nightdresses were examined by Mr. Foley and she believed also by Dr. Parsons* (10), the medical attendant of the family.

She thought the bloodstains had been effectively washed out, but on holding the dress up to the light a day or two afterwards she found the stains were still visible. She secreted the dress, moving it from place to place, and she eventually burned it in her own bedroom and put the ashes into the kitchen grate. It was about five or six days after the child's death that she burned the night-dress.

On Saturday morning, having cleaned the razor, she took an opportunity of replacing it unobserved in the case in the ward-robe (11). She abstracted her nightdress from the clothes-basket when the housemaid went to fetch a glass of water.

The stained garment found in the boiler-hole had no connection whatsoever with the crime.

As regards her motive for the crime, it seems that although she entertained at one time a great regard for the present Mrs. Kent, yet if any remark was at any time made which in her opinion was disparaging to any member of the first family, she treasured it up and determined to revenge it. She had no ill-will against the little boy except as one of the children of her stepmother. She declared that both her father and her stepmother had always been kind to her personally. . . .

She told me that when the nursemaid was accused she had fully made up her mind to confess if the nurse had been convicted; and that she had made up her mind to commit suicide if she was herself convicted. She said that she felt herself under the influence of the devil before she committed the murder, but that she did not believe, and had not believed, that the devil had more to do with her crime than he had with any other wicked action. She had not said her prayers for a year before the murder, and not afterwards, until she came to reside at Brighton. She said that the circumstances which revived religious feelings in her mind was thinking about receiving the Sacrament when confirmed.

This, then, was that detailed confession for which the public had been so eagerly waiting. But did it solve the mystery? Did it answer the questions? No, it did not. And neither did that other account of hers—that written earlier from Brighton in her letter to Sir John Eardley Wilmot. In that letter, so said Inspector Williamson,[1] she stated that after cutting the child's throat "she thought she had not cut it effectually and she then stabbed him twice". *Twice!?* If she did indeed say such a thing it only goes to show—as does her confession broadcast by Dr. Bucknill—that even *she* was not aware of *what had actually happened on that night.*

[1] See Inspector Williamson's report of the 24th of July, 1865: Appendix I.

Chapter 32

THE CONFESSION

Most of the writers who have focused at length on the case of Constance Kent have one thing in common: they find it impossible to accept her detailed confession as an explanation of the way in which the crime was committed.

Even at that time, immediately following the publication of the confession, *The Times* gave voice to those questions raised by her story and said:

> Such are the details now afforded us of this extraordinary crime, which seems not to diminish in perplexity and strangeness as it is unravelled step by step. It is evident that we have not yet obtained a complete account of all the circumstances. . . .

Regarding the girl's publicly stated motive for the killing, that journal goes on:

> . . . The motive assigned for the murder is not the least extraordinary part of the story. She repeats her assertion that she had received nothing but kindness from her father and the second Mrs. Kent, and she adds that she had no ill-will whatever against the boy. It was simply that "if any remark was at any time made which in her opinion was disparaging to a member of the first family, she treasured it up and determined to revenge it". These trivial vexations, and nothing else, were sufficient to incite her to take such a horrible revenge . . . [and] she murdered her little brother from no motives but those of the most trifling spite. . . . Let us hope that the mystery which remains may soon be unravelled, and the terrible tale consigned to a quick oblivion.

It is hardly surprising that Constance's published motive was not generally accepted. It was of course a lie. And Dr. Bucknill made this quite clear in a letter he wrote to Mr. Waddington at the Home Office on the 30th of August:

Sir,

In reference to the published confession of Constance Kent, I think it right to inform you that . . . the answer given of her motive of her crime was inserted by me at her request instead of what I consider the more truthful and sufficient motive which I mentioned to you. The reasons she argued for the variations from her statements to me in examinations were regard for the feelings and interests of her father and brother.

Thirteen years later in a lecture delivered at the Royal College of Physicians (April 1878) Dr. Bucknill made public the correct motive for the crime, saying:

. . . to save the feelings of those who were alive at the time, I did not make known the motive, and on this account it has been that the strange portent has remained in the history of our social life that a young girl, not insane, should have been capable of murdering her beautiful boy brother in cold blood and without motive. I think the right time and opportunity has come for me to explain away this apparent monstrosity of conduct. A real and dreadful motive did exist. . . .

And the motive now given by Dr. Bucknill was, as we know, the *correct* one, that Constance was wreaking vengeance on her stepmother—for that lady's disparaging remarks about the first Mrs. Kent. Said Dr. Bucknill:

. . . She thought of poisoning her stepmother, but that, on reflection, she felt, would be no real punishment, and then it was that she determined to murder the poor lady's boy. A dreadful story this; but who can fail to pity the depths of household misery which it denotes?

As has been clearly demonstrated, in giving her motive to the court at the time of her trial Constance had not hesitated to lie—for the protection of others. And just as she had lied about *why* she had committed the crime, so, in her detailed confession, she lied about *how* the deed was done. This can easily be seen in a brief examination of certain parts of that confession. It will *not* stand scrutiny. Consider those points which I have already singled out:

1. *She obtained possession of a razor from a green case in her*

father's wardrobe. . . . Why take the risk of stealing a razor when she could have appropriated a knife so much more easily? Also, as it is very doubtful that she would ever have seen her father shaving himself, how could she be so familiar with his razors that she could know which one she could safely borrow without its being missed?

2. *This was the sole instrument she used.* Then how to account for the stab in the side? It is impossible to stab with a razor. Said Dr. Parsons: The stab wound could only have been made with "a sharp, pointed knife".

3. *She took the child from his bed and carried him down-stairs.* . . . Savill must have weighed about thirty-five pounds. That she could have held him on one arm while she remade his cot, and then carried him from the room without him making any sound of protest or any other noise is hardly credible. He would have awakened at once.

4. *In the drawing-room she put on her goloshes. Having the child on one arm she raised the drawing-room window with the other hand, went round the house and into the closet, lighted the candle and placed it on the seat of the closet, the child being wrapped in the blanket and still sleeping.* Is it possible that she could have held that exceptionally heavy child *sleeping* on her arm (*a*) while she put on her goloshes; (*b*) while she opened a heavy window and climbed out of that window, and (*c*) while she struck a match and lit a candle? It *is* possible that she carried out those acts, but it is not possible that the child remained asleep whilst they were performed. Also, why should she take the longest route to the privy when that offered by means of the kitchen door was much safer and much easier to negotiate?

5. *While the child was in this position (i.e. lying asleep on her arm) she inflicted the wound in the throat.* The throat was severed by one clean cut, from ear to ear. Is it possible that a girl who had probably never used a razor in her life before could have used one for the first time with such efficiency? In any case, it is certain that she could not have inflicted such a wound while the child lay in the position she described.

6. *She thought the blood would never come and that the child was not killed.* . . . If the child's heart was beating, blood would immediately have *spurted*, spraying from the severed arteries. If the child's heart had *stopped* beating the blood would still have *flowed*

—at ónce—and it would have continued to do so for at least twenty minutes afterwards. It cannot be believed, therefore, that the throat wound was slow to bleed. Constance also said that after cutting the child's throat she thought he "was not killed". But Savill's throat was cut so deeply that his spinal column was clearly visible. Is it possible to almost decapitate one's victim and still think he "was not killed"?! It is a ludicrous suggestion.

7. *She thrust the razor into the left side.* . . . As stated above, it is impossible to stab with a razor.

8. . . . and *put the body with the blanket round it into the vault.* . . . But the blanket was not found wrapped around the child's body; it was lying on top of it.

9. *She . . . examined her dress and found only two spots of blood on it.* To hold a child on one arm, cut its throat almost to the point of decapitation and end up with only "two spots of blood" on one's clothing . . . such a thing is not possible.

10. *Her three nightdresses were examined by Mr. Foley and, she believed, also by Mr. Parsons.* . . . But Constance *did not know* what the two men actually saw. When Foley was asked whether she had been in the room while her linen was being examined he said she had not.

11. *On Saturday morning, having cleaned the razor, she took an opportunity of replacing it unobserved in the case in the wardrobe.* How did she do this? Her father's dressing-room door connecting with the landing was *sealed*, therefore the only means of gaining access to his wardrobe was by way of his bedroom. But Mrs. Kent was there. Mr. Kent had left her in that room when he went dashing off to Trowbridge and *she stayed there all day*.

Although certain parts of the girl's confession bear signs of truthfulness it must be acknowledged that other parts were the result of deliberate lying; or of hasty invention—which is not the same thing.

Then what was the truth? And why would she lie in her confession? Clearly, one needs to look deeper to solve the mystery.

In my own search for the answer I began by re-examining the medical evidence put forward by Dr. Parsons following the *post-mortem* examination. In his opinion, he said, the child had first been suffocated—this suffocation causing death or *almost* causing death. Following this had come the wound in the throat—which would have made death certain—and then finally the stab in the chest. As this latter injury had bled hardly at all and the sides of the wound had not retracted Dr. Parsons was quite certain that the child was already dead when the wound was inflicted. That, then, was the sequence in which he believed the injuries had taken place: suffocation, throat-cutting, chest-wound—a sequence which, I realized, has formed the basis of every hypothesis concerning that act of murder.

But was this sequence the correct one?

Seeking an answer to this I approached Professor Keith Simpson of Guy's Hospital, one of Britain's foremost pathologists, and asked him to examine the medical evidence. This he most kindly agreed to do. His subsequent comments proved most enlightening.

First of all it was necessary to look at the question of the blood found at the scene of the crime.

Everyone concerned at the time was in complete agreement that there were no signs of the spraying or spurting that would normally be the result of the severance of living arteries. The blood on the face and body showed that it had *run* or *trickled* there, while the small pool and the drops on the privy floor had clearly come from blood *falling straight down*. Says Prof. Simpson: "If there was no arterial spurting—real spraying as from arteries—the child must already have been dead." And he adds: "It would, of course, continue to lose blood until the blood clotted—maybe *twenty or thirty minutes later*."

One point is therefore established: the child was dead before the wound in the throat was inflicted.

Regarding the stab wound in the chest, Dr. Parsons, seeing that the sides of the wound had not retracted, was certain that it had also come after death. And in this he was correct. However, noting that the wound had bled hardly at all he stated that the body must have been "previously drained of blood", i.e. that it had *followed* the cutting of the throat. In forming *this* assumption, though, Dr. Parsons was *wrong*; Prof. Simpson says that the fact that the chest wound did not bleed does *not* indicate that the body was "previously drained of blood". He states: "Stab wounds *seldom* bleed much *externally* if the penetrating wound is, as here, into the abdominal and chest cavities, for there is *so much room* for any blood which flows to accumulate *internally*."

All this, of course, totally destroys Dr. Parsons' certainty as to the sequence in which the injuries occurred: 1. suffocation; 2. throat-cutting; 3. the stab in the chest. Indeed, says Prof. Simpson, there is nothing in Dr. Parsons' evidence to bear out such an opinion, and in actuality the stab in the chest might have been inflicted as much as *fifteen minutes before* the throat was cut.

So now there was an alternative possible sequence for Savill's injuries; a sequence that seemed to me to be the correct one: first the fatal suffocation of the child; then the stab in the chest—which bled *internally* and, on its own, would not have caused death; and lastly—and perhaps some time later—the wound in the throat—from which the blood would still have freely flowed. This sequence alone, I found, was consistent with all the other known facts, and with that realization I was drawn still closer to the answer I sought.

What, in fact, did take place in the early hours of that morning of the 30th of June, 1860?

Any theory advanced *must* take into account Mr. Kent's seemingly inexplicable behaviour and the certain knowledge that he knew before Savill's body was found that the child had been taken away in a blanket. And likewise Elizabeth Gough's behaviour too, for she had also surely lied about her knowledge of the blanket, *and* as regards her assertion that she had been able to see—by kneeling on her bed—that Savill's cot was empty. These are factors that have a part in the mystery—a mystery which is not solved by the many incongruities in Constance Kent's confession.

But *why* does Constance's confession not bear examination? It cannot be that her memory was bad. The incidents of that night must have been etched on her mind forever. Had she, then, set out to lie? If so, for what purpose?

The answer, when it came to me, set me on a course which answered so many questions.

The clue to it all, I realized, was to be found in what she had told Mr. Wagner and Miss Gream. To the Superior, Constance said she had murdered Savill with her father's razor, and Miss Gream later, on oath, relayed this information to the Trowbridge magistrates. Mr. Wagner, though, *refused* to tell what *he* had learned from Constance, saying that to do so would be a breach of the confessional. All *he* ever admitted was a knowledge of the girl's guilt in the affair.

But why did he refuse to divulge what the girl had said to him if Miss Gream had already told the truth of the matter? Did he take that recalcitrant stand just to bring notice to his much-hated means of worship—or was there a different, more important, and perhaps more laudable reason?

Look again at the words of Constance's written statement:

> I, Constance Emilie Kent, alone and unaided on the night of the 29th of June, 1860, murdered at Road Hill House, Wiltshire, one Francis Savill Kent. Before the deed none knew of my intention, nor after of my guilt; no one assisted me in the crime, nor after in my evasion of discovery.

True, succinctly she admits to being guilty, but most of the confession is taken up with protestations that she did it *alone*. Over and over again in these fifty-two words she seems intent on one thing, on asserting that she, *and she alone*, should be considered guilty. But would not one such protest have been enough? As Gertrude would have it: "The lady protests too much, methinks".

Now look at Mr. Wagner's letter to *The Times* regarding those accusations that he had betrayed Constance's confession. He wrote:

> It was at Miss Kent's own request, and by her authority, that I communicated to two persons only the fact of her guilt. Those two were Sir George Grey and Miss Gream. . . .

The accepted way of reading that first sentence is as follows:

> It was at Miss Kent's own request, and by her authority, that I communicated to *two persons only* the fact of her guilt. . . .

Mr. Wagner, it seemed, was putting this forward as his defence; that he was not guilty of betraying her secret as he had only told two people. But surely, a secret divulged to even *one* person is a secret betrayed. No, his letter, as I was reading it, didn't quite make sense. And then I suddenly realized that the error was *mine*: *I was putting the emphasis on the wrong words*. With the emphasis *shifted*, that sentence took on an altogether different meaning:

> It was at Miss Kent's own request, and by her authority, that I communicated to two persons *only the fact of her guilt.*

That was it: the *truth*. Wagner was not concerned with stating that he had *only told two persons*; he was stating that he had told those two persons—Miss Gream and Sir George Grey—*only the fact of Constance's guilt*. And this she had requested him to do. Constance had given *two different, separate accounts* of the happenings on that fatal night. One account was intended to go out to the world, while the other, *the true one*, she gave only to Mr. Wagner, in the confessional. Wagner had told Sir Thomas Henry this when Constance had given herself up at Bow Street, saying: "When speaking of Miss Kent's confession I wish it to be clearly understood that I was not referring to any *private* confession made to me, but to an open, public confession."[1] It was that private confession she had made to him that he was bound to keep secret. And that secret was the truth. It was the true story of the part she had taken in that most mysterious murder at Road.

Before attempting to reconstruct the pattern of events that occurred on that night of the 29th/30th of June it is necessary, for clarification, to briefly examine one or two other points.

First of all it must be remembered that much of Constance's detailed confession published in the press was the result of pure invention. So many of the things she "accounted" for could *not possibly* have happened in the way she would have one believe. But *why* did she lie? The answer is clear: for the same reason that she lied about her motive: protection of her father. Had Mr. Kent not become inextricably involved in the murder she could have told the truth. But he *was* involved and Constance, trying to hide the fact, had to somehow tell a story that would account not only for what *she* had done, but for what she believed her father had done as well. No easy task, and her confession shows just how unequal she was to that task. It comes over at once as an uneasy blend of fiction and fact. Just as there are sentences, phrases that smack of pure fabrication, so there are also parts that have an inescapable ring of truth about them. For example: Constance's statement that she found only two spots of blood on her nightdress when she got back to her room. This, to me, seemed to be based in truth. But why only *two* spots? This was a puzzle to me until I learned from Prof. Simpson that "some slight bleeding from the nose occurs in

---

[1] See page 266.

suffocation". With that information another piece of the jig-saw fell into place.

Why, also, did Constance say that, following the cut with the razor "she thought the blood would never come and that the child was not killed"? As remarked earlier, is it possible to almost decapitate one's victim and still believe him to be living?! Also as stated, although the blood might not have spurted—if suffocation had taken place—the blood would still have flowed, and *at once* Her statement here cannot possibly refer to the wound in the throat, but it *can* very easily refer to the wound in the chest. That same wound which she would naïvely have us believe she inflicted with a razor!

And on to the matter of the razor itself. Why did Constance say that a razor was the "sole instrument" she used? No such stab wound could have been made with a razor and neither would she have been able to cut the child's throat with a razor in the way in which she claimed it was done. Then why did she say she had used a razor for the purpose. The answer is because that is how she *thought* the wound had been inflicted.

The open razor today is rarely seen outside a barber's shop, but in those days, of course, they were common to almost every household. Further to that it was quite often used as a *weapon* and was a common means of suicide (means of suicide popular today: pills-overdose, etc., did not then exist); added to which fact when someone's throat was cut one at once assumed that a razor would have been the instrument used; in support of this is the fact that an open razor is quite commonly known as a "cut-throat". The truth is, Constance *assumed* that Savill's throat had been cut with a razor, and she therefore insisted—to protect her father—on taking the blame for it herself.

Make no mistake, apart from Constance, who played a leading role, Mr. Kent was most deeply involved in the happenings of that summer night—of which involvement, it would appear, there were many who harboured some suspicions. Wrote *The Devizes Advertiser* before the trial:

Serious rumours are afloat of a second person being implicated in this tragic deed. It would be highly imprudent to say anything more till the time of trial arrives; but the result of the investigation of the detective officers will, we believe, show that the Road jurymen were not so void of penetration or sympathetic feeling as they have been represented to be.

And from *Lloyd's Weekly London Newspaper*:

It is also said that criminal proceedings are intended to be taken against other parties, the nature of which it would be premature further to particularise at present, that will tend still further to increase the public interest in this extraordinary affair.

Mr. Kent, of course, was the object of these references. Indeed, so much of his behaviour had showed clearly how desperate he was to hide the fact of his complicity.

And what of Elizabeth Gough? At the time of the crime there were many, including some of the police officers, who had been convinced of *her* involvement. Had those suspicions been misdirected? No. She too played her part. Very early on in the investigations the Wiltshire police had voiced an opinion that two persons must have been concerned, and that one of them was a woman. This was only partly true. Captain Meredith *should* have said that *at least* two persons were involved. There were in fact *three*. Constance, Mr. Kent, and Elizabeth Gough.

Before showing the nature of this involvement there are certain indisputable facts that must be borne in mind:

1. At the time of the crime Mrs. Kent was eight months pregnant. In his marriage, therefore, Mr. Kent would have been denied sexual satisfaction for some considerable time. Also, as they had cohabited for about seventeen years it can be well imagined that their first passion had long since burned out. Therefore, although Mr. Kent appears to have been genuinely very fond of his wife there is no reason to suppose that such affection precluded his being drawn to the attractions of an available, good-looking and much younger woman like Elizabeth Gough. Whilst living with his first wife—and giving her a child almost annually—he had for many years pursued an intrigue with the then governess, Mary Pratt. Obviously then, the deceit required for an extra-marital fling was by no means foreign to him. Neither was he averse to it.

2. Mr. Kent was always the last member of the household to retire at the end of the day; he might go to bed at any time and

provoke no curiosity. Also, as he had only that afternoon returned home from a business trip his movements that night might be expected to be even less reliable.

3. Mr. Kent's financial situation was not sound and he was almost totally dependent for his livelihood upon his government position.

My theory, presented in the following chapter, not only takes into account the above factors but also answers all those many questions that must be answered. Some of those questions are as follows:

1. From Mr. Kent's behaviour on the morning of the 30th of June it is clear that the news of Savill being missing came as no surprise to him. Why was that?

2. His proven knowledge of the missing blanket, and then his *denial* of that knowledge, show that knowledge to be based in guilt. Why did he lie about the blanket?

3. Both he and the nurse insisted that there was never any conversation between them regarding the dead child. Was this true? And if so, what possible explanation could there be for such strange behaviour?

4. Why did Elizabeth Gough not raise the alarm when she found that Savill was missing?

5. Witnesses claimed that the following morning she appeared to be suffering from lack of sleep—yet *she* said she had slept soundly. How, then, can one account for her unrested appearance?

6. Savill's cot was only nine feet from the nurse's bed and she was, by her own admission, "a light sleeper". Also, the room was not in darkness for there was a nightlight burning. Is it conceivable then that the child could have been taken from his cot without the nurse being in the least disturbed by the activity?

7. Why did she first proclaim knowledge of the missing blanket and then later *deny* that knowledge?

8. She stated that she had seen from a kneeling position on her bed that Savill's cot was empty—but this was proved to have been impossible. Why did she lie?

9. Why, in the morning, did she put off till the last possible moment the necessary task of going to Mrs. Kent and asking for Savill?

10. Assuming Constance to be guilty, why did she take her flannel wash-cloth with her on her murderous errand?

11. What was the purpose of the blanket? Surely it could not have been for the child's welfare.

So, what exactly *did* happen on that night when Constance crept from her room with murder in her heart?

The following dramatic reconstruction gives, I am certain of it, the only possible solution to the mystery.

Chapter 33

THE SOLUTION

M r. Kent was not late to bed on that night of the 29th of June, and before midnight he was lying at the side of his wife. He was waiting for her to fall asleep.

Perhaps, as he lay there, his thoughts touched upon the future; on his application for a seat on the Board of Factory Inspectors. He needed that promotion. The past twenty-seven years had seen him continually travelling about the country in the service of the government. A seat on the Board would relieve him of much of that more exhausting part of the work but, most important of all, it would mean a substantial increase in salary. He had done all he could to ensure success, having prevailed upon nearly two hundred magistrates to support his application. And his chances were good. Things had gone better for him of late; all the scandal involving his first wife and the children's governess belonged now to another time, another place. In those earlier times it had threatened his very existence, but he had somehow ridden out the storms until time and distance had secured for him a certain measure of peace.

Not that he had always had peace here at Road. Only four years ago that sense of well-being had been snatched from his grasp in a blaze of publicity that had exposed his family to the eager scrutiny of everyone for miles around. Because of Constance. She it was whose recalcitrant and headstrong behaviour had jeopardized their new-found security; so determined had she been to remove herself from her stepmother's presence that—with William in tow —she had run away from home.

But even that scandal had passed. There was greater harmony now in the household, and with Constance spending most of her time away at boarding-school there was less opportunity for that harmony to be disrupted. Would that it might continue. . . .

Mrs. Kent's even breathing told him that she was asleep. He waited a while longer then rose up in the bed, put his feet to the floor and pulled on his slippers. Briefly she stirred. And then settled again. Leaving her there, sleeping, he took up his dark-lantern and crept silently from the room.

Noiselessly closing the door behind him he crossed the carpet, gently tapped on the door of the nursery and then made his way on to the spare bedroom. He and the nurse would be safe from discovery there, for although it was right next to the room where his wife lay asleep the rooms were separated by a deep chimney breast and a solid wall three feet in thickness.

In the nursery Elizabeth Gough satisfied herself that Savill and Eveline were sleeping and then slipped out and tiptoed to the room where Samuel Kent was waiting.

Upstairs Constance left her bed and took up her flannel face-cloth. Her hatred of her stepmother had steadily grown over the years to the point where it now consumed her very reason, and that hatred was soon to be expressed in one terrible, devastating act of revenge —revenge for her own mother's hurt, and the insults levelled against the dead woman's memory. The girl had formed plans for revenge in the past, but they had been only half thought out and never executed. This one would be realized. Now, silently, she opened the door and stepped out. She stood for a moment on the threshold, listening, then, closing the door behind her, moved across the landing and down the stairs.

On the floor below she stopped outside the nursery and grasped the door-handle. She knew that it would creak unless the greatest care was exercised, but she knew also the trick of it and under her fingers the handle turned noiselessly and the door opened.

Inside the room her first sight was of the nurse's empty bed with Eveline sleeping in the cot at its side. The discovery of the nurse's absence brought relief but this was swiftly dispelled by the realization that if the nurse had only slipped out to the lavatory she would soon return. Constance must act quickly.

A moment later she was standing above Savill's cot. In the glow of the nightlight she saw that he was sleeping soundly, mouth slightly open, his face to the wall. She still had a choice. Even now she could leave him and creep silently away and return to her own room. And no one need ever know. But she could not turn back now. Her hatred had brought her this far and she would see it through. Without hesitating for another second she raised the flannel and brought it down over the child's mouth.

Almost at once he began to struggle, fighting for breath. She could not risk his crying out, though, and she pressed the flannel even harder, covering his whole face. Then as he continued to squirm and kick she used her other hand and arm to hold him, pushing his body down into the feather mattress.

All at once she realized that he was no longer struggling and she released him and tentatively lifted the flannel. His eyes, she saw, were still closed and she wondered for a moment whether he was dead. But no; leaning closer she found that his heart was still beating. *He is asleep*, she thought. Even so, she could take no chances; he might awake at any second, and in case he should do so she must ensure that he could neither struggle nor cry out.

Lowering the flannel once more she thrust a part of it into his open mouth; it would stay there, secure, and he would be unable to make a sound. Then, pulling aside the quilt she withdrew the blanket and placed it on the side of the cot. After that she pushed back the sheet, laid the blanket on the boy and wrapped it tightly around him. And now he would be unable to move.

Hurrying to the door she quietly opened it and peered cautiously out onto the landing. All was dark, silent. Returning to the cot she lifted the child in her arms and left the room. To her dismay she found that she could not, with ease or safety, close the door behind her, so, rather than risk making a sound that might disturb those sleeping nearby she left it slightly open. She crossed the landing towards the main staircase which, with the heavy child in her arms, was more easily negotiable than the winding stairs at the rear of the house. Step by step she descended, arms tight about the boy, her right hand on the back of his head, pressing his face—with the flannel gag still secure in his mouth—firmly into her breast. He made no sound, no move.

On the ground floor in the gaslit hall she laid him, cocoon-wrapped, on the sofa, and taking her goloshes from the cupboard, pulled them on. This done she went towards the back of the house and unfastened the locks and the bolts that stood between her and the yard, then, returning to the hall she took Savill up into her arms again and carried him out, over the step, past the knife-box and into the night.

When the dog, awakened, rose up and shattered the stillness with his barking, Constance must have stood frozen with fear. He would be calmed, though, with a whispered word, and as he moved back to his kennel so the girl moved on across the yard and out through the gates. Turning to the left she made her way through the shrubbery—only a few steps—and into the privy.

She laid Savill's body on the seat. She did not know it but throughout her slow, careful journey from the nursery he had gone on suffocating in her arms, his breathing stifled by the flannel and the pillow of her breast. As frequently occurs in suffocation he had bled from the nose, some of the blood running onto the flannel and a little onto the girl's nightdress. Now, if he was not dead then he was on the very point of death. Constance, however, was unaware of this; to her mind her plan was yet to be fulfilled.

A few days before she had hidden in the privy a piece of candle and matches and now she placed the stub on a scrap of newspaper and lighted the wick. By the light of the flame she lifted the still, blanket-wrapped body and pushed it through the hole in the seat. It slid downward on the sloping, stained splashboard—and stopped.

Although she pushed, the gap between the splashboard and the rear wall was not wide enough. The body would not pass through. Only the flannel, becoming dislodged from the child's mouth, fell through the space into the vault and settled on the surface of the water below. It seemed to Constance that her plan to murder the boy was to be thwarted. The privy's cesspool had seemed the ideal means of both killing him and of disposing of his body, but try as she might she could not push him past the board.

What, then, could she do? She could not take him back to the house; she had gone past the point of return. Somehow she must complete the task she had set out to accomplish. But how? And then she remembered the knife-box that stood just outside the kitchen door. With the thought she turned and hurried back across the yard.

From the knife-box she chose a sharp-pointed knife then returned to the privy and lifted the seat. Savill was just as she had left him, lying on his back on the splashboard, left side uppermost. Leaning forward she pulled away the blanket to expose the white of his nightshirt. She raised the knife. And then she saw that his left arm was lying across his chest, in her way. Quickly she hooked the

point of the knife against the boy's fingers and, with her second
attempt, managed to move his hand aside. (This manœuvre resulted
in the two small cuts later found on the boy's forefinger, one little
more than a scratch, the second one deep to the bone.) And now
her way was clear. Raising the knife again she plunged it downward with all her force, driving it in, deep between his ribs. Un-
intentionally she twisted the blade as she inexpertly withdrew it
and for a moment it caught fast and she was forced to wrench it
free. Then by the light of the guttering candle she gazed down. She
had aimed for the heart and she expected to see the blood well-
ing up from the wound. Strange, there was hardly any blood at
all.

There was blood on the knife, though, and taking a piece of
newspaper (that served as toilet tissue) she wiped the blade clean.
The light flickered and went out and in the darkness she fumbled
for the matches, and the paper that had held the candle-stub. Outside she tossed the scraps of paper into the shrubbery then went
back across the yard and into the house.

In the spare bedroom Mr. Kent and the nursemaid had just parted.
At that hour of the night they could not, of course, take the risk of
being seen together so when Elizabeth Gough re-emerged onto the
landing she was alone. She got her first shock immediately she saw
the nursery door. She had left it securely closed. Now it stood
slightly open. The second blow—and far more devastating—followed almost at once. Savill. He was not in his cot.

In panic she hurried back to Mr. Kent where he still waited in
the spare bedroom and told him of her discovery. Then together
they went back to the nursery and looked into the empty crib—
both very much aware of the frightening meaning of it all; it could
mean only one thing: Mrs. Kent had entered the nursery, found
the nurse absent, and taken the child away. It was the only explanation, and they considered no other.

Perhaps the boy had cried, the nurse said, and although they had
not heard him Mrs. Kent, who had been nearer, had. That must
have been what had happened. True, Mrs. Kent had said only the
day before that she could not carry the child but clearly, now, she
had managed to do so. The nurse pulled the disarranged covers
aside. She has taken his blanket too, she said.

What could be done? Mrs. Kent knew of their liaison and Mr. Kent must return to his bedroom and face the music. Elizabeth Gough, however, would have to wait a little longer for *her* confrontation; for that moment—it must come with morning—when she would surely receive instant dismissal. With such certainty in her mind she was left alone, somehow to get through the long hours till daylight.

Quietly entering his bedroom—and still holding the dark-lantern —Mr. Kent was astonished to find that all was calm and quiet. He had prepared himself for a scene—and instead he found his wife soundly sleeping. Even more strange, though, was the fact that she was alone in the bed. Savill was not there. Savill was not even in the room.

Then where *was* he? And if Mrs. Kent had not taken him then who had? And then he recalled the loud barking of the dog in the yard. At the back of the house where he had been with the nurse he had heard it clearly. Now he realized that someone had been passing through the yard. Carrying Savill.

Quickly changing into shirt and trousers he left the room and moved silently towards the stairs. With increasing dread he knew well that whoever had taken the child had done so for no good purpose.

As Mr. Kent descended the main staircase Constance, having replaced the knife—which she had washed at the kitchen sink—and her goloshes, made her way carefully up the winding back stairs to her room on the top floor.

Inside she lit the candle beside her bed and studied herself in the glass. High up on the breast of her nightdress she found two spots of blood and, taking the garment off, she washed the stains away. After draping the nightdress over a chair to dry she took a clean one from the drawer and put it on. Then, blowing out the candle she climbed into bed and closed her eyes. She must not think about the thing that she had done; she must try to sleep.

A glance at the front door had told Mr. Kent that no one had forcibly entered there as also did the locks and bolts at the rear of the house. But had anyone broken in he would surely have heard the noise. Savill had been taken by someone *inside* the house—and he was sure who that someone must be. There was only one person who was at all likely to do such a thing. Constance. She who for so long had given such clear indication of her hostility and resentment—so much so that it had been impossible to suffer her presence at home. And those feelings of hatred had all been directed at her stepmother—whose favourite child young Savill was. Yes, Constance. She who only last year had crept into the nursery by night and stripped the socks and the bed clothes from the boy as he had slept.

The dog, no longer disturbed by the comings and goings of the house's inmates on this night, now made no sound as the man hurried through the yard. Mr. Kent opened the gates and went through. Immediately to his left was the shrubbery, and the privy. The privy. That place where Constance had hidden her clothes when she had absconded four years ago. In seconds he was inside and, holding high the lantern, staring, stricken, at the body of his son.

Setting down the lamp he stooped and lifted the warm, blanket-wrapped figure and laid it gently on the floor. He had no doubt that the child was dead. He could feel no heartbeat and when he brought the light closer he saw traces of blood on the nightshirt, the cut in the fabric. Constance had finally given her hatred full expression. For so long she had sought revenge, and now at last she had taken it.

He straightened, stood for a moment above the body, and then turned and walked blindly out into the night. In the quiet and the dark of the shrubbery he stopped, and slowly, on top of the horror of the moment, came the realization of his terrible dilemma. His son was dead, murdered, and he should inform the police immediately. *But how could he? His very knowledge of the death, at this hour, would at once proclaim his own guilt.* How, it would be asked, had he discovered the murder? What had he been doing at such a time to have made such a discovery? And the nurse, too. Why had she been absent from the nursery? Soon everyone would learn the truth.

Those scandals of the past would be as nothing compared to the scandal that would soon break over his head. Not only would there be the sensational news that his daughter had murdered his son, but it must also be known what he and the child's nurse had been doing while that murder was taking place. Once such shocking facts were known there would be nothing on earth that could save him. He was ruined.

Ruined. Not only had he lost his much-loved son, but soon he would lose everything else. Not only would he lose his chance of promotion but he would also lose the position he now held—his only means of livelihood. And with it would go his respect, and the affection of his wife. He would be shunned by his fellow-man. Soon, with everything gone he and his wife and children would be brought to poverty. Face to face with such annihilating catastrophe even Savill's death paled in its significance.

But perhaps there was a way out. If it could be believed that he had remained at his wife's side all night, sleeping, in ignorance of his son's death, that promised havoc might yet be averted. After all, it would only be his disclosure of his present knowledge that would betray his liaison with the nurse. Yes, that was it: the discovery that Savill was missing must be made later—and in as natural a way as possible. And when that "discovery" was made he, Kent, must be innocently in bed, and the "discovery" made and related by the nurse alone.

But what *then*? It would take even the most inept investigator only minutes to see that the murder had been committed by an inmate of the house, following which, and after the questions had been asked, it must be soon known that Constance was the guilty one. And there again lay Mr. Kent's undoing, for in that situation *also* lay the means of discovering the full story. If Constance was successfully prosecuted the truth would surely emerge—that she had been able to take the child from the nursery because the nurse had been absent.

There was no alternative. He must protect Constance from suspicion, for only by saving her could he save himself. He would do everything possible to direct suspicion away from her. More than that—direct it right away from the house.

Into his besieged mind came the memory of those stories he had heard since coming to Road—accounts of those several murders that had taken place in the neighbourhood—murders in which each victim had met death by having his throat cut. The killer had never been found, but whoever he was, Kent was determined, he must now carry the responsibility for yet another brutal death: the death of Savill.

Time was passing, though, and whatever had to be done must be done quickly. Hurrying back to the house he went into the kitchen, took one of the carving-knives and returned with it to the privy. There, crouching over the body he pulled back the head to expose the small, pale throat. The sharp blade was placed against the boy's skin, at the left of the jaw, below the ear—and then he had to look away, eyelids clenched, the tears streaming. It had to be done, though; there was no choice. After a moment he summoned all his courage and, in one movement, pressed the blade home and drew it across the throat. It was done.

It was done. And he had burned his bridges and dare not stray from the course to which he was now committed. If ruin had been certain before it would be even more certain should anyone ever know of the measures he had now taken. No one *must* know—*ever*.

He could not leave the body here in the open; it would be found too easily, too quickly, and he needed as much time as possible. Blood, he saw, was running from the wound in the throat into the folds of the blanket and also forming a small pool on the floor. Steeling himself again he stooped and lifted up the gory, blanket-wrapped bundle. As he did so the dead child's head fell backwards, the gash yawning, so that the blood dropped spattering onto the floor and the front of the privy seat. Quickly he laid the body back on the splashboard.

It might even be possible, he thought, that without the blanket the body might fall down into the vault—in which case discovery would be delayed for even longer. He pulled at the blanket, tugging it free and on the soil-covered splashboard the body revolved. But it did not fall. It stayed, coming to rest on its left side, right hand and foot slightly raised, head hanging down, the blood streaming into the vault.

Samuel Kent dropped the blanket onto the body and lowered the seat. His work here was finished. Picking up the lantern, wet with blood, from the floor, he returned to the house. There in the kitchen he did all he could to remove all traces of the deed, washing himself, cleaning the knife and replacing it in the drawer. The lantern, though, was another matter; he was unable to clean it satisfactorily; he would therefore have to find some way to dispose of it; there was danger in keeping it in the house.

From the kitchen he moved to the library and there sat staring into space, numbed by the horror of his predicament and the enormity of what had been done; what he had done. Slowly the night began to fade till, with four o'clock, came daybreak—and still he remained in his chair. Not only was he consumed by thoughts of the happenings of that past night but he knew he had yet more to do if he was to ensure survival. Somehow he had to mislead any coming investigators, to make them believe that a stranger had forced an entry into the house. But how could he do that? Such a move would entail the smashing of locks, the breaking of windows, actions that would at once alert every member of the household. Certainly that must be avoided at all costs.

In the end he went into the drawing-room and unfastened the shutters and raised the middle window—only a little, though, for it stuck and he could not risk the noise of forcing it higher. As it was, the sounds of his manœuvres did not go unheard. In her bedroom Mrs. Kent found herself awakened and realized that her husband was not at her side. Seeing, however, that it was daylight, she was not alarmed and after a moment or two she went back to sleep. Downstairs in the open drawing-room doorway Mr. Kent looked at his handiwork: open window, open shutters. It might not fool anyone, but it was the most he dare do.

It just remained now to get rid of the lantern, and this was only the work of a few minutes. Hurrying out into the early-morning air he left the grounds and made his way to the edge of an adjoining field. There where the earth was soft and bare he scooped out the soil, dropped the dark-lantern into the hollow and covered it up. Well away from the house as it was, it would never be found.

As soon as he was indoors again and had once more washed his hands, Mr. Kent went up to his bedroom, undressed and got into bed beside his wife. He had done all that he could.

Beyond the landing Elizabeth Gough slept fitfully. After Mr. Kent had left her alone she had paced the nursery frantic with anxiety. For a time she had wondered whether Mrs. Kent might bring Savill back again and in preparation had tidied the boy's cot. But it did not happen and in the end she had gone to bed.

She awoke later that morning about five o'clock and, unable to rest further, got up, dressed, said her prayers and read a chapter from her Bible—and then waited for the time when she must go to Mrs. Kent and ask for Savill. That was the moment she dreaded and she put it off as long as she could, until the very last possible moment. When she did finally pluck up the courage to knock on the door of her mistress's bedroom she was, naturally, stunned to discover that the child was not there.

The rest of the story is known. Constance, of course—as Inspector Whicher suspected and as she herself later confessed—destroyed her stained nightdress and retrieved the one from the laundry-basket to replace it. Regarding her father's intrigue with the nurse it has been suggested to me that Constance was perhaps aware of it and went into the nursery *knowing* that Elizabeth Gough would be absent. Well, it is possible, though there is no evidence to support such a theory. I am of the belief that, having returned home from school with the intention of killing one of her stepmother's young children she chose the night for the deed as she felt that that was the only time when she would be safe from observation. The fact that the nurse was absent from the nursery aided her considerably, though she was convinced, I'm sure, that even with the nurse present she could remove the child without disturbing her. Whether in fact she could have done so is of course extremely doubtful, but there, having successfully removed Savill's bedsocks and blankets while he slept on a previous occasion, without awaking the then nurse Emma Sparks,[1] she probably thought she could get away with it this time.

As for Elizabeth Gough, I am sure she was in complete ignorance of how the murder took place that night. She was only aware of her own part in the affair—and that she dare not disclose, ever. If she did it would mean her certain ruin. She was suspected, as we have seen, of having had an intrigue with Mr. Kent, and of *limited* involvement in the crime, but after telling certain lies—to cover the guilty part she did play—she continued to protest her innocence and her ignorance—for the most part real—and managed to survive.

Certainly Mrs. Kent could never have believed in the nurse's rumoured involvement—in any way. Had she ever seriously thought that Savill had been unprotected that night because the nurse was out of the room with the child's father she could never have borne

---

[1] This incident was related to Inspector Whicher by Mr. Kent (see p. 158). Although it is not substantiated by any other source I see no reason to doubt its veracity.

the sight of her—let alone beg her to remain at Road Hill House. No, she must have accepted Elizabeth Gough's story, that Savill had been taken away while she, the nurse, had been sleeping.

In the same way Mrs. Kent could never have suspected the extent of her husband's involvement—either with the nurse or in the mutilation of Savill's body. Kent could not possibly have told her what he had done, that he had first been in the spare bedroom with the nursemaid and then later had taken the body of his wife's favourite child and deliberately cut its throat. There was no necessity to tell her something so totally destructive, and it is inconceivable that he did so. No, to the day she died Mrs. Kent fully believed that Constance and Constance alone was responsible. Very soon after the crime, when her husband fell under suspicion, Mrs. Kent, when it was necessary, lied to protect him. Which is understandable— after all, she believed him to be quite innocent; guilty of nothing more than attempting to save his daughter from disaster, and the scandal that would result from it—and in the fulfilment of this aim she was pledged to aid him.

The measures taken by Mr. Kent to shield Constance have already been seen. His action of cutting Savill's throat made it even more essential to save his daughter, for she could tell her prosecutors that while she was guilty of having suffocated the child and stabbed him, she was *not* guilty of inflicting the throat wound. So it can be understood just why he was so desperate to help her. That was why, also, when she did come to be suspected—in spite of all his efforts—and her arrest seemed imminent, he widely implied that she was insane. His purpose here was two-fold. Insanity would account for the most unnatural act—even where murder was concerned—of cutting a defenceless child's throat, and also ensure that no reliance could be placed on anything she might say.

No wonder Mr. Kent was to distraught when, in 1865, he received Constance's letter telling him that she intended to publicly confess. At last he had come to believe himself safe, and now suddenly he was faced, after five years, with the prospect of that damning exposure he had done so much to avoid.

His acute distress, though, on that count, was for nothing. For her own sake Constance did what she had to do. By gaining a murder conviction for herself she brought some ease to her conscience and alleviated the weight of suspicion from others, and with a story fabricated from truths, half-truths and lies, she kept safe her father's secret. And she achieved salvation.

I agree with F. Tennyson Jesse who, in her book *Murder and its Motives*, writes:

> Constance Kent's salvation, like her damnation, came from within herself. . . . She was not—as the congenital female criminal invariably is—a *poseuse*. She did not commit the crime for the sake of notoriety. Neither, when she took the tremendous step of confessing, do we find her, to put it vulgarly, "out to make a splash". She went through with the thing as plainly as might be. There seems . . . no valid reason for doubt that it was genuinely the working of her conscience that drove Constance Kent to the confession that electrified England in the year 1865.
>
> I lay stress on these points because they are extremely rare in any criminal, and so rare as to be practically unique in a female criminal; and it is upon the inner evidence afforded to the mind by these points that Constance Kent deserves to be placed in the class of occasional criminals and not in that of the congenital criminal.
>
> Let there be no mistake about it—there was no necessity, save that of spiritual compulsion, for the confession of Constance Kent. The affair would never have been raked up again, and she had not that dire necessity which even the most hardened criminals would feel—of confession to save the neck of some innocent person.

Constance's remorse was of the deepest. She had rather face the gallows than continue to live with her guilt. So, it must be true that in the bleak prospect of those years of penal servitude stretching out before her she found some measure of peace, or at least of hope. She would never be free of the crime, never be free of her guilt, but perhaps the sacrifice she had made would enable her to live with herself again.

So she began her sentence, taking with her only the secret of what had happened on that summer night five years before. And as did those other two keepers of the secret, Mr. Kent and the Rev. Wagner, she would hold it safe for the rest of her life.

Part Four

THE AFTER-YEARS

*. . . for good or evil, her future life would
be remarkable.*

John C. Bucknill, M.D.

Chapter 34

THE PRISONS

While the *Madame Tussaud's* artists created an effigy of Constance Kent that September (which for some unknown reason would not be shown until after the death of Mr. Kent) the girl herself was still in the relative seclusion of the Salisbury gaol. The prison authorities were not happy with the situation but there was nothing they could do; Millbank prison, to which she had been allocated, was quite full; it was not until later in the autumn that there would be room to receive her there.

Her weeks in the small, parochial gaol at Salisbury could have done little to prepare her for the realities of prison-life, and the vastness of Millbank (built on that part of the Thames now occupied by the Tate Gallery), packed with convicts, must have been a great shock to her. Here it was that she truly began her life sentence of penal servitude.

Female prisoners in those times were divided into three classes, distinguishable by the colour of their clothes: the third-class (newly arrived) prisoners wore brown serge dresses, second-class wore green serge, and first-class—those whose good behaviour had earned them the best jobs and the greater privileges—blue serge.

During the first nine months of their imprisonment the convicts were confined to their cells, employed there with needlework and knitting, leaving that confinement only for half an hour each morning and afternoon when they were allowed walking exercise in the prison yard. And this period of solitary confinement did not end automatically when the first nine months were up; no, promotion to the second class was dependent upon good behaviour for that length of time.

Promotion also gained for the prisoner a slight improvement in dietary fare which, for the lowest class, consisted of a breakfast of bread and molasses-sweetened cocoa, a dinner of suet pudding or soup or boiled beef, and an afternoon dish of bread and gruel. For the second-class prisoner the much-hated gruel was replaced with a pint of tea.

Promotion from the bleak existence of the lowest class meant more to prisoners than getting a little better diet and the change from brown to green serge, however; it also meant that they moved about the building and the grounds, doing "housework", such as scrubbing, and various outside chores. As stated, the best-behaved woman were eventually promoted to the first class, and it was from this privileged position that they were selected for the best jobs—such as those in the laundry and the infirmary.

Constance Kent, after completing her initial nine months in solitary confinement, was not long in achieving promotion to the first class and employment of a more congenial nature.

Prison life must have been particularly hard for Constance. In her middle-class upbringing she had known only a rather sheltered existence, never coming into contact with the rougher elements of society. She had lived in the most elegant houses, with servants and carriages, an existence with so much emphasis on manners, refinement and style—qualities so prized by the Victorians. Apart from all the benefits of domestic comforts she had also had a good education and, both at home and at her various schools, had always mixed with individuals of a certain social level.

Her brief adult life had seen her in even more protective situations, for she had spent the latter years in the seclusion of religious homes. Imagine, then, after such experience, the impact upon her of prison life; the exchange of the sequestered quiet of St. Mary's for the bleakness of Millbank. So many of the prisoners within its walls were hardened criminals, immoral, illiterate and ill-bred, and it was in their company that Constance now found herself. She had given up the gentle ways of the nuns for those of her new fellows with their coarse manners and their language the language of the gutter. The only refuge she would have was in her work.

Major Arthur Griffiths, Millbank's Deputy Governor at that time, was later to write of Constance in his book *Secrets of the Prison House*:

Constance Kent, who I remember at Millbank, was first employed in the laundry and afterwards in the infirmary. A small, mouse-like creature, with much of the promptitude of the mouse or the lizard, surprised, in disappearing when alarmed. The approach of any strange or unknown face whom she feared might come to spy her out and stare constituted a real alarm for Constance Kent. When anyone went the length of asking, "Which is Constance?" she had already concealed herself somewhere with wonderful rapidity and cleverness. She was a mystery in every way. It was almost impossible to believe that this insignificant, inoffensive little person could have cut her infant brother's throat in circumstances of peculiar atrocity. No doubt there were features in her face which the criminal anthropologist would have seized upon as being suggestive of instinctive criminality—high cheek bones, a lowering, overhanging brow, and deep-set, small eyes; but yet her manner was prepossessing, and her intelligence was of a high order, while nothing could exceed the devoted attention she gave the sick under her charge as a nurse.

In tending the sick, Constance had found a task that suited her abilities and her capacity for caring. That experience was to serve her well in later years, when she was free. That freedom, though, now, was a very long way off—a life sentence away. All she could do was try to bring it closer.

In 1860 when her crime was committed the acknowledged term of a life sentence was fifteen years. With remission, however, that term could be reduced to twelve. On her arrival at Millbank Constance had been immediately informed of this and in addition was presented with a card on which were noted marks that might be earned by good behaviour and industry. The earning of these marks[1] could, she was told, lead to her release in twelve years. Twelve years. It was a long time, but she would still only be thirty-three; there would yet be time for a life of her own. She would earn that remission, she was determined.

While Constance was behind the high walls of Millbank those other participants in the Road drama went their own ways in the free world outside. Among them was the Rev. Arthur Wagner who,

---

[1] A maximum of six marks each day could be earned. Apart from helping to secure a reduction of a prisoner's sentence they also secured for that prisoner, on release, a gratuity.

proving the adage that it's an ill wind that blows nobody any good, had actually *gained* from the affair. His refusal to disclose what had been said to him in the confessional that day had never been put to the test in court and consequently, in spite of the strong feeling against him, he and his cause emerged triumphant. As Canon Hutchinson wrote years later in his foreword to H. Hamilton Maughan's booklet *Wagner of Brighton*:

. . . All the great guns were brought up and trained on Wagner of Brighton. . . .

He stood his ground, and a great—a truly great—victory was won. One might almost say that from that time the confessional in the Church of England remained unchallenged.

While Mr. Wagner was going from strength to strength Elizabeth Gough, cleared of the heavy suspicion that had hampered her progress, was building a new life, and on the 24th of April, 1866, in the parish church of St. Mary Newington, Surrey, she became the wife of one John Cockburn, a Kensington wine merchant.

Not all the changes that took place, however, were of such a happy nature. Only a few months later, in Llangollen, Wales, Mrs. Kent fell ill and died.

Due to "congestion of the lungs", her death occurred on the 17th of August. She was forty-six years old. Her husband was at her side.

The early years of that couple's relationship, with its background of adultery, had caused so much scandal, even so, it does appear that they had known a true and deep affection for one another. And that affection had lasted. Granted, Samuel Kent had not been one to be left unmoved by a pretty face, and with his constant journeying to other towns and the opportunities thereby offered it would be surprising if Elizabeth Gough was the only one with whom he had briefly strayed; which situation of course only goes to show that he was no different from so many of his fellows; human nature is human nature, and where it came to denying his sexual drives Samuel Kent was no stronger than the next man. There can be no real doubt, however, that his true feelings were for his wife—and she was a good wife to him, and a good mother to her children. Her failure sprang from her total lack of understanding of the needs of her stepchildren, from putting her own children always to the fore, and from bitter resentment of the first Mrs. Kent. Together these factors had spelt disaster and led to those "depths of household misery" mentioned by Dr. Bucknill.

On Mary Drewe Kent's behalf it might be argued that she herself had not had the happiest life; only during those few brief years at Road had she been free of the condemnation that society had for so long heaped upon her. To suffer constant denigration—whether the sufferer is blameless or not—must have its effect, and this might well have contributed to Mary Drewe Kent's attitude towards her predecessor and towards that woman's children.

And now she who had so unwittingly wrought so much havoc, and suffered from it, was dead.

After the loss of his wife Samuel Kent and his younger children moved further north in Wales, to Rhydycilgwyn issa, Llanynys, Denbigh. By this time Mary Ann, Elizabeth and William had quit the family circle and gone to London, the two sisters to live quietly together and William to pursue his chosen career as a naturalist.

In January 1872 William, then working at the British Museum, returned to Wales to visit his father who was gravely ill with a disease of the liver. Samuel Kent, at seventy-one years of age, was nearing the end of his life. His had been a passionate nature; he had been selfish and, oftentimes, in the pursuit of his desires, cruel, and blind to the desires of others. And yet in spite of all his errors, his blunders, he still manages to leave a picture of a man with some humanity and dignity.

On the 5th of February, 1872, he died. He was buried at his wife's side in the churchyard at Llangollen.

Later that year William married a Miss Elizabeth Bennett, eldest daughter of one Thomas Randle Bennett, which gentleman, at William's instigation, appealed to the Home Office for Constance's release. This request, made through the Attorney-General, Lord Coleridge, was denied.

It was about this time that Constance, now at Parkhurst on the Isle of Wight—to which prison she had been removed from Millbank—was working on a series of mosaics for certain churches in the kingdom, and the results of her work can be seen adorning the chancel of the Bishop's chapel at Chichester, the East Grinstead Parish Church, St. Paul's Cathedral and St. Peter's Church, Portland, in Dorset. St. Peter's was built solely by convict labour, which fact has led to the commonly held belief that Constance was at one time held in Portland prison. This is not so. She was never at Portland. Nor *could* she have been as it housed only *male* convicts. No, her beautiful mosaics, both designed and executed by her, were made in transportable sections at Parkhurst and then shipped to their destinations to be assembled and laid by others.

After Parkhurst Constance was sent to Woking—a prison where she was particularly unhappy—and it was while she was there, in October, 1875, that Bishop Webb, the Bishop of Bloemfontein, wrote to the Home Secretary:

> . . . Though both she and her family are unknown to me, I wish to know if there would be any possibility of her being allowed to go out as Laundry Matron to a Religious Establishment of the Church of England under my charge at Bloemfontein, South Africa. I should hold myself responsible for her in every way. . . .

The request was vetoed by the then Home Secretary, Sir Richard Cross, who noted on an internal Home Office memorandum: "I cannot think it would be right to let her out so early in such a case of murder as this was."

Constance had been informed of Bishop Webb's plea on her behalf and she had hoped, desperately, that it would meet with success. She had now been in prison for more than ten years. She was thirty-one years old. Life was passing her by. That the Bishop's plan failed, though, did not come as any great surprise to her; and for the simple reason that, in the second year of her imprisonment at Millbank she had learned—to her great dismay—that a life sentence was *not* the fifteen years she had at first understood it to be. No: in 1864 the period of a life sentence had been increased to *twenty years*. Constance's late awareness of this must have been a particularly bitter pill for with it came the realization that, had she been convicted at the time of her crime, she could have expected to have served that shorter term—fifteen years or, with remission for good behaviour, twelve. Now all she could do was hope that when she *had* completed twelve years—come 1877—the authorities, notwithstanding the new rule, might be moved to look more kindly upon her case.

During the next two years she was removed from Woking and returned to Millbank where, as the summer of 1877 drew near, she did all in her power to obtain her release. It was probably in the expectation of her release that the directors of *Madame Tussaud's* were approached by Constance's friends and asked if they would consent to remove her effigy which had been on display since 1872. This they agreed to do. At about the same time William's father-in-law once more wrote appealing for her freedom, on the grounds that she had "now completed the term of twelve years penal servitude". His letter of the 9th of July to the Home Office goes on: "I hear that her health is giving way. Should you feel it consistent with your duty to grant my appeal it will be a great boon to all her relations and friends. . . ."

This question of Constance's health led promptly to her being examined by the prison medical officer. He duly reported:

> . . . Constance Emily Kent is not at present in quite so robust a state of health as usual, and a few days ago I deemed it advisable to recommend that she might be employed for a time at needlework instead of in the kitchen. Although the case is not in the slightest degree pressing, and there is no reason whatever to feel the development of any disease or any permanent failure of general health, yet I anticipate that by way of precaution it will be desirable to remove her before long—though not to Woking, as the great dislike which for some reason or other she entertains to that prison would entirely neutralize any benefit that she might otherwise derive from change of air.

A week later, while William's father-in-law, Thomas Bennett, was still waiting for a reply to his letter, Constance, on the 25th of July, petitioned the Home Secretary for her release.

The *Petition* form was on blue foolscap, upon which would be noted relevant information about the petitioner after he had finished writing his appeal. A wide margin on the left-hand side was for the purpose of holding a concise summing-up of the words of that prisoner's appeal—this was usually done by the chaplain—and solved any problems that might arise from illiteracy etc.

Constance's petition in 1877 was as follows:

The Petition of Constance E. Kent r5 . . .

    HUMBLY SHEWETH— (and then Constance wrote—in the third person:) that she has undergone 12 years penal servitude, which time, when she received her sentence, was supposed to constitute life, she being then given a card with marks to that effect.

Your humble petitioner further sheweth that there was against her no evidence upon which any jury could have brought in a conviction, or even on which she could have been committed for trial; had there been, she would have received her sentence in 1860, long before the passing of the 20 years act, and then would have been entitled to a consideration of her case in 1872. The want of evidence was not the result of any endeavour on her part to thwart or obstruct the course of justice, or to cast suspicion otherwise; it being simply non-existent.

So many years of constant confinement are also impairing her strength, she not being at present able for hard labour. The mercy of a speedy release is therefore the earnest prayer of your humble petitioner

Constance E. Kent.

Her appeal was rejected. On the 2nd of November that year she left Millbank and went to Fulham prison where, the following year, on the 5th of July, 1878, she petitioned once again.

The Petition of Constance E. Kent r5 . . .
   HUMBLY SHEWETH—

that she has served 13 years of a life sentence, at the beginning of which she was given a card with marks which by good conduct and industry might be earned in 12 years (these marks she has long since earned), the longer period of 20 years not being till the 2nd year of her imprisonment officially known when she received a mark-card to that effect. To serve this period of 20 years she would not have been liable had there been any evidence to convict her at the time of the commission of her crime, she being then only 16 years of age.

Some years after when arrived at womanhood she fully felt the atrocious enormity she had been led to commit by giving way to the then unconquerable aversion to one who had taught her to despise and dislike her own mother, who robbed that mother of the affection both of a husband and of a daughter. The sense of wrong done to her mother when once discovered became yet more intensified after her death, her successor never alluding to that mother but with taunting sarcasm; she therefore sought to retaliate on its authoress the mental agony her own mother had endured, by a deed which nothing can excuse, the deepest repentance for which she ever feels and which induced her to give herself up to justice.

Your humble petitioner prayeth for pardon on the grounds 1st of her extreme youth at the time; 2nd, the great provocation she *then* thought herself under; 3rd, the impossibility of the discovery of her guilt except by her own confession which was not made till 5 years after when all inquiry had ceased, the early investigations in 1860 having rather tended to exculpate her.

4th, having friends ready to receive her. 5th, bearing a good prison character to which the officials can testify. She therefore most humbly implores to be set at liberty as she would have been had conviction followed on her crime, or at least she beseeches that some early period may be assigned to which she may look forward and obtain the privilege of gradual emancipation accorded by removal to the refuge;[1] a speedy release is in any case the earnest prayer of your humble petitioner Constance E. Kent.

This, Constance's petition, is of interest for several reasons. Not only do we have, in her own words, a reaffirmation of her motive for the crime, but her words leave the unmistakable impression that she *still* had not forgiven her stepmother. We also learn that Constance had "friends ready to receive her". We do not know who these friends were, though she was almost certainly referring to Bishop Webb of South Africa and also, probably, to the Rev. Wagner who, going by the Home Office file, was in contact with her throughout her prison years and visited her regularly—as also did Miss Gream up to the time of her death in May, 1873. Unfor-

[1] *Refuges* were institutions—the first ones established in 1864—designed to combat those "dangers which always await a female convict on her discharge from prison", and aid her rehabilitation. A contemporary memorial from the Committee of the Reformatory and Refuge Union to the Home Secretary in 1864 states: "To accomplish what is thus desired on behalf of female convicts, the Committee of the Reformatory and Refuge Union believe it to be essential that they should be placed under the charge of these charitable and religious societies, not when they are finally discharged on the completion of their sentence, but at that period when they would ordinarily be sent out on tickets of leave [released on parole], so that, during the unexpired portion of their sentence, the societies should be able to exercise over them a legal as well as a moral influence."

tunately Constance's prison records no longer exist so there is no
way of knowing who her other visitors were, though almost certainly William was among them—and probably Mary Ann and
Elizabeth too.

Constance's statement in her petition that she had been led to
believe that twelve years was the expected life term after remission
caused the memorandums to fly back and forth through the Home
Office corridors and an inquiry resulted in the Home Secretary
receiving the following report:

> . . . With respect to convictions since July 1864 the 20 years rule
> is understood to apply, *subject* of course to such exceptions as
> Secretary of State may think proper to make.
>
> Constance Kent was sentenced in July 1865 [but] for years after
> she was sent to Millbank the cases of Life convicts were sub-
> mitted for consideration after 12 years. She therefore may no
> doubt have been informed that her case would be submitted for
> consideration after 12 years, [though] no pledge of any kind can
> have been given her. . . .

To this the Home Secretary (R. A. Cross) added his instructions: "Too soon; follow according to rule." And then: "Should
not the matter be explained to her?"

The matter *was* subsequently explained to Constance, and she
could do nothing then but try to come to terms with the fact that
her freedom was, as yet, still a long way out of her reach.

On the 27th of March, 1880, she tried again, saying in her petition:

> . . . she has suffered just upon 15 years imprisonment (inclusive
> of time before trial), a longer period than has yet been undergone
> by any woman whose crime was committed before 20 and which,
> with one exception,[2] has not been exceeded by any well conducted
> female under a life sentence, while many have been released much
> sooner although convicted since 1864.

She then went on to urge again the fact that the mark-card she
had originally been given at Millbank was for a period of twelve
years and that she had been given to understand that that would

[2] This was Mary Cox. See p. 353.

be "the utmost length of her confinement". Her plea, however, as
before, did her no good.

There were several in positions of some power at the Home
Office who, judging by the various memorandums that circulated,
would have been happier seeing Constance Kent set free—pleaded
one gentleman: "It is a special case,"—but the final, all-important
decision, from the Home Secretary—now Sir William Vernon Harcourt—always put an end to any hopes. In October of that same
year the Rev. Wagner appealed on Constance's behalf to Mr.
Gladstone, the Prime Minister, but all that *that* gentleman could do
was to pass the letter on to the Home Secretary. And Constance
remained in gaol.

Fulham prison—part of which still stands today at the junction of
Rigault and Buer roads, London S.W.6—housed about four hundred convicts, all women, of whom Constance was among the best
known. Other notorious names on the prison roll at that time included Elizabeth Staunton who, like Constance, had had a death
sentence commuted to penal servitude for life. In 1877 she and her
husband Patrick, his brother Louis, and her sister Alice Rhodes,
had all been found guilty of the murder of Louis' mentally re-
tarded wife Harriet—by means of starvation and neglect. "A crime
so black and hideous," commented the judge, "that I believe in all
the records of crime it would be difficult to find its parallel." Even
so, Elizabeth Staunton found no difficulty in being accepted by her
fellows, and by the prison governors she was even allowed certain
privileges that were denied to other convicts. Not so Constance
Kent. Her story was a very different one. Notwithstanding the
general harshness of prison life at that time *her* experience as a life
convict was more bitter than most.

Because of the nature of her crime Constance was never accepted
by the other prison inmates at any time during her prison career.
It is a sad fact, and yet it is hardly surprising. It is well known that
prisoners who have committed crimes against children are almost
universally disliked by their fellow prisoners—and Constance was
no exception. One of the matrons of Fulham prison, Mrs. Bridget
Wright,[8] telling of her experiences in *Lloyd's Weekly News* in 1909,
said of Constance's situation:

[8] She was matron at Fulham prison from 1876 to 1883.

. . . She was not liked in prison. None of the matrons would have her in their work-parties. Year after year she sat alone in her cell with her needlework till at last, to the surprise of all, I had her appointed as my servant. Each matron had a prisoner to wait on her, and I could not have had a better maid than Constance Kent, who told me of her stepmother's harsh treatment and how she was goaded to her terrible crime.

Constance's fourth petition was made in June, 1881. She was thirty-seven years old now, a mature woman, one who must have looked back upon that murderous schoolgirl as upon a stranger. Twenty-one years had passed since her crime; over seventeen of those years spent behind bars. In her petition she urged her youth at the time of the murder and also the fact that no prisoners who were as young as herself when their crimes were committed had "undergone so long an imprisonment as she. . . ."

Like her previous appeals this one also met with no success, it being summarily dismissed by Sir William Vernon Harcourt with the single scrawled word: "Nil."

And Constance had to accept it. There was nothing else she could do. It was that or give up, give in to despair, and such a course was not her way. Throughout her life she had given numerous examples of her strength of spirit and that strength would sustain her now; it would be her salvation. Having already served so many years she was no doubt aided by the belief always that her release was imminent, that although she might fail in her appeal *this* year she must surely succeed the next. And so in cell number twenty-nine she would go on waiting, until it was time to try again.

Her next petition came the following year, 1882, in November.

The Petition of Constance E. Kent r5 . . .
  HUMBLY SHEWETH—

that she has been in prison for a longer period than she had lived when she committed the crime for which she suffers, she being then only just 16; it also exceeds the time served by any other woman whose crime was committed at so early an age.

Her long and rigorous confinement has much impaired her sight. Your humble petitioner earnestly prayeth for release from the lowest and most degrading association with which she has been constantly surrounded for so many years.

Your humble petitioner most deeply repents of the crime which her evil passions led her to commit, she having a stepmother who while living in the family some years before her mother's death always treated her mother with ridicule and disdain, teaching your humble petitioner to do the same until she was old enough to see how unnatural was such conduct. The revulsion of feeling caused an uncontrollable hatred towards her stepmother which was fanned and kept alive after her mother's death by her stepmother never mentioning her mother's name but with sarcastic contempt and in terms of disparagement, till at last your humble petitioner committed the terrible crime which she never ceases to deplore.

Your most humble petitioner throws herself on your clemency and will as in duty bound ever pray.

Constance E. Kent.

Acompanying her petition was the Medical Officer's report, which stated:

She has increased in weight seven pounds. I have sent for her and examined her eyes—her sight is somewhat impaired, the vessels of the retina are infected—and a slight inflammatory action set up—but her general health is good.

This appeal also elicited from the Home Secretary the one-word answer: "Nil."

In August of the year following (1883) came another appeal from Bishop Webb, now Bishop of Grahamstown, who offered to take her "to his diocese in South Africa, and place her there in a religious home where she would be under the care of some Sisters and usefully employed". This proposal was urged by several people, including Mr. Wagner, who wrote: "The party, consisting of a clergyman and some ladies, will start for Africa the first of October, so there is not much time to lose."

But the 1st of October came and went, and while the clergyman and the ladies set sail for South Africa Constance remained in Fulham prison. With one exception those at the Home Office who were concerned with her fate had been much in favour of the proposal to send her to join Bishop Webb. That one exception, though, was, as usual, the man who really mattered—the Home Secretary, and he had given his usual negative answer.

William's wife Elizabeth had died in 1875 at the age of twenty-five, only three years after their marriage. A year later, however, in the spring of 1876, he married again, his new bride one Mary Ann Livesey, a young woman of some financial means. She was to become a great champion of his work and when in the course of that work (probably sponsored by the government), he set sail for the Australian island of Tasmania in 1884, she went with him. Accompanying the Saville-Kents (William had made a slight adjustment to his name) was the twenty-nine-year-old Mary Amelia who, having spent some years in employment as a governess, was now seeking a new life abroad. In time some of her siblings would also make their ways to Australia's shores.

Constance in that year of her brother's departure was still in Fulham prison waiting for a glimpse of freedom. She had hoped that the offer from Bishop Webb would secure her release, but it had not, and so, growing increasingly desperate, she once more petitioned the Home Secretary. This petition, her sixth, dated the 23rd of July, 1884, shows clearly her acute misery:

The Petition of Constance E. Kent r5 . . .
 HUMBLY SHEWETH—

that she entered upon the 20th year of a long and rigorous imprisonment, without one single ray of hope to brighten a life which since earliest recollection has been passed in confinement, either of school, convent or prison, while before her only this, a gloomy future of approaching age—after a youth spent in dreary waiting and heart-sickening disappointment—in complete isolation from all that makes life worth living, amid uncongenial surroundings, from which mind and body alike shrink.

That her miserable fate is well deserved she most humbly owns, with deepest contrition for the past, knowing that she is utterly undeserving of the mercy she fain would crave, yet, let it not be accounted presumption in your humble petitioner that she now prayeth with tears in all humility, for one word, one single word of hope, however small, however distant.

Your humble petitioner has friends most willing to receive her as their late proposal to send her to South Africa fully proves.

Your humble petitioner, almost in despair, implores for hope, one glimmer of hope for pity's sake, and may the mercy of Heaven reward your clemency your humble petitioner will as in duty bound ever pray.

Constance E. Kent.

But, deeply moving as Constance's words were, as eloquent as was her plea, it all availed her nothing. Still she must wait. On April the 16th of the following year, 1885, she petitioned for the seventh and final time.

On reading this last petition one feels that perhaps she regretted her earlier pleading; perhaps she at last had come to realize that her entreaties were falling upon deaf ears and that it was useless for her to continue. The petition is the very briefest, and in it she makes no request for liberty. Instead, she merely asks that she may spend the remaining years of her imprisonment in the "refuge class", a privilege afforded so many other prisoners serving life sentences. Perhaps she had begun to doubt that she would *ever* be set free.

But soon she was to be given the news for which she had waited so long. On the 14th of May she was informed that she would be released on Licence (also known as "ticket of leave") in the coming July, on the 18th. On that day she would have completed twenty years imprisonment.[4]

In recent times only one other woman had served a full sentence of twenty years. She was one Mary Cox, whose crime, according to the Home Office, was "peculiarly brutal".[5] Constance's crime also had been most cruel but it might be argued in mitigation that when it was committed it was after years of provocation, and when she

[4] Her sentence dated not from the day of her trial, the 21st of July, 1865, but from the day the Assizes began: the 19th of July.

[5] Irish-born Mary Cox, 27, was convicted, with her husband John, of the murder of their neighbour, 82-year-old Ann Halliday. In the course of a robbery on the 10th of August, 1862, the old woman was savagely beaten to death as she lay in bed. John Cox was hanged, but Mary Cox, found to be pregnant at the time of her trial, had her death sentence commuted. She was released from prison in 1882.

had been in that period of transition from child to adult—a time when glandular changes can sometimes wreak such havoc on the mind and the emotions. Certainly her behaviour since reaching maturity showed indisputably that that bitter, confused, revengeful adolescent had been left far behind, that she had become a different, *normal* person. Furthermore, she had only gone to prison by dint of her own confession—born of true and deep remorse—which also clearly shows her own awareness that there was absolutely nothing in common between Constance Kent the schoolgirl and Constance Kent the woman.

Therefore, although it was of course quite right that she should pay a penalty for the dreadful crime of which she was guilty, it may well be argued that a shorter sentence would have sufficed. But it was not to be. A life sentence of penal servitude had been deemed fitting punishment and the full term, twenty years, must be served. And perhaps that punishment, though extreme, *was* fitting. Perhaps F. Tennyson Jesse was right when she wrote:

> . . . In spite of the extremely brutal and callous crime which she committed, modern psychology would have found many excuses for her, but it is perhaps better that she should have been treated in the simpler and harder manner of those days, for the stark spiritual solitude in which she wrestled with her soul must have—surely it is permissible to think so?—gained her more peace in the long run than she could have acquired under different methods.[6]

And now at last those twenty long, long years of confinement were coming to an end.

On the morning of Saturday, the 18th of July, 1885, the doors of Fulham prison were opened and Constance Kent stepped, wondering, out into the world once more. And surely she must have found some grain of comfort in the bare and rigid truth of those twenty years imprisonment behind her. Her crime had been extreme, but so had her punishment. Perhaps now she would be enabled to put what had passed into the past. Perhaps now, if it was not too late, she could at last begin to live.

[6] *Murder and its Motives*. F. Tennyson Jesse.

Chapter 35

EPILOGUE

The weather experts had forecast showers for that mid-July Saturday, but the rain did not materialize and the day remained fair and grew fairer with the passing hours.

It was a good day to be in London, and visitors to the capital and its suburbs found much to interest them. One of the main attractions was the International Inventions Exhibition at South Kensington, while those individuals who were more sport-orientated had only to cross the river to Wimbledon where they could watch the deciding round in the marksmanship competition or the men's singles final in the Lawn Tennis Championships; here Ernest Renshaw would try in vain to wrest the title from Herbert Lawford, the holder.

The evening promised further pleasures to persuade visitors to linger in the city, and as many of those visitors flocked to the Crystal Palace to view the spectacle of "ten acres of brilliant illuminations" so those of a more cultural bent could go to the Royal Opera House, Covent Garden, where the famous diva Madame Adelina Patti was making her second appearance in the title role of *Carmen*. Lovers of the drama were also well catered for with the illustrious Henry Irving and Ellen Terry both appearing at the Lyceum Theatre in Willis's play *Olivia*.

For all its attractions, though, there was nothing in London that could possibly tempt Constance Kent to remain there a moment longer than she had to. Her one immediate aim was to get away; and just as the Rev. Wagner had aided her in her plan to relinquish her freedom all those years ago so here he was now to help her reclaim it. As the doors of the prison were closed and locked behind her the Rev. Wagner stepped across the pavement towards her and escorted her to his waiting carriage. And so the sixty-one-year-old clergyman and the forty-one-year-old ex-convict set off together through the streets of London, bound for a train that would take them to Buxted in East Sussex (about twenty miles from

Brighton) where, close to Mr. Wagner's house, "Belvedere", he had established a religious community affiliated with St. Mary's. Here for the time being, it was decided, Constance would stay. It would be a safe retreat where she could try to come to terms with her unwonted freedom and, hopefully, determine what to do with it.

In *Somerset*, a book in his *The King's England* series, Arthur Mee writes of a visit to Road in the late nineteen-thirties when he was told by the villagers of that crime that had shocked the nation. Whilst there, he said,

> . . . we came upon a man who remembered an afternoon, long afterwards, when a little woman in black came riding in a carriage and had tea at the Red Lion Inn. She asked a few questions about the murder (as everybody does here), and about the witnesses, and though she gave no name it was enough to send a whisper round the cottages of Rode,[1] and old folk came to their doors to look as the woman in black drove away. A pathetic sight it was, said he who told us. It was Constance Kent come back—like the nurse in *East Lynne*, he said.

Of course it was *not* she. Constance, as has been shown, avoided publicity like the plague, and the last thing she would have done would be to sit casually drinking tea in the Red Lion Inn asking questions about a murder that she herself had committed! No, the mysterious woman was obviously just another of the many annual visitors to the village who showed a natural curiosity about one of the most sensational crimes of the age. But so the myths about Constance Kent abounded.

Hers was a life that had given birth to any number of myths, of course, but of her life after prison the greatest number of myths were concerned with what she did with that life. Constance's life after her release has always fascinated followers of the Road murder—and mainly because it has hitherto remained as mysterious as the murder itself. Practically every chronicler of the case has at some time touched upon the question. One writer, Charles Kingston, romantically states in his book *The Judges and the Judged* that she married her prison chaplain and lived a most happy and

---

[1] As stated earlier, it was to this spelling that the village's name was altered in the intervening years.

worthwhile life until her death in the late 1890's; while John Rhode put forward his belief that she "died within a year or two of her release". Both men were miles off the mark, as also was Yseult Bridges who was convinced that Constance changed her name to Emilie King and emigrated to Canada as a children's nurse. All three writers would have been wiser had they joined most of the other scribes who freely admitted that, as far as the end of Constance Kent's story was concerned, they knew absolutely nothing at all.

So what, then, was the truth? In looking for the answer I came across two or three other people who possessed certain facts relating to Constance's later life, yet none of those persons knew anything like the *whole* story; *that* was not known by anyone until, after much effort and much searching, I discovered it for myself. And now it can be told, that final chapter in Constance Kent's history. It is a fitting epilogue to what has gone before.

Twenty years earlier when Constance had been facing her life imprisonment Dr. Bucknill had voiced his opinion that although she was at that time perfectly sane, protracted prison life would probably cause her to lose her sanity. He was as wrong as he could possibly be. Constance emerged from her long confinement with her strength, mental and physical, unimpaired.

The following year (1886) William left his work in Tasmania to come back to England. It is not known whether the reason for his return was business, his sister Constance, or both, however, his stay was brief and when once more he set sail for Tasmania Constance was at his side. She did not, though, travel as Constance Kent; no, that name would be as much a prison as any prison she had known. A new name was now essential. Henceforth she would be Ruth Emilie Kaye, retaining only her second name—a link with the past. Indeed, for the rest of her life she would be known as Emilie, dispensing with the Ruth more and more until it became all but forgotten.

Over the next few years Constance lived with William and Mary Ann, his wife, first of all in Tasmania and then in Melbourne, Victoria, to which city they moved in 1887. She was with them too the following year when they moved yet again, this time to the Darling Downs in Queensland. Here, though, Constance did not stay. Apparently she saw no future for herself in Queensland and as William did not plan to remain there for very long there was little point in attempting to get settled. Besides that, she had been long enough dependant upon her brother; it was time she began to build her own life.

Making her decision, Constance returned alone to Melbourne where, she knew, her future would depend only upon herself, upon her own strength and resources. But she had no lack of either and somehow—perhaps aided by the knowledge that for the first time in her life she was absolutely free—she would survive; though what she would actually do with her life was a question that remained to be answered.

And then early in 1890, during a typhoid crisis, the Alfred Hospital put out a call for help in caring for the victims. Constance, having the required experience in nursing, responded to the plea, met all the demands of the very arduous and exacting work and, when the crisis had passed, realized that in answering the hospital's call she had found her own answer. She would make nursing her career.

When she began her training course at the Alfred Hospital Constance was forty-six years old—about twice the age of her fellow students. Even so, she "adapted remarkably well to her situation and even hid under the bed from the night sister, along with her more youthful colleagues".[2] Perhaps at last she felt she really *belonged*. Well, true it was that for practically the first time in her life she had entered into a worthwhile situation *freely*—not pushed or pulled by any kind of outside influence, be it parental, religious or any other. But whatever the reason for her adapting so successfully she entered wholeheartedly into the chosen situation and, under the supervision of nurses trained with and by Florence Nightingale, underwent the two strenuous years of training. Writing many years later she described her work:

> We came on duty at 6 a.m.—reported to the night nurse and had tea. One half went to breakfast at 8, and made our beds, the other half at half-past; worked till 1 p.m., had half-an-hour for dinner, then on till 6. At half-past those off had tea. We had otherwise [to work] till 8—now and then till 9. . . . We took

[2] *The Hospital South of the Yarra*, by Ann M. Mitchell.

night-work month and month about. We scrubbed lockers and polished brass. The last pro. had to attend to the fireplaces in the small wards. . . . Once a week we were on at 5 a.m. to put fresh wax on the floors which we kept polished.[3]

After completing her training in March 1892 Constance stayed on at the Alfred Hospital until August of that year, at which time she left to travel to a private hospital two thousand miles away in Perth, Western Australia. Here—and rather surprisingly, as she had only recently qualified—she took up the post of matron. Her brother William was also working in Western Australia at this time—which factor may well have contributed to Constance's decision to work there. Not, however, that she stayed there long. Just over a year later, in November 1893, she left the private hospital and, probably after spending a little time with William and his wife, made her way back east again—this time travelling the whole breadth of the continent, heading for the east coast where, at the Coast Hospital[4] in Sydney, New South Wales, she began work as a Sister. Later, with promotion to matron, she was transferred to the Lazaret, an annexe of the hospital reserved for the treatment of lepers.

Constance left the Coast Hospital four years later in 1898 at the age of fifty-four and then (having given her age as forty-nine!) commenced work as matron of the Parramatta Industrial School for Girls—a post wherein she was very happy and which she held for the next eleven years. It is interesting to note that this was an institution for girls who, generally speaking, had had problems with authority; the girls being placed at the school by the children's courts for misdemeanours ranging from running away from home to involvement in major crimes. Many of my readers, I am sure, will feel that Matron Ruth Emilie Kaye must have been eminently suited to her position. With her own experience she must have possessed an insight into so many of the problems that confronted her confused and unhappy charges.

It was in August 1909 that she left Parramatta and, going south to Mittagong, spent a year working at the tuberculosis sanatorium there. Following that, in 1910, she moved on to Maitland where in December of that year she took a lease on a property in Elgin

[3] Quoted in *The Hospital South of the Yarra*, by Ann M. Mitchell.
[4] Now known as the Prince Henry Hospital.

Street that had once been a home for nurses—reopening it as the same the year following. So it was that at sixty-six years old Constance, as matron of the Maitland Nurses' Home,[5] went into business for herself.

And this was not her only interest. Apart from having shares in a Maitland theatre company she was also a founder member of *The Free Trade and Land Values League,* a political body (with its own magazine, *Progress*), advocating, and working for, social reform. Notwithstanding her advancing age Constance, obviously, was keeping busy.

In England in 1913 an advertisement appeared in *Notes and Queries* asking for the "date and place of death" of Constance Kent. Not surprisingly no one came forth with an answer. Nor was there any response in 1924 when F. Tennyson Jesse asked the same question in her book *Murder and its Motives.* Constance, assuredly, could have put all the minds at rest—had she had a mind to and if she was not too busy working; also, of course, providing that she happened to have seen the publications.

There cannot be any doubt, however, that she read John Rhode's book, *The Case of Constance Kent,* which was published in September, 1928, and that she it was who subsequently wrote to the publisher Geoffrey Bles that extraordinary document—dated February 1929 and posted in Sydney, New South Wales—now known as the Sydney Document. Near the end of that fascinating, almost-three-thousand-words letter—all of which is quoted in Appendix II—the anonymous writer said to Mr. Bles:

Dear Sir,
    Do what you like with this. If any cash value send it to the Welsh miners, to men who our civilization is torturing into degeneration. Please acknowledge receipt in the Sydney Morning Herald under Missing Friends.

                                                    February, 1929.

Well, obviously a letter to be taken seriously; indeed, as the reader has seen, a most informative work and very persuasive as to its honesty and validity. It is hardly surprising, therefore, that John

[5] Previously, and later, known as the Pierce Memorial Nurses' Home.

Rhode, writing a further, brief, account of the case in 1936 for a book entitled *The Anatomy of Murder*, should make use of the document and quote from it extensively. He too was quite convinced that it could only have been written by Constance Kent herself.

In 1937 at the request of Mr. Rhode a handwriting expert, Dr. C. Ainsworth Mitchell, rather cursorily compared it with a letter written by Constance in 1860[6] but "in spite of a number of resemblances"[7] being evident in the two handwritings he thought it unlikely that they were from the same hand. According to him if the 1929 letter *had* been written by Constance then her handwriting over those intervening sixty-eight years had changed considerably. However, as he already regarded her writing in the 1860 letter as "curiously mature" he doubted that it would have changed very much in the years that followed.

Well, Dr. Ainsworth Mitchell was wrong. I have seen many examples of Constance's handwriting and over the years from her youth to her old age that writing is seen to be *greatly altered*.

Unfortunately it is not now possible to compare the handwriting on the Sydney Document with the existing known samples of handwriting from Constance's old age, and this for the simple reason that the Sydney Document no longer exists. After Dr. Ainsworth Mitchell had completed his examination of it it was returned to the Detection Club where it had been lodged in 1933 and there was subsequently destroyed by enemy action. Sadly, no photographic copy was ever made and it was only during the latter stages of my involvement with this book that a typewritten transcript of the complete document was discovered amongst the few surviving papers of the late John Rhode.[8]

However, even without the original document to re-examine, a brief reappraisal of those parts quoted in this book should be enough to convince anyone that it could only have been written by someone with *inside knowledge gained over many, many years*—which must surely preclude the notion (as suggested by some writers) that a former servant of the Kents was its author. It must also be

[6] The text of this letter can be found on p. 244.

[7] All quotations attributed to Dr. Ainsworth Mitchell are taken from his letter of the 20th of May, 1937, to author John Rhode.

[8] For many years up to the present it was believed, even by John Rhode himself, that the only parts of the Sydney Document to survive were those published in *The Anatomy of Murder*.

noted that much of the information given in relation to Constance is, apart from being somewhat sympathetic towards her, of a most intimate and personal nature, even telling of her thoughts and feelings. Furthermore, the comments made about her and those others involved in the affair are in no way objective. The whole thing is purely *sub*jective, everything and everyone appearing as if seen through one particular pair of eyes—the eyes of Constance Kent. With all this—and the knowledge that when the letter was posted in Sydney she was actually living in that area—it is impossible to avoid the conclusion that Constance and Constance alone was the source of it.

The document is equally persuasive when it deals with her later life. It says: "After her release she changed her name and went overseas and, single-handed, fought her way to a good position, and made a home for herself where she was well-liked and respected before she died." Which was all perfectly true—bearing in mind that the reference to her death in the past tense was simply a red-herring; she being in the very best of health at the time.

The document's reference to the crime is also most interesting:

She vowed she would avenge her mother's wrong if she devoted her life to it. After brooding over it for some time she resolved that as her stepmother had robbed her mother of her father's love, she would deprive her of something she loved best. She then planned and carried out her most brutal and callous crime, one so vile and unnatural that people could not believe it possible for a young girl.

And the reader will see that those words telling of her motive: ". . . her stepmother had robbed her mother of her father's love . . ." are almost identical in phraseology to those in her petition of the 5th of July, 1878.[9] This, surely, is further indication of the anonymous author's identity.

In 1896 William, with his wife, had left Australia to return to England. William's father and stepmother had always insisted that he would amount to nothing in his life. They were both so wrong. He had greatly distinguished himself in his career, particularly in

[9] See p. 346.

that work done in Australia; and he had been honoured for it, having at various times been the President of the Royal Society of Queensland and Commissioner of Fisheries to the Governments of Tasmania, Queensland and Western Australia. When he died in Milford-on-Sea in 1908 he left behind several books that are testimony to his brilliance and his dedication. Among his best known works are *The Great Barrier Reef of Australia* and *A Naturalist in Australia.*

At the time of William's death Mary Ann and Elizabeth were living together in Wandsworth, London, where they had been resident for many years. And they were still there on East Hill in February, 1913, when Mary Ann died of bronchitis. She was eighty-one years old. Elizabeth's sense of loss at the death of her sister must have been acute, for since the moment of her birth she had so rarely and briefly ever before been parted from her. Elizabeth's own death occurred nine years later, not long before her ninetieth birthday in 1922. With her burial in the peaceful Putney Vale cemetery the two sisters were at last reunited, and as they had been throughout their long lives together so they were once more—and now remain—side by side.

It was not till after Constance's eighty-eighth birthday that she retired from the matronship of the nurses' home in Maitland, though she continued to live on there for some years afterwards. However, even though she no longer concerned herself with the running of the home she still remained busy and active in her private life. And a strong force in that life was her religion. Ever since regaining her love of God all those years ago in Brighton it had never left her, and as she grew older so she became, and would continue to become, more devout. St. Mary's in Church Street was her centre for worship in Maitland and here it was that she could regularly be seen.

When she at last left the nurses' home in 1936 she went to reside at Cintra, a private hospital in Maitland's Regent Street. She did not remain there long, however, and after a brief stay at another Maitland nursing home, River View, moved to Loreto, a rest home in nearby Strathfield.

And there it was, in 1944, that she celebrated her hundredth birthday.

When she had first had her picture in the newspapers it was back in 1865 when she had given herself up for murder. Now, in *The Sunday Sun and Guardian* of the 6th of February, 1944, her face appeared again. With a different name, though—and for a very different reason.

Beside the photograph and its caption: "100 YEARS OLD: ONCE SHE NURSED LEPERS," is written:

Celebrating her 100th birthday anniversary today is a pioneer nurse whose varied career included four years nursing of women lepers at Long Bay. The old lady is Miss Ruth Emilie Kaye, of 'Loreto", 119 Albert Rd., Strathfield. She will celebrate with a party of friends and drink her own "health and long life" from a bottle of champagne which has been sent to her.

Only since her 99th anniversary has Miss Kaye given up walking to church regularly and taking part in outside social activities. She is still energetic, bright and a constant reader, though she does not wear glasses, and possessed of a particularly keen insight into politics.

She was born at Walton Manor, South Devon, England, in 1844. After travelling widely in Europe she came to Queensland in 1868 and lived for many years in the Darling Downs. She is the sole survivor of a family of fourteen children.

The newspaper's text goes on to give details of her nursing career in Australia, but it is that last paragraph quoted above that is of particular interest. It is such a strange mixture of truth and untruth. She was of course born at *Cliff Cottage*, South Devon, only later moving to Walton Manor—which was in Somerset. Also, as is now known, she did not arrive in Australia in 1868, but in 1886, nearly twenty years later; a discrepancy that almost certainly sprang from a wish to further conceal her true identity and also to "account" for those twenty years missing from her life. Nor was she "the sole survivor of a family of fourteen children", for there had been *fifteen* in all. Still, she could hardly admit—while hiding her real identity —that her youngest half-sister was still living!

However, to return to those tributes from the press. . . . *The Australasian Nurses' Journal* reported:

Congratulatory messages from the King and Queen and from His Excellency Lord Gowrie were received by Nurse Ruth Emilie

Kaye on her 100th birthday, Sunday, 6th February. Miss Kaye was born in Devonshire, England, and came to Australia in 1868, and trained as a nurse at the Alfred Hospital, Melbourne.

His Grace the Archbishop of Sydney called early on the morning of her birthday with a floral tribute and to give her the Church's blessing. A magnificent floral tribute from the Mayor and Council of Strathfield and other tributes from the Matron and staff of the Loreto Rest Home, the Pallister Girls' Home, St. Anne's, well-wishers, etc., the gardener and many other gifts made the day a memorable one. Miss Kaye said she had been greatly honoured, and felt very proud at the congratulatory messages she had received.

The Bulletin wrote:

> Surely on the honour roll of Australia's citizens the name of Ruth Emilie Kaye should hold a high place. Miss Kaye, who lives in Strathfield, was 100 years old last Sunday. She drank her own health in a glass of champagne, and, as she has given her life to the well-being of others, she deserves good health and happiness. . . .

One of the guests who was at the small party held to mark the memorable day told me that the old lady "looked very well but very frail; her eyesight was perfect, though she was very, very deaf".

Constance lived only two months after her hundredth birthday. She died at the Loreto rest home on Easter Monday, the 10th of April, simply of old age.

That same informant also spoke to me of her impression that Miss Kaye "had been determined to reach the hundred-year-milestone, for, having once achieved that final ambition she quite quickly declined".

The particulars on her death certificate are few; they name those parts of Australia in which she had lived—for "about sixty years", and state that her mother's name and father's name and occupation were "not known". Constance had taken her knowledge with her.

However, notwithstanding the lack of information regarding the old lady's earlier years, even the most casual observers knew that she must have known a quite remarkable life—if for no other reason than by way of the sweeping changes that had occurred within its

DEATH REGISTERED IN NEW SOUTH WALES, AUSTRALIA.

No.	Date and place of death	Name and occupation	Sex and age	Cause of death Duration of last illness, medical attendant, when he last saw deceased	Name and occupation of father Name and maiden surname of mother	Informant
481	1944. 10th April, "Loreto" Rest Home, 119 Albert Road, Strathfield -municipality of Strathfield	RUTH EMILIE KAYE	Female 100 years	(1) Senility (2) (3) Arnold S. Dynne (registered) (4) 9th April, 1944	(1) Not known Kaye (2) Independent Lena (3) Not known	Ellen Cullen No relation 119 Albert Road,
		Nurse				Strathfield

I, JOHN BRETTELL HOLLIDAY, HEREBY CERTIFY THAT THE

KEPT BY ME.

ISSUED AT SYDNEY, 2ND FEBRUARY 1978.

Death certificate of Ruth Emilie Kaye.

span. When that sickly girl child was born to Mr. and Mrs. Samuel Kent in Devonshire in 1844 the railways were in their infancy and the swiftest means of local travel required the use of a horse. When she died a hundred years later men were fighting a war from motor vehicles and aeroplanes while, at the nearby cinema Bob Hope could be seen in the motion picture *They Got Me Covered*. Constance had seen the innovation of it all: radio, gramophone, telephone, television; and now the atom bomb was being perfected.

As was to be expected, when the newspapers reported her death they were loud in praising the memory of the grand old lady and her remarkable story. No one, though, knew just how truly remarkable that story was.

And now it is at last told—the *full* story.

CERTIFIED COPY FURNISHED UNDER PART V OF THE
EGISTRATION OF BIRTHS, DEATHS AND MARRIAGES ACT, 1973.

rticulars of istration	When and where buried; name of undertaker	Name and religion of Minister and names of witnesses of burial	Where born and how long in the Australasian Colonies or States	Place of marriage, age, and to whom	Children of marriage
[illegible signature] April 1944 BURWOOD	(1) 11th April, 1944 Delivered to the Crematorium at Rookwood. Frank Murphy employed by Wood Coffill Limited (2) 11th April, 1944 Cremated at Rookwood Crematorium T.J. Massey (3) Superintendent	(1) C.M. Rogerson Church of England (2) Joseph Nevin J.C. Smith (3) A.E. Baker	Devonshire England about 60 years in Queensland Victoria, South Australia Tasmania and N.S.W.	(1) (2) --------Not married----------- (3)	years

A TRUE COPY OF PARTICULARS RECORDED IN A REGISTER

J. B. Holliday

PRINCIPAL REGISTRAR.

F. Tennyson Jesse in her book *Murder and its Motives* writes of Constance:

> . . . It is permissible to say that with a more understanding upbringing, such as she might have obtained nowadays, Constance Kent, with her determination, her force of feeling, and her rare power of secrecy, might have made a very fine thing of her life, instead of turning it into a sordid tragedy.

That writer did not know it but eventually Constance Kent was to do just that—she made a very fine thing of the remainder of her life. The knowledge we have of her later history shows that she was, in essence, a good person, a creature of understanding and imagination, one possessed of strength of will such as few are blessed with. Her great tragedy was that certain of those qualities, under the influence of outer forces that worked relentlessly upon a mind and emotions unbalanced, should briefly have become a power for evil, and that power, festering beneath the surface, eventually erupted, resulting in the most terrible of crimes.

But she did redeem herself. Although nothing on earth could right that wrong or bring the dead child back again she did all in her power to atone for the dreadful act—even offering up her own life in payment.

The sparing of her life and the substitution of a twenty-year term of imprisonment did not end the matter either—not for Constance Kent. And even though the law's administrators decided that she had fully paid for her crime she, obviously, did not feel the same way. So it was that after being released from prison she devoted herself solely to the welfare of others. And make no mistake, she did not *have* to do that. Having succeeded in finding and establishing a new identity she could, as Ruth Emilie Kaye, have regarded her debt as discharged. But she did not do so, and with all the choices so open before her she chose to give the rest of her life to humanity, devoting herself entirely to her fellows, caring for all who came within her embrace—the troubled adolescent girls, the typhoid victims, the consumptives and the lepers.

And surely the resulting satisfaction must have brought her some contentment. Or was her rue so bitter that, driving her on, it allowed her no peace, no rest? No one will ever know. After her arrival in Australia Constance confided in no one her deep dark secret, and no one outside her immediate family knew that she was anyone other than Miss Ruth Emilie Kaye. And that is how she is remembered today, for those who knew her as Constance Kent have long since gone from the face of the earth.

Gone, too—or greatly altered—are so many of the actual places associated with the story told here, those buildings whose very stones witnessed some of the most dramatic and poignant events ever known. The privy in the garden of Road Hill House was long ago swept away—as also since then was the little arbour built on its site in memory of Savill's untimely passing. The house itself, however, still stands, and is little changed from those days when the sightseers flocked from miles around to gaze upon it. Still there, too, are some of the cottages in the adjacent lane, those cottages whose proximity led Mr. Kent to start erecting fences for the protection of his privacy. The lane itself ends, as it did then, abruptly at a gate opening onto meadows beyond. Down in the village centre the Red Lion Inn is still standing, though the Temperance Hall, scene of so many dramas, was razed many years ago.

And gone, too, is the Trowbridge Police Court wherein Constance stood weeping before the magistrates; gone, too, No. 2 Queen's Square, the Brighton convent where she first met the Rev. Arthur Wagner; gone, too, the confessional at nearby St. Paul's in which, on her knees that day in 1865, she finally unburdened her soul to him.

Many miles away, in the quiet of the Wiltshire countryside, the shared grave of Savill and the first Mrs. Kent can still be seen in the tiny Coulston churchyard, though the gravestone itself has been so affected by time and weather that its inscription is now hardly readable.

Constance herself has no stone at all. The day following her death in Strathfield, New South Wales, her body was taken to the Rookwood Crematorium and, after cremation, her ashes held pending possible word from a claimant. None came, though, and after remaining unclaimed for one year, her ashes were buried in an unmarked grave.

Perhaps, however, now that the complete story is known, it is not too late to write for her an epitaph, and in doing so to quote the words of Mr. Rowland Rodway who, all those years before, had pled so earnestly for her life. Mr. Rodway never knew it, but he was later to be proven right. Constance Kent, he had said, in spite of what she had done, was, nevertheless, *"so fit to live"*.

APPENDIX I

Detective Inspector Frederick Williamson's report to Sir Richard Mayne of the Metropolitan Police, Scotland Yard, on the 24th of July, 1865.

I beg to report that on the 25th of April last I was sent for to Bow Street Police Court where I found Constance Emily Kent who had gone before Sir Thomas Henry and confessed that she alone and unaided had on the night of the 29th of June 1860 murdered at Road Hill House, Francis Savill Kent, her brother. Miss Kent was accompanied by the Revd. A. D. Wagner, Perpetual Curate of St. Paul's, Brighton, and Miss Gream, Lady Superior of St. Mary's Hospital, Brighton, of which place Miss Kent had been an inmate for the last 20 months.

Sir Thomas Henry remanded Miss Kent to Wiltshire; I on the same night, accompanied by Miss Gream and Sergeant Thomas, conveyed her to Trowbridge, at which place I arrived at 2 a.m. 26th and lodged the prisoner in the Police Station and at 12 o'clock the same day she was taken before W. H. H. Ludlow and R. P. Stancombe Esquires and remanded to Devizes Gaol until Thursday the 4th of May, to which place I conveyed her again accompanied by Miss Gream and Sergeant Thomas. At the desire of the magistrates I occupied myself in searching out and arranging for the attendance of the witnesses at the re-examination. On Thursday the 4th of May the prisoner was brought up before a full Bench of magistrates at Trowbridge and committed for trial at the ensuing Assizes for Wilts on the charge of wilful murder.

The prisoner was arraigned before Mr. Justice Willes at Salisbury on Friday last the 21st instant when she pleaded guilty and was sentenced to death.

Since she has been confined in Devizes Gaol awaiting her trial I am informed that she has made a written confession which is said to be in the hands of Sir Eardley Wilmot; the substance of the confession is that she has from her earliest childhood entertained a strong feeling of dislike towards the present Mrs. Kent, who was then her governess, her own mother being alive but partially imbecile from continued illness; after her mother's death Mr. Kent married the governess, then Miss Pratt, and from that time all her thoughts were turned towards avenging herself on her stepmother; twice, she stated, she intended to kill her but was prevented by circumstances, and then the thought struck her that before she killed her, she would kill the children as that would cause her additional agony, that it was with these feelings in her heart she returned home from school in June 1860, that on the night of the murder before going to bed she placed a candlestick and matches in the privy where the body of the child was subsequently found, that after all was quiet she went downstairs, opened the drawing-room door, after doing this she went to the nursery, took the sleeping boy from his cot, wrapped him in the blanket, took him out of the drawing-room window to the privy where she cut his throat with one of her father's razor's which she had previously possessed herself of. When she cut the throat the blood not coming as quickly as she imagined it would, she thought she had not cut it effectually and she then stabbed him twice. On her return to her bedroom she found there were two spots of blood upon her nightdress, she washed it in her foot bath and placed it in her drawer, taking out one of her clean ones which she put on, and her dirty [nightdress] was in the drawer when the police first came; she moved it from one place to another for some days and ultimately burnt it in her bedroom.

(signed:) Fredk. Williamson
Insp. Detective.

APPENDIX II

Unedited text of letter received by publisher Geoffrey Bles in 1929, following publication of John Rhode's *The Case of Constance Kent*. The original letter was presented to the Detection Club in 1933 and subsequently destroyed by enemy action.

Rhodes [*sic*] in his 'Case of Constance Kent' has made a great feature of insanity. Was Mrs Kent insane? Her two eldest daughters always vehemently denied it. No act has ever been mentioned to prove it. The second governess who was employed for the education of the two eldest daughters, arrived about the time of John's birth 1842. She was a pretty, very capable woman Considering Mrs Kents frequent confinements, also several miscarriages & that servants took advantage of circumstances, was it anything out of the way that Mrs Kent was only too glad to find someone willing and able to superintend the menage. Many wives are incompetent or unwilling as housekeepers, but are they therefore deemed insane? As Mr Kent ceased to live with his wife only about two years later, did he then consider her so?

The eldest son, who was training at a naval school, came home for his holidays about a year before Sidmouth was left, rising early one morning he met his father coming out of the governess' room which was next to his. Highly indignant he did not mince his words to his father, who promptly sent him back to school. Soon after the two elder girls were sent to two different boarding-schools, the governess' position was much canvassed in the town. The governess had made a great pet of Constance who was very fond of her, but soon trouble began. The governess had a theory, that once a child said a letter or spelt a word right, it could not forget it and she conscientiously believed it was her duty to treat any lapse as obstinacy. The letter H gave Constance many hours of confinement in a room while she listened longingly to the music of the scythe on the lawn outside, when words were to be mastered punishments became more severe 2 days were spent shut up in a room with dry bread & milk & water for tea, at other times she would be stood up in a corner in the hall sobbing I want to be good I do I do, till she came to the conclusion that goodness was impossible for a child & could only hope to grow up quickly as grown-ups were never naughty. At times she gave way to furious fits of temper & was locked away in a distant room and sometimes in a cellar, that her noise might not annoy people. [Walking] was a great delight to Constance, when sent into the garden & told to keep in sight, she would slip away to explore in the park and woods half hoping half fearing, she might see a lion or a bear. She slept in a room inside that of the governess, who always locked the door between when she came to bed. Mr Kents bed & dressing room were on the other side & when he was away the governess said she was frightened to be alone & Constance had to sleep with her.

Mrs Kent had a bed, bath-room & sitting room to herself at the other end of the house, only when in winter a fire was forbidden in her sitting room, she sat in the dining room with her 2 eldest daughters & the eldest boy when home & her youngest son to whom she was devotedly attached. Mr Kent and the governess occupied the library where Constance had her lessons but all generally met at meals When the youngest boy was about 5 he was sent to school with relatives of the governess, he was a delicate child and suffered from an abcess on one of his legs, also he had very pronounced Hutchinsonian teeth*, the youngest daughters teeth were also slightly so affected, may not the fact that five children pined away (merasmus) in infancy, have been owing to the same cause. Mrs Kent never saw her little son again, he grew to manhood and displayed a very strong constitution The governess always spoke of Mrs Kent with a sneer, calling her a

---

* *Hutchinson's teeth* is the term applied to the narrowed and notched permanent incisor teeth which are one of the signs of congenital syphilis. Such teeth are named after Sir Jonathan Hutchinson (1828–1913) who first described them. In her anonymous letter Constance clearly implies that at one time one or both of her parents was syphilitic, and suggests that the disease may have been the cause of the early deaths of several of her siblings. She also implies that she and her brother William were affected by the inherited organism. It was evident in William, she suggests, in the malformation of his incisor teeth and in a chronic abscess on his leg; in herself it was evident in her teeth.

Certain Person, ridiculing her. Constance was sometimes rude to her mother & would tell the governess what she had said, she made no comment other than a Mona Lisa smile.

A good deal of company was kept at Sidmouth, there was none afterwards, only gentlemen came down for the shooting The two eldest girls made friends with some young people from 2 neighbouring families, but as they would not call at the house they were forbidden to meet them, the same ban was placed on the younger children. One day Constance and her brother were supposed to be attending to their little gardens behind some shrubbery, they heard some merry laughter from a neighbouring garden, they went to the hedge & looked over longingly at the children playing with some visitors, they were invited to join but were afraid, they were seen and their disobedience punished, the little gardens were uprooted and trampled down, Constance made some futile efforts to revive hers. No pets were allowed, two little tropical birds sent by the eldest son to his sisters were consigned to a cold back room & died. The few relatives who visited got into disgrace over the governess & their stay was brief. Once Constance was told to make friends with a girl about her own age who lived nearly a mile away but friendships are not made to order, after a period of mutual boredom, the girl falsely accused C of trying to set her against her mother. At school she was happier with companions but as she was always resentful of authority she was still ever in trouble, and looked on as a black sheep, she had nothing to do with the gas escape which was probably owing to the taps having been forgotten when the meter was turned off, she gave nicknames to her teachers & made rhymes on them which were not complimentary increasing her unpopularity with them tho' there were exceptions one of the masters who attended the school, had a great quantity of black hair and rugged countenance, she named him Bear in a bush & when taken to a fashionable chapel for Bible class, the minister who became a Bishop, she called the Octagon Magpie from the shape of the building when they were told they only laughed & the minister thinking he might bring some good out of her took some extra pains with her, but seeing the other girls were jealous she gave stupid replies on purpose & so fell from grace. Then she thought to turn religious & got 2 of her companions to join her in learning chapters of the Bible, but it did not act to make her as good as she had hoped, she was given to read a book by Baxter which convinced her that she had committed the unforgivable sin, so it was useless to try any more. She did not always come home for the holidays on one occasion when she did so no one took any notice, she might have just come in from a walk. She was sitting at a window rather disconsolate when her step-mother wanted her to do some mending, she refused, her step-mother said, do you know only for me you would have remained at school when I said you were coming one of your sisters exclaimed What! that tiresome girl so you see they do not want you. About this time she read a book on Evolution by Darwin & much scandalized her family by expressing her belief in his theory of Creation. She longed for a more active life than the one she led so dull and monotonous, she was not wanted, everyone was against her, she had read of women disguised as men earning their living & never found out till they were dead she felt fit and strong and made up her mind to dress as a boy & get a billet as cabin boy on the first ship that would take her, she thought there would not be much fuss if she disappeared, there was none when her eldest brother ran away, so she persuaded her young brother to join her in her wild enterprise, they intended to go to Bristol they reached Bath that night and went to a hotel to get accommodation, a gentleman recognised her brother & as she told anyone who questioned her to mind their own business, she was treated as a bad boy who had led the other astray. The next morning they were both driven home. C. had always wished she were a boy to go to sea. Soon after she was sent to school to some relatives of her step-mother, they were extremely proper & she delighted in shocking them, it was only too easy, she was considered blasphemous because she would always speak of Sara Bernhardt* as La Divine Sara, she was not with them long as they considered her incorrigible. It was about this time she began to think much about her mother there seemed to be some sort of mystery. Why did her mother when speaking to her often call herself "your poor mama" which the governess said was silly Why

---

* Constance's memory is at fault here. She could not, while still a schoolgirl, have spoken of Sara Bernhardt, for Bernhardt was not then known as an actress; she was too young. She was born in the same year as Constance, 1844. Constance's references to her must have been made in later years.

was the governess taken out for drives, her mother never Why was her father in the library with the governess while the rest of the family was with her mother, she remembered many little incidents which seemed strange, one was during a thunder storm when the governess acted as tho' she were frightened & rushed over to her father, who drew her down on his knee and kissed her, she exclaimed O! not before the child Tho' her mother seemed to feel being placed in the background, why did she not resent it and assert herself? C. came to the conclusion that she must have been a saint. She vowed she would avenge her mothers wrongs, if she devoted her life to it, after brooding over it for some time she resolved that as her step-mother had robbed her mother of her fathers love, she would deprive her of something she loved best, then she planned and carried out her most callous and brutal crime, one so vile & unnatural that people could not believe it possible for a young girl, in fact she failed to realise till she came under religious influence 5 years later after when filled with deep sorrow & remorse she told the clergyman of the place that in order to free others of any suspicion cast on them, it was a duty to make a public confession of her guilt. She was told she was right to obey her conscience & make amends [if] she could her life if spared could only be one long penance and he exclaimed What an awful wreck you have made of your life No likeness or description of C. is accurate she always as much as possible concealed her features & slipped out of sight if strangers came near Major Griffiths description of her is nearest the truth, her best points were a fresh complexion and a quantity of golden brown hair, other girls were often taken for her & on more than one occasion interviewed. After her release she changed her name and went overseas and single handed fought her way to a good position and made a home for herself where she was well liked and respected before she died to

Geoffrey Bles
Publisher
22 Suffolk St
Pall Mall
London S.W.1

Dear Sir
   Do what you like with this, if any cash value send it to the
Welsh miners to men who our civilization is torturing into
degeneration Please acknowledge receipt in the Sydney Morning Herald under Missing Friends

February/ 29

A

At one time at Baynton C's place of punishment was in one of the
empty garrets, the house was built in the shape of an E & there
was a parapet round the best part of the house, she used to climb
out of the window & up the bend to the top of the roof & slide
down the other side, she tied an old fur across her chest to act the
monkey & called it playing Cromwell to return she got through
the window of another garret but the governess was puzzled at
always finding the door unlocked, the key was left in, the servants
were questioned but of course knew nothing, one day she found
C and her brother out on the leads, told them not to as it was
dangerous Next time when she did her climb she found the
window fastened, she could not climb back the way she came just
where the parapet ended was the window of a room where the
groom slept she leaned across and climbed thro' tho' she was
upset & broke a jug on the wash-stand, the cat got the credit,
afterwards she heard that her father did not approve of the
window being fastened to trap her & said that when unruly she
could be shut in the study a room where her father wrote and kept
his papers, being on the ground floor she easily got out of the
window & passed her time climbing trees in the shrubbery also
displaying a very cruel disposition by impaling slugs and snails on
sticks in trees and calling them crucifixtions [*sic*] The affection
between the governess and C no longer existed

B

Re Mr Kent living beyond his means It was not generally known that he was the owner of Saville [*sic*] Row in London built by his grandfather on a 99 years lease which expired a year or so after he came to Road when a landlord made a free gift of it to the ground landlord

C

C. did not take her punishments very seriously she generally managed to get some amusement out of them. Once after being particularly provocative & passionate, the governess put her down in a dark wine cellar, she fell on a heap of straw & fancied herself in the dungeon of a great castle, a prisoner taken in battle fighting for Bonnie Prince Charlie & to be taken to the block next morning, when the governess unlocked the door and told her to come up she was looking rather pleased over her fancies. The governess asked what she was smiling about Oh she said only the funny rats. What rats said the governess, she did not know there were any there They do not hurt said C; only dance & play about After that to her disappointment she was shut in a beer cellar a light room but with a window too high to look out of, but she managed to pull the spigot out of a cask of beer, after that she was locked up in one of 2 spare rooms at the end of a vestibule & shut off by double doors, she liked the big room for it had a large 4 poster bed she could climb about, but the little room was dreary, the rooms had a legend attached to them, were said to be haunted & on a certain date a blue fire burned in the fire place

APPENDIX III

On the following page is the text of a letter written by Constance Kent just two months before her hundredth birthday, and four months before her death. As in the letter she wrote anonymously to Geoffrey Bles in 1929 it illustrates her disinclination to punctuate her sentences, her preference for the symbol "&" for "and", and for the use of Roman numerals for numbers. In the transcription below, I have omitted some names to preserve the anonymity of their owners.

9.11.43.

199 Albert Rd
Strathfield

Dear ----

Thanks for your nice long letter, you made up for silence By this mail I am sending you an Xmas parcel early you will say but things got so mudled [*sic*] last Dec:. I bought a mecano [*sic*] early as advised, then when I had it sent on they said they had to sell it, & toys were banned for the duration At another big firm I bought something. When it was called for they had sold it again Dirty tricks I call it. I looked thro' a list of books in a childrens library, it seemed all fancy fiction on monstrosities The ugly gollywog has banished the beautiful Fairy So much that is grotesque bizzare & hideous is printed for children, then they are expected to grow up artistic

I am very disappointed in the book for --- I expected illustrations of nests, eggs & in a popular form It is a mere bird catalogue It came from Dymocks [?] so that firm in Newcastle might be willing to change it for something of your choice I am so sorry I am out of bed but not yet trotting round the ring Miss Oxley [?] is balancing her bugget [*sic*] with munition workers she has only about 4 or 5 nurses My hand is all waddle & wait so must conclude Wishing you & family a Merry Xmas and a Happy New Year & many of them and a special weight of well fair [?] for yourself and little --- , from

Yours very sincerely
E Kaye

9 . 11 . 43   119 Albert Rd

S Kathyiele

Dear ~~----~~

Thanks for your nice long letter, you made up for silence. By this mail I am sending you an Xmas parcel early you will say but things got so muddled last Dec! I bought a meccano early as advised, then when I had it sent on they said they had to sell it. Toys were banned for the duration. At another big firm I bought something, when it was called for they had sold it again. Dirty tricks I call it. I looked thro' a list of books in a children's library, it seemed all fancy fiction or monstrous ters. The ugly golly wog has banished the beautiful fairy. So much that is grotesque bizarre & hideous is printed for children, then they are expected to grow up artistic. I am very disappointed in the book for ~----~. I expected illustrations of nests, eggs &c in a popular form. It is a mere bird catalogue. It came from Depts I wish so that firm in Newcastle might be willing to change it for something of your choice. I am so sorry I am out of bed but not yet trotting round the ring. Miss Oxtes is balancing her budget with munition workers. She has only about 4 or 5 nurses. My hand is all wobble & wait so must conclude. Wishing you & your family A Merry Xmas an a Happy New Year, & many of them and a special weight of well fair for yourself & little ~----~ from

Yours very sincerely

E Kaye

BIBLIOGRAPHY

BOOKS

ARCHER, FRED, *Killers in the Clear*, W. H. Allen, 1971.

ATLAY, J. B., *Famous Trials of the Century*, Grant Richards, 1899.

BIRMINGHAM, GEORGE A., *Murder Most Foul*, Chatto and Windus, 1929.

BRIDGES, YSEULT, *Saint—With Red Hands?* Jarrolds, 1954. Published in the U.S.A. in 1955 by Rinehart under the title *The Tragedy of Road-hill House*.

BURNABY, EVELYN, *Memories of Famous Trials*, Sisley's, 1907.

COBB, BELTON, *Critical Years at the Yard*, Faber and Faber, 1956.

DETECTION CLUB, THE, *The Anatomy of Murder* (inc. essay: 'Constance Kent, by John Rhode), John Lane, The Bodley Head, 1936.

GRIFFITHS, ARTHUR, *Memorials of Millbank*, Chapman and Hall, 1884.

—— *Secrets of the Prison House*, Chapman and Hall, 1894.

HARTMAN, MARY S., *Victorian Murderesses*, Robson Books, 1977.

JESSE, F. TENNYSON, *Comments on Cain*, William Heinemann, 1948.

—— *Murder and its Motives*, George G. Harrap, 1952.

KINGSTON, CHARLES, *The Judges and the Judged*, John Lane, The Bodley Head, 1926.

MARTIN, J. P. and GAIL WILSON, *The Police: A Study in Manpower*, Heinemann Educational Books, 1969.

MAUGHAN, H. HAMILTON, *Wagner of Brighton*, Coelian Press, Dublin, 1949.

MAYCOCK, WILLOUGHBY, *Celebrated Crimes and Criminals*, George Mann, 1890.

MEE, ARTHUR, *The King's England: Somerset*, Hodder and Stoughton, 1940.

—— *The King's England: Wiltshire*, Hodder and Stoughton, 1939.

MITCHELL, ANN M., *The Hospital South of the Yarra*, Alfred Hospital, Melbourne, 1977.

PARRISH, J. M. and JOHN R. CROSSLAND (Editors), *The Fifty Most Amazing Crimes*, Odhams Press, 1936.

RHODE, JOHN, *The Case of Constance Kent*, Geoffrey Bles, 1928.

RHODES, HENRY, *Some Persons Unknown*, John Murray, 1937.

ROUGHEAD, WILLIAM, *Classic Crimes*, Cassell, 1951.

STAPLETON, J. W., *The Great Crime of 1860*, E. Marlborough, 1861.

SUSSEX ARCHAEOLOGICAL SOCIETY, *Sussex Archaeological Collec-tions, vol. XCVII* (inc. essay: 'The Wagners of Brighton and their Connections', by Anthony R. Wagner), Sussex Archaelogical Society, 1959.

WALBROOK, H. M., *Murders and Murder Trials*, Constable, 1932.

WILLIAMSON, W. H., *Annals of Crime: Some Extraordinary Women* George Routledge, 1930.

JOURNALS

Annual Register, The
Australasian Nurses' Journal, The
Bath Chronicle, The
Bath Express, The
Bath Herald, The
Bath Journal, The
Brighton Gazette, The
Bristol Daily Post, The
Bristol Times, The
Bulletin, The (Sydney)
Central Somerset Gazette, The
Cornhill Magazine, The
Criminologist, The (Vol. 9, No. 32)
Daily Telegraph, The
Devizes Advertiser, The
Devizes and Wiltshire Gazette, The
Express, The
Frome Times, The
Fulham Chronicle, The
Keene's Bath Journal
Lloyd's Weekly London Newspaper
Lloyd's Weekly News
London Review, The

Morning Advertiser, The
Morning Herald, The
Morning Post, The
Morning Star, The
News of the World, The
Penny Illustrated Paper, The
Penny Illustrated Weekly News, Th
Saturday Review, The
Somerset and Wilts Journal, The
Spectator, The
Standard, The
Sunday Sun and Guardian,
   The (Sydney)
Sydney Morning Herald, The
Times, The
Trowbridge Chronicle and
   Volunteers' Gazette, The
Trowbridge and North Wilts
   Advertiser, The
West Sussex Gazette, The
Wiltshire County Mirror, The
Wiltshire Times, The

PAMPHLETS
The Road Murder, by "A Barrister-at-Law"
The Road Murder, by James R. Ware.

DOCUMENTS
Scotland Yard file MEPO 3/61   Home Office file Ho 144/20/491
Lord Chancellor's file: Assizes 25/46/8

INDEX

True crime – now available in paperback from Grafton Books

Professor Keith Simpson
Forty Years of Murder (illustrated)   £2.95 ☐

Vincent Teresa
My Life in the Mafia   £2.50 ☐

Robert Jackson
Francis Camps   £1.95 ☐

John Camp
100 Years of Medical Murder (illustrated)   £2.50 ☐

Colin Wilson
A Criminal History of Mankind   £3.95 ☐

Stephen Knight
Jack the Ripper: The Final Solution (illustrated)   £2.95 ☐
The Killing of Justice Godfrey (illustrated)   £2.95 ☐

Peter Maas
The Valachi Papers   £2.50 ☐

John Pearson
The Profession of Violence (illustrated)   £2.95 ☐

Sir Sydney Smith
Mostly Murder (illustrated)   £2.95 ☐

Stewart Tendler and David May
The Brotherhood of Eternal Love (illustrated)   £2.50 ☐

Roger Wilkes
Wallace: The Final Verdict (illustrated)   £2.50 ☐

To order direct from the publisher just tick the titles you want
and fill in the order form.

The best in biography from Grafton Books

Henry Cecil		
On the Level (illustrated)	£2.50	☐
Bryan Robson		
United I Stand (illustrated)	£1.95	☐
Dudley Doust		
Ian Botham	£1.50	☐
Kitty Hart		
Return to Auschwitz (illustrated)	£2.50	☐
Roger Manvell and Heinrich Frankel		
Hitler: The Man and the Myth	£2.95	☐
Desmond Morris		
Animal Days	£1.95	☐
Axel Munthe		
The Story of San Michele (illustrated)	£3.95	☐
Professor Keith Simpson		
Forty Years of Murder (illustrated)	£2.95	☐
Elizabeth Longford		
The Queen Mother (illustrated)	£3.95	☐
Greville Wynne		
The Man from Odessa (illustrated)	£2.50	☐
Livia E Bitton Jackson		
Elli: Coming of Age in the Holocaust	£2.50	☐
Graham Gooch		
Out of the Wilderness (illustrated)	£2.50	☐

To order direct from the publisher just tick the titles you want
and fill in the order form.

Mysteries of the universe – revealed

Charles Berlitz

Without a Trace	£1.50	☐
The Mystery of Atlantis	£1.50	☐
The Bermuda Triangle (illustrated)	£2.50	☐
Doomsday: 1999	£1.50	☐

Henry C Roberts

The Complete Prophecies of Nostradamus	£2.50	☐

Jenny Randles

The Pennine UFO Mystery (illustrated)	£1.50	☐

Colin Wilson

Mysteries	£5.95	☐
Starseekers	£1.95	☐
The Occult	£4.95	☐

Graham Philips and Martin Keatman

The Green Stone (illustrated)	£2.50	☐

B Butler and others

Sky Crash: A Cosmic Conspiracy (illustrated)	£2.95	☐

To order direct from the publisher just tick the titles you want
and fill in the order form.

Famous personalities you've always wanted to read about – now available in Grafton Books

Dirk Bogarde

A Postillion Struck by Lightning (illustrated)	£2.50	☐
Snakes and Ladders (illustrated)	£2.95	☐
An Orderly Man (illustrated)	£2.95	☐

Muhammad Ali with Richard Durham

The Greatest: My Own Story	£1.95	☐

Fred Lawrence Guiles

Norma Jean (illustrated)	£3.95	☐

Becky Yancey

My Life with Elvis	£1.95	☐

Shelley Winters

Shelley	£1.95	☐

Stewart Granger

Sparks Fly Upward	£1.95	☐

Billie Jean King

Billie Jean King (illustrated)	£1.95	☐

Stephen Davies

Bob Marley (illustrated)	£2.95	☐

Pat Jennings

An Autobiography (illustrated)	£1.95	☐

Ann Morrow

The Queen (illustrated)	£2.50	☐
The Queen Mother (illustrated)	£2.95	☐

Pat Phoenix

Love, Curiosity, Freckles & Doubt (illustrated)	£1.95	·☐
All My Burning Bridges (illustrated)	£1.95	☐

To order direct from the publisher just tick the titles you want and fill in the order form.

Titles of General Interest – in paperback from Grafton Books

Malcolm MacPherson (Editor)		
The Black Box: Cockpit Voice Recorder Accounts of Nineteen Air Accidents	£1.95	☐
Isaac Asimov		
Asimov on Science Fiction	£2.50	☐
Roy Harley Lewis		
The Browser's Guide to Erotica	£1.95	☐
Charles Berlitz		
Native Tongues	£2.50	☐
Carole Boyer		
Names for Boys and Girls	£1.95	☐
José Silva and Michael Miele		
The Silva Mind Control Method	£2.95	☐
Millard Arnold (Editor)		
The Testimony of Steve Biko	£2.50	☐
John Howard Griffin		
Black Like Me	£1.95	☐
Desmond Morris		
The Naked Ape	£2.95	☐
The Pocket Guide to Man Watching (illustrated)	£5.95	☐
Ivan Tyrell		
The Survival Option	£2.50	☐
Peter Laurie		
Beneath the City Streets	£2.50	☐

To order direct from the publisher just tick the titles you want and fill in the order form.

All these books are available at your local bookshop or newsagent, or can be ordered direct from the publisher.

To order direct from the publishers just tick the titles you want and fill in the form below.

Name _____

Address _____

_____

Send to:
Grafton Cash Sales
PO Box 11, Falmouth, Cornwall TR10 9EN.

Please enclose remittance to the value of the cover price plus:

UK 60p for the first book, 25p for the second book plus 15p per copy for each additional book ordered to a maximum charge of £1.90.

BFPO 60p for the first book, 25p for the second book plus 15p per copy for the next 7 books, thereafter 9p per book.

Overseas including Eire £1.25 for the first book, 75p for second book and 28p for each additional book.

_____

Grafton Books reserve the right to show new retail prices on covers, which may differ from those previously advertised in the text or elsewhere.